THE PRACTICAL GUIDE

Marvellous and maddening,
full of secrets and surprises,
peopled with the whole spectrum of humanity
. . . . This is Cairo, my home.
Please come in and enjoy it.

Omar Sharif

THE PRACTICAL GUIDE

Edited by
Claire E. Francy

in collaboration with
Joshua Mortensen, Maher Nashed
Joan Ahmed, Sas Browne

1997 Edition

Original 1975 edition edited by
Deborah Cowley and Aleya Serour

THE AMERICAN UNIVERSITY IN CAIRO PRESS

First Edition 1975
Second Edition 1977
Third Edition 1981
Fourth Edition 1984
Fifth Edition 1986
Sixth Edition 1988

Seventh Edition © 1997 by
The American University in Cairo Press
113 Sharia Kasr el Aini
Cairo, Egypt

Dar el Kutub No. 3726/96
ISBN 977 424 394 3

Design, layout, and maps by Penguin Advertising Agency, Cairo
Cover photograph by Thomas Hartwell

Printed in Egypt

CONTENTS

1 WELCOME TO CAIRO   1

SKIMMING THE SURFACE OF EGYPT AND CAIRO   1

PRACTICAL MATTERS FOR ALL VISITORS   8

GETTING AROUND CAIRO AND ENVIRONS   13

GETTING OUT OF TOWN   15

STAYING HEALTHY   17

SPORTING AND COUNTRY CLUBS 89

3 LIVING IN CAIRO 91

BASIC DECISIONS 91

PRE-DEPARTURE CHORES AND CHOICES 91

THE SHIPPING NEWS IN CAIRO 93

AS SOON AS YOU ARRIVE 94

HOUSING DECISIONS 94

SCHOOL DECISIONS 100

CARS IN CAIRO 103

PREFACE

More than a thousand years of history are mirrored, and mired, in the blooming, buzzing confusion of modern Cairo. Evidence of thousands more loom at the city's doorstep and beyond: the stark grandeur of the Great Pyramids, Alexandria, city of dreams, the marvels of Luxor and Aswan. Throughout the city, remnants of ancient Egypt abut reminders of the caliphs and sultans who made medieval Cairo the hub of Arab commerce and culture. Elegant souvenirs of eighteenth- and nineteenth-century French and British influence form graceful counterpoints to superb mosques. More recent history shows up in stylish examples of the Art Deco look Cairo wore in the 1930s.

The spectacle is clear evidence that through the ages, Cairo has been a magnet for foreigners and Egyptians alike. Today, it is bursting at the seams with both, reaching ever further out into the desert and up and down the Nile to accommodate us all. Making sense of modern Cairo's sheer size and complexity calls for this, the seventh edition of *Cairo: The Practical Guide*. Like its predecessors, it offers English-speaking visitors and residents verbal and visual maps to the how-tos of life, work, and leisure in Cairo. But it differs in providing more selective listings to help sort out the unprecedented boom in goods, services, and culture over recent years. To make the *Guide* less of a catalog and more of a companion, we have expressed opinions—our own and others'—to entertain and perhaps provoke both wide-eyed newcomers and jaded old-timers.

Cairo's magic contradictions—its minarets and Marlboro signs, its vastness and surprising intimacy, the dust of its past and the cacophony of its present—can best be savored step-by-step. Walk! (But watch the traffic and the potholes.) Meander the Byzantine alleyways, parks, and markets—all surprisingly safe and genuinely friendly. And when a Cairene stranger says "Welcome in Egypt," smile in return, and thank whatever fate brought you to al-Qahira ('The Vanquisher'), 'Mother of the World,' whose diversity, mystery, and warmth will touch your heart if you let them.

HOW THIS BOOK IS ORGANIZED

No guide is all things to all people. As its title suggests, *Cairo: The Practical Guide* focuses on the nitty-gritty realities and practicalities of life in Cairo. The audience? Short-term visitors who want more than a tourist's perspective, foreign residents new and old who need help with making a life and a home in Cairo, and Cairenes themselves who, for business or personal reasons, want to tap the pulse of the large foreign communities of Cairo.

To make the publication as useful as possible for these three groups, we have divided it into two stand-alone units packaged together:

1. The *Guide* itself, including:
   Welcome to Cairo (arrival, health, basic background, restaurants and lodging, shopping and sightseeing)
   Leisure and Learning (entertainment, sports, kids' activities, the arts, hobbies)
   Living in Cairo (househunting and furnishing, schools, neighborhoods, household help, cooking and cleaning, shopping lists in Arabic)
   Work and Research (office etiquette, doing business, permits, privatization, job-hunting)
   Cairo Arabic (the basics one really needs)
   Directory (a consumer listing of goods, services, and interests, with phones and addresses, by category and neighborhood and with map coordinates; in the chapters, Directory categories are cross-referenced in bold, e.g., **Banks, Museums, Shoes**)
   Subject Index
2. The *Maps* booklet

Readers who have comments, corrections, or ideas they would like to see reflected in the next edition of *Cairo: The Practical Guide* are cordially invited to submit them by mail (*Cairo: The Practical Guide*, AUC Press, PO Box 2511, Cairo 11511, Egypt) or by e-mail (cairo97@acs.auc.eun.eg).

If you cruise the information superhighway, you will soon be able to access *Cairo: The Practical Guide* on the World-Wide Web (inquire at cairo97@acs.auc.eun.eg).

ACKNOWLEDGMENTS

For their expertise, ideas, effort, encouragement, patience, and sheer entertainment, grateful thanks to Aleya Serour, Anita Girgis, Ann Owen, Anne and Curt Beech, Anne Dorra, Bessie O'Rourke, Beth Miller, Bob Kingsley, Bridget and Rob McKinney, Carol Sidky, Carole King-Reed, Cetra Rees, Chris Bell, Colette Belanger, Cosima Lukashevich, Delores Clardy, Diana Digges, Dr. Ehab Fayek, Dr. Karim Shaalan, Dr. Sherif Zakher, Ennas Omar, Gini Stevens, Hamida and Menem Moafi, Hanan Shouman, Hassan Ahmed, Ian Portman, Jacki Sutton Shirbini, James and Elham MacIntyre, Jane McCarthy, Jo Nessim, Jon Hill, Josse Dorra Fiani, Judi Holtze, Larry and Polly Cunningham, Leslie Zehr, Lorraine Chittock, Luanne Napoli, Maria and Peter Hartmann, Mark Linz, Mike Dixon, Nagwa Kami, Neil Hewison, Nicola Kutner, Patricia Lawrence, Peter Reynolds, Remah Talaat, Simon O'Rourke, Soha El Gawali, Tessie El Gabi, Wael Salem. Special thanks to Daney, Kusuma, Brad, and Marina.

CHARTS

RAINFALL Cairo 2.5cm (1 in.) per year, usually Dec–Mar; Alexandria 18cm (7 in.) per year, Oct–Apr; Aswan and Luxor almost none.

TEMPERATURE Cairo hottest June–Sept (normal daily maximum 35–38°C, 95–100°F), coolest Nov–Feb (normal daily maximum 10–18°C; 50–65°F), with very significant nighttime drops, especially in winter and spring.

HUMIDITY 30-60%.

KHAMSIIN This nasty hot sandstorm blows variably, usually Feb–Apr, lasting 3–8 hours, but rarely more than once a week.

1997 HOLIDAYS AND BUSINESS HOURS

Banks, government offices, and most businesses are closed on public holidays. Banking hours are 8:30 am to 2 pm Sun–Thurs; some hotel banks are open 24 hours. Many shops are closed on Sundays; most do not open until at least 10 am, but stay open until late at night. Government shops close during Friday prayers. Normal office hours, government and private, are approximately 8:30 am to 4 pm, with great variations, and all normally close on Fridays. Many private businesses also close on Saturdays, including foreign embassies and consulates. Ramadan this year is expected to begin on 10 January and end on 8 February.

PUBLIC HOLIDAYS

9–11 February*:	*'Id al-Fitr*, the Small Feast
18–21 April*:	*'Id al-Adha*, the Great Feast
25 April:	Sinai Liberation Day
28 April:	*Shamm al-Nisim* (spring festival)
1 May:	Labor Day
9 May*:	Islamic New Year
18 June:	Evacuation Day
17 July*:	*Mulid al-Nabi*, the Prophet's Birthday
23 July:	Revolution Day
6 October:	Armed Forces Day

* Dates of Islamic holidays are approximate

0		Sifr
1	١	waaHid / waHda
2	٢ / ٢	itneen
3	٢ / ٣	talaata
4	٤	arba'a
5	٥	khamsa
6	٦	sitta
7	٧	sab'a
8	٨	tamanya
9	٩	tis'a
10	١٠	'ashara
11	١١	Hidaashar
12	١٢	itnaashar
13	١٣	talattaashar
14	١٤	arba'taashar
15	١٥	khamastaashar
16	١٦	sittaashar
17	١٧	sab'ataashar
18	١٨	tamantaashar
19	١٩	tis'ataashar
20	٢٠	'ishriin
21	٢١	waaHid wi 'ishriin
22	٢٢	itneen wi 'ishriin
30	٣٠	talatiin
40	٤٠	arba'iin
50	٥٠	khamsiin
60	٦٠	sittiin
70	٧٠	sab'iin
80	٨٠	tamaniin
90	٩٠	tis'iin
100	١٠٠	miyya
101	١٠١	miyya wi waaHid
120	١٢٠	miyya wi 'ishriin
125	١٢٥	miyya khamsa wi 'ishriin
200	٢٠٠	miteen
273	٢٧٣	miteen talaata wi sab'iin
300	٣٠٠	tultumiyya
356	٣٥٦	tultumiyya sitta wi khamsiin
400	٤٠٠	rub'umiyya
500	٥٠٠	khumsumiyya
600	٦٠٠	suttumiyya
700	٧٠٠	sub'umiyya
800	٨٠٠	tumnumiyya

900	٩٠٠	tus'umiyya
1,000	١,٠٠٠	alf
2,000	٢,٠٠٠	alfeen
3,000	٣,٠٠٠	talattalaaf
10,000	١٠,٠٠٠	'ashartalaaf
100,000	١٠٠,٠٠٠	miit alf
1,000,000	١,٠٠٠,٠٠٠	milyoon

CURRENCY CONVERSIONS

Effective July 1996

LE	Aus$	FFr	J¥	UK£	US$
1.00	0.38	1.49	32.35	0.19	0.29
5.00	1.90	7.45	161.75	0.95	1.45
10.00	3.80	14.90	323.50	1.90	2.90
25.00	9.50	37.25	808.75	4.75	7.25
50.00	19.00	74.50	1,617.50	9.50	14.50
75.00	28.50	111.75	2,426.25	14.25	21.75
100.00	38.00	149.00	3,235.00	19.00	29.00
250.00	95.00	372.50	8,087.50	47.50	72.50
500.00	190.00	745.00	16,175.00	95.00	145.00
750.00	285.00	1,117.75	24,262.50	142.50	217.50
1,000.00	380.00	1,490.00	32,350.00	190.00	290.00

Aus$1 = LE2.63   FFr1 = LE0.67   J¥1 = LE0.031   UK£1 = LE5.22   US$1 = LE3.39

TRAVEL INFORMATION

LONG-DISTANCE BUSES

(Fares are one-way and some vary slightly depending on time of day and amenities; check on air-conditioning in summer):

Superjet, 772-663. To: Alexandria, LE19–21; Port Said, LE15; Hurghada, LE40–45; Sharm al-Sheikh, LE50. Stations: Cairo Airport, Almaza (Heliopolis), Midan Abd al-Mum'im Riad (near Ramsis Hilton), Midan al-Giza.

East Delta Bus Co. 482-4753. To: Ismailia, LE5.75; Suez, LE5.75; al-'Arish, LE13–21; Sharm al-Sheikh, LE27–40; Nuweiba, LE31. Stations: Qulali (near Midan Ramsis), Almaza and Tagnid (Heliopolis) for Ismailia and Suez; Sinai Bus Station in 'Abbasiya for al-'Arish, Sharm al-Sheikh, and Nuweiba.

West Delta Bus Co. 243-1846. To: Hurghada, LE30; Safaga, LE35; Qusir, LE38; Luxor, LE35; Aswan; LE50. Stations: Midan Abd al-Mum'im Riad (near Ramsis Hilton), Almaza (Heliopolis).

TRAINS

Information: Ramsis Station, 147 or 575-3555.

CAIRO–LUXOR/ASWAN:
French overnight deluxe sleeper trains depart 7:40 pm and 9 pm. To Luxor, LE294 foreigners, LE129 residents; to Aswan, LE300 foreigners, LE141 residents. Spanish deluxe trains (no sleepers) depart 6:45 pm, 8:45 pm, 9:45 pm. To Luxor, LE51 first class, LE31 second class; to Aswan, LE63 first class, LE37 second class.

CAIRO–ALEXANDRIA:
Turbini trains (non-stop express) depart 8 am, 2 pm, 7 pm. LE22 first class, LE17 second class. French trains (stopping at Banha, Tanta, and Damanhur) depart regularly throughout the day; first class LE20, second class LE12.

CAIRO–PORT SAID:
Trains depart 6:20 am and 8:45 am; LE45 first class, LE26 second class.

PLANES

Information: Egypt Air, 390-0999 (Adly), 390-2444 (Opera).

Roundtrip fares: Aswan, LE991 foreigners, LE300 residents; Hurghada, LE780 foreigners, LE220 residents; Luxor, LE780 foreigners, LE220 residents; Sharm al-Sheikh, LE821 foreigners, LE246 residents.

LANDMARKS

To give directions, or to get them from passers-by, you will be more successful if you say or show the name in Arabic. Cairo is often better navigated by landmarks than by actual addresses.

Abdeen Palace	'aSr 'abdiin	قصر عابدين
American University	il-gam'a il-amrikiya	الجامعة الامريكية
	(specify Tahrir or Zamalek)	
Botanical Garden	gineent il-urmaan	جنينة الاورمان
Cairo Plaza	kayru blaaza	كايرو بلازا

Cairo Tower	burg il-qaahira	برج القاهرة
Cairo University	gam'at il-qaahira	جامعة القاهره
Camel Market	suu' il-gimaal	سوق الجمال
Citadel	il-'al'a	القلعة
City of the Dead	il-'araafa	القرافة
Coptic Cairo	maSr il-'adiima	مصر القديمة
Duty Free Shop	il-suu' il-Hurra	السوق الحرة
Egyptian Museum	il-matHaf il-maSri	المتحف المصرى
Fish Garden	gineent il-asmaak	جنينة الاسماك
Gezira Club	naadi giziira	نادي الجزيرة
Heliopolis	maSr il-gidiida	مصر الجديدة
Islamic Cairo	il-Huseen	الحسين
Islamic Museum	il-matHaf il-islaami	المتحف الإسلامى
Manial Palace Museum	matHaf 'aSr il-manyal	متحف قصر المنيل
Ministry of Foreign Affairs	wizarit il-khargiyya	وزارة الخارجية
Mogamma	il-mugamma'	المجمع
Old Cairo	maSr il-'adiima	مصر القديمة
Opera Complex	daar il-ubra (fi-l-giziira)	دار الاوبرا
Pyramids	il-haram	الهرم
Ramsis Train Station	maHattit ramsiis	محطة رمسيس
Shooting Club	nadi iS-Seed	نادى الصيد
Swissair Building	mabna swiseer (fi-l-giiza)	مبنى سويس أير
Tahrir Square	midan it-taHriir	ميدان التحرير
Television Building	mabna it-tilivizyoon	مبنى التليفزيون
World Trade Center	markaz it-tigaara	مركز التجارة
Zoo	gineent il-Hayawanaat	جنينة الحيوانات

BOOKS

In general, travel guides are cheaper if purchased abroad before you come to Egypt.

Blue Guide Egypt. V. Seton-Williams and P. Stocks. London: A. & C. Black, 1988 (2nd ed.). LE128. The ideal tome for the serious scholar-traveler interested in history, natural history, and above all, archaeology and architecture.

Let's Go: The Budget Guide to Israel and Egypt. J. Willard, ed. New York: St. Martin's Press, 1996. LE65. Great for budget travellers and anyone wanting a cheerfully jaded-youth perspective as well as the lowdown on prices.

Egypt and the Sudan: A Travel Survival Kit. S. Wayne and D. Simonis. Hawthorn, Aus: Lonely Planet Publications, 1994 (3rd ed.). LE70. More appealing layout and design than the Let's Go guide, covering much of the same ground but with more depth and style, especially on Cairo.

Fodor's Exploring Egypt. A. Sattin and S. Franquet. Fodor's Travel Publications, Inc., 1996. $21. The best writing, layout, design, insights, and right-on facts in an all-around guide, including walks and cultural nuggets.

A Guide to the Egyptian Museum, Cairo. Cairo: Egyptian Antiquities Organization, 1988. Worth its LE10 price: even though printing, table of contents, and organization system are poor, items in the museum are covered in order and with good basic descriptions.

Lorraine Chittock. *Shadows in the Sand: Following the Forty-Day Road.* Cairo: Camel Caravan Press, 1996. A must for every camel-and-adventure-lover's coffee table. Two intrepid women trek the Western Desert with a camel caravan. Fantastic photographs.

Paul William Roberts. *River in the Desert: Modern Travels in Ancient Egypt.* New York and Canada: Random House, 1993. $25. Simply a wonderful book—a rollicking travelogue and paean to Egypt ancient and modern by a wry and erudite Egyptophile. Read it!

Ola Seif. *Khan al-Khalili: A Comprehensive Mapped Guide to Cairo's Historic Bazaar.* Cairo: AUC Press, 1993. LE30. The shopaholic's key to every nook and cranny of the maze-like Khan.

Alberto Siliotti. *Guide to Exploration of the Sinai.* Luxor: A. A. Gaddis & Sons, 1995. le95. The best guide on Sinai so far, with especially good inland coverage.

Cassandra Vivian. *Islands of the Blest: A Guide to the Oases and Western Desert of Egypt.* Cairo: Trade Route Enterprises, 1990. A lot has changed since this excellent guide was published, mainly tourism development with its amenities and horrors. But Vivian's book remains a major resource, with excellent maps.

Marcelo M. Giugale and Hamed Mobarak, eds. *Private Sector Development in Egypt.* Cairo: AUC Press, 1996. LE70. Essays by experts on various aspects of Egypt's privatization drive.

Saad Eddin Ibrahim. *Egypt, Islam, and Democracy: Twelve Critical Essays.* Cairo: AUC

Press, 1996. LE70. A fascinating collection of essays on modern Egyptian politics and society by one of Egypt's leading analysts.

Phillip Moore. *Egypt: Investment and Growth*. London: Euromoney Publications PLC, 1995. Highly readable low-down on Egypt's economy and opportunities. Though written for investors, this well-produced book minces few words while adding immeasurably to one's grasp of Egypt's economy, politics, and infrastructure issues. For a copy in Cairo, contact Egyptian Fund Management Group, 3 Ahmad Nisim Street, Giza. Tel: 349-1162.

COOKBOOKS

Samia Abdennour. *Egyptian Cooking: A Practical Guide*. Cairo: AUC Press, 1984. Has a certain matter-of-fact charm as if a busy Egyptian mother-in-law were showing her son's foreign bride how to cook while skimping on essential details—perhaps intentionally so!

Maadi Women's Guild. *What Cooks in Cairo*. Maadi, Egypt, 1996. LE30. A really handy cookbook for Cairo. Nothing fancy, but all doable with local ingredients. Mostly down-home American-style recipes plus a few Egyptian favorites. Excellent "Hints and Substitutions" section and conversion tables, plus pretty thorough English-Arabic food names. All proceeds to Egyptian charities.

Tess Mallos. *The Complete Middle East Cookbook*. London: Peter Ward Book Exports, 1991. LE105. Tempting photos and recipes in a well-organized format which clarifies the connections among the many cuisines of the Middle East. Contains an excellent glossary which gives the many Arabic names of similar dishes from different countries.

Sue Torgerson. *Flavors of Egypt*. Maadi, Egypt: Sue Torgerson. LE50. Homey hints, great Egyptian recipes, and exquisite illustrations by Jemila Yosri, with a handy list of ingredients and cooking utensils in English and Arabic script. All proceeds to scholarships for Egyptian students.

FICTION

Noel Barber. *A Woman of Cairo*. London: Coronet Books, 1984. A painless overview of the turbulent politics of Egypt from 1919 to 1953 in the cloak of an enjoyable romantic saga.

Mohamed El-Bisatie. *A Last Glass of Tea and other stories*. Cairo: AUC Press, 1994.

Lawrence Durrell. *The Alexandria Quartet*. Various editions.

Yusuf Idris. *The Cheapest Nights and other stories*. Cairo: AUC Press, 1990.

Naguib Mahfouz. Any of seventeen titles by Egypt's Nobel laureate, all published in Cairo by the AUC Press and in the United States and Britain by Doubleday.

NON-FICTION

For the general, eclectic reader rather than the scholar.

Nayra Atiya. *Khul-Khaal: Five Egyptian Women Tell Their Stories*. Cairo: AUC Press, 1984. LE40. From the mouths of mostly poor women, narratives of their own lives with perspectives at once philosophical, humorous, devout, cynical, resigned.

Nicolaas H. Biegman. *Egypt: Moulids, Saints, and Sufis*. London and New York: Kegan Paul International, 1990.

Donna L. Bowen and Evelyn A. Early, Eds. *Everyday Life in the Muslim Middle East*. Bloomington: Indiana University Press, 1993. Excellent anthology from wide range of social-anthropological sources, many from Arabic translations, and including customs, fiction, poetry, rituals, and reflections on exactly what the title says.

Geraldine Brooks. *Nine Parts of Desire: The Hidden World of Islamic Women*. New York: Anchor Books, 1995. Fascinating. The author's anger, affection, and curiosity make a rich soup of her delvings into this contradictory world.

Elizabeth Warnock Fernea, ed. *Children in the Muslim Middle East*. Cairo: AUC Press, 1996. LE70. Fables and lullabies, sociology and statistics: a book both for and about children as well as for scholars and general readers concerned with the future generations of the Middle East.

Katherine Frank. *A Passage to Egypt: The Life of Lucie Duff Gordon*. New York: Houghton Mifflin, 1994. $27.50. Moving and informative biography of this nineteenth-century writer who came to Upper Egypt to cure her tuberculosis. Sadly, it didn't work, but in the meantime, she conveyed through letters home her love for and fascination with rural Egypt and its people. An evocative legacy well worth reading.

Albert Habib Hourani. *A History of the Arab Peoples*. Cambridge: Harvard University Press, 1991.

Max Rodenbeck and Guido A. Rossi. *Egypt from the Air*. London: Thames & Hudson, 1991. LE200. Gorgeous coffee-table book featuring bird's-eye views of Cairo and Egypt accompanied by fascinating textual tidbits.

QURAN

Muhammad Asad. *The Message of the Quran*. 1980. Cited by the Blue Guide as "a superb English interpretation of the Arabic text."

The Koran Interpreted, translated with an introduction by Arthur J. Arberry (Oxford and New York: Oxford University Press, 1983) is a version widely preferred by students of Middle East Studies.

Two other good English translations are Marmaduke Pickthall's and Yusuf Ali's.

1 WELCOME TO CAIRO

BASIC FACTS AND STATISTICS

Although this is a practical guide, Egypt elicits a touch of the poet in anyone remotely susceptible to its charms. So we precede our bare-bones statistics and facts by urging the reader to first picture a large, nearly square expanse of desert. Superimposed on the square is an eternally blooming lotus flower with a very long curling stem, the River Nile, stretching from south to north. The Delta is the triangular lotus flower, just below which is one large nodule, the city of Cairo, and in the far south, near the Sudanese border, is another, Lake Nasser.

The Delta and the banks of the Nile are almost the only arable land in all of Egypt's one million square kilometers. Nearly all of the country's 62.4 million people (95 percent) live within this three percent of the land, a good quarter of them (16–18 million) in Cairo. No single flower could feed so many, and in fact Egypt imports over half the food it needs for its burgeoning population.

Egypt, or Misr (pronounced 'masr' by its people), is officially known as the Arab Republic of Egypt. It occupies the northeastern corner of Africa, with the Mediterranean Sea its northern border and the Red Sea and its gulfs (of Aqaba and Suez, with the arrowhead of the Sinai Peninsula between them) occupying the bulk of its eastern border. Israel and the Gaza Strip touch Egypt's northeastern corner, Sudan lies to the south, and Libya to the west. Egypt's coastline is nearly 2,500 kilometers long, with the Suez Canal linking the Red Sea to the Mediterranean—a marriage of geographical accident and human technology vital to both Egypt and the world.

PEOPLES AND CULTURES

According to 1995 estimates, the population of Egypt is 62.4 million. Over a third (37 percent) is under fifteen years old. With its youth and its fertility rate of 3.67 children per woman, it is not surprising that Egypt's annual population growth rate is nearly two percent. This means that every year, despite some of them dying (on average, at age 59 for men, 63 for women), the number of people in Egypt increases by 1.25 million.

Who are the Egyptians? The progeny of peasants and pashas alike assert half-jokingly but nevertheless proudly that they are descended from the pharaohs. The boast is not intended literally; it signifies that they consider themselves ancient Egyptian rather than Arabs or Africans. (Given the fecundity and polygyny of some of the pharaohs, though, the claim may well have some genetic merit!) Throughout Egypt's history, though, and particularly in the urban centers, its people have influenced, been influenced by, and intermixed with people from the east, north, and south as well.

Southward toward Sudan, the tall, dark-skinned Nubians are more evident. Upper Egyptians who are not Nubians refer to themselves proudly as *Sa'idis*. *Fellahiin* is the general term for the agrarian peasants, many of whom have migrated from the countryside to the cities to find work. In the deserts and oases there are Bedouins and Berbers. Cairo's mix is notably harmonious, showing little or no overt prejudices, although stereotypes, biases, and plenty of good-natured jokes based on differences abound. The deep divide in Egyptian society is neither racial, geographic, nor religious. It is economic, and it is profound.

In addition, Egypt has always been hospitable to foreigners—sometimes to its detriment. Today, there are aproximately 10,000 Americans, 3,500 Britons, 3,000 French, 3,000 Germans, and thousands of other Europeans and Africans living and working in Egypt. There are also many Latin Americans and larger numbers of Middle Easterners, who maintain residences and do business in comparatively free-wheeling Cairo, plus Asians from India to the Philippines.

RELIGION

Islam's profound influence is visible—and audible—at every turn: the haunting calls to prayer five times a day from every minaret (now mostly a matter of loudspeakers rather than the unadulterated song of the muezzins) . . . the minarets themselves, spiraling to the skies and putting modern skyscrapers to shame by their beauty . . . the sight of men in gallabiyas or Brooks Brothers suits, on sidewalks, in shops, and in office buildings, breaking to prostrate themselves in prayer . . . the incantations of *in sha'allah* ('God willing') and *il-hamdulillah* ('thanks be to God') punctuating all conversations as naturally as breathing . . . the sudden and total absence of food, drink (even water), and cigarettes all during the days of Ramadan, and the night-long revels that follow . . . the blood of sacrificed animals on the doors of new homes in hovels and highrises alike. All exert their undeniable effects on Muslims and on non-Muslims as well, demanding our attention and respect.

Reliable estimates place the percentage of Egyptians who are Muslim between 90 and 94 percent, virtually all of whom are Sunni rather than Shi'a Muslims. The divide between these two branches dates to shortly after the death of the Prophet Muhammad (AD 570–632). When he died, the heirs and devotees of the charismatic Prophet, who named no successor, began a family squabble of epic proportions, replete with assassinations and counter-assassinations. Adherents of the Prophet's son-in-law, Ali, became the Shi'a, while those who sided with a series of elected factional leaders became the Sunnis. During all this internecine intrigue, though, Islam spread far and fast, partly as a result of the power of the message of the Quran, partly due to the Prophet's and his followers' military and political stratagems.

The Quran is regarded by Muslims as immutable and infallible. It is the recorded collection of God's revelations given to the Prophet by the angel Gabriel. These the Prophet passed on orally to his followers, who eventually codified them in AD 651; since then no changes whatever have been introduced. In addition, there are two other important bodies of work: the Hadith, the sayings of the Prophet; and the Sunna, precepts based on the example of the Prophet's life. Islamic law (Shari'a) is based mostly on the Quran, partly on the Hadith and the Sunna.

All Muslims are required to follow the Five Pillars of their faith: to declare publicly that 'There is no god but God and Muhammed is His Prophet' (anyone thus proclaiming is immediately accepted as a Muslim); to pray five times daily toward Mecca; to fast during the month of Ramadan, which was when the Prophet received his first revelations; to make at least one pilgrimage to Mecca during one's lifetime; and to give alms to the poor or for the defense of Islam.

In principle, Islam is a highly tolerant religion. Both Moses and Jesus are regarded as prophets under Islam, and Jews and Christians are respected as 'people of the Book.' In practice as well, the vast majority of Muslims, particularly in Egypt, are tolerant of other religions. It is illegal, however, for foreigners to attempt to proselytize, and deportations have been known.

Modern Egyptian law is based partly on the Napoleonic Code and partly on the Shari'a. The center of Islamic jurisprudence is in Cairo at al-Azhar University, the oldest in the world. Muslims from all over the world congregate to study here as they have for over a thousand years. The newest sheikh of al-Azhar is Muhammad Tantawi, appointed in 1996. He is well regarded by President Mubarak and is considered moderate compared to his highly conservative predecessor.

In addition to Islam, Coptic Christianity (an Orthodox rite) has had a long and enduring influence in Egypt. Current estimates put the number of Coptic Christians at six to ten million, spread throughout the country, with large concentrations in Middle Egypt around Minya and Asyut. The number of Coptic monasteries thriving today, including those at Wadi al-Natrun north of Cairo, provide fascinating glimpses of Coptic Egypt past and present. Other Christian sects, including Protestants and Roman and Greek Catholics, are evident in the many crosses that mingle in neighborly fashion with the minarets spanning the skyline. Most of Egypt's substantial and influential Jewish community left the country (along with large numbers of Italians, Greeks, and Maltese) in the adverse political climate of the 1950s. The total Jewish population of Egypt was estimated in 1990 at sixty.

MODERN GOVERNMENT AND POLITICAL PARTIES

Egypt's strongly centralized government operates in principle as a political democracy with executive, legislative, and judicial branches. In practice, and along with official democratic features such as a multiparty system, free elections, and a bicameral National Assembly, power resides heavily in the office of the president, supported by a large military bureaucracy, ministry heads appointed by the president, and a heavily nationalized industrial complex as part of a huge public sector–based economy.

President Muhammad Husni Mubarak is serving his third six-year term (through 1999), and is the head of the ruling National Democratic Party (NDP). There are about ten legal opposition parties, the strongest of which are the Wafd Party (center-right), the Socialist Labor Party (socialist), and the National Progressive Unionist Party (leftist). More influential in some senses is the outlawed Muslim Brotherhood party. The NDP swept the last elections (in November 1995) and continues to dominate the National Assembly.

Egypt is divided into twenty-six governorates, each with a governor, local councils and ministerial representatives, and other appointed and elected officials. Greater Cairo is divided among three governorates, Giza (west of the Nile), Cairo (east of the Nile), and Qalyubiya (in the northern districts).

ECONOMY

Ever since President Anwar Sadat's 'Open-Door Policy' was introduced in 1974, Egypt has been shifting slowly from a public to a private sector–driven economy. The shift to privatization and foreign investment poses real and imagined threats to the labor force and to the status quo of the powers that be—threats that to date have been effectively staved off by regulations, paperwork, and a legalistic framework that tends to thwart rather than support these changes.

Recent estimates report that 36 percent of the work force of 16 million are employed in the public sector, including the government itself and the military. Agriculture accounts for a further 34 percent, with only

3

20 percent in private services and manufacturing and 10 percent 'other.' The 'other' includes the 2.5 million Egyptians working abroad whose remittances are the country's largest source of foreign currency. Revitalizing the economy might well stem the 'brain drain' of professionals and skilled labor, whose contributions are sorely needed at home. Income from the Suez Canal and tourism follow expatriate remittances as the major sources of foreign currency.

Egypt's most important natural resource is its people—too much of a good thing at present, but representing an enormous labor force and a huge market for local and foreign goods. But since Egypt is otherwise relatively resource-poor as a major world market supplier of anything except cotton (and to a lesser extent gas and oil), the economy is in something of a vise: Egypt produces far more people than it can support and too many of them lack the skills to support themselves. Unless both these situations change, this resource cannot be 'exploited' to its own advantage.

One more vital natural resource needs to be mentioned: location. Egypt's position on the geographical and political map has always been of paramount significance, but never more so than today. Hence the health of the Egyptian economy is closely monitored—and in fact supported—by the major world powers. Egypt is near or at the top of the list of international foreign aid recipients overall, and, after Israel, is the largest recipient of US foreign aid. The goal of much of this aid is to help Egypt become economically self-sustaining. It is a goal that will be extraordinarily difficult to reach, in no small part because it is at cross-purposes with another: the donor nations' desire to assure political alliances with Egypt through partial economic dependence.

GEOGRAPHY AND TOPOGRAPHY

Very simply, Egypt is a desert and Egypt is the Nile. The Nile's banks and its Delta are among the richest agricultural land in the world, and beyond is desert almost everywhere.

Each area of the country has its own character. The Sinai Peninsula is perhaps the most dramatic in terms of color and topography, with wadis, mountains (including Mount Catherine, the highest in Egypt, at 2,642 meters), and massifs or high plateaus. The Eastern Desert is largely stony sand punctuated by crags revealing eons of striations to the naked eye and low-lying purple and black mountains set back from the Gulf of Suez. The Western Desert is by far the largest. Parts of it are below sea level, and it is here that the major oases are found. The Nile Valley, no more than ten kilometers wide on average, is the narrow, fertile ribbon that, along with the Delta, supports the vast majority of Egypt's population. The Nile Delta is the green fan beginning just north of Cairo where the Nile splits into its remaining two distributaries, the Rashid (Rosetta) and the Dumyat (Damietta) branches. The Fayyum is a fertile depression in the Western Desert watered by an offshoot of the Nile, the Bahr Yusif.

The Aswan High Dam, completed in 1971, is largely a blessing, partly a curse. It created Lake Nasser, one of the world's largest artificial lakes, but drowned villages and archaeological sites. It allowed for controlled irrigation and hence increased the growing season, but raised the water table throughout the Nile Valley, lifting buried salts to the surface that are gradually poisoning the land. The people of the river are now subject less to the whims of nature, but more to the effects, both good and bad, of human technology. And rarely, as if to reassert its dominance, Mother Nature cries long and hard. It rains, even in the deserts, flooding ancient tombs, washing away roads and villages, and reconfiguring the land.

EGYPT PAST

Assuming that most visitors and residents will explore their particular interests in Egypt's vast history with more detailed guides, we sketch only a cursory chronology to help readers situate themselves in place and time.

c.4000 BC: Agricultural settlements along the Nile and around Fayyum,

c.3100 BC: Unification of the Two Lands. Upper (southern) and Lower (northern) Egypt, probably under a pharaoh from the south who subjugated Lower Egypt, founding the capital of Memphis and the first of thirty dynasties.

c.3000 BC: First evidence of the early pharaohs and hieroglyphic writing

Old Kingdom (c.2686–2181 BC) (Third to Sixth dynasties). Over a mere five hundred years, centralized and nepotistic rule produced the organization, wealth, and military might that were epitomized in the construction of the pyramids—Dahshur to Saqqara to Giza.

Middle Kingdom (c.2010–1786 BC) (Eleventh to Seventeenth dynasties). Pressures internal and external led to a period of decline, which was reversed by the pharaoh Mentuhotpe, who reunited the Two Lands and built the new capital of Thebes—modern-day Luxor. The necropolis of the Valley of the Kings was begun during this time under Tuthmosis I.

New Kingdom (c.1567–1085 BC) (Eighteenth to Twentieth dynasties). The end came for the Middle Kingdom when the Hyksos peoples, probably Levantine, invaded Egypt and ruled until Ahmose chased them from their Delta strongholds in c.1567 BC and reestablished Thebes as his capital. The New Kingdom saw the golden age of art and architecture: Hatshepsut's mortuary temple in the Valley of the Queens, the temples of Seti I (Abydos), Ramsis II (Karnak, Thebes, and Abu Simbel), and Ramsis III (Thebes). Also during this period, Amenhotep IV (c.1369–53 BC), better known as Akhenaten, temporarily wrested power from the priesthood and instituted the worship of one god, Aten, the sun disk. His young successor, Tutankhaten, bolstered by the priests of Amun, reverted to Amun's worship and is known to history as Tutankhamun.

Third Intermediate Period and Late Dynastic Period (c.1085–343 BC) (Twenty-first to Thirtieth dynasties). Seven hundred years of war and dissension led to the disintegration of the old order and Egypt was conquered by the Persians, who in turn were conquered by Alexander the Great in 332 BC; he commemorated his achievements by founding Alexandria.

The Ptolemaic Period (322–30 BC). Upon Alexander's death, his Macedonian general, Ptolemy, succeeded him. Although he bowed to Egypt's past and built temples at Edfu and Kom Ombo, his dreams lay northward—the Mediterranean, the Near and Middle East, and Europe—and Alexandria became the jewel of the Ptolemies, of whom Cleopatra was the last.

The Roman and Christian Periods (30 BC–AD 641). Augustus Caesar's defeat of Antony and Cleopatra made Egypt the vassal and granary of Rome. Augustus and his successors left their imprints on the pharaonic and Ptolemaic temples. Christianity appeared under St. Mark in the Roman garrison of Babylon, the present-day Old (or Coptic) Cairo; Trajan redredged the earlier canal linking the Red Sea to the Nile (AD 115). Egypt came under Byzantine and (very briefly) Persian control. Meanwhile, Christian hermits started crowding the deserts and eventually, around 320, began uniting for defense in monastic fortresses throughout much of Egypt.

The Arrival of Islam: Arabs, Mamluks, and Ottomans (641–1798). After its conquest in the name of Islam in 641, Egypt was ruled by a succession of foreign overlords—the Abbassids (Sunni Muslims), the Tulunids, the Fatimids (Shi'a Muslims), the Ayyubids (including Saladin), the Mamluks, and finally the Ottoman Turks. The many glories of Islamic architecture are exemplified by the mosques they built throughout the expanding city of Cairo. Under the Ottoman Turks, who hung the last Mamluk sultan from Bab Zuwela in 1517, Egypt foundered, temporarily ignored by the ascendant Europeans in their pursuit of New World riches.

Europeans in Egypt (1798–1952). Although the French were officially in Egypt for only three years under Napoleon Bonaparte, they exerted a profound influence on subsequent culture and reopened the rest of the world's eyes to Egypt's wonders—and strategic geographical position. The Ottoman Turks returned to nominal power in 1801, and under the farsighted usurper Muhammed Ali Pasha, who founded his own ruling dynasty that lasted until 1952, modern Egypt had its beginnings: railroads and aqueducts; Cairo transformed by a building boom in the 1860s; and the Suez Canal built under Ismail Pasha in 1869. But less than ten years later, Egypt sold its shares in the Canal to the British to finance mountainous debts. The British ruled in fact and then, from 1882, in name as well. Beginning in 1919, the banner of independence was raised repeatedly. The British Protectorate officially came to an end in 1936, but real independence was not achieved until a bloodless coup by the Free Officers, led by Gamal Abdel Nasser, ended the British-backed reign of King Farouk in 1952. Egypt at last was Egyptian again.

EGYPT PRESENT

Nasser solidified his power and his heroic stature by successfully nationalizing the Suez Canal and resisting the joint British–French–Israeli invasion that resulted in 1956. The windfall, economic and political, allowed him to build the Aswan Dam with the help of the Soviets, to whom Nasser leaned but never capitulated. Although he was tarnished in his own eyes by the loss of the Sinai Peninsula to the Israelis in 1967, he retained his esteem and his presidency until his death in 1970. The country's economy, however, took a nose-dive during Nasser's rule thanks to his autocratic form of socialism. Takeovers of private lands and industries alienated aristocrats and industrialists, many of whom left Egypt for good, and created the ponderous state and military bureaucracies that still shackle Egyptian society.

Egypt's second president, Anwar Sadat, had a more international and democratic outlook than his predecessor. He enhanced his power at home greatly by recapturing part of the Sinai Peninsula from the Israelis during the October War of 1973. But in 1977, when he made the overtures to Israel that produced the Camp David accords in 1978, Sadat's fate was sealed in the Arab world. He became a pariah. And despite massive infusions of Western aid, the plight of Egypt's poor worsened. His 'Open-Door' economic policies did not make up for the loss of food subsidies, and the hungry poor were ripe prey for the blandishments of Islamic nationalism and militarism.

Sadat's assassination in 1981 brought the current president, Muhammad Husni Mubarak, to power. He was elected to an unprecedented third term in 1993. Mubarak has adroitly managed a series of domestic and international crises. Relations with Egypt's Arab allies in the Middle East, though tense, are holding, and the country's preeminent position among them has been firmly reestablished. This despite Mubarak's continuing efforts to broker the peace between Israel and all its neighbors, including the Palestine National Authority.

The same pragmatism that characterizes Mubarak's regime in the region is working internally as well. Ever so slowly, he is making good on the economic reforms initiated by Sadat. Partly as a result of a 1991 agreement with the International Monetary Fund, inflation and trade tariffs have been reduced considerably. More importantly, Egypt is the beneficiary of one of the largest foreign debt write-offs in history as a direct result of Egypt's alliance with the West during the 1990–91 Gulf War. Egypt is also required as part of the deal to revert to a privately fueled capitalist economy. In the mid-1990s these efforts might best be described as unduly tentative, but relentless nevertheless.

EGYPT FUTURE

Egypt's path toward 'progress' as the twentieth century closes is beset by some enormous boulders, political and socioeconomic. The definition of progress itself is a key one. Will it be based upon a largely secular democratic model, or upon a conservative Islamic model with strongly socialistic overtones? Each view ignores the other at its peril. And each will ultimately have to accommodate the other to devise palpable solutions to severe problems. Among them: overpopulation; a true unemployment rate of at least 20 percent plus endemic underemployment; a rise in headline-grabbing terrorist attacks; severe degradation of the environment, whether land, air, or water; tremendous income disparities between rich and poor; and illiteracy rates of 66 percent among women and 37 percent among men. To put this catalog into perspective without minimizing any of it, it might be noted that many of these problems are shared by a number of 'highly developed' countries as well.

With financial and technical help from its foreign allies, Egypt is making some headway in addressing its problems. To bolster the economy overall, both foreign investment and privatization of much of the public sector are being pursued more aggressively than in the past. And to offset the economic and social upheavals these moves entail, the Social Fund for Development (SFD) was inaugurated in 1991 to address five interlinked issues: family planning, health, education, women in development, and poverty alleviation. The idea seems to be that the SFD will cushion the blows of economic reform until its benefits trickle down to the poor, while simultaneously empowering them to influence their own lives through education, training, microenterprise development, and so on. Untold numbers of non-governmental organizations, plus many charitable organizations (including the Muslim Brotherhood), also work directly on these development projects.

CAIRO TODAY

Tourists in Egypt generally ignore its capital for the most part. A quick ride from the airport, two nights in a lowdown or upscale hotel, one at each end of the trip, a nod if that at the Egyptian Museum—more likely shopping in Khan al-Khalili instead—and then off to Luxor and Aswan for cultural enlightenment or to the Red Sea resorts for fun in the sun. But Cairo, marvelous and maddening, and always throbbing with life, is well worth exploring for its own sake.

Cairo is a city-lover's city. Its most obvious asset is the river that runs through it, its genuinely accessible banks dotted with cafes and gardens everywhere. Then there is the architecture: Cairo is home to some of the world's most splendid Islamic monuments. Museums and galleries? There are plenty more than those listed in most guidebooks. Although Cairo may not rate as a gourmet's paradise, there are hundreds of appealing places to get a good meal, a few in the 'splurge' category, but many more quite reasonable. Night owls will be relieved to find the nightlife hot and heavy if one knows where to look. Sports fanatics find themselves in good company in Cairo, with the weather and wealth of facilities cooperating fully. A daunting and unique array of shopping, the Opera Complex, green enclaves, a 'neighborhood' feel, contrasts galore—all at one's doorstep in Cairo. The problem is one of an embarrassment of riches, among which one must learn to pick and choose.

Cairo has its 'too much' problems as well, with one significant exception—and that is crime, of which until now there has been mercifully little. But there is too much noise, pollution, traffic, and dirt, and far too many people. Overall, though, Cairo works, and it is working on its problems as well. Lead-free gasoline and emission controls are being introduced to make the air cleaner. Trucks are banned from the city's streets during the day. Most of the garbage in middle-class neighborhoods gets picked up by the *zabbalin* garbage-collectors, and an army of street-sweepers keep the dirt at bay—barely. And the Metro is a marvel—clean, quiet, and safe—which, as it expands its tentacles, will further alleviate the traffic.

Less successful is the attempt to get the Cairenes out of Cairo and into the new desert cities. Cairo dwellers are a gregarious and urbane lot, unwilling in the main to exchange their crowded but lively and familiar conditions for the starkness and isolation of raw new cities in the desert. Thirty years ago, though, all of Giza was a suburb—the sticks—and look at it now. The comparison is not fully apt, however, as the new cities lack something, besides people, that exerts a powerful psychological pull: the Nile. But because Cairo changes with dizzying speed, future editions of this book may well paint a completely different picture and report on the restaurants, shopping, and nightlife in the exciting exurbs of 10th Ramadan and 6th October.

In the meantime, we hope this new edition of *Cairo: The Practical Guide* convinces you to share the belief of the majority of Cairo residents both native and expatriate: that modern-day Cairo is an eminently livable and even lovable city.

PRACTICAL MATTERS FOR ALL VISITORS

CLIMATE—AND AESTHETICS

The **Climate** chart at the front of the book gives the hot and cold facts. But what newcomers want to know is how the weather feels and how to dress for it. Many visitors are chagrined to find they have not brought remotely the right clothing for the climate, weather-wise or culture-wise. We therefore address both here.

Fall and early spring are touted by many guidebooks as being the best seasons in Cairo, but in fact they are almost nonexistent in terms of temperature moderation. Winters are marvelous—crisp, breezy, and invigorating, sometimes stretching from late October into April. You will, believe it or not, probably appreciate having a winter coat for this season—maybe not fur or down, but warm nevertheless. Fortunately, Cairo shops carry a good selection of coats and jackets, thereby obviating the stuffed-sausage look caused by excess layering. A turtleneck shirt plus a sweater over it suits warm-blooded mammals of both sexes, both indoors and out, as do cozy bathrobes and slippers inside the house. For women, longish skirts are stylish and warm, as well as much easier than slacks for visits to the loo. Handy additions and alternatives might include that old fifties standby, the sweater set, or leggings with long tunics. For women's feet, socks plus suede boots work well with skirts or slacks and are easy to dust off with a brush. Since Cairo's sidewalks and streets are incredibly dusty at best, filth-strewn at worst, you will stay not only warmer but cleaner in these get-ups than with pantyhose and pumps. Men can have their shoes shined on any corner for a song, but we've never seen a woman having it done.

Summer in all its sullen heat and humidity can suddenly smack right up against winter. For Cairo, this definitely does not mean a blithe baring of the flesh for either men or women. Unless of course you wish to be allied with tourists of an age—and avoirdupois—to know better, who clump about in the garden of the Egyptian Museum in spandex bike shorts and neon tank tops showing off their sunburned flab, their bra straps, and their banana-shaped money-belts. Ugh! Instead, dress comfortably in loose, graceful, cotton clothing: lightweight sport shirts and slacks for men, casual dresses or loose slacks and tunics for women. The sleeveless issue for women is a matter of personal taste and comfort, with many expatriate residents prudently advising against it, and other chic Cairenes saying modest sleevelessness is fine in the city. One can comfortably straddle the issue by carrying a short-sleeved jacket or bolero.

Outside Cairo, it's another matter entirely. There is almost no shade anywhere, and the sun is punishing, so make your own, winter or summer. If you have the élan to carry off a parasol, do so; otherwise, some sort of floppy hat plus a loose, light-colored jacket or long-sleeved blouse work well. But since the temperature plummets late afternoon through early morning the further you go into the desert, warm sweaters are vital except perhaps in high summer. The modesty factor increases in the countryside as well, with men, as usual, having more leeway than women.

A note on shoes: the best foot forward is not sandal-clad except at home or perhaps at a beach resort. Feet get sunburned and filthy very fast, and sand is gritty and uncomfortable. We hate to admit it, but sneakers are a practical alternative. If you deplore the look, though, rubber-soled loafers, espadrilles, and rubber-soled ballet flats for women work well. They look okay, can be slipped off easily for mosque visits, and allow for a reasonable amount of clambering about pyramids and monuments.

Rain is usually a non-issue in Cairo except for rare, brief, and welcome showers in winter and early spring (though on rare occasions the city can suffer sudden downpours that flood the streets). But the *khamsiin,* the hot southerly wind from the desert, is another matter. When it pays a visit, usually between February and April, it gusts and whistles into every nook and cranny— doors, windows, eyes, nose, and mouth. The skies turn a murky yellow with sand and dust. For fans of strange weather phenomena, it is quite appealing and dramatic in its way. The *khamsiin* can blow for seven or eight hours at a time, but two or three is more common, and it is rare to have more than one or two a week. Do not go into the desert during a *khamsiin,* obviously. It is dangerous. And even in the city, beware of loose signboards, rickety scaffolding, and dancing garbage.

Pollution, too, affects the weather and one's lungs, nose, eyes, and skin. A couple of large cement plants near Cairo spew their cloying dust into the air. Cairenes smoke like fiends indoors and out, but a few restaurants now actually have non-smoking areas. Traffic fumes are unpleasant and unhealthy; Cairo traffic cops' blood has among the highest lead levels in the world, and their sperm counts are consequently among the lowest. Airborne sand particles from the desert are the housekeeper's bane, but also contribute to Cairo's magnificent sunsets. In all, Cairo is not ideal for contact lens wearers, and sensitive skin suffers some here. Coping mechanisms include eye drops at the ready, heavy-duty all-over moisturizers, and sunscreen always.

Finally, although they are rare, earthquakes do occur. A very bad one hit Cairo in 1992, causing significant damage and loss of life. A milder one struck in November 1995 near Sharm al-Sheikh, but shook up Cairo considerably as well, with aftershocks lasting into the next week. Supposedly, buildings constructed in Cairo after 1992 are quakeproof: they'll shake, rattle, and roll, but not tumble. You are supposed to head for a reinforced corner or stand under a doorway during earthquakes. But realistically, they are over so fast that there is barely time to do so.

TRAVEL AND TRANSPORT

ARRIVAL BY AIR

Airfares from Europe and North America to Cairo vary wildly depending on season, political climate, and your bargain-hunting skills. Budget travelers know to check the fine print in the travel sections of major newspapers for the best deals, and then to check again carefully before forking over any money. Recent economy class round trips New York–Cairo hovered between $1,300 and $1,600, but one friend recently got an open-ended fare of $900 on Olympic Air. London–Cairo round trips are generally in the region of £300. And Europeans on organized tour can get great deals on airfare and hotel rates direct to Sharm al-Sheikh: around £430 for a week.

Cairo International Airport, twenty kilometers northeast of the city, is undergoing major expansion. It improved by leaps and bounds when the new Terminal 2 for international flights opened (before that, it vied with Bombay as one of the world's least pleasant airports). So even though it is short on amenities now—a flower shop, an inconvenient restaurant, and a duty-free hole-in-the-wall that tends to shut down for 'inventory' just as three jumbo jets arrive—look for improvements in the near future and be glad you are not arriving from abroad ten years ago.

You can certainly get through customs and into Cairo on your own, but if you are short on patience or pluck, or cannot meet Aunt Ida yourself, you can opt for a meet-and-assist service (**Airport Meet-&-Assist**) like American Express's. Charming people will whisk you through passport control and customs and deposit you into a limo car for a hassle-free ride to your destination. For meet-and-assist alone, American Express charges LE30 for one or two persons; transport to downtown Cairo is about LE55 extra, less to Heliopolis, more to Maadi. If you are willing to pay for the convenience, it is a godsend. No lines, no excessive pawing of luggage, no haggling with taxi drivers. If the American Express office is not busy, you can even arrange this on the spot for yourself by dialing ext. 2127 as soon as you get off the plane.

If you do take a taxi, LE15–30 (per trip, not per passenger) is the going foreigner rate to downtown, the lower one only for those with well-honed bargaining skills and enough patience to indulge in the pastime. Age, sex, clothing, skin color, facility in Arabic, number of passengers, amount of luggage, and time of day may all be involved in the taxi driver's reckoning. When traffic is light (before 7 am, very late at night, or on Fridays), you can be at the Nile in twenty minutes, but otherwise, count on close to an hour. And during the pilgrimage-to-Mecca season, which lasts for about two weeks around the 'Id al-Adha seventy days after the end of Ramadan, it could take nearly that just to get into or out of the airport, as carloads of wellwishers waving white flags cram the roadways to joyously send off or greet the departing or returning pilgrims. The sooner you adopt the patience, good humor, wile, and sociability that characterize Egyptians' attitudes in situations like these, the sooner you will start enjoying your stay and feeling like a plucky Cairene yourself.

Buses and minibuses from the airport are also available. Inquire at the airport or consult one of the more budget-oriented guides for details. One can, of course, jump right into the fray by renting a car at the airport. But it is expensive—about $35–85 per day depending on model—and an international driver's license is necessary. Read the section on **Cars in Cairo** (Chapter 3) before making your decision.

Reconfirming airline reservations for both domestic and international flights, by the way, is taken somewhat seriously in Egypt. Even though it can be difficult to do so by phone, persist, or have a travel agent persist for you and make a note of the confirmation code number. Overbookings and flight cancellations are commonplace, and reconfirming may give you a competitive edge and a seat. (See **Airlines**.)

GETTING IN AND OUT BY OTHER MEANS
Ferries may still run between Alexandria and ports in Europe (Istanbul, Piraeus, Venice) on Adriatica Lines. But the two travel agents in Cairo who used to handle this in Cairo (De Castro and Mena, both on Sharia Tal'at Harb) said "no" or "maybe" in mid-1996, and advised checking in Alexandria. You can still travel overland by bus to Jordan and to Jerusalem from Cairo reasonably comfortably and very inexpensively. But border crossing formalities can take forever, especially to/from Israel.

Travel to Israel may necessitate either a second passport or an Israeli visa stamped on a separate piece of paper, as having an Israeli visa in your 'real' passport could cause difficulties when entering certain Arab countries. Check with both the Israeli Embassy and your own (**Embassies & Consulates**) for the most up-to-date details.

VISAS AND PERMITS
Put off your introduction to Egyptian bureaucracy for as long as possible by getting visas when you arrive at the airport (Cairo, Luxor, or Hurghada). It is cheaper and easier than getting them at Egyptian consulates abroad. Visas are good for at least three months, your passport must be valid for at least that, and you can get a multiple-entry stamp, but it costs more than double the price of the single-entry visa ($15 currently for Americans). All that anyone except diplomats can get is a thirty-day visitor's visa initially. If you are staying longer, or plan to work and live here, the necessary visa extensions and changes are done here, not from abroad. Even if you are Mr. or Ms. Hotshot from MegaCompany with reams of paper and letterheads that show your official status, either let your company handle the visa or do it here yourself. Otherwise, you can spend long hours and more money and make numerous return visits for absolutely nothing more than you will get more quickly on arrival.

The formality of foreigners having to register at the local police station upon arrival was suspended for many nationalities (including US and UK citizens and most Europeans) in July 1996. Check with your hotel or your company to ascertain current regulations.

THE MUGAMMA
This daunting paean to classical Soviet architecture on the south side of Midan al-Tahrir strikes terror in the heart of any

Kafka fan. But fear not: it can be efficiently negotiated with a bit of know-how, and all sorts of complexities have been considerably streamlined. Just the same, if your company or educational institution offers support in obtaining visas and passport registration, by all means take advantage of it. The Mugamma is open from 8:00 am until 3:30 pm except Fridays (closed), but individual windows can close at any time, especially after 1:30 pm. Go early to avoid the crowds.

To extend a tourist visa or pay fines, head straight upstairs to the first floor. Proceed directly to the 'forms' section and buy the proper paperwork before going to the visa windows. This will save a lot of time. A visa application with all the stamps will cost around LE15. Current fees for the most common infractions are LE28.40 for late registration, LE58.40 for overstaying a visa. To give you that in-the-know veneer of confidence, here are the functions and numbers of various windows:

	Windows
Temporary residence for work-permit seekers	1–8
Temporary residence for tourist visa extensions	23–29
Payment of fines	40
Form purchase	42
Stamp purchase	41

Why this emphasis on residence, temporary or otherwise? Because as a resident, you pay Egyptian rather than foreigner rates for in-country airfares and hotels throughout Egypt—for example, LE200 ($59) versus $211 for a Cairo–Luxor roundtrip air ticket.

If you are lucky, you may find someone who speaks some English at the Mugamma. A patient Arabic-speaking friend or a Mr. Fixit makes things easier. And certainly go armed with reams of passport photos. Some small remuneration will be in order if you decide to avail yourself of the services of the 'guides' outside who offer their Mugamma expertise, but the negotiations involved in doing so might be more protracted and ultimately unpleasant than just doing it yourself.

CUSTOMS—CAVEATS AND CURIOSITIES
Alcohol is seen as *haram*—forbidden, a sin—by most Muslims but its consumption is tolerated here more than in many other countries of the Middle East. Hence the fairly moderate approach described below with respect to its importation.

Currently, adults may bring one liter of alcohol and two cartons of cigarettes in their luggage. Presumably, this includes what you buy from the duty-free airport shops abroad, and you are liable for customs duty and/or confiscation on the excess. At the duty-free shop in Cairo Airport, you may purchase an additional four cartons of cigarettes and four liters of alcohol. If you don't take advantage of this, you can also take your passport to one of the **Duty-Free Shops** in Cairo within thirty days of arrival, where you can purchase yet more cigarettes, but only three liters of alcohol, not four. (Or you can do both if they neglect to stamp your passport at the airport duty-free.) A carton of imported beer can be substituted for one liter of alcohol at any of the duty-frees.

If you will be living and working in Cairo and are sending air or sea shipments of household effects, or if you have diplomatic status or some of the privileges thereof, these restrictions do not apply. Depending on your nationality, you may be able to ship as much wine and other spirits as you like. But do inquire first with your shipper (see **Movers** for Cairo-based ones) and your employer, as these regulations change frequently. In the summer of 1995, for example, one woman's sea shipment was held in Alexandria while customs agents broke all of a number of cases of wine she had shipped and charged her something like LE3,000 for the service. A luckier colleague whose shipment arrived a few months later, when apparently some rules had changed, had no problem. (More details on shipment of household goods are found in Chapter 3.)

Cellular telephones require permits at present, but this may well change shortly, so check carefully before departure. Fax machines and photocopiers do not require import permits, but they are problematic—although computers (including laptops) and normal telephones are not. CDs and video-cassettes, but not video games, may attract the attention of customs agents and censors, but then again, since censorship does not officially exist, they might not. If all this seems arbitrary and vague, it is—at least to the newcomer. To be on the safe side, declare major items of electronic equipment when you enter the country or on your shipping lists.

GETTING AROUND CAIRO AND ENVIRONS

The pros and cons of your many options for transport in and about Cairo are reviewed here.

Walking: This is the best—the most fun—and, over walkable distances, the fastest. Do consider it once you have recovered from your alarm at the chaotic traffic and the condition of most sidewalks. Crossing the streets encircling Midan al-Tahrir is the best way to practice the art of pedestrian survival; it doesn't get any worse, and once you have mastered it, you are a pro. Simply wait for a crowd or a bus crossing where you want to cross, and blend right in. The crowd or the bus will be your buffer against certain death. After a few successful crossings, you will be ready to take on the Leader of the Pack role yourself. Then reward your-

self with a cold Stella at the shisha terrace of the Nile Hilton (there is now a LE10 minimum during the day, but believe us, you'll feel you deserve it). There are also underground Metro tunnels criss-crossing this large round square (!), but then you miss the astounding patter of the potato-peeler salesman, the flirting of the AUC students, and the throbbing hubbub of this one of Cairo's many hearts.

The Metro: Cairo's miracle. Thirty piasters (less than $0.10) will take you up to nine stations. So far, though, there is just one north–south line, on the east bank of the Nile, with 32 stops between Helwan (home of cement plants and sulfur baths south of the city) and al-Marg. There are stations in Maadi, Coptic Cairo, Midan al-Tahrir, Ramsis Train Station, and Saray al-Qubba, within easy reach of Heliopolis. One long-awaited Nile-crossing artery is under construction under Sharia al-Tahrir in Dokki, and others are planned. The Metro is clean, safe, cool, and relatively quiet and frequent. The first two cars are reserved for women, but women can also ride in the others, mostly without being bothered. If someone annoys you, a loud shout of *'eeb* ('for shame!') will do the trick. In sum, riders of London's Underground and New York City's subways will think they have died and gone to heaven. But remember that the Metro caters to workers and residents, not tourists; hence, with few exceptions, it does not stop at prime tourist spots. And remember to keep your ticket for exiting.

Heliopolis Metro: There is an above-ground trolley system known as the Metro in Heliopolis, but it is very slow and no longer connects with Midan al-Tahrir.

Buses: One look at Cairo's old municipal buses—rusted sardine-cans on wheels—will put off anyone with more than a few piasters in their pocket. Avoid them unless you want a vivid reminder of what many resilient Cairenes cheerfully put up with.

And if you do decide to try the buses, wear sneakers, carry no money, and steel yourself for a world-class athletic event to board and exit. Destination boards and route numbers are written in Arabic. Useful routes: Tahrir to airport #400 (terminal 1), #949 (terminal 2); Tahrir to Pyramids/Mena House #900, #913; Tahrir to Citadel/Ibn Tulun #174.

Minibuses, microbuses, and service taxis: These are the choice of budget-conscious Cairenes and foreigners when their feet will not quite cover the distance. The government-run white-with-an-orange-stripe minibuses have fixed routes, fixed fares, and fixed stops; microbuses and service taxis are government-licensed, privately-owned vans and Peugeots that also operate on fixed routes but have scaled fares and no fixed stops—you just get in and get out where you want. You can get to the Pyramids from Tahrir on minibuses #82 and #83 for less than le1 in the same time it will take a taxi for LE5–8. If you are living in one part of town but working in another, find the nearest minibus stop or just look for the microbus vans on main thoroughfares and shout out your destination to fellow passengers. This is the cheapest plausible way to get to Heliopolis (minibus #24 from Tahrir).

River buses: These stop at various spots on both banks of the Nile between the Television Station building and Old Cairo, as well as going north to the Nile Barrages at weekends, when they're crammed with young, noisy revelers. They only operate up to 4 pm.

Taxis: Since most foreign visitors and residents will use taxis exclusively, as do many middle- to upper-middle-class Cairenes, some exposition of this subject is required.

First off, hotel taxis generally charge a lot more than a taxi you hail on the street. A kilometer away: LE10; airport: LE60; Saqqara round-trip: LE100. If you are rich and temporary, it doesn't matter, but if you live here, it does. On the other hand, some of the most useful people you will meet initially come from the hotel taxi ranks. Most know their way around, have decent cars, and speak at least a bit of English. The older drivers tend to have more foreign language skills and far better manners than the younger ones, some of whom are surly and aggressive once they have wheedled you into their car and then act unable to get you anywhere but where they want you to go. In their defense, though, they have very tough jobs—dependent on the ups and downs of tourism, having to cope with maddening traffic, in competition with their colleagues, and regularly dispensing baksheesh to the pashas who rule the hotels' driveways and curbsides.

Once you have an idea of what to pay, it is easier and cheaper to hail the black-and-white taxis on the street. What to pay depends not only on the distance traveled but also on time of day, state of the traffic, and number of passengers: as a rough guide, most journeys within the Dokki–Mohandiseen–Zamalek–Downtown area normally fall in a LE2–5 range; Downtown to Heliopolis or Maadi LE8–15; Downtown to the Airport LE15–25. During rush hours, don't hesitate to share. Just call out your destination to any cab, occupied or not. Disregard the meter, even if it is on. Since meters are rarely used, neither is tipping. Don't haggle over the price before getting in; it is a futile pastime that will last the entire length of the ride and beyond. Just get in knowing about what to pay, and pay when you exit. If the driver asks beforehand, tell him what you will pay—and if he balks and you know it is fair, hail the next cab. Women should avoid sitting in the front seat, unless you get to ride with one of Cairo's few women taxi drivers. The hourly rate for Cairo running is LE10-15.

Taxi drivers the world over are a cynical lot, with good reason, and Cairo's are no different. But the bulk of them are surprisingly kind, affable, and patient. For every negative anecdote you will hear, there is a corresponding one about a guy who returns a stranger's full wallet untouched, makes sure his passenger does not get swindled in the markets, or watches over a cranky toddler with good humor, skill, and affection while Mama confers with the butcher. Many drivers have phones at home, and once you establish a relationship, you can call them up for efficient, reliable service—and perhaps eventually be invited home for *kushari*. Finding a few good taxi drivers early on may help your adjustment to Cairo.

Limos: They sound like a glamorous and expensive alternative, but they are neither. Limousine Misr (**Taxi & Limousine Services**), for example, charges LE55 for half a day's Cairo running, in good cars with English-speaking drivers.

CAIRO FOR PEOPLE WITH PHYSICAL DISABILITIES

. . . is murder! Major hotels and a few of the major tourist attractions are getting better in this regard, but it is tough getting around. The sidewalks and streets are hard on pedestrians, period; those using wheelchairs or canes require even more determination than usual. If you have a hearing loss, you are spared some of Cairo's cacophonous noise, but you must be extraordinarily attentive to traffic. Likewise for the blind, although people are generally very accommodating when you want help. But it is probably unwise to submit a seeing-eye dog to the general mayhem.

NAVIGATING BY LANDMARKS

Not many Cairo streets carry street signs, and when they do they are often only in Arabic. Street names sometimes get revamped to honor this or that politician,

and the same street can also change names from one end to the other. Furthermore, the giving and getting of directions, seemingly regardless of whether you speak Arabic, results in a great many well-meant social exchanges, but not usually in getting you where you want to go. Finally, terms like 'next to,' 'behind,' 'across from,' and so on, can be very broadly—like, a kilometer broadly—interpreted. What to do? Navigate by landmarks. The **Landmarks** chart at the front of the book gives the most familiar ones in English, Arabic transcription, and Arabic script. As you create your own cognitive map of Cairo, learn how to pronounce the names of landmarks relevant to you so that you can at least give directions. Also ask your friends to give you directions referring to common landmarks in addition to their street addresses. Old Cairo hands already do this as a matter of course.

Lastly, a thought that might cheer you up as you are on the verge of tears after being hopelessly lost for an hour exactly a few blocks from where you know you have to go: if you were to ask in perfect Arabic for the Villa Borghese Gardens or the Empire State Building or the Little Mermaid in Rome, New York, or Copenhagen, the locals would be just as stymied as they are here when you ask in English. Learn the names of 'your' landmarks in Arabic.

GETTING OUT OF TOWN

Wonderful as Cairo is, you will want to leave it briefly sooner or later. Despite the city's enormous size, it is delightfully easy to escape to the countryside for a dose of nature, peace, and quiet (which you can also find without leaving it; see **Green Cairo**, p. 59). A few means of transport are evaluated below, and the **Travel Information** chart at the front of the book gives stations, times, prices, and amenities.

Buses: These are a great alternative to the trains or more expensive private transport for destinations outside of Cairo. You can book a seat in advance, some buses are air-conditioned, and some have videos blaring to help while away the journey.

Trains: The trains are also good and cheap, but they are limited to the north–south line of the Nile—Port Said, Alexandria, Cairo, Luxor, Aswan, and stops in between. Reserved seats or berths are essential in first class and must be purchased in advance—at Ramsis Station, through a travel agent, or very easily at the Wagon Lits office at the Helnan Shepheard Hotel. You can also buy tickets for major destinations in some telephone exchanges— Bab al-Luq, for example, near the American University in Cairo. Although the train station is beautiful from the outside and the crowds offer great people-watching fodder, you will not want to spend much more time there than strictly necessary. The café, where service is poor and a cup of coffee expensive, is unappealing.

Planes: Obviously faster, but EgyptAir is notorious for canceled and late flights. And it is often impossible to get through to them by phone to get updates, so you can spend a lot of time cooling your heels at the airports. What kind of service can one expect of a monopoly?

Tourist buses: Very comfortable but comparatively expensive—for example, a trip to the Pyramids is $20–30 per person. These afford the opportunity to strike up temporary new acquaintances as well as excessive forced 'opportunities' to stop at the perfume-bottle factory, rug shop, kebab restaurant, and so on. The destinations are strictly limited to the major tourist attractions. Contact any travel agent or hotel for what's on when.

Organization-sponsored trips: Cairo's many community and other **Organizations** always have a large roster of interesting trips in and around Cairo. The Community Services Association (CSA), American Research Center in Egypt (ARCE), the Women's Association (WA), and the British Community Association (BCA) are among the most active in this regard. Their trips are always reasonably-priced, well-planned and -guided, and usually anyone can sign up. These outings are an excellent way to get your feet wet, meet people, and learn something. But you do have to sign up ahead of time. Just call, or see the "In Cairo" section in *Egypt Today* magazine for a very thorough listing.

Taxi and limousine services: For privacy and convenience, these are ideal. You do have to know where you want to go, and to make sure the driver knows as well. For any place off the beaten track, this can be problematic, but not insurmountably so with a little persistence. Unless you are able to resist very politely, you will also be subject to visits to Ali's uncle's alabaster shop and his sister-in-law's restaurant.

Travel to the oases: The major oases of the Western Desert—Kharga, Dakhla, Farafra, Bahariya, and Siwa—are all major jaunts requiring three to four days minimum, good planning, and a fair amount of cash until you are experienced enough to venture on your own. Contact CSA or WA (**Organizations**) to see if any trips are planned, or call one of the travel agents specializing in desert-and-oases travel—specifically MAX Travel, Abercrombie & Kent, Ali Saad, Isis Travel, Maadi Adventures, or SIAG Travel (**Desert & Diving Safaris**). Just be aware that these agencies charge between $100 and $200 per day all-in, except for Isis and Maadi Adventures, which are both closer to $55 per day. Most Cairenes, even those who regularly travel the globe, have never been to the oases. Their allure seems to appeal more to foreigners, some of whom even live there. Check out the prospects for oasis travel carefully beforehand, as it can be restricted from time to time.

STAYING HEALTHY

BASIC PRECAUTIONS

The first and best advice is preventive: make sure family immunizations, especially children's, are up to date before you come, as not all vaccines are always available here. Contact the Center for Disease Control or its equivalent in your country to ascertain the most current recommendations regarding health precautions and immunizations for travel in Egypt. Currently these are: Typhoid, Meningitis (A and C), Rabies preexposure, Havrix monodose, Hepatitis B, Polio, and Diphtheria/Tetanus. Note especially the preexposure rabies vaccinations with Imovax, which involves three shots over a one-month period. You can also have this done in Cairo by a doctor or a pharmacist. The preexposure shots (imported from Merieux of France and available locally at As-Salam pharmacy in the hospital of the same name) confer almost indefinite immunity in three shots at LE70 each.

We do not wish to sound alarmist, but since rabies is common among stray animals in and out of Cairo, caution is warranted, especially for children. As you probably know, rabies is inevitably fatal unless treated very quickly. Postexposure treatment involves first and foremost washing the scratch or bite (or even a preexisting cut that may have been licked by a stray animal) for at least ten minutes with soapy water, then immediately getting started on postexposure injections. But the postexposure treatment with injections of RIG (Human Rabies Immunoglobin) is not consistently available in Egypt, which means you might have to leave the country to get treated—so it is well worth having the preexposure treatment.

Yellow fever is only required if you plan on traveling to sub-Saharan Africa or to Thailand. It is available at the Old Airport Clinic.

You will also need to be tested for HIV if you are planning to work here. An HIV certificate is required by the Ministry of Labor when issuing a work permit for the first time, but not for subsequent renewals, providing you have not been out of the country for more than six months. HIV certificates issued abroad are accepted providing they are legalized by an Egyptian consulate in the country in which they were issued; you can also have HIV tests in Cairo. Tourists do not need to have an HIV certificate.

Upon arrival, two simple rules suffice for tourists, plus one more for residents: be moderately careful about food, carry a small bottle of water everywhere, and, if you will be living here, find the most decent hospital closest to your home and make sure everyone in the family knows how to get there. Another way to guarantee quick access is to rent your flat from a doctor who also lives in the building; he or she will have a direct financial interest in keeping you healthy!

Much is made of 'pharaoh's revenge'— diarrhea—and dehydration in Cairo. Rule one above will probably not prevent one short bout of diarrhea shortly after arrival, but will keep it mild. Dose yourself and your loved ones with Kapect rather than Immodium should the pharaoh strike; both are available at all pharmacies, but Immodium should not be given to small children. Obviously one carries water in the desert to prevent dehydration, but it is also easy to get dehydrated trekking around the Pyramids and throughout Cairo. It is a law of nature that exactly when you feel faint from thirst after hours of shopping or exploring, there is not a place in sight from which to buy water—even in the heart of downtown Cairo.

Although Baraka is the most common

brand of bottled water, its very high mineral content gives it a taste some people don't like. Siwa and Delta are better (lower mineral content), with Delta having a distinct price advantage that makes it taste even better.

Tap water in Cairo is fine, but highly chlorinated and very occasionally an unappealing beige color. Accustom yourself to it in small doses gradually, and you will be far better off than visitors who keep their systems virginal and end up sicker than they need be from a sudden fall from grace in a five-star hotel.

Details on hygienic food handling are in Chapter 3 for people living, cooking, and buying food here. Eating out involves the usual commonsense precautions: no raw unpeeled fruit and vegetables; meat fairly well cooked; hot food hot and cold food cold. Also, try to eat where food handlers are more likely to wash their hands. Lastly, and discreetly or not, immediately spit out anything that tastes funny, especially seafood or alcoholic beverages.

SEAFOOD AND ALCOHOL

As two prime sources of potential health problems, these need to be addressed separately. The Nile is polluted and carries both giardia and schistosomiasis, both nasty things you do not want to get. Don't eat fish from the Nile and don't swim in it. And because of variations in storage and cooling, don't eat any seafood from anywhere that has even a faint off-taste. Shrimp are particular culprits here.

In lieu of anything else, and because of the very high price and limited availability of imported alcohol, people who drink do drink the local wine and beer, both produced under government auspices. The local beer, Stella, is produced in local and export versions, the difference being that Stella Local comes in green bottles, tastes better,

and is cheaper than Stella Export (Local is around LE3 per bottle in stores where it is sold, and ranges from LE5 to LE10 per bottle in restaurants of various categories). If it is flat (a frequent occurrence) or if it really has too many tidbits floating in it, send it back politely but insistently. The restaurateurs will grouse to their suppliers, who will grouse to the producers, and eventually consumer-driven quality control will trickle down. Fastidious readers might be interested to know that a friend who visited the Stella brewery in Cairo reported that he was absolutely staggered to think that anything fit for human consumption could possibly be produced in its filthy, dungeon-like atmosphere—and then proceeded to celebrate this observation with a nice cold Stella! (Both Stella and Egyptian Vineyards are up for privatization at the time of writing.)

The local wines, variously labeled Gianaclis, Reine Cleopatre, Cru des Ptolemées, and Omar Khayyam, come in red, white, and rose versions. All are awful; it is simply a question of deciding which ones are less so, and that is a matter of personal taste. Remember the comments on soil salinity earlier on? Apparently the vineyards are among its first victims, resulting in the ruination of what was once palatable Egyptian wine. With a little ice and club soda, the wines can be drinkable—barely—but the whites go off very quickly.

Both local wine and locally made hard liquor have been clearly implicated in a number of cases of methanol (wood alcohol) poisoning that caused at least two deaths since Christmas 1995. Avoid all but clearly imported hard liquor purchased from a traceable source—duty-free shops or trustworthy bars. Do not give empty liquor bottles to the garbage collector, the housekeeper, your friendly bootlegger, or anyone. Instead, break and discard them. Include a bottle-cutter among your household goods if you live here, or at least soak off labels before discarding bottles. Because adulterated wine caused one of the deaths, wine is now being sold less openly than before. If you want to drink it, do so gingerly, in moderation, and make sure it is from a reputable source. This last is relative, since a vaguely clandestine air surrounds all alcohol purchases other than at the duty-free shops, where it is a gay free-for-all among foreigners and Egyptians both.

MOSQUITOES

Egyptian mosquitoes can produce pyramid-sized welts on the tender flesh of the susceptible. Some sources swear that garlic pills and vitamin B-12 supplements ward off mosquitoes. You can also avoid them by using insect repellent on the skin and plug-in vapor repellents (which stink, but work) in the bedroom. Mosquito nets are effective too, but work and look best with a four-poster bed and a net big enough to puddle on the floor. Don't believe people who say that living high up in a highrise is a deterrent. Mosquitoes easily ascend to at least the tenth floor and can be particularly maddening in Maadi due to all the greenery.

COMMON AND UNCOMMON AFFLICTIONS

Following the relatively low risks of diarrhea and dehydration given sensible precautions, the Cairo cough or cold caused by low humidity and pollution is more common and less avoidable. We are not at the gas mask stage as in Tokyo or Mexico City, but when you drive south on the Corniche toward Helwan, you will think twice about it. The dust from the cement plants colors everything gray-white. People susceptible to allergies will notice them flaring up more here. As suggested earlier in the Climate section, those with dry skin and those who wear contact lenses will have to make the appropriate moisturizing adjustments. Finally, and again, sunscreen is always vital, especially for the fair-skinned.

MEDICAL CARE IN CAIRO

Overall, medical care in Cairo is excellent. Doctors train here by doing one year of pre-med in the Faculty of Science of their university followed by five years of medical school in the Medical Faculty, followed by a one-year internship and then two to four years of residency, depending on specialization. A license to practice medicine is awarded after completion of the internship phase. Internships and residencies are done abroad (UK, Germany) by many, and the great majority of doctors in Cairo speak good English.

Egyptian nurses may have either a government diploma (which is somewhat equivalent to a Licensed Practical Nurse's degree in the United States) or a Higher Institute of Nursing degree (three years) involving much more theoretical knowledge, but less patient-care practice. Egyptian doctors—and most patients, too—fault the low standard of nursing care as a major problem in Egyptian hospitals. Clearly the doctors themselves, as well as the Ministry of Health and the Medical Syndicate, could and should actively address this, as might the nurses themselves. But as elsewhere, 'women's work' is undervalued, and nurses have traditionally come from the lower classes, although that is beginning to change. Experienced nurses with Higher Institute degrees are paid between LE200 and LE300 per month in the government hospitals. It is customary, therefore, as you might well imagine, to tip everybody below doctors when you stay in hospital or have an operation. Doctors often prefer to work in private hospitals because there they can treat private patients, and charge private-patient fees for their services.

If you do have to spend time in hospital, it is quite normal to take in a companion. He or she can plump up your pillow, make sure that a needle dropped on the floor does not go into your arm, and keep an eye on you when the busy doctor is away from the hospital. Many people recommend using a foreign-trained nurse to monitor post-operative progress; your embassy should have a list, or contact the Community Services Association (CSA) in Maadi to get theirs (**Nurses; Organizations**).

More and more, the better hospitals are trying to attract foreign Directors of Nursing to upgrade and professionalize nursing care. One recently offered such a position to a well-qualified candidate at a very high Egyptian salary, LE2,000 per month, but it was not high enough by the foreigner's standards; an international oil company paid her far more.

Pharmacists are the buffer zone between the people and the rest of the medical establishment. They too are generally well trained, most speak excellent English, and all in all, they are a godsend. Find a good one in your neighborhood if you live here, and your life will be much simpler. They deliver (medicines, not babies), they consult and diagnose intelligently, and they even make housecalls to give injections to you, your kids, and your pets. Veterinarians do the same for pets.

Alternative or holistic medicine is booming in Cairo, as it always has in the countryside. A large number of foreign and Egyptian practitioners of everything from acupuncture to yoga ply their specialties formally and informally, and have large and devoted followings (**Alternative Therapies**). Egyptians have always used herbalists as well, who fall into the 'can't hurt, might help' category, and certainly they have centuries of practice from cosmetics to embalming to call upon in Egypt. The Harraz Herb Shop in Bab al-Khalq is reput-ed to be the best in Cairo for all sorts of advice and remedies in this line.

Foreigners notice two big differences about medical care in Cairo. One is hygiene standards, which are distinctly lower than most Westerners are used to. It is not common even in the fanciest clinics, for example, for the doctors to wash their hands as a matter of course before examining or touching a patient. Although you might feel reluctant, you should nevertheless diplomatically request that this be done. You can and should also request disposable needles for injections; this is pretty standard by now anyway. The other big difference is access:

ACCESS AND BEEPER ACCESS TO DOCTORS

Do not get sick in the morning or the afternoon if at all possible! Doctors traditionally keep only evening hours, saving the daytime for teaching and hospital attendance, and many jump from clinic to clinic. Hence tracking them down can be frustrating. Some of them also cancel or do not show up for their two-hour stint at Clinic X if there are not enough appointments scheduled to make it worth their while. Call just before leaving to make sure the doctor is due. Waiting times will vary depending on the luck of the draw. Patients may be better off seeing younger but well-qualified doctors who have not yet built up their reputations. The Anglo-American Hospital already has doctors attending in the mornings.

Improved access to doctors is increasingly available via beeper, which a great many doctors now have. And while you may hate them, they are particularly useful here for emergencies. Here is how they work: all doctors with beepers are available through the same three central dispatching numbers, which are on the front page of this book's Directory as well as right here: 777-474, 575-1851, and 575-9010. Dispatchers speak

English and French, but do not know doctors' names, only their beeper numbers. Which means you have to know their beeper numbers; clearly, it would be a vast improvement if the dispatching station kept lists by both number and name. In the meantime, we have provided as many as we could get in the Directory. If you know your doctor's beeper number and if you have a touch-tone phone, simply dial 010, then the beeper number; then wait for the tone signal and enter your own phone number followed by two pound signs (# #). Will you be able to remember all this in an emergency? No, so write it down or photocopy the front page of the Directory and keep it by the phone.

One last note on making medical appointments: do clarify whether your 10 o'clock appointment is am or pm—it is much more likely to be the latter!

MEDICAL FEES AND INSURANCE

A prominent Cairo physician acknowledged that the sight of a foreigner conjures up dollar signs in many a doctor's eyes. At the very first visit, clarify exactly what the fees are for a range of clinic and laboratory services. Make clear whether or not you have insurance, and whether you have a residence visa stamp in your passport, which should make you eligible for Egyptian fee rates. Some hospitals expect a cash guarantee that you will be able to pay their fees, often a minimum of LE1,000. Many companies working here issue a payment card for use in such a case, and in a few cases you can use an AMEX or VISA card, though you will probably have to pay the 5 percent extra commission on the card.

For Egyptians, medical insurance is supplied by the government, by employers, and through private insurers. Foreigners working here often have some form of insurance through their companies, but not always. One excellent alternative is the British Community Association's (BCA) (**Organizations**) medical insurance scheme. It is open to anyone who joins the BCA for a mere LE30 per person or LE40 per family, plus a one-time application fee of LE100 per person and an annual fee of LE220 per person for the medical scheme. This entitles you to unlimited visits to the BCA Clinic (**Clinics**) at the Anglo-American Hospital, Zamalek, and to the clinics at the affiliate Hospitals (As-Salam, Nile Badrawi, Pyramids, Hayat Medical Center, Misr International, and Cairo Medical Center). In addition, the usual deposits—often quite hefty—for treatment and/or stays at these hospitals are waived on presentation of the BCA medical membership card, and patients can claim refunds of up to LE500 for treatment costs.

The International Association for Medical Assistance to Travelers (IAMAT), a Canada-based organization, has member clinics in and around Cairo. Fees are set by the organization and tend to be comparable to overseas medical fees—for example, $55 for an office visit, $75 for house calls, and $95 for holiday/Sunday house calls; residents may be eligible for lesser fees. One IAMAT doctor, Dr. Nabil Ayad al-Masry, specializes in tropical diseases and fevers; his IAMAT Clinic is conveniently located near the Coptic Hospital off Sharia Ramsis just north of Ramsis Station (see **Clinics**).

Foreign-based medical insurance for independent travelers or residents is also available, but in general is quite expensive, as it usually includes medical evacuation options. For this kind of insurance, consult classified ads in the international newspapers or your embassy's consular section.

EMERGENCY CARE

The best emergency care is the closest. You realize this the first time you are caught in a major traffic jam and you hear the blare of an ambulance siren—and nothing moves! Including, of course, the ambulance. Inquiries to taxi drivers regarding this phenomenon yielded the observation that 'big shots' commandeer ambulances when they want to get somewhere fast. So of course everyone ignores them. Whether or not this belief has any validity, the result is the same as if it were true. In addition, ambulances in general do not have paramedical professionals or life-support apparatus on board, but there are exceptions: specifically, As-Salam and Nile Badrawi hospitals in Maadi send emergency room physicians with their ambulances. (See **Medical Emergencies**, front of Directory.)

Please note that telephone lines in Cairo are overloaded, including those at hospitals, clinics, and particularly emergency rooms. So in a real emergency, don't bother calling. Just go as quickly as you can.

PLASTIC SURGERY

To bring you down from emergency alert to a more frivolous level, a word on plastic surgery in Cairo. If you have been considering the odd nip and tuck, you have come to the right place. Cairo is becoming something of a center for plastic surgery among well-heeled Egyptians as well as among Europeans and Middle Easterners, men as well as women. Face lifts, liposuction, collagen treatments, laser and sclerotherapy for varicose veins, radial keratotomy for the nearsighted on an out-patient basis—all are available at considerably more reasonable cost than abroad. If you are curious but feeling tentative, ask to interview a few happy patients after you have discussed your requirements with a plastic surgeon.

You can even have permanent lipstick, eyeliner, or an alluringly-situated beauty mark applied through the wonders of tattooing. Who would expect anything less in the land of Cleopatra and Nefertiti? (An Egypt-

ian friend reports that eye-liner tattooing is agonizing, but she is very happy with the results!).

What price beauty? In the most expensive shops, tattoos range from LE200 to LE600, fruit acid peels to clear and smooth the skin are LE166 per application, and collagen injections are LE300 each. Various overhauls, all according to prices at Shaalan Surgicenter, which is far and away the most expensive: face lift, LE7,000–10,000; breast reduction or augmentation, LE3,000–4,000; eye lift, LE3,000–5,000; rhinoplasty (nose job), LE2,000–3,000; liposuction, LE1,500–3,000.

BEST HOSPITALS AND CLINICS

We have listed in the Directory only hospitals, doctors, laboratories, and clinics that come well recommended by foreigners and Egyptians. For additional recommendations, consult any of the **Nurses** in the Directory or your embassy, but note that some embassies tend to be impractically limited or perhaps hidebound in their recommendations. The US Embassy, for example, recommended exactly two pediatricians in all of Cairo in late 1995. The Kasr al-Aini Teaching Hospital, the post-modern brick-and-aluminum fortress on the Corniche in Garden City that opened in March 1996, was too new at the time of writing to make realistic recommendations. Its great potential rests heavily on the government's ability to keep up its state-of-the-art equipment, which is currently being serviced under contract with the French, who funded the hospital.

BRAND NAMES FOR COMMON DRUGS AND PHARMACEUTICALS

Trade names for reliable Egyptian-made brands are given below, preceded either by their common American names or by their effects. They are much cheaper than imports, and often made under license to a foreign pharmaceuticals company. New drugs, imported and locally produced, come on the market every day, so consult with your pharmacist on what is available and best. Prescriptions are rarely necessary, even for some controlled substances like codeine, Valium, and Prozac. Warning: This does not mean that our readers or anyone else should self-medicate.

Ibuprofen: Brufen; comes in 200, 400, and 600 mg coated tablets and in syrup for children

Tylenol: Paracetamol.

Aspirin: Rivo (original and micronized formulas), Aspocid, Asponasr.

Antidiarrheals: Kapect, Lomotil, Entocid, Streptoquin.

Worm treatments: Flagyl, Fluvermal.

Antifungal creams: Canesten, Dactarin.

Rehydrators: Rehydrans (sold in packets of powder to be mixed with juice or water).

Antihistamines: Claritine, Flurest, Allergex, Hismanel, Histadine (most come in both sedative—for sleeping—and non-sedative formulas).

Topical analgesics: Xylocaine (2 percent and 5 percent), Lignocaine.

Anti-inflammatories: steroidal: Diprosole, Betaderm, Dermatop, Fucicort; non-steroidal: Voltaran, Olfen, Feldene (both come in tablets and ointments).

Antibacterial ointments, creams: Fucidin, Garamycin, Fucicort.

Antibiotics: Septrin, Taravid, Ceclor, Peflacin, Augmentin (note, please, that antibiotics are only effective against bacterial infections, not viruses, and that they must be taken for five to ten days to work, and so as not to build up an immunity to them; don't self-medicate, especially with antibiotics, but if you cannot reach a doctor, rely on careful consultation with a careful pharmacist).

Antivirals: NoVirus (tablets and ointments,

intended for herpes and other viral infections).

Multivitamins: for adults: Vitamax, Supravite, Geriatric Pharmaton, Theragran; for children: Theragran liquid, Multisenestol; for all: Seven Seas brand vitamins in a large range of formulations.

Mosquito repellents: Off Spray (contains 15 percent DEET).

Tampons: the only brand available so far in Egypt is Tampax; Egyptian women generally resort to sanitary pads, but the cultural prohibitions against tampons may lessen in the face of advertising and education, thereby inreasing market choice.

Baby wipes: Fresh Ones brand comes in big boxes, and now also in pocket- and purse-sized dispensers; very convenient anywhere and everywhere.

Please check the Directory under the specific appropriate heading for anything you need or want to investigate—for example, **Alternative Therapies**, **Doctors** (under which each specialty is listed alphabetically), **Clinics**, **Pharmacies**, **Veterinarians**, etc.

MONEY MATTERS

CURRENCY AND CURRENCY EXCHANGE

Cairo (and more so the rest of Egypt) is still largely a cash economy as soon as you descend from five-star altitude. The best place to change foreign currency is at the innumerable exchanges throughout the city. They have much better hours, better rates, and shorter lines than the banks, and they do not charge any commission. The rate you see posted is what you get. Travelers' checks limit your flexibility in this regard, as many exchanges—and banks—will not take them, or will charge a lot for doing so. Carry cash instead, with caution. Note too that there has been a recent influx of good-quality counterfeit $100 bills, so this denomination is very carefully scrutinized; you are better off with $50 denominations. Hotel personnel can also usually be trusted, by the way, to change foreign currency for you when the hotel's exchange service is closed, as it often is. They just go to an exchange or a bank, get the cash, and bring you the receipt, deserving, of course, a tip of a pound or two for their trouble. Just make sure the person who does this for you is traceable.

You will need something other than a normal wallet to carry your wads of Egyptian pounds (*gineeh*, referred to by some as 'L-E'). Some sort of make-up case with dividers works well. It is hard to get either of the two largest denominations, LE50 and LE100 bills, and harder still to change them. Denominations of LE20, LE10, and LE5 are more common, then near the bottom of the scale, with le1 bills, the scarcity again increases. Get at least LE100 in singles as soon as you can for taxis and so on, to save yourself the nuisance involved in making change. One hundred piasters (*'irsh*) make one pound, and paper currency also comes in 25 and 50 piaster notes. Coins of smaller denominations are rare, often superseded by matches, gum, and candy for change from a purchase. The **Currency Conversions** chart at the front of the book gives Egyptian equivalents of major foreign currencies.

A FEW CURRENT SALARY SAMPLES

Before proceeding to tipping (baksheesh), the humanitarians among our foreign readers might be interested in what some Egyptians earn. The 1996 estimated per capita income hovered just over $600 per year, or $50 (LE170) per month. Look around at prices, consider inflation and the likely devaluation of the Egyptian pound, and then imagine raising a family on monthly salaries like the following:

Cairo University tenured professor, Ph.D. with twenty years' experience: LE700

Egyptian housemaid, full-time: LE100–250

Accountant, recent university graduate, large private international accounting firm: LE400

Government schoolteacher; mid-level public servants: LE300

Laborer at Stella bottling plant: LE100

Laborer at private company: LE670

Bawwab (before tips): LE100–150

Sales clerk, mid-range clothing shop: LE200

Tea boy, private company: LE350

TIPS ON BAKSHEESH

There are a lot of people in Cairo. Quite a number are obscenely rich. But the vast majority of them are poor, or barely scraping by. You will probably note that wealthier Cairenes tend to tip generously. If you are a foreigner, who most likely falls into this same relative category, you might do the same. We note, for example, that Cairenes who can well afford it routinely tip 10 percent over the restaurant bill directly to the waiter, who theoretically receives the 12 percent service charged at most places (the old theory/practice dichotomy is unlikely to work to the waiter's advantage, is it?).

'Parking attendants'—both the ones who really do guard and move your car as well as those who suddenly appear out of the woodwork—expect 50 piasters or a pound, depending on how long you have been parked, how bad the parking situation is, whether they have cleaned your windshield, and so on. If you are taxi-ing, notice that the taxi driver tips these fellows, and take that into account when you pay him. One Egyptian acquaintance routinely waves off the out-of-the-woodwork parking attendants, another routinely—but ever so discreetly—

tips a pound to her neighborhood traffic cop as he stops traffic for her. Watch, figure out what the locals do, and let your conscience be your guide, along with the specifics below:

If you are a weekend guest, it is traditional to tip the domestic help of your hosts; LE20 is generous and fair for foreigners.

When someone carries your packages, tip them 50 piasters or a pound. When it takes three people to carry the same packages, tip a pound altogether. Bellhops in the big hotels get more—LE2–5 depending on the number of bags.

Avoid self-appointed 'guides' at museums and monuments. They are the bane of tourists in Egypt, expert at nothing except haranguing you. A sepulchral 'I vant to be alone' à la Greta Garbo usually does the trick after the tenth time or so. And should you have to pay to have the lights turned on at the Islamic Museum even though you have already paid LE8 admission (for foreigners) under the foolish assumption that visibility is part of the deal? Apparently so.

If you are at a hotel for a considerable length of time, about LE10 per week for the person who cleans your room is good. Prorate for other services from doormen and concierges.

It is not uncommon to tip the fellow who fills your petrol tank or the man who prepares your deli order at the supermarket. Supposedly this assures you of continued good service, but at Sunny's Supermarket, for example, this is not an automatic guarantee.

The much more complex baksheesh issues that arise when you live here are covered in Chapter 3.

dren, children everywhere. And as usual, rumors abound of beggar kings and beggars' auctions and drug involvement in the whole business. Whether the rumors are true or false, the pathos and plight of many beggars are obvious, of some others, not so. Since it is one of the Five Pillars of Islam to give alms to the poor, and since a strong streak of fatalism runs through Egyptian society, there is little shame, if any, associated with begging. It is just the beggars' lot in life, with which they cope quite cheerfully in the main.

Be aware of one strong deterrent to giving money to beggars: you will frequently and immediately be surrounded by ten more, especially when children are involved. And the old ploy of giving food rather than money to someone mimicking eating with a hands-to-mouth movement is usually met with derision and scorn, so don't attempt to control the process in this fashion (although we did witness one enterprising young girl of eight or so, under her mother's watchful eye, deftly and with great aplomb scooping hearty leftovers from the tourists' plates during Ramadan in Khan al-Khalili; not begging at all, but recycling).

If you feel that you cannot face it on a daily basis and decide to simply ignore all beggars, you might consider salving your conscience by a generous donation of food, toys, clothing, time, or money to the many charities that help the poor, or to take one neighborhood family discreetly under your wing in some useful fashion—shoes, books, and vitamins for the kids; food, especially meat, for one of the feasts. This is a customary, practical, and personal form of charity here in Cairo.

BEGGARS

Beggars are a fact of life throughout Egypt. The elderly poor, the handicapped, mothers with fly-bespecked babes in arm, and chil-

PRICES AND BARGAINING

A number of sources we contacted, particularly among expatriates, claimed that bargaining is on the wane in modern-day Cairo.

They must have been referring to Cairo, Illinois!

Virtually everything is negotiable in Cairo and throughout Egypt, from airline tickets to hotels, a length of fabric from any shop in any price category, to a kilo of tomatoes at the corner grocer's. Arabs the world over are known for the trading skills and wiles they have honed over centuries, and though the Egyptians do not identify themselves as Arabs, they are nevertheless experts at the art of bargaining.

Even where prices are clearly marked, and even in upscale shopping venues like the World Trade Center, some people bargain to good effect. 'Discounts' are often made available to 'friends.' Doctors' fees are negotiable. And of course, bargaining is *de rigueur* in all the *suqs* (markets), the epitome of which is the tourist-infested but nevertheless wonderful Khan al-Khalili. Are there any rules of thumb? Probably not. Knowing exactly what one wants to pay is the only possible advantage the buyer can claim over the seller. If you enjoy the complex dance steps of bargaining for its own sake, you offer far less than you will actually pay and then gradually spiral up to agreement with the seller. If not, you state and then implacably stick to your price, but this may well be regarded as so crude that sellers will cut off their noses to spite their faces rather than sell to an ignoramus who seems oblivious to the whole concept of 'face.' Remember, this is supposed to be fun; it is the social heartbeat of the Middle East.

A few unusual aspects of pricing and commerce that may run counter to some foreigners' intuition: A whole lamb—head, eyes, hooves, wool, and all—will cost the same per-kilo price as a choice cut, at least at the numerous butchers we have patronized. Volume discounting, unlike discounting by any and every other rationale, does not seem to be the norm here. Returning merchandise is also frowned upon, although it can be done. It is a question of more-persistent-than-thou, and of stressing your value as a customer to the management. Customer relations and consumer activism are fairly new concepts in Egypt, so caveat emptor is the rule.

MISCELLANEOUS POINTERS ON MONEY

Learn the Arabic number symbols immediately if not sooner. Some establishments have no qualms about rounding up even well-marked prices if they think it will fly.

Travelers' checks are a real nuisance in Egypt. Avoid them.

Don't be alarmed by a staggeringly high bill at a reasonably priced restaurant; it just means that prices are tallied in piasters rather than pounds, so simply move the decimal point two places to the left for a better deal.

Look at the menu. It is all too common for the gullible *khawaga* to be soaked by the friendliest waiters and managers of charming restaurants. If they say they do not have a menu or that it is in Arabic only, leave or ask the price first.

Don't accept torn or otherwise mutilated bills from banks or exchanges, as shopkeepers will not accept them.

BANKING IN CAIRO

Even if you live here as a foreign resident, you can almost avoid banking here. Cash rather than checks are used to pay bills, so a checking account, known here as a current account, is useful mostly as the destination for funds from your paycheck or overseas. Bank cards and cash machines are now routine at the larger **Banks**, which provides an additional reason for having a checking account, but it must be in Egyptian, not foreign, currency—that is, you cannot draw Egyptian pounds from a dollar account via cash machine.

With a Visa or American Express (preferably gold) credit card you can, by maintaining a positive balance on the card account, withdraw money readily at the American Express Bank office or at hotels that honor those cards. It's free!

Savings accounts and fixed deposits (CDs) are available in Egyptian pounds and dollars at most banks. The interest rates for these are expected to go down slightly in 1997, but in mid-1996 they were hovering around 4 percent for dollar savings accounts (5 percent for CDs with one- to twelve-month maturities). In Egyptian pounds, these options were more interesting: 10.25 percent for savings accounts and about 9.5 percent for CDs. It beats inflation, but if the rates do go down as promised, it will not.

Banking tends to be a time-consuming and inefficient process regardless of the bank. In fact, banks with the biggest reputations, like Commercial International Bank (CIB), are the worst offenders in this regard. Each slightly different transaction requires going to a different department. Long lines await at each—no one-stop shopping yet. While waiting, though, it is entertaining (at least initially) to watch as businessmen stuff briefcases, suitcases, and gym bags with huge wads of cash. Even without lines, very simple transactions like cashing a check can and do take forty-five minutes, as various minions ponder your signature, confer with colleagues, do not have the denominations needed at hand, and so on. And international banks like (but not by any means limited to) Citibank charge very high fees for the privilege of getting your foreign-bank check (even from another Citibank!) deposited into your local account: 16 per mil, which translates into $16 per thousand dollars. It also takes a minimum of two weeks, and more commonly four weeks, for a check from abroad to clear, so remember this when calculating your cash-flow needs.

Finally, do not assume that because you have an account at one branch of a bank, you can simply wander into another branch of the very same bank to cash a check. You cannot—well, you can, but you have to go through a lot of rigmarole with the manager of each branch first.

If you must bank, it is the same situation as with hospitals, for similar reasons: the best bank is the one closest to home or work. And the best time to hit the bank is shortly after it opens at 8:30 when most customers are still sleeping but employees are in place. MIBank, Egyptian British Bank, and the Bank of Nova Scotia come well recommended within the context of the comments above.

CRIME IN CAIRO

This section can be mercifully brief: Cairo is an astonishingly safe city, considering its size and the poverty of many of its inhabitants. There is virtually none of the horrifying, anonymous violence that plagues some of the world's major metropolises. The first reason given in response to "Why do you love Cairo?" by a veteran foreign journalist (female) living here was: "I feel safe. I can walk anywhere, any time, alone, without feeling threatened."

That said, here are a few caveats and observations worth considering, as petty non-violent crime seems to be on the rise of late.

Foreign pedestrians of either sex should be wary of a few pickpocketing scams: being approached by a playful 'drunk' who is bobbing and weaving too closely; the old "There's mud—or pigeon dirt, or ice cream—on your leg/back" ploy; and, of course, being targeted in crowded bus or train stations or in the conveyances themselves where foreigners stand out. Should you suddenly find yourself being victimized, quickly shout "IlHa'uuni! Haraami!" meaning 'Help! Thief!' You will be helped, not ignored, by passersby.

If your car breaks down—even (or especially) in Maadi, we hear—don't fall prey to the 'helpful' stranger who lifts the hood to have a look and may walk off with the vital part he has just removed, only to have his 'brother' appear a short time later to sell the part back to you at an exorbitant price. Such ruses are rare, though; more typically, Egyptians of all classes will genuinely and competently help you charge the battery or replace the flat tire and absolutely refuse any money for it.

Differing somewhat with our friend the journalist, we strongly advise women—even with male companions—to avoid Khan al-Khalili at night during Ramadan. First, it is a madhouse; you risk being literally stampeded to death should you accidentally trip or fall. And even if you don't, rowdy bands of teenage boys tend to get way out of hand—that is, their collective hands can feel you up faster and more thoroughly than you would ever dream possible.

This brings us to a note on sexual harassment in general, a topic on which there is little consensus among the women we interviewed. Many feel violated, at least symbolically, by the hisses, stares, and sotto voce comments one sometimes gets on the streets of Cairo. Others barely notice it, or just ignore it if they do. Although harassment, sexual or otherwise, is a punishable crime in Egypt, do not expect much sympathy from those who should know better. The magazine *Egypt Today* in March 1996 published a frankly hair-raising piece quoting such eminent personages as the head of the vice department and a (female!) AUC professor, who seriously opined that really 'decent' women do not get harassed or attacked. The rest of the article makes very clear that they do. Advice: be friendly but on guard in response to friendliness; totally ignore rude stares and comments; react with loud outrage the moment an unwelcome male hand is placed upon you; and do not sit in the front seats of taxis unless the driver is a woman.

Finally, the police: it is unlikely you will ever have to resort to them, but if you must, you are in for a pleasant surprise. Real policemen, English-speaking or not, are unfailingly courteous and as helpful as they can be on the whole. Please keep this in mind as you digest the following paragraph.

Unfortunately, there also seems to be a number of people—real but renegade policemen or impostors, who knows?—who use their uniforms to first intimidate and then rob their victims of money, passports, and jewelry, sometimes with the unpleasant twist of having first planted an alleged drug like hashish or cocaine on them. *Do not* get into an unmarked car or taxicab with anyone in a police uniform. *Do not* hand anything over to them. *Do not* give them your address or take them to your home. Insist politely, and then loudly, that you must first walk to a telephone to call the local police station and talk with an English-speaking officer, and ask them to give you the number. Act cool or act clueless, but attract an audience and be stubborn. Your persistence will eventually drive these creeps away unrewarded. Then, to reduce the frequency of this new phenomenon, report it to the real police and to your consular section.

TERRORIST ATTACKS

On April 18, 1996, all Cairo was put on violent notice that attacks against tourists would resume after a long and peaceful lull of four years. Eighteen people were shot to death outside a Pyramids Road hotel in broad daylight, having apparently been mistaken for a group of Israeli tourists by the gunmen.

It remains to be seen how effectively the

Egyptian government cracks down on this very serious threat to its vital tourism dollars. In the recent past, the response has been swift and hard. For this, both residents and tourists in Egypt must be grateful while they, and the world at large, wait for an enduring end to the myriad conflicts in the Middle East.

COMMUNICATIONS

MAIL SERVICES

The good news is that, basically, the postal system in Cairo works. The bad news is that it is slow and can be unreliable. To illustrate: a few years ago, a couple we know were delighted to receive an invitation in the mail in early December to a lavish New Year's Eve do. All decked out in their holiday best, they showed up very fashionably late on December 31st at their host's door—like, a year too late. The invitation had been mailed over one year earlier.

Pity the poor postal workers. They have to sort mail written in two different alphabets. Given that, they do a pretty good job. To enhance the chances of your in-Cairo mail arriving, print the address very clearly or type it, and allow a week for delivery, although lots of things take only a day—amazing! You can put it in the red (local mail) mailboxes one finds around town, but it is probably better off taken to your local post office. Many Cairo residents, local and foreign, advise against using the local mail, but from our experience, this is unwarranted. We and other people we know routinely receive flyers, notices of meetings, and even letters from overseas unscathed.

Letters for overseas can be successfully mailed from any big hotel, which may work better than from a post office or the blue airmail mailboxes. Overseas stamps, available from hotel newsstands and the post office,

are 80 piasters; letters take seven to ten days to Europe and ten to fourteen days to North America. For your regular overseas correspondents, you could send them address labels written in both Arabic and English—a handy present to family and friends and a gentle reminder to write. Larger **Stationery Stores** along Sharia Abd al-Khaliq Sarwat downtown can make such labels for you.

Receiving packages or well-stuffed envelopes from overseas is dicey and a nuisance at best. They are inspected by customs officials and censors—CDs, videotapes, and computer games especially—and hence rarely arrive intact, if at all. You receive a notice and must go to the dusty, cavernous customs clearing house downtown or out near the airport to pick up the package, run around to various windows, and very possibly pay duty worth more than the package's contents. This is true even if packages are sent to a business address, by the way. All in all, not worth it.

COURIER SERVICES

To send important mail, and especially packages, with the greatest expectation of its getting through, you will probably have to resort to expensive courier services (**Couriers**). Federal Express's charges from Cairo are typical, and even competitive: a minimum rate of LE120 for anything up to 250g (8.75 oz). A full kilogram (2.2 lb), by comparison, is 'only' LE160. Ten percent sales tax is added to all prices. For this, though, you are promised (but almost never get) 24-hour door-to-door delivery to anywhere in the Middle East, Europe, and the United States. Lower rates can be negotiated if you set up an account.

TELECOMMUNICATIONS

Telephone density throughout Egypt is low: 3.47 telephones per 100 people—but much higher in Cairo—compared to 55 per 100 in the United States. But service in Cairo is, at long last, relatively good. Egypt ranks among the five most expensive countries in the world for international calls. And cellular phones at this writing still require registration, although they are no longer illegal. Nevertheless, Egypt's telecommunications infrastructure is developing—and being embraced—rapidly, while government restrictions on its use are being chipped away at slowly but surely.

Under each heading below, we first cover those aspects of the topic relevant to visitors, and then move on to considerations for residents. But first off, we strongly advise all new residents to do a thorough hands-on check of their telephones and phone lines before signing a lease on an apartment. Just because there is a telephone physically present on the premises does not guarantee that it works, that the number is valid, or that it has the long-distance or international capacities promised by either lease or landlord. Private lines mysteriously become party lines, your number becomes someone else's, 'temporary' turns into forever—and we all nevertheless manage. So will you.

DIRECTORY ASSISTANCE AND DIRECTORIES

Phone numbers in Cairo have been undergoing major revisions over the last several years. In one year alone, the phone numbers in Nasr City changed *three* times; the subscribers themselves were reportedly not informed of these changes. Finding a given number, therefore, is not easy. There are English-language directory assistance numbers for Greater Cairo (140 and 141). Unfortunately, the lines are often busy, and usually exactly the number you want is the one "not in the diary," as the helpful but stymied operator advises you.

There is also an English/Arabic *Cairo Yellow Pages* put out by Egypt Yellow

Pages in conjunction with Tele-Direct International Ltd, a Bell Canada Company. It is only minimally useful as a consumer directory, concentrating as it does on manufacturing, and listing only some Egyptian ministries and foreign embassies but no other government offices.

A new set of directories, the *Focus Guides*, is somewhat better. There are separate books for different neighborhoods, but again, the emphasis is on business rather than consumer listings. The guides are LE12 each and not always easy to find, but can be obtained from the publishers.

The Maadi Women's Guild publishes an annually updated residential and consumer directory called *The Maadi Women's Guild Telephone Directory* (LE20). It is very useful for Maadi residents, less so for others as the majority of its listings are for Maadi.

For businesses, the situation is far better. In addition to those mentioned, three other business directories exist: the American Chamber of Commerce in Egypt's *Membership Directory*, *EgyptTrade*, and the two-volume *Kompass Directory*. The last is by far the best and most comprehensive—the Rolls-Royce of business directories, carrying a high—and highly justified—price (LE450). (See **Directories** for information on the above publications.)

Cairo: The Practical Guide's Directory will begin filling the large gap for consumer listings with this and our subsequent editions; we hope that community-minded readers will send their additions and corrections to AUC Press, PO Box 2511, 113 Sh. Kasr el Aini, 11511 Cairo.

LONG-DISTANCE AND INTERNATIONAL CALLS

Long-distance calls within Egypt and overseas calls can be made from any of the big hotels, but at considerable mark-ups over the already high rates. Use an international calling card like MCI or AT&T when calling from hotels. Calls can also be made from any telephone exchange (known as 'centrales') either by purchasing time in advance (with a minimum of three minutes) or, better, by purchasing prepaid calling cards. Purchasing time from the centrale operator costs about LE24 for three minutes to Europe or North America; when using the operator you must pay for at least three minutes if you connect, including to wrong numbers and answering machines. And, of course, in using centrales, be prepared for long waits and lines; the low telephone density means that many Cairenes must use the centrales. See the front of the Directory for neighborhood centrale numbers. Prepaid calling cards are much cheaper and are not subject to a minimum amount of time; LE15 gives 2.5 minutes. The cards do not work from some phones, though, even for within-Egypt long-distance calls. Trunk calls can also be made from home but require a trip to the centrale first to pay a deposit, usually a percentage of the estimated length of the call.

CALL-BACK SERVICES

We are happy to report that to make international calls you no longer have to go to your local centrale, have an international line, or bother your neighbors who have one. You do not even need a calling card like MCI or AT&T. Much cheaper and simpler is using one of the various **Call-back Services** now available direct from Egypt and through US and European companies. Call-back companies essentially act as long-distance wholesalers, using the principles first developed by direct-to-the-public travel wholesalers. The system has become quite sophisticated, complex, and cutthroat, both as a business proposition and in terms of the technology used. But for the end-user, it is easy. You just dial a local or toll-free number to the call-back company, then hang up. The company immediately calls you back; then you give your personal ID number, wait for a signal, and dial the long-distance number. All this in many cases without the intervention of a single human being. A very recent (July 1996) glitch in the form of a lawsuit filed by major long-distance carriers against these call-back upstarts may throw a wrench into the works. But in the meantime, it is working.

These services are lifesavers for Cairo residents, many of whom cannot get an international line or can do so only at exorbitant costs and after inordinate waiting periods. Call-back services offer greatly discounted long-distance rates and can be used from both hotels and home. The requirements (deposits, minimum charges, billing, etc.) differ from company to company, so shop around to find the one that is most suitable. Cross Communications in Heliopolis has a fully-automated Egypt origination system in place, with rates of under $1 per minute for long-distance to the United States; they also deliver bills in person by appointment. Keep in mind that using call-back services usually requires a touch-tone phone. Phones that can switch between tone and pulse are available from most stores that carry phones in Cairo. Tone devices can also be purchased at many electronic stores in the United States and Europe and are often available from the call-back companies themselves.

If you are coming from abroad or using an overseas-based call-back service, put it into effect to the extent possible before you leave. This whole business is expanding and changing rapidly, so check the ads in the *Economist*, *International Herald Tribune*, *Financial Times*, or *Wall Street Journal* for what is available to and from Egypt, as rates and availability can vary widely.

LOCAL AND IN-EGYPT CALLING

These are fairly straightforward procedures, but there are a few bleeps. It is not uncommon for lines to get crossed so that Mr.

Mustafa across town is getting your calls and you his. Your line, unbeknownst to you, may actually be the *bawwab*'s line 'temporarily' being run up to your flat from the basement. And unless you specify—and check—beforehand, you (rather than the landlord) might get hit with the hook-up charges for long-distanceservice.

CENTRALES, BILLING, REPAIRS, AND SERVICE

Each neighborhood in Cairo has its own centrale, which is responsible for all repairs and service problems, billing and purchase of new or additional lines, and long-distance calls. Phone bills are issued every six or twelve months depending on the type of phone service one has and the conditions of its installation. If you are renting, your landlord will know when the bills should come. It may be advisable to allow him or her to handle payment, or to have a Mr. Fixit or your *bawwaab* make the payments and thereby save you a lot of standing around at the centrale.

Complaints and requests for repairs can be made by calling 188 or by calling your centrale directly.

TELEPHONES AND ANSWERING MACHINES

We suggest that readers buy their telephones (**Appliances, Small**) abroad if possible, as they are usually cheaper there than in Cairo and the hook-ups are the same; just plug them into the phone jacks in new flats or purchase an adapter for their use in older phone jack systems. BT devices from Britain may not work in Egypt, though. International brand-name phones with all the bells and whistles are available here— the Ogel stores have a decent selection—but make sure you are buying what you want: for example, a real Panasonic rather than a Panesonic or a Panasunic, which are cheaper Chinese knock-offs without warranties.

If you are bothered by crank callers, an answering machine with a male-voice phone message is a good way of warding them off.

FAX SERVICES

All hotel business centers and **Business Service Centers** provide fax, all at a hefty price. If you do a lot of personal or business communicating to overseas destinations, or even locally, strongly consider getting your own fax machine or fax modem set-up. The convenience is invaluable. It is illegal to have a second telephone line in residences (although some people do have them), so you may also want to acquire one of those gadgets that identify and route incoming faxes to the fax machine.

THE WORLD-WIDE WEB, INTERNET, AND E-MAIL

Egypt has joined this brave new world with a vengeance. And so far, it is uncensored. Until recently, there were only two ways to hook into the Internet other than through some private embassy systems: for academics, through the American University in Cairo and the Egyptian Universities Network; and for businesses, through the state-owned RITSEC (Regional Information Technology and Software Engineering Center). Both are free to users who can get an account, but access to the Web is limited by browser limitations. Now, RITSEC has opened up the arena by deciding to provide its services only to government affiliates, and allowing private **Internet Service Providers** (ISPs) to enter the fray. Which they have done, to the extent that Cairo now boasts its very own Cyber Café (**Cafés**).

The prices for entry now that there is competition for subscribers will almost surely drop over time. Price quotes in April 1996 from one of fifteen new ISPs, Video On Line, were in the range of LE125 per month with unlimited time and two free months, with quarterly or yearly payment upfront. Another, ESTINET, is cheaper still, and reliable for e-mail. Gradually, there may be some weeding out of the new providers, and, hopefully, a drop in prices.

One ISP, Internet Egypt, is cheaper than some because it has its own node—unlike others so far, who are simply reselling time they buy from the government's Information Decision and Support Center (IDSC—parent of RITSEC). Companies can lease a data line from Internet Egypt straight from their home or office to Internet Egypt's computer—you do not pay phone call fees—for LE15,000 per year. Individuals who do not need their own dedicated data line pay much less, of course. Internet Egypt and the Cyber Café (see below) might be the first place to check for the most current news on what's new in this world.

America On-Line (AOL) has just become available in Egypt. Other commercial services (like Prodigy and Compuserve) can be reached here only through costly ($15/hr) dial-up services. In the meantime, a whole host of providers are just starting up. We list a few and the services they offer or plan to offer here, giving their contact numbers and addresses under **Internet Service Providers** in the **Directory**. Since they are all brand new, though, check them out by word of mouth for prices, service quality, and so on.

ENSTINET provides e-mail only and is very inexpensive.

Internet Egypt: the whole gamut—Web pages, e-mail, Internet, dedicated lines, and the Cyber Café.

RITE: Internet access, e-mail, company database

Video On Line: Internet access, e-mail, company database

Anyone who is 'wired' and, ideally, has a browser like NetScape need not suffer Cairo's limitations of daily news access from print, TV, or radio sources. The world is at your fingertips, so type away on your keyboard to get:

Reuters and other wire services: http://www.yahoo.com

CNN news: http://www.cnn.com

Time-Warner (publishers of Time magazine): http://pathfinder.com

Voice Of America: http://gopher.voa.gov:70/11/newswire

For cultural and literary criticism from leftish points on the political spectrum, just a few of the hot 'webzines' are:

Hotwired: http://www.hotwired.com

Feed: http://www.feedmag.com

Salon: http://www.salon1999.com

Slate: http://www.slate.com

There are only about 120 (!) Egypt- and Egyptology-related web sites. Try any of these:

General information: http://pharos.bu.egypt

Government statistics on health, population, economics for all twenty-six governorates: http://163.121.21.50

Local news: http://www.synapse.net/~filou/samir/index.html (the normally rational Middle East Times avers not only that this is the best local news home page, but that it comes from—*The Egyptian Gazette!*)

Hieroglyphics: http://weblifac.ens-cachan.fr/Portraits/S.ROSMORDUC/nomhiero.html (just type in your name phonetically and you get it back in hieroglyphs!)

Soccer (stats, game schedules, etc.) on two sites: http://www.io.com/~wadood/egypt.html *or* http://www-ceg.ceg.uiuc.edu/~haggag/soccer.html

Economics: http://163.121.10.42/amman/indicat (company listings, product directories, but no investor information, from the Egyptian Business Center)

Coptic Orthodox Church of Egypt:

http://cs.www.bu.edu/faculty/best/pub/cn/Home.html

THE CYBER CAFÉ

If it lasts, this looks to be the best bet for access to the cyberworld and its denizens. It is part of Internet Egypt under the direction of Dr. Ahmed Bahgat, and is staffed by Egyptian digerati from 9 am to 9 pm. In addition to eight PCs (IBM clones), the Cyber Café offers a big stereo with Mariah Carey, Yanni, Michael Bolton, and Egyptian pop music CDs, a lounge full of computer magazines, non-alcoholic beverages, and a classroom for computer training. You cannot smoke, except in the lounge, and currently you need your own e-mail address to get or send mail, but this too may change. All this and the company of one's fellow nerds for a mere LE10 per hour—cheaper than a game of pool or bowling.

MEDIA

Increasingly, the scope and variety of English print and other media are improving. International daily newspapers usually arrive only one day late on Cairo newsstands. For residents, it is cheaper and more convenient to get subscriptions to these, which can be done through al-Ahram (see below), and they really do arrive most of the time. The local English-language daily *(The Egyptian Gazette)* is not up to par, but a few weeklies and some magazines, plus television, radio, and the World-Wide Web keep ignorance at bay. Note that unless one is in an expat neighborhood or tourist area, international publications are hard to find.

NEWSPAPERS AND MAGAZINES

Here's a hint: if you want to keep track of interesting people, places, and events in Egypt, get a loose-leaf binder and a hole puncher from the stationery shop; as you read the publications described below, cut out whatever interests you and file it in your binder to spare yourself the 'now-where-was-that-great-article-on-the-Camel-Market' syndrome. See **Newspapers** and **Magazines** in the Directory.

If you read Arabic, up-to-the-minute local and international news and commentary are available, with lively coverage from all points on the political spectrum. If not, you will probably resort to *The Egyptian Gazette*, a daily that purports to offer international and local news. The *Gazette* is most notable for its detailed reporting on the affairs of the president (the banner headline every day of the year), its unique approach to editing, and its . . . umm . . . striking editorial content. The *Gazette*'s somewhat Dickensian headquarters have been the spawning ground for a number of distinguished journalistic careers, though, so anyone with a fair command of English and printer's ink in the blood might well check out writing and editing opportunities with the Editor-in-Chief. A French daily, *Le Progrès Egyptien*, also originates here. LE180 for annual subscriptions to the *Gazette*, LE92 for Le Progrès.

Two weekly papers, the *Middle East Times* (MET) and *Al-Ahram Weekly* (both LE39 for annual subscription), supply more sophisticated renditions of regional and local news plus good cultural coverage, listings, and features. The *Weekly* tends to toe the government line, whereas the MET flaunts its occasional failure to do so by leaving a white space in place of a piece deemed objectionable by the censor. The *Weekly* has the better international coverage, MET the better upcoming events coverage. The *Weekly*'s French-language cousin is *Al-Ahram Hebdo*.

Another weekly, the *Middle East Observer*, proudly announces its mission: "Economic covering the Middle East, Arab Gulf and African Markets." It may well do so, but the syntax, grammar, and punctuation conspire to keep the mission a mystery (LE175 annual subscription—and only $375 abroad!)

Much better on regional business news, including Africa, is the monthly magazine *El-Wekalah*, with articles in both English and Arabic.

The general-interest English-language magazine market is cornered by *Egypt Today*, *Business Today*, and *Sports and Fitness*, all published by the same company. Glossy, well written, and even a teeny bit provocative on occasion, each has the hands-down best listings on events, activities, and organizations relevant to its audience. For *Egypt Today*, it is the cosmopolitan Cairene; for *Business Today*, anyone doing business in Egypt; and for *Sports and Fitness* athletes of all ages. Subscriptions are much cheaper than newsstand prices and the magazines come unscathed and on time monthly (LE45–60 for annual subscriptions).

Pose is a newer entry aimed at Cairo's jaded youth and anyone else interested in who is wearing what and where they are going while wearing it. *Live Colours* is a less literate version of the same, which, strangely, could use help with color separation of its live colors. Teenage girls and the well-born love-lorn would seem to be the main market for both.

For expatriates, a magazine from the United Kingdom called *RA: Residents Abroad* addresses this audience cogently and entertainingly. An airmail subscription is expensive, though: £61 per year.

TELEVISION AND RADIO

As one might infer from the satellite dishes that now far outnumber minarets on the skyline, television is rapidly altering not only the silhouette but the culture of Cairo and Egypt. Cairo was long the hub of television

and film production in the Middle East, but the advent of satellite broadcasts as a direct result of the Gulf War has changed all that. Big battles backed by big money, largely Saudi, are shaping up over who will control this megamarket and whether secular or Islamic influence will prevail.

Satellite and cable television offer a variety of programming, but satellite usually offers a few more channels (albeit in Turkish or Russian). Check with several companies to see who has the best programming. Cable television is available through Cable Network Egypt (CNE) (see **Television**) for around LE80 a month, which includes MNET, CNN, K-TV, MTV, and Super-Sport. A number of other services originate by satellite from London (MBC—Middle East Broadcasting Company), Italy (ART—Arab Radio & Television), and Cyprus (Orbit, which includes a number of English and French channels). For CNE and any others, though, you must also purchase a decoder box; the larger one with more features including remote control is LE799 and the smaller one without remote is LE399. Satellite is available from a number of different companies; in mid-1966, Samsung outlets in Cairo were offering a package deal of television set, receiver, and a fixed dish for about $740 (LE2,515). Flats rented to expatriates in Cairo now frequently include satellite dishes as part of the furniture—but to get a wide variety of channels via satellite, you need the remote that turns the satellite dish. (Whew! Our advice: read books instead.)

Avoiding cable and satellite, couch potatoes still have a reasonable choice, including Nile TV, which broadcasts in English and French. Channels 1 and 2 are the national channels emanating from the Television Building on the Corniche, with Channel 2 having news in English and French. Channel 3 is the Cairo local channel, and 4 through 8 are broadcast from Ismailiya,

Alexandria, Tanta, al-Minya, and Aswan respectively. All channels carry a variety of programming, including foreign language films and serials. A daily schedule for the two national channels and the Cairo channel is available in the *Egyptian Gazette*. Foreign serials appear often but tend to change frequently so check scheduling to see what is currently available.

FM 95 carries Cairo's European service radio, and features programming in English, French, German, Italian, Greek, and Armenian. The news is available in both French and English in the mornings. The *Gazette* prints a daily program schedule.

The BBC world service is also available throughout the day on several different AM frequencies. The *Middle East Times* prints a weekly schedule and a list of frequencies. Additional BBC information and schedules are available from the British Council (**Organizations**).

MANNERS, MORALS, AND CUSTOMS

Egypt is a complex blend of Mediterranean and Arab with respect to its manners, morals, and customs. Anyone coming from these traditions will find it easy to adapt; others may not. But Egyptians are quite open-hearted and open-minded (even if occasionally confused and amused) about the foibles of foreigners. Arrogance and bluntness, especially on the part of foreigners, though, are not well tolerated, and people who display these traits are rightly regarded as boors. It is also considered extremely gauche to criticize or display anger in public; the concept of saving face is as strong here as in many Asian countries. Most Egyptians, in other words, display considerably higher levels of tact, sensitivity, and good manners than certain Westerners do. Our advice: When in Cairo, do as the Cairenes do. Watch how they talk, watch

their body language, observe the interactions among guests and hosts, men and women, adults and children, and follow suit. Mostly, you will find yourself becoming more civil and civilized as a result. Below, we describe general customs, manners, and morals, and give a few specific pointers on how foreigners can make a positive impression for their own and their compatriots' sakes.

HOSPITALITY WITH A CAPITAL H

Even among the hospitable and generous Arabs, Egyptians take pride of place. They entertain lavishly or not at all—and up to, sometimes beyond, what they can afford. At no dinner parties in Cairo will you find anything remotely resembling nouvelle cuisine with its minimalist selections and starvation-ration portions. Instead, expect at least two or three offerings of every course, often served buffet-style, and heavy on the sweets Egyptians adore. To please your hosts, come with a hearty appetite, dieting for days ahead if necessary. Cairo is no place for finicky eaters, so mind your manners and try a little of everything. If you really cannot stomach liver or *kubeba* or pigeon or *mulukhiya*, just pray they are not all served at the same dinner, and say "I love most Egyptian food, but I'm allergic to X, I'm afraid."

It is polite to refuse the first offer of tea or a drink or hors d'oeuvres. Your host will press you, and you then graciously accept the second or third time. You will note quickly that two minutes after you are invited to an Egyptian home, even just to borrow a screwdriver, you will be offered something to eat or drink. You may refuse graciously, but do make the same offer yourself when people are in your home. This holds for business meetings as well, by the way.

Children are far more in evidence on social occasions than in the West, including those that go on until all hours. Your little darling will occasion the kind of acceptance and affection that nothing else can. The only place it is not appropriate to bring kids is to an official or semi-official party or an obviously adults-only event. When in doubt, ask three ways: "Shall we bring the children?"—But of course!—"Will any of the other children be there?"—Oh, a few.—"We have a baby-sitter anyway."—Oh, well, if you'd really rather not . . . .

Never be so rude as to show up on time to any social event, except the Opera or an *iftar* meal (see **Holidays** below). If you are invited for 8 pm, arrive between 8:30 and 9, but not much after. If it is for dinner, dinner may be served between 11 and 12 anyway. It is also likely that the men and women will eat and socialize quite separately at parties; the more traditional the home, the more likely this is, but even among Westernized Cairenes, it is common. Invitations are issued primarily by telephone. If you are entertaining, it is not untoward to call a few days ahead to remind your guests of the invitation.

Potluck dinners are not an Egyptian custom, nor is offering guests 'doggie bags' to take home, nor is offering to bring something for the dinner, except to the closest of friends. On the other hand, one never ever shows up empty-handed for dinner at someone's home—even Mom's. Foreigners may wonder what their Egyptian hosts do with all the flowers, candy, and pastries they are laden with. Wonder on, if you will, but bring them nevertheless. A fancy cake from a fancy bakery is the safe, chic thing. If you know for certain that your hosts drink alcohol, a bottle of scotch or some exotic liqueur—imported only—is a welcome alternative. Wine—again, imported only—is less so unless you are sure of your hosts' tastes. Fruit is not acceptable except among close friends, as it might suggest that the hosts cannot afford to buy their own.

If you spend the weekend as someone's guest, it is considerate to tip the household help. LE20 is generous unless you have made a real mess or they have gone above and beyond the call of duty in the care and feeding of your children. And don't bring Fifi or Fido; even if your hosts adore the little mutt, some of their other guests or neighbors might well not.

EGYPTIAN FAMILY LIFE

The importance of this cannot be overemphasized, particularly to Northern Europeans and North Americans, many of whose upbringings lead them to prize independence over family ties. Exactly the opposite is the case here. It is almost unheard of in Egypt, for example, for family members to go for months without seeing each other as adults. The cradle-to-grave family bond is not only inescapable, it is inconceivable that one could live otherwise.

An Egyptian's children, parents, and spouse—usually in that descending order—are exalted above all else. Egyptian mothers are at least as avid, for example, in their attention to their children's studies as Japanese women, this even if they are holding down full-time jobs themselves. It is not uncommon for little Ahmad's mother to learn German herself, say, in order to help Ahmad with his German homework. In the countryside and among the poorer classes, when a mother bears a son she is proud to be called, for example, Umm Mustafa, 'mother of Mustafa,' and does not remotely view this as a negation of her own identity; on the contrary, it enhances and ennobles it. The mother–son bond is traditionally closer than any other, and, as in many other cultures, is paralleled by the father–daughter bond, although fathers generally play a far less active role in their children's upbringing. Adoption, by the way, is illegal under Islamic law and in Egypt.

The job of Egyptian parents is to set their offspring up for life. They do everything they possibly can financially and socially to make sure their children marry well, get good jobs, and—very important—have a home and its many accouterments to embark on and renew the cycle. For all but the wealthiest, these efforts entail great sacrifices, which are usually undertaken more than willingly. Without a home of his own, usually paid for by his parents, a middle-class young man cannot hope to attract a suitable bride. If the parents of the young lovers (a strictly poetical term) cannot agree on exactly where the home is located and who pays for what bit of the furnishings, the marriage is off. Hence among the middle and upper classes, a broken engagement or two is not uncommon before the right personal and financial terms are reached to produce marriage.

We see, then, that the emotional stake parents have in their children's welfare is intensified by their considerable financial stake all up and down the economic ladder. As in much of the world, arranged marriages are the norm. That is not to say that romantic love does not enter the picture, but it is frequently a secondary consideration. Divorce is certainly not unheard of among Muslims, especially in Cairo, but it is comparatively rare and regarded as a calamity, except, perhaps, among the jaded nouveaux riches. The Coptic church does not allow divorce. An unmarried child is almost as much of a tragedy, childlessness a curse. Much is made of all this on the very popular Egyptian soap operas.

Although Islam permits the taking of up to four wives, this is rare now, particularly as one climbs the social and economic ladder.

SOCIAL CLASS AND MOBILITY

Is Egypt a class-conscious society? Yes, very much so, according to rich and poor alike. But especially since the 1952 Revolution, there are two routes to upward mobility: a military career and education. None of Egypt's four presidents was born to wealth or aristocracy, but they reached the acme of success through their military, and hence political, ambitions and connections. And some lucky few of the poor whose intelligence is recognized and fostered in school can also jump the class barriers to illustrious careers. Top civil servants, for example, are no longer necessarily of the aristocratic class as they invariably were before 1952, nor are members of the professional classes. 'Marrying up,' though not unheard of, is a less common ticket to a different life, given that marriages are more or less arranged.

Nevertheless and overall, despite the postrevolutionary increase in social mobility, Egypt's social structure retains many of its feudalistic divisions, and the Quran teaches all to accept their given stations in life. A couple of examples of how these class divisions work on a daily basis might illustrate the point: upper-class mothers do not take their children to the many public amusement parks appealingly scattered around Cairo—they take them to 'the club' instead. And the bulk of the café–casino–restaurants dotting the banks of the Nile, with their ideal settings, shade, and charm, are frequented only by the odd foreigner and the lower-middle classes—at least according to a number of upper-class Egyptians who would not be caught dead there.

THE BIRDS AND THE BEES

Cairo is much like the rest of Egypt and the Arab world with regard to relations between men and women. Marriage is the sole permissible venue for sexual relations, and platonic friendships between the sexes are rare. Light flirtation, though, is quite commonplace, as long as its limits are made eminently clear, and Egyptians are famous for their bawdy jokes and earthy sense of humor. But public displays of affection beyond a little clandestine hand-holding among young lovebirds are greeted with censure and even downright hostility. An Egyptian friend who gave her fiancé a quick peck in the car when he told her he had finished his doctorate was spat on by the middle-aged couple in the car next to them! (Our friend later used this experience to her advantage when she wanted street lights installed in her midan; she explained to the local council that her aim was to prevent the leafy street from being used as a 'lover's lane'—and quickly got her street lights.)

Adultery is illegal and can carry severe penalties, especially for the adulteress. Homosexuality is illegal too, but generally a blind eye is turned. Women of all classes are expected to be virgins at marriage. An Arabic saying loosely translated warns: 'A girl is like a match—you can only light it once.' To make sure the match lights on the wedding night, for the poor there is chicken blood, for the rich, re-virginization operations—and for the great bulk of brides there is genuine chasteness. Engaged couples can go out alone, in public, but the Western practice of dating prior to engagement does not exist; in effect, the couple only begin getting to know each other after they have committed publicly to marriage—another reason that broken engagements are not uncommon.

Males are circumcised with great fanfare among country people between ages five and ten, although among wealthy urban dwellers it is commonly done in infancy. And yes, female circumcision is practiced to a considerable extent in Egypt among both Muslims and Copts.

The removal of all bodily hair (including that of the head) was regarded by the ancient Egyptians as an act of spiritual purification for men and women. Today, men tend to limit it to shaving the underarm and sometimes the pubic hair, but fastidious women regularly have their bodies depilated completely using a sugar-and-lemon taffy-like substance called *Halaawa*. Many a Western bride has been somewhat chagrined to learn that her Egyptian husband views this as an essential aspect of his wife's toilette, as do her mother- and sisters-in-law.

WEDDINGS AND FUNERALS

Egyptian weddings are wonderful and exceedingly noisy bashes, whether held on the village street or at the Nile Hilton. Invariably, they are joyous, raucous, open-handed affairs designed in part to demonstrate the wealth and generosity of the families involved. And like Western weddings, they frequently break the bank of the parents. The groom's family usually pays for the wedding, the couple's house or flat, kitchen, lights, and electrical appliances. The bride's family handles the engagement party, furniture, and carpets. But the groom also has to come up with 'bride money,' or *mahr*, usually equaling one room of furniture, and a wedding gift, usually gold, for his bride, called the *shabka*; in rural areas, it is the *kirdaan*, or wedding necklace, and it has to be 21 or 24 carat gold, whereas in the city one can get away respectably with only 18 carats.

Foreigners are frequently invited or merely dragged along most welcome to Egyptian weddings. Your only obligation if dragged along is to enjoy yourself, dance, and be gracious. If you are invited, a gift is required. Here are a few gift guidelines from an upper-middle-class Egyptian perspective: A boss invited by a junior associate whom s/he doesn't know particularly well should give a minimum of LE200. To one's secretary of some years' duration, a minimum of LE500. Gifts of cash are appropriate, but silver tea sets, ashtrays, vases, and the like are also welcome. For the wedding of friends, it is perfectly all right to ask what they would like. Gifts are delivered to the couple's or families' home, not taken to the wedding, and they are not formally acknowledged.

Funeral customs are comparatively simple, but there are a few things to be aware of. Among Muslims, women receive women at home and men receive men either at home or in a specially-erected tent nearby on the day of the burial and for the following two days. It is customary to offer condolences then sit quietly for half an hour or so before leaving. Sugarless coffee is traditionally served. Only the men go to the mosque, where prayers are said, then they walk to the cemetery or part way carrying the bier. If one cannot attend a funeral when it is expected that one should—and this is an obligation to which great weight is given—it is customary and virtually required to send a telegram, fax, or note of condolence right away to the family of the deceased. An important commemoration takes place on the fortieth day after the death, and if you were not able to pay your respects at the time, you should certainly do so now. Coptic funeral customs differ slightly in having a church service, attended by men and women, but otherwise condolences are paid in the same way on the three days at the time of the death and on the fortieth day after.

HOLIDAYS AND HOLIDAY CUSTOMS

Although Egypt is not the country with the most holidays in the world (Sri Lanka holds that distinction), it is up there—thanks to the mix of secular, Muslim, and Coptic traditions. Egypt also uses three different calendars for different purposes: the Gregorian or Western calendar is used for most secular purposes, the Islamic for Muslim religious events, and the Coptic, the ancient pharaonic calendar, for farming and Coptic observances. Each is slightly different in duration, and each starts at a different time of year, so some holidays shift considerably on the Gregorian calendar from year to year. In our description below, public holidays are indicated; banks, schools, government offices, and many businesses close on these days. The holidays are given in 1997 Gregorian calendar order. (See also the **Holidays** chart at the front of the book.)

Coptic Christmas. 7 January. Copts attend midnight mass. Monasteries are closed for fasting during the 43 days preceding.

Ramadan. 10 January–8 February*. See below for a full description.

Laylat al Qadr (Night of the Worth). 26th night of Ramadan, commemorating the Prophet's receiving of the first chapter of the Quran. It is believed that prayers are answered on this night.

'Id al-Fitr, or the Small Feast (public). 9–11 February*. Three-day holiday feast marking the end of Ramadan. Grocers' shelves are emptied out, and supplies are not restocked until after the feast. Many people take off for the country or seaside, so travel reservations need to be made well ahead of time, and the roads to and from Cairo are packed. Tourists take heed—not the ideal time for a spontaneous visit. This 'Id is also one of the two annual sale times, when everyone is supposed to get a new set of clothing, thereby providing storekeepers with funds for feasting. At this feast, it is traditional to give one's Muslim domestic help, building employees, etc., gifts of food and/or money, as much as a month's salary if not dispersed piecemeal during other holidays. This is much more vital than Christmas baksheesh, which will nevertheless also be solicited.

'Id al-Adha, or the Great Feast (public). 18–21 April*. This four-day feast, occurring

Exotically Egypt.

Uniquely Inter·Continental.

At our three luxurious hotels in Egypt you will experience a philosophy which focuses clearly on understanding the needs of the business and leisure traveller by providing consistently high levels of comfort, service and facilities.

The Semiramis Inter-Continental Cairo, Hurghada Inter-Continental Resort & Casino, and the Sharm El Sheikh Inter-Continental Resort & Casino are superbly located, offering both business and leisure facilities in an atmosphere which reflects the unique customs and cultures of this exotic country.

For reservations call
London: 0181 847 2277 Outside London: 0345 581444

Regional Sales Office Egypt
Tel: [20] (2) 355 7171 Fax: [20] (2) 356 3020

There are over 180 Inter-Continental Hotels and Resorts worldwide in Europe, Middle East, Africa, Asia Pacific and the Americas

seventy days after the end of Ramadan, marks the prophet Abraham's sacrifice of a sheep in place of his son. It is celebrated by the slaughter of sheep, naturally, the meat of which must be shared with those who cannot afford to slaughter their own. Hence the streets are filled with temporary pens holding the sheep until they are slaughtered. Like the Small Feast, this is not the ideal time for spur-of-the-moment travel.

Eastern Palm Sunday. Coptic Christian holiday. 20 April.

Sinai Liberation Day (public). 25 April.

Eastern Easter. 27 April.

Shamm al-Nisim (public). 28 April. The pharaonic rite of spring, Shamm al-Nisim or 'sniffing the breezes,' is the origin of some Western Easter practices, including the dyeing of eggs.

Labor Day (public). 1 May.

Islamic New Year (public). 9 May*.

Evacuation Day (public). 18 June. Celebrates the evacuation of the last British troops from Egypt in 1956.

Mulid al-Nabi, the Prophet's Birthday (public). 17 July*. Great festivities countrywide, with a big, colorful procession held at al-Azhar.

Revolution Day (public). 23 July. Anniversary of the 1952 Revolution.

Coptic New Year. 11 September (12 September in leap years).

Armed Forces Day (public). 6 October.

* *Dates of Islamic holidays are approximate.*

Ramadan, the holiest month and holiday of Islam, celebrates the beginning of the revelation of the Quran to the Prophet through the Archangel Gabriel. Business and schooling come largely to a standstill, starting late and ending early. Devout Muslims fast totally (no food, drink, cigarettes, sex, or impure thoughts) from sunrise to sunset, in accordance with one of the Five Pillars of Islam. The streets empty completely just before sunset, when everyone breaks the fast with a festive meal called *ifTaar.* Then, in the very early morning (1–2 am), a second meal, *suHuur,* is taken, often in restaurants with friends.

Tents and tables line the streets of the city as wealthy merchants and philanthropists lay out night-long feasts for the poor every single evening—an amazing and impressive logistical and charitable feat. The wealthy congregate in special tents set up outside fashionable restaurants and hotels and in the Opera House gardens to eat, socialize, and smoke shisha. Otherwise, most restaurants close during the day, except for those in large hotels. Alcohol is removed from the shelves of all stores, and people carrying Egyptian passports will not be served alcohol anywhere, day or night. As a mark of respect, foreigners should refrain completely from eating, drinking, or smoking in public during the day in Ramadan; if they do not, they will hear about it, usually politely, from the taxi driver or passersby.

Since they do not get much sleep during Ramadan, some people tend to get a bit cranky during the day, especially when Ramadan falls during the summer with its long hours of daylight and high temperatures. Young children, travelers, the sick, and pregnant and menstruating women are exempt from fasting, although many women fast a few days beforehand to account for the days of their menstruation during Ramadan. Stores are laden with special foods, especially nuts and sweets, in anticipation of the nightly feasts, and special Ramadan lanterns decorate all the highways and byways. Husayn Square and Khan al-Khalili are packed from dusk to dawn with revelers—an amazing riot of noise, music, entertainment, food, and shopping, but only for the sturdy and crowd-tolerant.

All in all, Ramadan reveals a unique set of contrasts: piety and gaiety, charity and ostentation, sacrifice and indulgence. Especially for foreigners interested in Islam,

Cairo during Ramadan is fascinating—and exhausting. Tourists should note that the streets are very noisy at night, that businesses keep odd hours, and that sustenance during the day is hard to come by.

YET MORE HOLIDAYS!

Fathers and mothers, farmers and doctors, artists and engineers also get their special days marked in Egypt, but on these, life goes on an usual. Another type of feast, the *mulid*, is celebrated by Copts and Muslims to honor their special saints. They are colorful religious celebrations involving dense crowds, parades, food stalls, animal acts, whirling dervishes—the works. Well worth seeing, but keep a very low profile, as religious zeal as well as great merriment runs high during a mulid. The biggest ones in Cairo are al-Husayn and Sayyida Zeinab.

HOW TO DRESS, DRINK, AND COMPORT ONESELF IN GENERAL

Egyptian movies from the thirties through the sixties reflect an Egypt that embraced Western ideals. In real life, too, affluent couples danced the night away in the smoke-filled boîtes of Cairo and Alexandria, and women copied the latest fashions from Paris and New York. Now, their daughters and granddaughters voluntarily veil themselves, join Islamic study groups, and take great pride in their religious heritage. Young men whose fathers have huge stocks of Johnny Walker Black at home spend their nights in vigil at the mosque and work for Islamic reform. So what is a foreigner to do?

You will generally avoid embarrassing yourself and others by keeping one thing uppermost in mind at all times: Egypt is a predominantly Muslim country in which Islamic ideals are becoming more and more the yardstick for behavior. It might also be useful to remember that most Egyptians' ideas about foreigners are colored much more by what they see on television and at the movies than by what they experience directly. Hence the average Westerner has love affairs and illegitimate children, takes drugs, carries a gun, has money to burn, and dresses just like they do on *The Bold and the Beautiful*.

To dispel these myths is not easy, particularly as some tourists perpetuate them by their dress and manners. Foreign residents, especially women, should dress considerably more modestly than they might at home, as detailed in the **Climate** section early in this chapter. For men and women, shorts are for sports and resorts, period.

Alcohol is another source of pitfalls. Obviously, many Muslims drink, just as many Christians ignore some of the tenets of their faith. But it is best to assume they do not until one has evidence to the contrary. If you are hosting a man with a prayer bruise on his forehead or a woman wearing the 'Islamic' head-covering, don't offer alcohol, and drink orange juice yourself if you need the contract. Even where alcohol is offered, imbibe moderately; this is especially important for women. One foreign consultant quickly lost her job in Cairo, in no small part because she mistakenly assumed she could slug 'em back with the boys at cocktail parties just like she did back home.

Muslims do not eat pork and would not knowingly relish anything cooked with alcohol, so save the bacon, grandemère's soufflé Grand Marnier, and your famous lasagna with pork sausage and red wine for compatriots.

EXCEPTIONS AND CONTRADICTIONS

Some of what has been said above might suggest to Westerners in particular a strait-laced, restrictive, intolerant society. Nothing could be further from the truth. Egypt, and Cairo in particular, embraces many exceptions and contradictions to the basic (and basically conservative) rules. A few examples. The extraordinary courtesy that prevails overall occasionally gives way to public screaming matches of epically obscene proportions. Young and old Egyptian cosmopolites of both sexes dance, smoke, drink, and even get drunk in the trendy bars of the World Trade Center. Hordes of Gulf Arabs out for a good time pack the belly-dancing clubs on the Pyramids Road and along 26th of July Street downtown. Prostitutes from all parts of the world including Egypt ply their trade in special 'hooker bars' scattered around town. Drugs are all too readily available, with wealthy (often foreign) teenagers being frequent targets of the dealers. For some rich men, a mistress is as essential to the wardrobe as an Armani suit. And the shop selling headscarves and long dresses is flanked on one side by a display of daring lingerie, on the other by sequined cocktail dresses of even more daring dimensions. In other words, Cairo is a big city. Don't expect consistency. And if you choose to explore the seamier side of its many-faceted personality, do so prudently.

A FEW SPECIFIC DOS AND DON'TS

Do see your guests to and beyond the door at the close of an evening. It is rude to abandon them before the elevator door closes.

Don't ask for 'Turkish coffee' in Egypt. Until barely a hundred years ago the Ottoman Turks ruled the Egyptians, who are still a tad touchy about it. Ask for *'ahwa* ('coffee') instead.

Women's Lib has not had quite the same impact in Egypt as it has in some Western countries. This produces some charmingly chivalrous behavior toward women on the part of men—opening doors, carrying packages, etc.—but can also cause the poor

things acute embarrassment if a woman offers to or insists upon paying for dinner. Defer to the custom of the country or your male companion's sensibilities on this issue.

Don't send flowers when someone dies. Flowers connote happiness and are therefore inappropriate on sad occasions.

Don't wonder aloud why your colleague is washing his or her feet, hands, ears, and face in the lavatory so often. It is done by devout Muslims before each prayer. Neither should a woman put a man in the awkward position of having to shake hands, as a woman's touch must also be washed away before prayer. Wait for him to make the first move. Egyptians are big kissers, but in public it's mostly same-sex greeting and departure kisses.

Don't barge in and discuss money or ostentatiously count your change as you might in other countries. These are not safety precautions: it is simply considered extremely rude to be hasty or frank about money, or to act as if someone might cheat you. This holds regardless of the facts that a) many Cairenes think nothing of asking foreigners what they have paid for their flat, their dress, their kids' school, or their laundry detergent, and b) the buyer–seller relationship is very much a caveat emptor one in which the wise buyer does count the change—but surreptitiously!

Be complimentary, but not unduly so, about other people's possessions. Excessive admiration attracts the evil eye and puts the owner in the position of having to follow the Egyptian custom of offering the item to the admirer with a gracious "Here, take it." A lengthy exchange of "Oh, no, I didn't mean . . . ," "But I insist . . ." must then follow.

Likewise, don't gurgle and coo over an adorable infant or toddler. Au contraire: either say nothing or, if you know the parents well, say something like, "Oh, what an ugly baby; this is the ugliest baby I have ever seen!" They will understand that you mean exactly the opposite and appreciate your thoughtfulness.

Unless you want to advertise that you have just had sex, don't go out of the house with wet hair.

ACCOMMODATIONS

Cairo has a huge number of restaurants and hotels, the range and variety of which, however, are somewhat less than dazzling for a city of this size, diversity, and crossroads-of-the-world location. The novelty-seeking sybarites among our readers should adjust their expectations accordingly. For the rest of us, good beds and good food in a wide range of prices are easily found throughout Cairo. Rather than supplying an exhaustive review, we highlight here the main five-star hotels and some less expensive, well-recommended alternatives in different areas of town.

Although the high-end hotels are managed by major international chains, most are government-owned by the Housing, Tourism, and Cinema Holding Company under the direction of the Ministry of Public Enterprise. Hotel staff members generally reflect the friendliness for which Egyptians are justly famous, but service standards overall are comparatively low—undelivered newspapers and messages are common, telephones calls go unanswered or misdirected, restaurant service is slow to inept, and so on. You will find exceptions, certainly; when you do, bring them to the attention of the management, reward them with good tips, and they might become the rule.

A suggestion to all the hotels from the many belly-dancing fans whose passions—and pockets—are not being fully exploited: to boost revenues that could pay for staff and management training, why not add early-bird dinner-and-belly-dancing shows

that start at 8 pm and finish by 10 or 11? This way, the bleary-eyed tourists and foreign business people who lack the admirable Egyptian capacity to stay up until the wee hours could enjoy the shows too. As it is, the only early-evening venues are the Nile riverboat cruises, which are fine, but a bit constrained on space and variety.

THE MAIN FIVE-STAR HOTELS

All of these have the usual amenities, including some with 24-hour casinos, executive floors, and basic to state-of-the-art health clubs. Sample 1996 rack rates for non-residents: $200 for executive floor singles, $230 for doubles with Nile views, $25–35 less for city views, $25–35 less for regular rooms. But don't be alarmed by these unduly high prices: corporate, government, tour-group, resident, and long-term rates are half or less, with seasonal and bargaining skill variations.

CENTRAL CAIRO

Cairo Sheraton: Despite its other-side-of-the-river location in Giza, this is a strong favorite among business and embassy types. Could it be because of Fifi Abdou, the resident belly-dancer reputed to be Cairo's best? Along with the Meridien, the Cairo Sheraton is one of the two non–government-owned hotels in Cairo. There is a duty-free shop on site.

Gezirah Sheraton: This is the round-tower Sheraton at the southern tip of Gezira island. Its river's edge restaurants—Italian, Lebanese, and Chinese—have great views and decent food.

Pyramisa Hotel: For some reason, this is not much frequented by Westerners, although it is just a block south of the Cairo Sheraton. It is a very pleasant hotel, more intimate and less impersonal than some of the others, with a particularly nice little shopping arcade and a comfortable, friendly pub, Jimmy's, where the service is actually excellent. The pool area is so-so.

Nile Hilton: Its 1960s-style acqua-and-white exterior lacks any charm whatever, but the rooms facing the Nile have delightful balcony views, and the secluded pool area may be the best in town—pool-side service is among the worst in town, though. There is a small new upscale shopping arcade that is very agreeable, with a good coffee shop, Café Olé, that is ideal while waiting for the Egyptian Museum next door to open. With the Corniche traffic to the front and Tahrir Square to the back, all rooms are quite noisy with the windows open. Ali's Alley, the shisha terrace at the back of the hotel, is the place to see and be seen—and smoke shisha—on a summer's afternoon.

Ramsis Hilton: Rising above a welter of fly-overs and a bus station, this Hilton is more centrally-located than those in search of peace and quiet might wish. Windows On The World, the top-floor restaurant, is reputed to be the best place in town for business lunches (LE65 fixed price), and its views are spectacular. But the LE38+ minimum charge deters the many local patrons who would otherwise pack the place to enjoy the sunset with tea or a beer. At night, Windows becomes a popular hangout with a jazz singer on hand, finally justifying the minimum. The Ramsis Hilton has the largest shopping arcade of any of the hotels, in its separate annex, but it is pretty tawdry. There is a good movie theater in the annex that shows Western films.

Cairo Marriott: Built originally in 1869 as a palace for the French Empress Eugénie, the Marriott has by far the most lavish hotel decor of any in central Cairo, as well as the most serene location (on the east side of Gezira) and the best garden—in fact, the only garden of any size. Probably the best choice for travellers with small kids. Harry's Pub is a wildly popular expat and Egyptian hangout for reasons we cannot fathom. Perhaps it is the karaoke nights or the ear-splitting music. The terrace café is more understandably popular and much quieter. Major and much-needed room refurbishing is being done, but we hear that the housekeeping is also in need of same.

Meridien le Caire: Bar none, the best views of Cairo, thanks to the hotel's north-facing location at the tip of Roda Island. The waterside terrace is the perfect place for sunset cocktails—if you can get the waiter and do not mind the din of seemingly eternal construction work on the garden while you are sipping. Popular with French and Japanese tour groups. The Champollion is reputed to be one of the two best French restaurants in Cairo. This privately owned hotel falls somewhat short on general maintenance and professionalism.

Semiramis Intercontinental: Very convenient to the many embassies in Garden City, and boasting one of the better lobby-lounge areas and overall layouts of the in-town hotels. The posh Grill Room restaurant has sweeping Nile views and good food.

Helnan Shepheard: This is the well-relocated reincarnation of the fabled Shepheard's of yore, which was burnt down in 1952, but there is otherwise little to entice nostalgia buffs.

HELIOPOLIS

Mövenpick Heliopolis is a popular community center for residents as well as being ideally located close to the airport and the many businesses that line the roads to it; it also holds frequent garage sales or flea markets as does the Mövenpick in Giza.

The *Meridien Heliopolis* is a favorite of Heliopolis's large French community; its Le 51 Bar is a favored watering-hole.

Rounding out the upscale choices are the *Swissôtel Cairo El Salam* and the older *Baron Heliopolis*, famous for its bakery.

PYRAMIDS AREA

Forte Grande: Close by the Pyramids and with eye-popping views of them from the pool and some of the rooms. Excellent tennis courts, a large pool with a swim-up bar, lavish bathrooms, and an elegant lobby. Grounds maintenance and pool-side service get a D-minus, though.

Mena House Oberoi: Rising in Moorish splendor at the foot of the Pyramids, this is the choice of many Cairenes for a weekend getaway without leaving town. Lovely gardens, a great pool, golf, tennis, and the Moghul Room for some of the best Indian food in Cairo. Since it is not in the heart of town, it does not attract the business crowd, but does get many tour groups. Service is similar to the other hotels but the ghosts of all the greats who have stayed there, plus the spectacular decor and setting, make up for this.

Mövenpick Jolie Ville: Pyramid views from some rooms, good programs for kids and for Giza residents, from whom the hotel garners good customers in addition to its tour-group business. A popular flea market is held on Fridays in the parking lot.

OTHER CHOICES AROUND TOWN

MAADI

Sofitel: Popular with the many oil companies in and around Maadi and for its advantageous pool membership with residents. We understand the Sofitel management, which recently took over the hotel from Pullman, keeps the place clean, but that food is not yet up to snuff.

The *Cairotel* has the best pool, with reasonable membership rates as well.

The *Residence Hotel*, home of the popular La Cassetta restaurant, is a real residential hotel with large two- and three-bedroom flats, often used by incoming/outgoing expatriates for temporary living quarters. Many rooms are in dire need of refurbish-

ing, particularly kitchens and baths; the Annex of the Residence is reported to be far better than the main building.

ZAMALEK

The *Hotel Flamenco* is deservedly a favorite for its food, service, and lovely views; its Florencia Restaurant on the tenth floor is rated the best in Cairo by many residents—superb steak au poivre, real paellas, great shrimp bisque—and there is an interesting cocktail lounge and a billiards room on the same floor.

The *President Hotel* is also highly regarded top to bottom—from the sixteenth-floor balcony rooms facing west, one can see the Pyramids in the mist, and the Cellar Bar is a good one. Also recommended is the *Safir Zamalek*, which rents apartments as well. And if you want to be literally on the water and get a taste of what houseboat-living might be like, the *Imperial Hotel* boat is a reasonably cushy way to experiment. Way down on the star scale, but perfectly okay, is the Pension Zamalek above the Meringo Bakery; for the budget-conscious young and young-at-heart, it cannot be beaten at le40 single and le70 per night with breakfast.

DOKKI AND MOHANDISEEN

We like three in this area: the *Hotel Nabila* right off Midan Sphinx on Sharia Gam'at al-Diwal al-'Arabiya is very clean and appealing with a nice little nook of a bar–coffeeshop outdoors. The *Atlas Zamalek* is nearby, not in Zamalek at all, and houses the popular disco Tamango. Also it is right next door to al-'Umda for cheap, good Egyptian fare. Finally the *Jasmin Hotel* near Midan Libnan is a charmer.

DOWNTOWN AND GARDEN CITY

The best source for a thorough rundown on the many very cheap hotels around Midans Tahrir and Ramsis is Lonely Planet's *Egypt and the Sudan*. But for the more fastidious and/or over-the-hill who nevertheless eschew luxury in favor of 'atmosphere,' the same names keep coming up word-of-mouth from long-term foreign residents: Windsor, Odeon, Cosmopolitan, and Garden City House.

The *Windsor Hotel* (singles $22–$32; doubles $32–$42) behind Cinema Diana echoes its history from the moment you get past the garbage-strewn street leading to it, enter the welcoming portals, and see a genuine old-fashioned switchboard in working order behind the reception desk. Formerly an annex to Shepheard's of old, it served as the British Officers' Club before the 1952 Revolution. The hotel has been owned and managed by the Doss family since the 1950s; they keep the large rooms and baths clean. Although opinions differ, we find the cavernous bar positively funereal, ill-lit, and definitely not the place to pay LE7.50 for a Stella—a price the waiters feel compelled to warn Egyptian patrons of in advance.

The *Cosmopolitan Hotel* (singles $41; doubles $51) is another remnant of another world smack dab in the middle of today's, but mercifully quiet.

Garden City House (singles LE64; doubles LE103) is convenient to AUC and Garden City embassies.

The *Odeon Palace* is efficient, central, and reasonable (singles $34; doubles $43); like many others, it is amenable to discounts for longer-term stays, and the 24-hour rooftop bar is a popular Cairo institution.

FOOD AND DRINK

Cairo boasts some fine restaurants and new ones open every week to take advantage of Egypt's bounty of fresh, excellent produce available almost year round. Another plus: most foreigners will find that, except at the very highest levels, restaurant prices are mostly very reasonable.

For foreigners who prefer the tried and true, all the large hotels offer 'continental' cuisine like one finds the world over in their coffeeshops and plush restaurants. Breakfast buffets in particular are designed to satisfy the peculiarly wide range of what people eat in the morning: fish for the English and Scandinavians, cheese and charcuterie for the Germans, croissants for the French, scrambled eggs and cereal for Americans, plus steaming copper vessels of fuul, the Egyptian breakfast of champions. Note, though, that these buffets are not cheap—between LE25 and LE40—so if you indulge, eat heartily. Some of the hotels throw in breakfast with the room, which represents a considerable saving particularly when traveling with children, so do try negotiating this.

Continuing in the tried-and-true vein, foreign readers will be either relieved or appalled to see the familiar logos of McDonald's, Arby's, Wimpy, Pizza Hut, KFC, Baskin Robbins, TCBY, and local variants thereof on virtually every corner of Cairo. Well, not in Islamic and Old Cairo ... yet. Will the Golden Arches rise up next to Bab Zuwela one day? Perish the thought. These fast-food joints are wildly popular among Egyptians and foreigners, and the in thing for toddlers' birthday parties is for the little critters to invade one of these places with their harried mothers in tow. Curiously and most refreshingly, service at both the Egyptian and international fast-food and take-away restaurants is far superior to that found in many of the upscale places.

EGYPTIAN FOOD

Before discussing what Egyptians eat, it is handy to know when they eat. Lunch at home or in restaurants other than those in hotels is usually not served until at least 2 pm and can start anywhere up to 5 pm after that. But some places close between 3:30

and 7 or 8 pm. For dinner, restaurants are deserted until at least 8, when tourists start trickling in, but 10 or 11 is when Egyptians start arriving, and it is not at all unusual for whole families to be working through their dinners at 1 or 2 in the morning. Office workers often have breakfast at their desks around 10, so 11 am might be the ideal time to approach government offices in particular so as not to disturb the morning's rituals.

Egyptian cuisine is a melange of Middle Eastern fare with local variations in spice. In general, the food is not overly hot-spicy, although it can be very salty. There are loads of good places around town to try, each with its own adherents who swear that this place has the best *kufta,* that stand the best *Ta'miyya.* We describe here some of the dishes you will encounter, and reliable places in which to do so, but we hope you will discover your own favorites and maybe even report back to us.

Breakfast often consists of a *fuul* sandwich—stewed broad beans with spices and salt added, slathered into *'eesh shaami* or *'eesh baladi,* respectively the delicious white and brown Egyptian versions of pita bread. The bread is sold in bakeries and supermarkets, but it is also hawked by children on every corner, and young boys wheel around Cairo on their bikes balancing huge piles of it on door-sized frames on their heads. *Ta'miyya,* fried patties of ground broad beans, parsley, coriander leaves, and other greens mixed with spices and sometimes egg, is also eaten at breakfast and throughout the day. Another way of preparing broad beans is to allow them to sprout and then marinate them in oil and spices: this is *fuul naabit,* a good snack often served free with drinks in bars (the Cellar Bar in the President Hotel is reputed to serve the best).

Speaking of bread, and to torture our readers who love it, the very best bread in Egypt, and perhaps in the whole wide world, is called *'eesh shamsi*—*'sun bread.'* Bread cognoscenti compare it favorably to France's *pain Poilane.* Left to rise on the hot sand in the sun, it is chewy and brown, with a crispy crust and a marvelous bite and aroma—divine. But you cannot get it in Cairo, so there! It is made only in Upper Egypt, a whole hour away by plane. Who will be first to make a mint by marketing *'eesh shamsi* in Cairo and Alexandria? In the meantime, leave an entire suitcase empty to carry loaves of it home with you from Hurghada, Aswan, and Luxor.

Lunch and dinner always begin with selections of *mazza,* or appetizers, which can in themselves make a great meal. *Babaghannuugh* and *TaHiina* dips are standard, the former being smoked mashed eggplant (aubergine) with garlic and oil, the latter a ground sesame seed paste with mild spices. Both are eaten with plain or toasted pieces of *'eesh baladi,* as are soft feta cheese dips with tomato and garlic. *Wara 'inab* are grape leaves stuffed with minced meat and rice, served both hot and cold; our favorites are from Estoril downtown and Paprika on the Corniche. Sometimes you see *baTaarikh,* the semi-dry pressed Egyptian salmon roe—very strong, salty, and somewhat expensive, but otherwise not much like caviar—served with hard-boiled egg. *Tabbuula* is usually delicious in Egypt; either as the salad course or part of the *mazza,* this mixture of parsely, tomato, onion, lime juice, oil, and usually bulgur wheat, tastes like health incarnate. *Mazza* also might include pickled carrots, radishes, onions, and olives. A few of the desert monasteries make and sell fantastic olives, but the ones in Cairo stores and restaurants tend to be more bitter than their European cousins.

More substantial fare includes *kufta,* spiced, grilled meatball fingers that kids love along with adults, and *kushari,* a great, cheap, and filling dish of rice, pasta, and

Exotically Egypt.

Uniquely Inter·Continental.

At our three luxurious hotels in Egypt you will experience a philosophy which focuses clearly on understanding the needs of the business and leisure traveller by providing consistently high levels of comfort, service and facilities.

The Semiramis Inter-Continental Cairo, Hurghada Inter-Continental Resort & Casino, and the Sharm El Sheikh Inter-Continental Resort & Casino are superbly located, offering both business and leisure facilities in an atmosphere which reflects the unique customs and cultures of this exotic country.

For reservations call
London: 0181 847 2277 Outside London: 0345 581444

Regional Sales Office Egypt
Tel: [20] (2) 355 7171 Fax: [20] (2) 356 3020

There are over 180 Inter-Continental Hotels and Resorts worldwide in Europe, Middle East, Africa, Asia Pacific and the Americas

brown lentils served with tomato sauce and dry-fried onions. The very best is said to be at Guha on Sharia 'Imad al-Din near the Windsor Hotel, and the Nile Hiton's is especially good and amazingly cheap at LE5 for a heaping plate (not on the menu, but available), as is al-'Umda's. Kids also usually like kushari, and it is certainly healthy. *Mulukhiyya* (which is Jew's mallow, a leafy plant that somewhat resembles mint in appearance but not in taste) is a uniquely Egyptian dish, usually made as a soup served with rice. It is green, it is slimy, it is an acquired taste, but the amazing thing is that tots who normally refuse any remotely green food simply gobble up this unusual staple of the Cairene diet, so take note and try it. Stuffed pigeon is another popular delicacy; all those tall narrow mud-brick towers with holes in them one sees in the countryside are pigeon coops, whose little denizens, once nicely roasted, grace many a buffet table. More common still is simple spit-roasted chicken, sold at any number of holes-in-the-wall throughout the city and usually delicious. Andrea's in Maadi and on the Kirdasa road serves up a particularly good version in a more serene setting.

Meat, particularly lamb, can be excellent; the beautiful fat-tailed sheep one often sees being herded through Cairo's quieter streets make delicious eating and are highly prized during the many feasts, since the average Egyptian's diet is heavily vegetarian for economic reasons. The sheep's testicles are considered a great delicacy; Ghanem on 26th July in Zamalek and Alfi Bey on Sharia al-Alfi downtown serve some of the best. Beef and veal are very lean, hence healthy, in Egypt, although the veal is not milk-fed. In many places, beef tends to be less tender than its European and American counterparts, but Florencia, Angus, and Pub 28, all in Zamalek, serve superb steaks—juicy, tender, and cooked as ordered. Mixed grills served kebab-style on skewers are

very popular, as are mountainous barbecued meat platters, but this cooking method tends to bring out the toughness and dryness of all cuts. Lovers of offal—kidneys, brains, and above all, liver—will find that many Egyptians also enjoy these delicacies; one of the best (and cheapest) places to try these is al-'Ahd al-Gadid on Sharia Muski near Khan al-Khalili.

Fresh fish from the Mediterranean and the Red Sea is widely available, but restaurants catering to foreigners tend to limit their offerings to grouper, or sea bass, and shrimp (prawns) and calamari. Lobster is also available, but is generally unremarkable and always expensive. Shrimp tends to be expensive, too—around LE100 per kilo at seafood restaurants like the Sea Horse on the Corniche. Calamari is much cheaper, generally more reliable, and positively addictive when lightly fried and served with lime wedges. One of the best places for a delicious bouillabaise-like stew loaded with seafood is Tia Maria in Mohandiseen; their whole menu, in fact, is very good, and consequently this restaurant is almost always crowded. The Flying Fish in Aguza also serves excellent seafood; it is reputed to be Omar Sharif's favorite Cairo restaurant. And in Shubra, every Cairene swears by Asmak Amir, a completely unpretentious place with the best, freshest seafood in town. To find it, take a left onto Sharia Khulusi from the Shubra bridge-tunnel and follow Khulusi to its end in Midan Dawaran Shubra.

Last but certainly not least is dessert. Egyptians love sweets of all sorts and make some delicious pastries. Wandering around Cairo, one immediately notices that pastry shops are nearly as prevalent as shoe stores, and that they are often quite glitzy and sparkling affairs, even in poorer neighborhoods. There used to be a clearer divide between pastry shops and bread bakeries, but some now overlap and offer both. Certainly try *kunafa,* a shredded wheat–like confection drizzled with honey, and *fiTiir,* a delicious and versatile soft puffed pastry with various fillings and toppings; much better, in general, than the baklava found throughout the Middle East and in Cairo as well. Perhaps the favorite dessert, along with the enticing confections from La Poire and Bon Appetit, is *umm 'ali* ('Ali's mother'), a soothing and subtle Egyptian version of bread pudding with rich cream, coconut, and nuts—not for the calorie-conscious, or at least not often; instead of as a dessert after a big meal, try it warm on a cold winter morning for breakfast. It is delicious.

Bottled water or soft drinks, including tonic water straight, are the beverages of choice with meals, all usually served at room temperature. A few delicious alternatives are *karkadeeh,* a hibiscus-flower infusion with a lovely ruby color drunk cool or warm, and in summer, fresh lime juice with sugar and water. Tea *(shaay)* and Turkish coffee *('ahwa),* both strong, are drunk prodigiously, usually with loads of sugar. For coffee with no sugar, ask for *'ahwa saada; 'ar-riiHa* is with very little; *maZbuut* is medium; and *ziyaada* is very sweet. More places are now offering filter cofee, called 'American' for some reason, but most places still have only one alternative to Turkish coffee—Nescafé. Simonds coffeeshop in Zamalek has very good capuccino for less than LE2; it is a fun place for a grocery-shopping break and to watch local businessmen on their leisurely breaks.

In addition to places we have already mentioned, another comes well recommended for authentic Egyptian food: Tab'i, with two branches, one on *Sharia 'Urabi* downtown and the other on Sharia Gam'at al-Diwal al-'Arabiya across from the Mustafa Mahmud Mosque in the same green-and-white building as the new Abu Shaqra restaurant, which is also good.

To close our discussion of Egyptian cuisine, we suggest that adventurous readers try two irresistible street foods. First, all over the city and almost all year long, but especially in summer, you will see net bags of fruit, and carrots, suspended from the rafters or piled on the counters of little juice stands. Orange, banana, mango, apple, pineapple, apricot, pomegranate, sugarcane juice . . . go ahead and indulge in anything that grows off a tree or is peeled. If the carrots are peeled, they are probably okay, but it is probably wise, regrettably, to avoid the tempting strawberries, as they are notoriously hard to clean. Nothing beats these refreshing vitamin-packed juice treats after a morning of climbing up and down dusty minaret steps in the heat. Second, in winter, the aroma of roasting sweet potatoes wafts from donkey carts with small charcoal-fired ovens aboard. There is some suggestion that the charcoal or the lighter fluid the vendors use may be carcinogenic, but for those who take a so-what-isn't-these-days attitude, these treats comfort cold hands and stomachs.

MORE RESTAURANTS AND CAFÉS

INTERNATIONAL PLACES

On the international 'ethnic' food front, options are limited but growing. The five-star hotels all have their versions of ethnic restaurants, and they are generally about as authentic as one would expect, with a few exceptions. There are at least three really good Indian restaurants: the previously mentioned *Moghul Room* at the Mena House, and *Taj Mahal* and *Kandahar* in Mohandiseen. *Asia House* at the Helnan Shepheard is also praised for its Indian, but not its Chinese, food. There are a number of Chinese restaurants. Consistently cited favorites: *Peking*'s various branches (the one in New Maadi is beautiful and food is great), *Chin Chin* at Four Corners in Zamalek, and *Lan Yuan*'s and *Maxie's Long*

Feng, both in Maadi. There are other Chinese restaurants downtown as well.

There is exactly one Thai restaurant, *Bua Khao* in Maadi; luckily, it is a good one. There are also a couple of pretty good hybrid Korean/Chinese/Filipino places, including *Susana* in Dokki and *Hana* in Zamalek. Mexico is ill-served in Cairo by *Los Amigos* in the Semiramis, and by *Chili's*, with three branches and counting—the food here is consistent and not bad, but bland. Japanese? Three are okay: *Yamato* at the Ramsis Hilton, *Sapporu* in the Cairo Sheraton, and *Sushi Yama* at the World Trade Center, but all are expensive. It is logical that Lebanese food would be easier to come by, and there are a number of places offering it: *Papillon* and *Maroush,* both in Mohandiseen, are cited most frequently for food, atmosphere, and service. There is also a Moroccan restaurant, *al-Fanous* in Giza, which gets raves for atmosphere and mixed reviews for food and service.

For French and Italian food, choices are limited. There is one excellent French bistro, conveniently called *Le Bistro*, downtown. Haute cuisine can be found at *Justine* and at *Champollion*. Justine has a good reputation and high prices to match; it is the place to wine and dine someone you want to impress, and Champollion's views are worth a splurge. For Italian food, two places are pretty good: *La Mama* at the Cairo Sheraton may be the best, along with *Al Dente* in Zamalek. *Tia Maria* and *Le Tabasco*, though not really Italian, have far better pasta dishes than some of the 'Italian' places, especially *La Casetta* and *Il Cortigiano*. The latter two have large portions of drab pastas, but are pleasant enough; don't automatically expect a glass of wine, though, as only the La Casetta in Maadi serves alcohol. *Da Mario* in the Nile Hilton is consistently reliable if not thrilling, with the additional plusses of very nice waiters,

an agreeable outdoor café, and very good beef carpaccio.

INTERESTING PLACES

For people-watching—Egyptians as well as tourists—and to soak up atmosphere and local color, here are a few of our favorites, and not-so favorites. We like *Estoril* downtown because: it looks like it has never changed, it has a lovely mashrabiya medallion on the ceiling, the Egyptian–continental food is consistently excellent, it is quiet but not lugubrious, and the owner and bartender recognize you in their low-key way after you have been in a few times. *Arabesque* is a beautiful restaurant, and the menu is more diverse than Estoril's. Both of the *Groppis* are just awful—dirty, dark, and sad; even nostalgia buffs would do well to simply take in the lovely tilework at the entrance to the one on Midan Tal'at Harb and have their pastry and coffee elsewhere. *Felfela* is okay and still attracts locals due to its convenient locations and reasonable prices, but there is a distinctly world-weary air on the part of the staff. Much better Egyptian food and good service can be found at *Paprika* near the Television Building; it is a delight. All the places on the square in Khan al-Khalili make for great places to observe the human condition, as do the famous *Fishawi* café and the far ritzier *Naguib Mahfouz Café* in the Khan itself. The food at Mahfouz is quite good, and quite expensive, operated as it is by Oberoi. *Asmak Amir* in Shubra (see **Egyptian Food** above) is not only a great fish place, but a great vantage point from which to join Cairenes from all walks of life engaging in their favorite pastime. *Gladiola* in New Maadi right next to Peking is new, blue, comfortable, and could be the perfect place to take someone you might not want to take home to Mother; a nice change in wholesome Maadi.

OUTDOOR PLACES

Sidewalk cafés abound in Cairo, but you will notice right away that women do not frequent any of them except the ones in the Khan. But there are many other places for agreeable al fresco dining, for which Cairo's climate is ideal, except perhaps on the very hottest and coldest days. Mosquito repellent is the best perfume for outdoor dining, and a light shawl or sweater is almost always welcome at night, especially by the water.

Popular waterside spots include the *Sea Horse*, the top deck of *Le Pacha 1901*, the *Imperial Hotel*, and the *Meridien* terrace. Many agreeable, somewhat more local places dot the river—*Casino Cleopatra* and *Casino al-Nahr* in Zamalek, *Mamoura Torz* near the Manial Palace on Roda, and *Casino Kasr al-Nil* on the Giza side of Gezira, but if you are a foreigner, do check the menu prices before tucking in. 'Casino,' by the way, is the term also given to riverside restaurants, many of which have belly-dancing in the wee hours.

Places with large or small gardens include *Five Bells* in Zamalek, *Maroush* in Mohandiseen, *Andrea's* and *Felfela Village*, both tour-bus-and-barbecue joints on opposite sides of the Maryutiya Canal heading toward Kirdasa, *Christo's* near the Pyramids and with great views of same (but the food is only passable unless you are with one of the bigwigs who frequent the place), and *Rossini's* and *Le Chantilly* in Heliopolis.

The very best outdoor restaurant of all is the one you make yourself: a home-made picnic, take-out from any restaurant or hotel, or even direct-to-the-dock delivery from Abu Shaqra on Qasr al-'Aini. Find a felucca with a nice table and comfy cushions, bring your own drinks, and for romance, a lantern and the partner of your choice. Mosquito repellent is a must at night unless you find itching irresistible. Heaven on the Nile from LE15 per hour. (And we have been asked to note that some of the felucca men prefer a liquid tip to money.)

TRENDY PLACES

To rub shoulders with the young and the beautiful—and the old, rich, and famous or notorious—there are three places in Dokki, all within shouting distance of each other. The newest is *Le Tabasco*, which also, perhaps not coincidentally, has some of the better food in Cairo, including the best Mexican on Wednesdays, and definitely the best music selections always. Tabasco needs to do something drastic about its ventilation system, though; go early to eat, as the smoke late at night is distinctly unappetizing. *El Greco*, a beautiful restaurant with fair-to-good Greek–Egyptian seafood, has live fish darting under the glass floor to guide you to the bathrooms and is straight across Midan Amman from Le Tabasco. *El Yotti* is staid, comfortable, and elegant until about 11 and then rocks out with live music and dancing, serving up good quasi-French–Egyptian food throughout; ring the bell at the end of a lamplit passage to enter.

In the World Trade Center there are also three chi-chi joints, all with live music later in the evening. *On the Rox* is an intimate, great-looking place with good versions of nouvelle cuisine, great bathrooms, and a bar full of young and old rakes; there is a miniscule dance floor with music geared to please a sophisticated (read 'over-35') crowd. *Katcho'z* on the ground floor is larger, louder, and kind of overdone overall, but very 'in'; food is pretty good but tends to be as gussied up as the decor. *Piano Piano* has a large bar, large piano, and large windows offering sweeping vistas of the Nile. All three get packed regularly, but Monday nights are less frantic than others. For more deafening noise and sardine-tin crowds after dinner, head up to *Upstairs*, the baroque-hip disco, to join a frenetic crowd including nymphets of all nationalities, Euro-trash, school-teachers, government ministers—the whole gamut. Unfortunately, Upstairs seems to impose an arbitrary 'members-only' entrance policy depending on the doormen's mood or their opinions of the looks of potential patrons. And then if you pass muster you are privileged to pay LE25 for a can of Carlsberg, the only beer on offer; this way-out-of-line price seems not to deter the trendies in the slightest.

The best restaurant reviews are to be found weekly in the *Middle East Times*. Their critics give detailed, balanced run-downs of both the well-known and out-of-the-way places. *Egypt Today*'s monthly Restaurant Guide is also good, but tends to repeat only the better-known places and to be glowing rather than balanced. Truly die-hard gourmets and gourmands will be pleased to know that there is an Egyptian branch of the international Chaîne des Rôtisseurs club in Cairo. It is notoriously difficult for foreigners to gain membership to this exclusive club, which is offered strictly by invitation or by examination for restaurant professionals. Its present *bailli*, or judge, is Mr. Bahram Mahmoud, whose restaurant recommendations include Katcho'z, Justine, the Café St. Germain at the Meridien Heliopolis, Taj Mahal, and the Pergola at the Sonesta in Nasr City. A knowledgeable friend who is a member of the club also offered his recommendations for our readers: the Moghul Room as one of the finest Indian restaurants in the whole world; the Gezira Grill at the Marriott for nouvelle cuisine; Champollion at the Meridien for French haute cuisine; Arabesque for Mediterrranean–Middle Eastern food; Le Bistro downtown for good bistro fare, and especially pork; and Carroll's and Estoril for generally excellent, reasonable food in casual settings. He also noted that in a number of places where wine is not sold (or even if it is) patrons may bring their own for a corkage fee in the LE30 range.

SIGHTSEEING

A large number of books, especially those in the **Book List** on p. xxi, cover this ground in thorough detail. So, rather than reinvent the wheel, we confine ourselves here to worthwhile sights in and around Cairo that consistently come recommended by native Cairenes and expatriates.

PYRAMIDS

How could we start with anything other than the Great Pyramids at Giza? Nothing prepares even the most jaded traveler (Mark Twain excepted) for their grandeur, their sheer awesomeness. Go. Here are some don'ts, followed by dos, to make your pilgrimage to the Great Pyramids what it should be.

Do not let the incredible hassles from touts of every description spoil the experience; just look dazed and ignore them totally. Do not take a guided tour unless it is with an organization like the Egyptian Antiquities Organization (EAO) or the American Research Center in Egypt (ARCE). Skip the Sound and Light show unless you are highly partial to such displays. Don't go early in the morning (early being anytime before 9:30 or so). One would think dawn would be the ideal time for the quality of the light and the tranquillity, but, especially in the cooler months, the pyramids are often shrouded in mist until 10am—and regardless, the security people and ticket takers do not care to accommodate early risers and can be quite obdurate about it, even at dawn on New Year's Day. Don't bring a videocamera: the pyramids do not move. If you must go into a pyramid just to say you have done so or because you are an archaeology or architecture buff, go ahead, but it is quite a claustrophobic experience and there is nothing to see anyway. Young visitors in particular like the Solar

Boat Museum (from the outside it is an eye-sore, as is all the touristic claptrap that infringes too closely on the pyramid complex).

Do go way, way around the back, approaching the pyramids from the southwest, about a ten-kilometer trip from the real entrances. We are not suggesting that you do not pay the entrance fee (LE10 for foreigners, and about to go way up in 1997), but you can do it on your way out rather than in and have the taxi that gets you there meet you back at the main entry gate. Sunset and moonlight are the best times to go—when, of course, the pyramids are officially closed, the tourists being shooed out or penned in at 4 pm in winter, 6 pm in summer, to clear the premises for the Sound and Light Show, for which foreigners pay an additional LE30. Non-riders will not appreciate this advice, but one of the best ways to avoid pyramid paranoia is to simply rent a nag for LE10 per hour any time of the late afternoon or night and ride around with a guide. It is easy on the feet—there is a lot of ground to cover—and not all that hard on the butt. You can also do this by camel, but the guys at the horse stables are generally a far more agreeable, low-key lot than the camel drivers. Good riders can go all the way from the Giza pyramids to Abu Sir or Saqqara and back; for anyone else, this is arduous, but fantastic on a full-moon night; many of the clubs and associations in town arrange such parties now and then.

Many pyramid fans prefer the smaller, older, more isolated step pyramid complexes at Saqqara and Abu Sir and the one lonely pyramid at Maydum, near Fayyum, with its much more interesting mastabas. Saqqara is the only one of the three much frequented by tourists, but it is still far less of a hassle than the Giza pyramids, and, to many eyes, more beautiful. Abu Sir, off the road to Saqqara, was still not officially opened at this writing, but for a reasonable considera-tion to the man who sometimes watches over the place, this need not deter a visit. It is an exquisite, magical place at sunset, which will still be true even after the tour buses invade, as, like Saqqara, it will also close at 4 or 6 pm. Maydum, thought to be the first attempt to build a true pyramid, is quite splendid in its isolation, as a grand development scheme seems to have stopped for the moment. Only the very sure-footed should attempt the descent and ascent into the corbeled vault. It is "fifty-seven meters down, ten meters up," as your helpful guide will repeatedly reiterate and illustrate in the sand.

The museum at Memphis near Saqqara is on the tourist circuit, but is not a must-see. It is a rather paltry affair except for the fallen colossus of Ramsis II and the alabaster sphinx in the courtyard. It is sobering, though, to think that the site of the small dusty village that is modern Memphis was the seat of power for centuries during the Old Kingdom and after. What wonders must still lie buried in the sandy hills nearby. All around the routes to Memphis and Saqqara are dozens upon dozens of carpet schools and showrooms. Avoid them if you can.

THE CAMEL MARKET

There are at least two ways to get to the new camel market, which moved from Imbaba a few years ago and whose new location has remained largely a mystery to all but the camel drivers until now. Thanks to Supriya Chawla, the adventure travel consultant (**Travel Agents**) who first published directions in the BCA magazine, we can offer this relatively simple route, which takes you thirty kilometers northwest of Cairo, past the village of Birqash. The market is open on Monday mornings as well as Friday mornings, starting at 7 am.

Traveling west from the city on the Pyramids Road, turn right (north) onto the

Mansuriya Canal road. Set your odometer to zero at this point and keep following the canal road for about twenty-five kilometers. You will pass, in succession, an amusement park on your right (1.6 km), a crossing (8 km), a small village with a big graveyard (19.5 km), and a T-junction with a small mosque minus minaret but with a small garden on your right (21.6 km). Keep straight all the while until you come to another T-junction at 25.4 km with a sign for Nimos Farm nursery; here you turn left. At 27 km, turn left again onto an asphalt road that is heavily sanded and under a canopy of trees. At 29 km, there is a fork in the road with a horse-head sign. Bear left, and at 30.3 km, you have arrived. Foreigners pay LE3 to enter plus LE2 for a camera and LE15 for a video camera—one of the very few occasions on which video footage might be well worth it. The Sudanese traders, the beasts themselves, and your fellow gawkers make for quite a show; luckily, portable video cameras still do not come equipped with Smell-o-Vision.

SOME MAJOR AND A FEW MINOR MUSEUMS

One realizes quite quickly that huge tracts of Cairo are in effect great outdoor museums, particularly the whole of Islamic Cairo. We give brief descriptions of some 'real' museums, then take a look at Old (Coptic) Cairo and Islamic Cairo, sketching the major sights therein.

THE EGYPTIAN MUSEUM
Literally hundreds of elegant, exquisitely decorated mummy cases stand as silent sentries over the thousands of visitors who daily pay homage to Egypt's treasures. The whole museum is overwhelming in its sheer volume, and is even more so with the knowledge that in the basement lurk many more uncatalogued treasures than fill the public spaces. Although the traffic in the museum is heavy and very noisy at all times, with guides exhorting and enlightening their charges in a cacophony of languages, it is easy to wander off into near-isolated halls to contemplate parts of the collection in peace and quiet. For a first visit, it is worthwhile hiring a guide or going with a tour group to get an overall sense of the place, which takes about two hours. Depending on the level of detail you want while looking at displays, a guidebook like the museum's own (LE10) or the Blue Guide is a necessity, as the legends are limited, illegible, or nonexistent. On subsequent visits, tourists' lunch time (12–2, except on Fridays, when the museum is closed) is a good time to go. There is an additional fee for the Mummy Room, high but well worth it, and the Tutankhamun display is duly dazzling, but always very crowded. The fee for taking in a camera is LE5, for a video camera much more; since the museum is for the most part not well lit and flash is prohibited, neither is worth carrying. Buy postcards instead. Though the museum is theoretically open from 9 to 5, the guards start herding people out at 4:30. There are very few places to sit in the museum, but there is a decent restaurant on the second floor for relaxing and digesting what you have seen. The gift shop and T-shirt shop are okay, a bit pricey, but if you haven't time for Khan al-Khalili, both serve souvenir-seekers well enough. The sculpture and statuary garden in front of the museum is full of lovely things, but none are labeled.

THE ISLAMIC ART MUSEUM
This is a delight for lovers of exquisite ceramics, illuminated manuscripts, and mashrabiya. Strangely, it is often deserted. The bulk of the items are not from Egypt but from Turkey and other parts of the Ottoman Empire. A strong flashlight and a

sunny day are required to view the collection, as the museum is dark and the windows appear not to have been washed since the last century. Although guards and 'guides' dog your steps, their main function seems to be offering to turn the lights on, many of which don't work anyway. As of this writing, the museum is undergoing major, much-needed renovations, and a large portion of it is closed.

THE COPTIC MUSEUM, OLD CAIRO, AND THE NILOMETER

The easiest way to reach the Coptic complex in southern Cairo is by Metro to the Mar Girgis stop or by river taxi to the Masr al-Qadima landing. Here you are walking on historic ground, for this area is what was once the Roman fortress of Babylon, and after that al-Fustat, the early Arab city. We highly recommend touring this part of Cairo with William Lyster, an engaging scholar and lover of Old and Islamic Cairo, who often gives tours and lectures (contact ARCE or the Women's Association to arrange). In addition to the museum, the area accommodates Egypt's first mosque ('Amr Ibn al-'As), a number of Coptic churches (the most famous of which are the 'Hanging Church' of al-Mu'allaqa and Sitt Barbara), the oldest synagogue in Egypt (Ben Ezra), and two Roman towers—all coexisting peacefully. Very little of what stands today is original, except for the Roman towers, but the area nevertheless has a wonderful feel to it.

The Coptic Museum is refreshingly clean, beautiful, and serene, housing the world's largest collection of Coptic art, along with some Nubian paintings saved from the flooding of Lake Nasser. A morning spent in the district and the museum might conclude with lunch at the nearby Sea Horse on the Corniche followed by a quick visit to the Nilometer at the southern tip of Roda Island. This column measuring the Nile's

level to determine flooding and harvest dates from the ninth century AD and was in use up until the building of the Aswan High Dam, which put an end to the annual flood. Since it gets few visitors, the area is an oasis of calm; the building housing the Nilometer itself is almost always locked up but can be opened with a baksheesh key.

MANIAL PALACE AND MUSEUM (NOT MAJOR, BUT A GOOD OUTING)

A short walk south from the Meridien Hotel on Roda is the vast former residence of King Farouk's uncle, Prince Muhammad Ali. Dating from the turn of the century, it houses an eclectic collection of weaponry, insects, china services, portraits, and mounted trophies. Very little is labeled, but it doesn't really matter as there are no historically significant treasures to speak of. Nevertheless, this museum is quite visitor-friendly, evoking the rococo-Oriental splendor in which the royal family lived and played. The gardens could use a lot more tending, but they are quite nice as they are. This is a good museum for tots, as the animal and insect displays intrigue them and they can gleefully run up and down the long esplanades and galleries, all on the ground floor. Cap your visit with a late lunch at Mamoura Torz across from the entrance to the palace, checking menu prices carefully first. Or wander up to the Meridien's terrace, stopping along the way at one of the pretty nurseries on the bank of the river.

THE POSTAL MUSEUM

Just off Midan Ataba is the Postal Museum, a quirky philatelist's dream, with a unique collection of stamps and mannequins dressed in postmen-through-the-ages costumes. Nearby is Muktallat, at 14 al-Ataba al-Khadra, the philatelists' café, where priceless stamps are bartered and traded over coffee and shisha.

ISLAMIC CAIRO

It would take a number of full-time months and a lot of energy to do a serious exploration of this fascinating area, which harbors not only a great many treasures of Islamic architecture, but a throbbing, endless parade of street life. To get an initial sense of both, look from on high from the Muqattam Hills, the Citadel, or the roof of the Ibn Tulun mosque. Then consult a detailed map to get an orderly perspective (SPARE, the Society for the Preservation of the Architectural Resources of Egypt, produces an excellent series of 3-D maps of Islamic Cairo). Finally, go exploring, but a little at a time, especially in summer's heat. Go on foot only; the medieval streets were never intended for cars. Wear easily removed, comfortable, rubber-soled shoes. The ancient steps of many minarets are slippery, sandy, and dark, ideal for ignominious and even dangerous falls in leather-soled shoes, as we ruefully discovered. Carry a small bottle of water and your map, however discreetly, since it is unproductive to stand at the footbridge between Khan al-Khalili and al-Ghuriya asking ten people for directions to the Street of the Tentmakers in semi-perfect Arabic only to find not one who has a clue that it is less than five hundred meters away. (It is best to ask for Bab Zuwela in this case, using the navigate-by-landmarks principle, and once there ask for Sharia al-Khayyamiya.) For women entering mosques, a headscarf is a respectful touch, but it is no longer expected, especially of foreigners.

The energetic can 'do' Islamic Cairo in three days, one each at the southern, middle, and northern sections. In the southern part, start at the mosque of Ibn Tulun and the Gayer-Anderson House behind it, then proceed toward the Citadel. At Ibn Tulun, climb as high as you can and clamber about the roof for spectacular views of nearby minarets and of the impressive courtyard of the mosque itself. Everyone finds the Gayer-Anderson House, (*beet al-kiritliyya,* 'House of the Cretan Woman'), charming; it is a well-cared-for anachronism of the nineteenth and early twentieth centuries in the midst of all the medieval stones, full of art and artifacts lovingly collected by the owner and displayed in a fanciful series of rooms he designed.

Walking toward the Citadel on Sharia al-Saliba, and drinking in the sights and smells all the while, one comes to Midan Salah al-Din, which fronts the Madrasa of Sultan Hasan, a splendid example of Mamluk architecture, and the mosque of al-Rifa'i, which is lavish in the extreme but otherwise unremarkable. It gets loads of tour buses, though, as it houses the remains of Shah Reza Pahlevi of Iran (who was denied burial in Iran by the late Ayatollah Khomeini) in multi-marbled splendor. The last two kings of Egypt, Fouad and Farouk, plus their father and grandmother, are also buried here.

The fortress of the Citadel *(al-'al'a)* stands as the cynosure of Cairo, evoking from a distance visions of the Thousand and One Nights with its glistening domes and minarets. It was originally constructed with the labor of captured Crusaders under Sultan Salah al-Din in the twelfth century. Within the two enclosures, referred to as the Northern and Southern enclosures but more accurately east and west respectively, one finds a staggering array of mosques, palaces, and museums. The main mosques are the nineteenth-century mosque of Muhammad Ali, or the Alabaster Mosque, with its enormous square courtyard; the mosque of al-Nasir Muhammad (1335); and the mosque of Sulayman Pasha (1528). In addition, there are the remains of many more historic buildings, and a number that have been converted into an odd assortment of museums: the Carriage Museum, the Military Museum, the National Police Museum, the Seized Museum (a mish-mash of contraband), and the Jewel Palace, scene of a grand dinner after which Muhammad Ali slaughtered his four hundred Mamluk guests for dessert.

The middle section of Islamic Cairo is about a kilometer north of the southern part and can be reached from it by walking along Sharia Bab al-Wazir. Two areas, Bab al-Khalq and al-Ghuriya, comprise this section, which is home to many more mosques and lively markets. The better-known include the Blue Mosque of Aqsunqur (1347) and al-Azhar mosque and university. Between the two is the imposing Bab Zuwela (1092), one of the gates of the Fatimid city; from its minarets one can get a great view of the whole area and then wander over to the nearby Street of the Tentmakers.

For over a thousand years, al-Azhar has been the seat of Islamic scholarship. Roam around in the University's expansive courtyard, but do so well covered, as the women students do. Just to the west of al-Azhar is the old caravanserai of Wikalat al-Ghuri, an eye of calm amidst the hubbub of the streets surrounding it. It is now an artists' cooperative. Nearby is the Ghuri Palace, now a cultural center where, on Wednesdays and Saturdays around 9 pm, the famed al-Tannura whirling dervishes put on a free display of their mesmerizing talents. It is also now being used for other musical productions on off-nights—a great place to hear Arabic-fusion jazz by Fathy Salama.

The northern section of the region begins across the green footbridge over Sharia al-Azhar. It is very easy—and highly recommended—to simply get lost here, keeping a few landmarks in mind: Sharia al-Azhar is the main east–west street coming from Cairo, worth avoiding in favor of the largely car-less side streets; just past and under the footbridge are the mosque, midan, and parking lot of al-Husayn, with Khan al-Khalili abutting it; and the main north–south street is Sharia al-Mu'izz li-Din Allah, on either side of which is a staggering array of mosques and madrasas in varying states of repair, but all a lovely counterpoint to the shops and shoppers jostling each other. If you are on a gawking rather than a shopping expedition, Sunday mornings are ideal for a relatively peaceful visit, as many of the shops are closed then. A full-moon night will find Sharia al-Mu'izz crowded, but it is also one of the best times to contemplate the stunning beauty of the place—a religious experience regardless of one's religion. The northern end of the street, known as Bayn al-Qasrayn, 'between the two palaces,' is the setting for the first volume of Naguib Mahfouz's moving Cairo Trilogy, *Palace Walk*. In an alley off al-Mu'izz is the lovely Bayt al-Sihaymi, a seventeenth-century merchant's house with a cool courtyard. The highlight of the area is the graceful complex of Qalawun, Barquq, and al-Nasir, just north of Khan al-Khalili on the left of Sharia al-Mu'izz. At the north end of the street is the mosque of the caliph al-Hakim (c. 1000), notable for its size (the second largest in Cairo) and for the controversy its recent and fairly appalling restoration caused. The Suq al-Futuh, around the Bab al-Futuh ('gate of conquests') marking the northern boundary of Islamic Cairo, is the locals' as opposed to the tourists' Khan al-Khalili, where many of the same things can be found in a more authentic and lower-priced setting.

For engaging walking tours, contact William Lyster, a font of arcane expertise on all of Islamic Cairo.

THE CITIES OF THE DEAD

Just east of the regions described above are the teeming Cities of the Dead, home to hundreds of thousand of alive-and-well Cairenes. A visit to the beautiful northern cemetery makes it easy to understand why: no high rises, no traffic, some stupendous architecture, low (no) rent, and some very quiet neighbors. Here are the mausoleum of Sultan Qaytbay with its large, lace-inscribed dome (1474) and the mausoleum of Barquq (1411), plus many lesser but nevertheless impressive ones. The southern cemetery is far less grand; in fact, it is a slum, but a unique and friendly one. The Friday morning flea market around the mosque of Imam al-Shafi'i draws the innumerable aficionados of broken bicycle parts, used gallabiyas, and plastic-mosque alarm clocks that deliver the call to prayer at the appropriate times. Go early; things get even more dusty, hot, and full of buses after 10 am.

GREEN CAIRO

One of the most surprising and wonderful aspects of Cairo is how green it is. Considering the rainlessness, the dust, and the pollution, every tree and garden is a tribute to the Cairenes' love of greenery. Much has been lost with development, with everyone except high-rise builders decrying the loss of the gardens and villas of Garden City, Zamalek, and Maadi, but an awful lot remains. When the noise and the heat get you down, head to the nearest park, many of which are often empty, for a jog or a contemplative walk, or just to let the kids run off steam.

Virtually all the parks, midans, clubs, and cafés offering respite are on the Giza side of the city, many on the island of Gezira (which includes Zamalek). The largest is the Gezira Club, which except for swimming can be used by non-members for an admission fee of LE10 (see **Sporting Clubs** in Chapter 2 for details on membership and amenities). Don't drive—or if you do, park at the Marriott or on a nearby street, as you can spend easily half an hour waiting in a car queue to enter the parking lots. The club is full of leafy glades, comfortable chairs and tables, and cheap refreshment stands, which is handy since no food or drink may be brought in. Also on Gezira is a small riverside amusement park with a Ferris wheel, trees, a café, and seating just south of Le Pacha 1901 and Casino al-Nahr. The Fish Garden has hilly grottoes that make it a favorite of young lovers. The lovely gardens on either side of Sharia al-Burg on the way to the Cairo Tower on Gezira are virtually deserted, but safe, with vine-covered arbors, walkways, and a couple of formerly grand but now ramshackle Victorian greenhouses. You can easily skip the Cairo Tower itself; with its two distinctly seedy restaurants and foreign admission of LE14, it is underwhelming and annoying, even though the view from the observatory is spectacular. At the southern tip of Gezira is a nice, formally laid out garden which also appears to be a nursery; it is referred to as al-Hurriya Gardens.

In Giza, the Orman Botanical Gardens at the south end of Sharia Dokki near Cairo University house a large array of rare trees and plants collected by Ismail Pasha, whose green thumb also expressed itself in the creation of the Gezira Club. The gardens are usually more peaceful than the nearby Zoo, but even that is fine except on Fridays, when it is overrun with schoolchildren playing boisterous games of soccer. Refreshments are available at both places, and though it is a bit run down, the Zoo is an oasis for humans—perhaps less so for the other animals. The Agricultural Museum in Dokki (first available right off the 6th October Bridge coming from Cairo) is neglected by most visitors, making it a terrific place to visit. There are three small, fun museums set in a lovely garden—another good place to bring small children. All around this area of Dokki, and in Mohandiseen as well, one finds a large number of residential areas surrounding lovely midans. Two particularly nice ones are Midan Ibn al-Walid, with a few nice shops and restaurants, just south of the Shooting Club (Nadi al-Seid), and a large jungle of a place at the corner of Sharia Midhat Abd al-Hamid and Sharia Fawzi Ramah in Mohandiseen. The Shooting Club itself is a vast sports and social complex similar to the Gezira Club, but it has very little shade.

Roda, the 'garden island,' no longer has much in the way of gardens except for those in the Manial Palace, which suffice well. And Garden City, alas, has no gardens at all for walking, but a few of its tree-shaded boulevards recall Paris, traffic congestion included. At the American University in Cairo (AUC) right off the mayhem of Midan al-Tahrir, the students and anyone else who can pass for one or for a professor can enjoy its agreeable courtyard.

Maadi is the greenest of Cairo's suburbs, but there is no real public park. The side streets, however, make for pleasant walks, as a great many avid gardeners show off their skills along the garden walls. The Nile Country Club outside of Maadi has a golf course which non-golfers can probably walk. Further afield, a visit to the Japanese Gardens in Helwan offers sanctuary to the serenity-starved, and further still, the Saqqara Palms Country Club and the Saqqara Country Club make an agreeable afternoon's outing.

A COMPLETELY ARBITRARY COMPENDIUM OF FAVORITE PLACES

When we asked long-time residents about their favorite places to take visitors in or around Cairo, the answers were mostly outside of Cairo, reflecting the city-dweller's need to escape the city now and then. What topped the in-Cairo list was felucca rides any time of the night or day—but from late afternoon on is probably ideal. The Gezira Club was also popular, especially for moth-ers with small children; moms can talk and drink fresh lime juice while the kids run safely amok. Saqqara got high marks from many, much more so than the Pyramids at Giza. Picnics in the desert in the petrified forest off the Qattamiya Road behind Digla; moonlight horseback riding at the Pyramids; the secondhand bookstalls at the back of the car park at the top of the hill beyond al-Azhar; Ataba Market for varied sights and smells at bargain prices; having a beer and watching the river traffic at one of the Casino restaurant terraces; AUC's annual classic film series; taking advantage of the cultural offerings at the Opera Complex and in the many galleries downtown and in Zamalek; a visit to the al-Zahraa Stud Farm near Heliopolis during the annual Arabian Horse auction in May; the Wissa Wassef studios for the indigenous architecture, the weavings, and fresh country air . . . . The list is long and varied, showing that for many, Cairo is a great place to live.

Going further afield, there are many high spots in addition to the obvious ones of Luxor and Aswan. Despite the far more numerous wonders of the former, many residents prefer the latter for its grandeur and isolation, particularly at Abu Simbel. Other highly recommended jaunts reflecting a variety of interests and effort: the Bedouin market at al-Arish; antiquing in Alexandria, but only in the winter months; the elegant new resort of El Gouna (near Hurghada, and far preferable to it); day trips to Fayed on the way to Ismailiya; cheap weekend camping at Basata on the Gulf of Aqaba with Israeli hippies; luxury in the Moorish simplicity of the Qusir Mövenpick, south of Hurghada; the water sports and nightlife at Sharm al-Sheikh; birdwatching at Lake Qarun; the terrible beauty of the British cemetery at al-Alamein; duty-free shopping in Port Said; sunrise from the top of Mount Sinai; watching the canal traffic at Ismailiya; exploring all of the Sinai Peninsula; Farafra Oasis and the psychedelic sculptures of the White Desert; cruising Lake Nasser by houseboat *(dahabiya)*. This list, by no means comprehensive, nevertheless illustrates that there is no excuse for boredom in Egypt. Stamina, enthusiasm, and a good sense of humor are baggage essentials, though. Keep in mind the happy-go-lucky approach of one Cairo tour guide, Barbi Eysselinck: "The detour is the tour." This will save you much psychic wear and tear as you discover Cairo and Egypt.

SHOPPING

All of Cairo is an enticing bazaar that fascinates and confuses most newcomers. To help our readers make sense of it, we have used a few exclusionary criteria and an organizational system we hope makes sense to you as well.

There are two sections of this book devoted to the fine art of shopping. This one is more for shopping-as-entertainment—souvenirs, local handicrafts, clothing, and so on—whereas the one in Chapter 3 is for the more humdrum items that householders need. To clear up any confusion this may cause, the Directory lists categories alphabetically, with specific sources for each. We have concentrated on quality rather than quantity, so our comments, advice, and listings are by no means comprehensive. Instead, they reflect the eclectic recommendations garnered from our many Egyptian and foreign-resident informants. So check the Directory for listings after reading our general comments, then reread the **Bargaining** section earlier in this chapter, and—happy hunting.

THE MAJOR SUQS OR MARKETS

Almost all the old *suqs* sell almost everything under the sun, with some specializing.

Except for Khan al-Khalili, they are all authentic marketplaces where Egyptians have done their household shopping in the same way for centuries. Even as one modern, lookalike shopping arcade after another is built, these will not change. Prices are lower than at supermarkets or arcades only if you are an experienced or Arabic-speaking shopper. The modern arcades, by the way, are also described in Chapter 3.

Khan al-Khalili: This bazaar dating from the fourteenth century may be a greater tourist attraction than the Pyramids. Look up at the glorious medieval stones and wood surrounding you as you browse and bargain. And go up—up the many often smelly, dungeon-like stairways, and up the not-so-secret stairways in many of the shops. It is there that many of the Khan's really interesting stuff is on offer. One unarguable benefit of tourism: the Khan also, unlike most of the non-tourist markets, offers even the footsore and hungry female many places to sit down, gather sustenance, and watch the world go by.

Al-Muski (Ataba Square to Khan al-Khalili): Everything; lots of small electrical shops, and lots of car fumes and traffic. Right off Husayn Square to the west and parallel to Sharia al-Muski is one full of paper products with nary a tourist in sight. Nearby are shops full of buttons, bangles, bows, sequins, bridal supplies and all kinds of sewing notions.

Suq al-Futuh: At the northern end of Sharia al-Mu'izz li-Din Allah near Bab al-Futuh; very worthwhile. This is where the shisha pipes that fill the cafés of Cairo are made and sold.

Perfume and Spice Market: Part of the Khan just north of Sharia al-Azhar where it meets Sharia al-Mu'izz li-Din Allah; sometimes called the Suq Sudani.

Suq al-Khayyamiya: The Tentmakers' bazaar behind Bab Zuwela.

Note: All of the above suqs, plus many

more—gold, coppersmiths, etc.—are very near each other, but nevertheless distinctive. It takes more than a few trips to make your own cognitive map of the area.

Ataba Market (Downtown): Large, mostly indoor food market with household goods, clothing, and hardware on the fringes. Wear gaiters or something similar for sloshing through the fish and butcher stalls.

Bab al-Luq (near Falaki Square): Covered food market.

Dokki Market (Sharia Suliman Guhar): Small, shady, manageable indoor–outdoor market with all types of food, hardware, jewelers, etc.

Midan al-Tahrir: Airlines, tourist traps, and major bus station. Tal'at Harb and Qasr al-Nil streets off it to the northwest have mostly clothes, travel agents—and shoes, shoes, shoes.

Tawfiqiya Market (near 'Urabi Square): Outdoor food market.

Wikalat al-Balah: Just north of the Abu-l-'Ila Bridge, about half a kilometer south the World Trade Center, a diagonal street branches to the right. Fabric, clothing, car covers, spare parts, and who knows what else.

OTHER SHOPPING STREETS AND AREAS

Heliopolis: Is turning into one giant shopping mall! In the Suq al-'Ubur on Sharia Salah Salem are branches of every store imaginable. Midan Roxy, Kurba, and Sharia Baghdad are chockablock, too (don't drive; no parking). More everyday shopping is along Sharia Harun al-Rashid and on Midan al-Gami', and Heliopolitans now boast the best supermarket in all Cairo, Fairway.

Maadi: Road 9 for everything, with the places on the Nile side of the railroad tracks for interesting utilitarian shopping.

Midan Libnan area (Mohandiseen): Mostly upscale furniture and clothing stores and many restaurants.

Sharia Muhammad Farid (Downtown): Many carpenters and a colorful outdoor food market.

Sharia Abd al-Khaliq Sarwat (Downtown): Stationery shops, printers, computer accessories, and electronics.

Sharia Gam'at al-Duwal al-'Arabiya (Mohandiseen): Modern strip-mall street: mostly clothes, shoes, car showrooms, lighting shops, no shade whatsoever.

Shooting Club vicinity (Mohandiseen and Dokki): An up-and-coming shopping area. On and off Sharia al-Thawra on the north side of the club is Creek's Restaurant, the very chi-chi Mohammed Jr.'s beauty salon, and two elegant couturier-type women's clothing stores, Melodie's and Boutique Viola. On Suliman Abaza veering off the club's northwest corner are Clarine's antiques, Queenie's couturier clothing, La Beauté for cosmetics, Bunny's for kid's clothes, etc. Off the southwest corner between Sharia Nadi al-Seid and Muhi al-Din Abu-l-'Izz are fancy fabric and home accessories shops.

Zamalek: As befits its status as a foreigners' and diplomatic enclave, Zamalek has the most concentrated range of elegant shops and good restaurants in the city. Expensive, yes, but you save on cab fare by walking. Alef, for unique home furnishings and accessories, is an exquisite shop in a league all its own.

SHOPPING ITEMS

ANTIQUES

Zamalek is the antique-lover's stomping ground. There are no bargains here, but there are dozens of wonderful shops full of genuine antiques and excellent reproductions, mostly European and Egyptian in origin. Serious hunters favor Alexandria's 'Attarin district over Cairo for antiques; the rare mind-boggling bargain, like a Beidermeier chair for LE70, can still be unearthed there. As with furniture in general, many Egyptians prefer the lavish and ornate to the simple, and this is true of antiques as well, but art deco pieces are also popular. All the shops listed in the Directory are good, but a few that are mouthwatering, with gourmet prices to match, are Clarine in Dokki, Hamdy al-Dabb in Khan al-Khalili, Atrium and Mit Rehan in Zamalek, Morgana in Maadi, as well as the best shops downtown, including Mahrous, Hassan and Ali, Ahmed Zeinhoum, and Philippe Devlay. Other favorites for accessories, as opposed to furniture, are Nostalgia in Zamalek and Samia Imports in Mohandiseen, which both have charming owners and are wonderfully funky places to dig around in. The Old Shoppe in the Khan is more like a dusty warehouse, but they have some great stuff, including an abundance of tables, mirrors, chests, and chairs with mother-of-pearl and wood inlays.

If you are already an expert, try Osiris Auction House downtown to compete with the professionals. If not, start by taking an antique shop tour with Rosemary Younes of the Women's Association.

APPLIQUÉ WORK
The Street of the Tentmakers behind Bab Zuwela is the place to find it all, concentrated in one place that is a riot of color. Cushion covers, bedspreads, wall-hangings, toaster covers(!), and yes, even tents for your wedding or your balcony can be found ready-made or custom-made. Colors tend to be bright to garish, and quality of work varies, but one place that has been recommended is Farghaly at 2 Sharia al-Khayyamiya. Dry-cleaning and ruthless bargaining strongly advised.

ARTS AND CRAFTS
Many places called galleries are either arts and crafts, furniture, or antique shops—a holdover from the French. Egyptian craftspeople used to be among the best in the Middle East, but many of them have either died or gone to greener pastures. Nevertheless, quite a lot of good work can still be found, much of it originating in the oases and among the Bedouin, where buyers go directly for their wares. Such items include rugs and weavings, silver jewelry, Bedouin shawls and wedding dresses, and baskets. With few exceptions, Khan al-Khalili is definitely not the place to go for good-quality handicrafts. Instead, try these, where quality and taste are on exhibit and representative crafts from around the country are well-displayed: al-Ain in Dokki; Nomad, whose lovely shop on Saray al-Gezira is like falling into a seraglio (the one in the Marriott around the corner is smaller and less enticing); Asila in Dokki, mainly for the pottery of Nabil Darwish (also see **Pottery** below); Ethno in Maadi; Shahira Mehrez in Dokki; Senouhi near Opera Square; and two exceptions in and around Khan al-Khalili, the Bayt al-Sinnari and Wikalat al-Ghuri artists' workshops. Another good place to get an overview of the crafts scene is at the monthly meetings of the Women's Association held in the Aida Ballroom of the Marriott. The first hour is usually devoted to shopping from a varied roster of vendors selling some kitschy, some classy goods.

BASKETS
Really beautiful baskets come from the Nubians in Aswan; a common type is a round, flattish cone used for serving and protecting food, but it also makes an elegant sun hat. More pedestrian but highly utilitarian baskets can be found on donkey carts at many Cairo street corners; they usually come from Fayyum, where they are cheaper and there is more variety.

BEADWORK AND EMBROIDERY

Thanks to the belly dancers and to Egyptian women's penchant for dressing up, these needleworker's arts still thrive here. Bedouin women use both extensively on their dresses, of which Hazem Hafez in Heliopolis has some lovely examples with silver and gold coins, buttons, and cross-stitch. For kinky dress-up fun, haggle with the belly-dance costume sellers in Khan al-Khalili. For the real thing at sky-high prices, go where Fifi Abdou goes, to Hafez at Bekhita in the Marriott. More restraint and style, but still with plenty of dazzle, can be found at Fantastic in Zamalek and Boutique Viola in Mohandiseen (**Clothing, Women's Evening**).

Soutache-like embroidery *(itan)* with silk and metal thread embroidery *(sirma)* are available by order from Atlas and Aseel respectively in Khan al-Khalili. These are unique couturier touches that one would pay a queen's ransom for in Europe, but are quite reasonable here. Another uniquely Egyptian craft, machine-woven ribbon called *ekkada*, can be found in a number of shops. You choose the colors and designs, and the ribbon is custom-made. It is a whole evening's entertainment to explore and haggle in one of the dusty ateliers, where you should end up spending between LE4 and LE10 per meter, depending on width, with silk and wool being more costly. Use it to border cushion covers, gallabiyas, or curtains.

BRASS AND COPPER

Pardon the pun, but Cairo, specifically Khan al-Khalili, really shines here. Aspiring Julia Childs clones can form a complete batterie de cuisine with gorgeous copper cookware, all tin-lined, from the shops hidden away up a dank stairway near the Naguib Mahfouz Coffee Shop, and at prices far more reasonable than abroad—for example, less than LE100 for a large oval casserole. The same is true for brass. Quality, as determined by

weight and work, varies, but it is all pretty nice and makes for beautiful cache-pots for your houseplants.

BOOKBINDING

This art that is dying in the West is still going strong in Cairo. Ask for Hisham Ragab at L'Orientaliste (**Books**),who works fast, well, and at a reasonable price. NADIM (see **Mashrabiya**) also does excellent bookbinding.

BOOKS

Bibliophiles in search of the old and arcane are very well served in Cairo, especially at L'Orientaliste, Lehnert and Landrock, and Reader's Corner, all fascinating browsing grounds. Those in search of a really wide selection of modern literature and non-fiction are less well served, although Danielle Steele, John Grisham, and Tom Clancy abound. Books in English and other foreign languages are expensive here, as most are published and printed abroad. Luckily, there are the two AUC bookstores, on the main Tahrir campus and in the Zamalek hostel, which are well thought of. Volume One in Maadi is a clean, well-lit place with a good selection, and other worthwhile places are listed in the Directory (**Books**). Used treasure can be unearthed at the bookstalls at the back of the car park at the top of the hill beyond al-Azhar and outside of Groppi's on Midan Tal'at Harb, and in the wonderful shops listed under **Books: Used** in the Directory.

CAMELS

Well, you never know when one might come in handy. The going rate is quoted as between $300 and $600 (LE1,000 to LE2,000), with females being more valuable. The new camel market (directions in **Sightseeing** section) will give you the widest selection, but there is still a small urban camel market in a little *midan* not too far from the southern section of the City of the Dead. Camel meat, by the way, is much eaten in Egypt, and is not only delicious but is said to be virtually cholesterol free.

CARPETS AND RUGS

For those in search of a bargain, Cairo is not the place to buy oriental carpets, although many beautiful shops selling them abound. However, richly colored Bedouin carpets and simple camel-hair moquettes are a buy—for example, less than LE50 for a 1 x 1.5 meter one of the latter at Kirdasa, handled by a hopeless non-bargainer. Cairo shops charge quite a bit for the Bedouin carpets, so it is better to go to al-'Arish or to the carpet markets west of Alexandria on the coast road. One is at al-Hammam (seventy kilometers west of Alexandria), the other at Burg al-'Arab (fifty kilometers). It is fun and worth the trip, as what sells in Cairo for LE600 can be found there for around LE200. Finally, and to dispense with floor covering altogether, cotton rag rugs are a great buy here: LE10 for a really big bathmat from the Association for the Protection of the Environment (APE) in Heliopolis or through the Marketing Link Project in Zamalek.

CLOTHING, ETHNIC

Gallabiyas, the ubiquitous long, loose tunics worn by men and women, make wonderful nightshirts, loungewear, and evening wear. In plain cotton, they are less than LE20. Traditional Bedouin wedding dresses dripping with embroidery and coins are also fun for evening. Hazem Hafez in Heliopolis has a great selection and is knowledgeable about both costumes and customs of the Bedouin. The beautifully woven wool scarves that farmers wear wrapped around their necks all winter make surprisingly sophisticated, warm coat scarves for men and women; they are available throughout the Khan.

For really glamorous take-offs on ethnic Egyptian styles, there are three great places to go. Ethno in Maadi has an excellent design duo who reinterpret Bedouin dresses, producing unique costumes that are stylish and even sexy. Abbas Higazi in Khan al-Khalili sticks to traditional patterns done in the fabric and decoration of your choice, including silks; his finishing work is generally superior to that at Atlas, where cuff and hem facings are ignored and seams are not well finished. Finally, Ed-Dukkan, with its jewel-box of a shop hidden away in the Yamama Center and a branch at the Ramsis Hilton Annex, has astonishingly beautiful things at high but well-justified prices. This is the perfect place to steer clueless husbands for a lavish birthday or anniversary gift à l'Egyptienne.

JEWELRY

Cairo is home to hundreds, perhaps even thousands, of jewelry shops, and to some jewelers with international reputations. Work quality and design are generally good to excellent, and the government monitors the weight and purity of all gold and silver sold, so you are pretty safe as a consumer. Jewelry in gold and silver only is sold by gram weight, with work and age adding marginally to its cost. The current price for 21-carat gold is about LE45 per gram, for sterling silver LE2 per gram. The addition of precious stones sends the price spiraling upward, as none are native to Egypt, but semiprecious stones like onyx, amber, jade, and turquoise are very reasonable here.

Gold is available from 18 carats and up; very little under that is sold. Sterling silver is 95 percent pure. Shops selling the one usually do not sell the other. The three top gold jewelers are Sirghany, with a number of branches, including one in the Khan, Hassan Elaish (four branches), and Nassar Brothers in the Khan. Another in the Khan, Mihran and Garbis Yazejian, is much used by AUC staffers, and Lalik, in Dokki and

Heliopolis, is also very good. Only at Yazejian should you ask for a gold cartouche with your name in hieroglyphs; the others would turn up their noses at such a request from anyone except wealthy Gulf tourists, on whom they depend for far more substantial purchases.

Silver jewelry, mostly in ethnic but some modern designs, is a bargain here. Saad of Egypt (three branches, including one in the Khan) is known for its design, quality, and high prices. Throughout town are many excellent shops; two favorites are Qasr al-Shawq in Zamalek and Kafr al-Nada near the Shooting Club in Dokki; the young owner of the latter makes beautiful silver necklaces combined with semi-precious stones and beads at very reasonable prices.

Shops selling beads and more beads, by piece and by weight, abound in the Khan. You choose and lay out, they string. Late in the evening, these places take on a comically mysterious air as people from all over the world sit on the floor to shuffle through the baskets, endlessly reconsidering their precious trinkets. Caveat emptor: ivory is on sale, too, along with ersatz camel-bone ivory. Most places will repair and restring your own heirlooms for very little in hopes of earning your good will. Try Mr. Beads at Turquoise for his friendly if well-practiced banter or the other shops listed in the Directory under **Khan al-Khalili**.

There are also a number of jewelry designers who work by word-of-mouth only and show by appointment only. Often members of the Women's Association can steer you to them, or they place notices in the *Maadi Messenger*, the *BCA Magazine*, or *The Niler*, the US Embassy staff magazine. Marie Louise Ibrahim is also a good source and an expert herself.

LITHOGRAPHS

L'Orientaliste on Qasr al-Nil has the biggest collection of original David Roberts lithographs in the world, as well as excellent reproductions. Originals range from LE300 to LE5,000, depending on rarity, size, and condition, with reproductions a mere LE10 to LE50. Comparison shopping? At a well-known New York dealer, originals start at $1,600.

MARQUETRY (INLAID WOOD) AND MOTHER-OF-PEARL

These are very popular decorative touches on all sorts of furnishings, often in combination with mashrabiya (below). Zillions of small boxes displaying this work are hawked in every gift shop and all over Khan al-Khalili. Most are of poor quality on close inspection and very inexpensive; but beautifully done pieces—chests, mirrors, screens, tables in all sizes—can still be found in the Khan and elsewhere. Check the Old Shoppe to get an idea and ask the salespeople to educate you in what to look for.

MASHRABIYA

The best place to go to get a good overview of this lovely, painstakingly hand-lathed woodwork designed originally to hide the girls from the guys is at NADIM in Dokki, behind the Coca Cola bottling plant off Sharia Sudan. The acronym NADIM stands for National Art Development Institute for Mashrabiya, but it is also really the name of the folklorist owner, Mr. Nadim, who preserves this craft along with his wife, an anthropologist. They have greatly expanded their showroom–workshop, and it is a fascinating place to while away a few hours. The best mashrabiya is of beech, for its hard, tight, fine grain, but walnut, teak, and oak are also used. Sample prices: three-panel screens, LE2,000–3,500; large octagonal coffee table, LE800–1,000; small bench, LE1,000. Prices are more or less fixed, and you can find nice things for less elsewhere if accompanied by a knowledgeable Egyptian friend, but you cannot beat NADIM's quality. They also do bookbinding and brass and copper work.

MUSICAL INSTRUMENTS

For authentic Egyptian and Middle Eastern instruments, head for Sharia Muhammad 'Ali downtown. Real musicians head directly to the source for these and Western instruments of all types as well: the Abdel Ghafar Group, which has moved to new location in Sharia al-Bustan near Midan Falaki. You must make an appointment to see the manager, Mr. Hatem Abdel Ghafar.

MUSKI GLASS

The vivid greens and blues, as well as the rarer reds and more common translucent whites of this handblown glassware make nice vases, pitchers, and casual drinking glasses. It is cheap, easily breakable, and available all over the Khan. Two places stand out: the Mosque Glass House for variety and volume, and Sayed Abd El-Raouf for the red Muski glass for your Christmas tree decorations. The glassblowers' district nearby is a treat for kids and grownups too.

NEWSSTANDS

The three with the best selection of international papers and magazines are outside of Groppi's on Midan Tal'at Harb, off Midan al-Tahrir just next to McDonald's, and on 26th July Street in Zamalek in front of Simonds. The major hotels all have adequate but more limited selections. So far, there are no good newsstands for non-Arabic readers on the Giza side of the river.

PAINTING AND SCULPTURE

Egypt nurtures an enormous number of talented artists, whose work is regularly on display at the many fine arts galleries throughout Cairo. The gallery owners are highly knowledgeable, accessible, and often wonderfully eccentric characters themselves. Check the 'Where To Go — What To See' listings in the *Middle East Times* or just browse using our by-neighborhood **Art Galleries** entries in the Directory.

PERFUMES

Create your own from essential oils diluted with alcohol or opt for perennial favorites like Cleopatra's Kiss. Among the (again) hundreds of perfume purveyors in the city, many of whom are in the Khan and around Midan al-Tahrir, you take pot luck, but one place to start educating yourself is at Abd al-Hady in the Khan. A well-dressed Egyptian woman would feel naked without her perfume, and after living here a while you may start to feel the same way. In no time, your dressing-table or bathroom counter could be full of the fragile perfume bottles that are nearly as numerous in Cairo shops as shoes are.

POTTERY

There are a few superb artist–potters, Nabil Darwish being one of our favorites. His studio near Saqqara is a delight, and prices are better than at Asila, where they are going through the roof. Mohammed Allam, who calls himself 'the Crazy Artist,' also does idiosyncratic and amusing pots (and metal and wood and whatever strikes his fancy at the moment) of all sorts in his atelier on the Saqqara road; just look for the large white paint-splattered chicken coop on the right (he also has an outlet, 'Fagnoun,' in the World Trade Center). Folksy figurines of dubious charm are widely available, especially at the Mud Factory in Mohandiseen, where large, pretty Islamic–Persian-style vases are also made for lampshades and display, but prices for these are unduly high for the quality—LE300–500.

SHOES AND LEATHER GOODS

For those of us with the illness, Cairo at first glance would seem to be a shoe fetishist's dream. But alas, on closer examination, it is a nightmare! In a city with nearly as many shoe stores as feet (surely an understandable overreaction to the eleventh-century reign of the caliph al-Hakim, who banned the manufacture of women's shoes in order to keep the women inside, barefoot, and presumably pregnant), it is almost impossible to find decent shoes. Overall, poor manufacturing abounds, as do synthetics. And the heels! Either completely clunky and mismatched to the shoe or with a staggering proliferation of gold plastic curlicues, pyramids, and spikes that would fit right in on an S&M version of *Star Wars*. (Obviously, we are referring here primarily to women's footwear.) The only exceptions we have found after much footsore research are: the BTM department stores all around town, which sell Italian imports with prices to rival Italy's; T & A in Dokki and the World Trade Center, with good work and materials and restrained styling, but still tending to clunkiness; al-Baraem (two branches), which has good Italian shoes at reasonable prices; Santana (two branches), with some nice Egyptian-made shoes and boots; and perhaps the best, La Scarpa in Maadi, with excellent quality of work, soft leathers, and wearable styles, but limited stock and sizes.

The wives of oil emirs are luckier: they can go to Antonio in Mohandiseen and slap down a mere LE2,700 for a heavenly pair of crocodile pumps, but most of what Antonio sells, for somewhat less money, would appeal more to Cinderella's stepsisters or even Minnie Mouse. It used to be possible to have shoes custom-made all over Cairo, but the old shoemakers are disappearing or selling out due to too much competition from the thousands of shoe stores. A few remain, including Abdel Moneim Abu Zeid (quality varies, mostly so-so) and El-Aziz (who makes cowboy boots) in Zamalek. Men fare far better in the shoe department, with Egyptian-made Bally shoes at around

LE150 and up available at Bally in Zamalek.

Cairenes who can afford to do so bring shoes from abroad. We suggest you follow in their footsteps, and just buy your *shibshib* (slippers) from street kiosks or in Ataba market, or try the Moroccan-style ones from Khan al-Khalili.

Luckily, we can end our shoe diatribe on a high note as we consider other leather goods and clothing. Clothing of all sorts in leather and suede (chamois) of excellent quality and in a variety of styles, sizes, and colors can be bought off the rack or custom-made in many places throughout town. Prices are very reasonable—for example, men's bomber jackets in very fine suede for LE350 at the Leather Corner (two locations), a good shop with lots of choice and good service. Handbags, wallets, and briefcases are also well-styled, with good prices. At Choice and Seven K (numerous branches), with consistently superior styling and work, prices tend to be somewhat higher than elsewhere, but worth it.

TEXTILES, TOWELS, AND EGYPTIAN COTTON

These are generally good buys and make great gifts, given the worldwide cachet of Egyptian cotton. For towels, our favorite place is Salon Vert on Sharia Qasr al-Nil, which stocks (but not always) deliciously thick, simple white towels and bathmats and good dish towels, all at reasonable fixed prices. They also have excellent matelassé-like bedspreads in cotton at LE32 for a double-bed size, but the size is a little skimpy and better on a single bed. Beautiful embroidered all-cotton sheet sets in all sizes (no fitted sheets, but they can be converted) are available. See Madame Linda, a charming, French-speaking vendeuse of the old school, at Salon Vert. And don't be put off by the less-than-prepossessing look of the place. It exemplifies what happened to Cairo's grand old emporia under nationalization, but many of the older salespeople retain their original courtliness and professionalism despite the drab surroundings. Be patient as they direct you through the complexities of actually paying for and obtaining your purchase. Good fitted sheets can be found at branches of Carpet City.

Excellent-quality men's all-cotton shirts, custom- and ready-made, are at the various Shirt Shop outlets for around LE65. The cheap place to go for fabric by the yard is the bowels of the Wikalat al-Balah (see above under **Major Suqs**), where the occasional treasure amidst lots of sleaze can be found, and at Ouf in the Khan. More elegant surroundings for household but not dress fabric, with better selections at higher prices, can be found at the numerous fabric shops in the World Trade Center, which also all have branches in Dokki just to the south of the Shooting Club. There are excellent fabric shops of all kinds along Qasr al-Nil between Midan Mustafa Kamel and Midan Tal'at Harb. See **Fabrics** in the Directory, but for great dress fabric, two stand out: Champs Elysées (includes linen, silk crepe, and wonderful washable silk), and (in Mohandiseen) Salem. Now all you need is a good tailor or dressmaker—a problem we address in Chapter 3.

The best-designed Egyptian-motif fabrics are at Tanis in the World Trade Center. All cotton, silk, and linen only, all made and printed in Egypt, and all just wonderful. Not cheap, but not outrageous. See Ahmad, whose English is very good, and who can arrange to have what you need made up.

WALL HANGINGS AND WEAVINGS

Museum- and lesser-quality folk-art weavings can best be seen at the Wissa Wassef Studio off the Saqqara road. Run by the late artist–architect's daughter Suzanne, who is also a professional potter, the compound is worth a visit as much for its excellent indigenous architecture and cool gardens as for the beautiful museum and its art. You will get an informative, no-pressure guided tour, best done by appointment. The best large pieces that are for sale are in the LE25,000 range, but smaller samples by younger, less seasoned artists are far more affordable. There is also batik, but most of it is unremarkable, as is true all over Cairo.

WATER-PIPES

Wonderfully tacky but impractical shisha pipes are seen all over. For functional but plain ones, go to Sharia al-Mu'izz li-Din Allah north of the Khan, where a number of small shops sell coffeeshop supplies, including shishas and all their accessories. Or design your own and make it the centerpiece of a living room or terrace corner festooned with floor pillows and lanterns: go to Mahmoud Eid El-Qalamawy & Sons in front of Qasr Bishtaq in the Khan to create your masterpiece. Then don a gallabiya, fill the pipe with water, light the charcoal, have your choice of smoke at the ready—appletobacco is cool and smells heavenly—and turn on some oud music or the cigarette girls' chorus from *Carmen* for an exotic evening.

2 LEISURE AND LEARNING IN CAIRO

CAIRO FOR KIDS (OF ALL AGES)

If you find yourself in a Cairo hotel or apartment with lively offspring, you will need some escape routes before you all start bouncing off the walls. Suburban children who have been used to a yard or local park may find the constraints of city living particularly hard to adjust to. At first glance, the busy streets might not seem welcoming, but there are spaces to roam and, unlike those in many cities, they are safe. In Cairo you can let your heirs out of your sight for a whole minute—hours, even—without becoming paranoid that they will be abducted by weirdoes. Do not underestimate the resulting peace of mind, and be grateful for it.

Your first and easiest option is to join a sporting club, or, simpler and cheaper, just go in on a daily fee basis. Indeed, if you live in town with small children this may be essential to your sanity. Tennis, swimming, gymnastics, karate, and just plain rolling around like puppies are only a few of the activities on offer, not to mention space for roller-blading and bike-riding. In Maadi, if you are fortunate enough to have access to the Cairo American College (CAC) facilities, your children can also explore the adventure playground there. On Fridays, try Victory Fields, which are open to the Cairo Softball League and Cairo Rugby members and their friends. There is a great family atmosphere around the ball games, and enthusiastic American-style support for the teams. Meanwhile, over on the Cairo Rugby field you will often find a game of cricket underway on Cairo's only public cricket pitch, where the thwack of leather on willow and the ripples of polite applause evoke quite a different world.

The Cairo Zoo, built in 1891, is one of the oldest in the world. Its maze of beautiful mosaic paths and many enclosures can be suitably exhausting for children. While the care of the animals does not perhaps reach the standard of world-class zoos, and the tendency of some parents to allow their kids to tease the animals may annoy, it is one of the few zoos where one can actually feed the animals. The keepers of hippopotami, giraffes, camels, and ostriches will sell you handfuls of the appropriate vegetation. (Political correctness aside, there is a great deal to be said for the velvety feel of a baby goat's lips on a child's hand.) In the reptile house, brave souls may even handle snakes. The zoo is crowded on Fridays and might, for the shy newcomer, be avoided on public holidays, when the plumage of obviously foreign visitors is likely to attract more attention than that of the animals.

If your family's interest in animals extends to wanting one in your own home, you can visit the Friday Pet Market. The easiest way to reach it is to take the Autostrade out of Maadi, and just near the turn to Muqattam (at the Esso petrol station) you will see two large concrete water towers on the left. Take the next left and then the next right to follow the railway tracks past brick-makers. It is no more than a kilometer from the main road. The Pet Market makes for an interesting outing, but it is definitely not for the squeamish or for animal rights activists, who will be upset by monkeys in cages far too small for them and endangered species of birds of prey offered for sale. Cairo's most popular pets, fish and birds, are in great abundance along with all their necessary equipment—and at prices far cheaper than can be found elsewhere.

The Fish Garden on Hasan Sabri Street in

Zamalek was formerly a khedival garden. It features fish tanks lodged in grottoes and is a perfect place for hide and seek. The fish are of less interest than the discreetly courting couples who rendezvous there, but the hilly park itself is great for walks and jogs.

There are a number of rather tame amusement parks in Cairo suitable for smaller children. Cookie Park is behind the Mövenpick Jolie Ville by the Pyramids. It is open daily from 3 pm except Fridays, when it starts at noon. Sindbad and Merryland Parks in Heliopolis are good for tots too. Merryland is on Sharia al-Higaz near Roxy; for Sindbad, take the first left turn at the beginning of the Ismailiya Road off Saleh Salem.

If the kids are really bouncing off the walls, take them instead to the trampolines at the Felfela in Maadi, which also has bumper cars.

Cairo National Circus was founded following Nasser's trip to the Soviet Union in the 1950s. Nightly performances take place under the faded big top on the Corniche in Agouza, except during the summer, when the circus moves to Alexandria.

There is also the Puppet Theater in Midan Opera. The singing performances in Arabic attract a noisy crowd and are much loved by Egyptian children. Language is largely irrelevant in these lively Punch and Judy shows, and a good time is had by all. Command performances can even be arranged by contacting the French Cultural Center (**Organizations**). A charming group of multilingual puppeteers who go by the acronym ZASSY can also be engaged for birthday parties and whatnot to entertain both kids and grownups (**Children's Entertainment**), but note that prices from these AUC graduates are on the American, not Egyptian scale.

Dr. Ragab's Pharaonic Village on Jacob's Island, Giza, makes for a fascinating and educational day out. Definitely cut out the ten-percent-off coupons frequently found on the first page of the *Egyptian Gazette*. Take

the floating guided tour past scenes from life in ancient Egypt and statues of gods and goddesses before alighting to visit a pharaonic temple and a replica of King Tutankhamun's tomb. Have your photo taken if you must in period costume—a very popular Christmas card idea for the folks back home—and then lunch in the restaurant. This is a good pre-Luxor outing. Some kids sneer at it, others love it.

For children at the upper end of that awkward post-diaper, pre-disco stage—eight to fifteen years' duration depending on precocity—the situation is bleak, as it is and has been throughout history, always and everywhere, in their eyes. Realistically though, Cairo offers a great deal to pre-teens and teens who eventually do decide to get off their butts after boring even themselves silly by whining, "There's nothing to do-oo-o!" For their health, and for their parents' sanity, there is a nearly infinite variety of sports, including some—such as horseback riding, tennis, squash, scuba diving, and gymnastics—that are far more affordable here than abroad, and generally of a high caliber in terms of facilities and instruction.

For some good, dirty (i.e., sweaty), family fun, escape the pollution and get out into the desert by joining the Hash House Harriers for their Friday afternoon jogs. The first Friday in the month is the family run, after which a refreshingly insincere effort is made to tone down the post-run dirty jokes. While getting winded, you will discover some great picnic locations.

In summer, many hotels have day rate entrances or seasonal family memberships, but limited space for kids to run and with unduly steep day rates in many cases—for example, the Marriott charges LE64 per person. A better solution may be the Saqqara Palm Club or the Saqqara Country Club, both near Saqqara, or the Nile Country Club, twenty minutes past Maadi toward Helwan. Facilities vary but are generally good and include a wide range of sports. The Saqqara Country Club in particular has an excellent equestrian program. Facilities aside, teens will be inclined toward whichever place their friends go. (**Sporting & Country Clubs**)

The first water park in Cairo was Crazy Water on the road to 6th October City. It has slides for all ages, a wave pool, quasars, go-karts, and video games. The latest to date is Aquapark on the Ismailiya Road, which is safe, clean, and very crowded on Fridays. Another antidote to the July heat: the Cairo Opera House has presented Walt Disney's World on Ice show at the Cairo stadium for the last few years; check the newspapers for these and other special events.

Less strenuous alternatives: snooker and/or pool halls (known as '**Billiard Halls**') have recently sprung up all over the city. Few serve alcohol—sigh of relief—and most require no membership. You just pay and play for le10 to le20 a game. Ten-pin Bowling is the latest imported craze, and some places have snooker and food outlets on site. The Bustan Center (9th floor), the Nile Bowling Center in Giza, and Maadi Grand Mall (MGM) are the main ones. Several cinemas show recent English-language films: Karim, Radio, and Metro downtown, Tahrir in Dokki, Ramsis Hilton, Cairo Sheraton, Horreya and Normandy in Heliopolis, and MGM in Maadi. And there are plenty of venues for hanging out at the mall; those currently in favor seem to be the World Trade Center, MGM in Maadi, 'Ubur in Heliopolis, and Yamama in Zamalek. Reasonably well-behaved teens can also work on their computer and social skills at the Cyber Café. (**Computers**)

Note: The Planetarium, situated in the Opera House complex, has been closed for some time and no one seems to know when or if it will reopen.

HOBBIES, INTERESTS, PASTIMES, AND SELF-INDULGENCE

The array of things to see and do in Cairo is inexhaustible. Newcomers who tend to hit the ground running will be inspired to explore Islamic Cairo, improve their tennis game, sign up for Arabic lessons, and get their flats redone all at once. Shortly thereafter, they find themselves exhausted and overcommitted. A better strategy is to get selectively busy with just a few things at first. For non-Arabic speakers, one of them should certainly be learning some conversational Arabic in a group setting. It is a great way to meet other people in the same boat and to start learning the ropes from each other.

Because of what is wryly referred to as the E-factor (E for Egypt), it is hard for everyone, native Cairenes included, to pack in as much as one would like in the course of a day. Much of this has to do with the traffic. It can take ten minutes or over an hour to get from Dokki to Midan al-Tahrir; don't attempt it between 1:30 and 3 pm during school sessions or during the morning rush hours of 8 to 10 am if you can avoid it. Another element of the E-factor is time, a lot of which is spent waiting—for stores to open, plumbers to show up, classes to start, lines to get shorter, and so on. Take it easy and always have a good book at hand.

In addition to the gamut of activities in this and the next two sections (**Arts, Entertainment, & Night Life** and **Sports & Fitness**), up-to-date inspiration for what to do is available in the back pages of *Egypt Today* (which carries excellent listings of everything from cultural centers to bars to art galleries), *Cairo's* (a small but useful pamphlet publication), and *Al-Ahram Weekly* and the *Middle East Times* (for excellent cultural listings). Note, thought, that times, phone numbers, and programs are subject to

The American University in Cairo Press

Illustrated Gift Books

Our gift books provide a special pleasure for anyone interested in Egypt's rich cultural heritage.

Life of the Ancient Egyptians
Eugen Strouhal
With photographs by Werner Forman
21 x 28cm. 289 illus, incl. 219 color. 279 pp.
Paperback: ISBN 977 424 380 3; LE90 / $29.50
Hardback: ISBN 977 424 285 8; LE175 / $42.50
For sale only in the Middle Eastt

The Mosque
History, Architectural Development and Regional Diversity
Edited by Martin Frishman and Hasan-Uddin Khan
22x30cm. 365 illus, incl. 170 color.
Hardbound.
ISBN 0 500 34133 8
Not for sale outside Egypt
LE195 / $59.50

Egypt
Text and Photographs by Mary Cross
25.x 35.5cm. 150 color illus. 301pp.
Hardbound.
ISBN 977 424 352 8
For sale only in the Middle East
LE225 / $60.00

Margo Veillon
The Bursting Movement
Art Works 1925–1996
25x31cm. 160 illus, incl. 120 color. 260 pp.
Hardbound.
ISBN 2 940033 20 X
Not for sale outside Egypt
LE350 / $125

Alexandria
Michael Haag
20x28cm. 95 color illus. 64pp. Paperback.
ISBN 977 424 339 0
Not for sale outside Egypt
LE40 / $22.00

The American University in Cairo Press
113 Sharia Kasr el Aini, Cairo, Egypt.
Tel: 357-6891/4/5/6; fax: 354-1440

change and that last-minute cancellations are not unheard of. Call ahead if you can, and have a back-up plan regardless, to keep frustration within manageable limits.

If your particular esoteric interest is not included here, the many community and social organizations invariably welcome anyone with the enthusiasm and expertise to organize something new.

ALTERNATIVE MEDICINE

Alternative Therapies are enjoying a resurgence in Cairo, mirroring a world trend. Herbs have been used to treat chronic ailments in Egypt for centuries, particularly by people too poor to see a doctor. At the Harraz Herb Shop in Bab al-Khalq, patients from all points on the social spectrum line up to discuss their ailments before picking up an individual herbal remedy. Business is booming, particularly among the better heeled, according to Ahmed Harraz.

Western-trained therapists come and go but aromatherapist and reflexologist Rawya al-Gamma runs a clinic in Zamalek that also deals with sports injuries and massage. She maintains a list of other alternative medical practitioners.

Acupuncturist Dr. Adel Badr is an Egyptian doctor who studied for two years in China. He has an alternative healing clinic in Mohandiseen. Another is Dr. Emad R. al-Zoghbi, with clinics in Heliopolis and Mohandiseen. Chiropractor Shamil Fahmy in Maadi comes well recommended, as does hypnotherapist Polly Cunningham in Dokki. Osteopathy is more in the medical mainstream for treating what ails you, while chi kung and reiki, the therapeutic placing of hands on one's chakra points, are less so, but all have their adherents and their recommended practitioners in Cairo.

Sand bathing is special to Egypt. The late Aga Khan visited Aswan every year to lie immersed in a shallow pit of sand as a cure for his aching bones and joints. It used to be very fashionable for the élite of cold, damp Europe to seek such cures, and the practice is back in vogue with hotels such as the Oberoi and the Amoun having special pits. Similar cures are offered at Siwa Oasis, where you can be buried up to your neck in sand at Gebel Dakrur, although the accommodations at the nearby hostelry are rather more basic than those at Aswan.

ARCHAEOLOGY

Could there be a richer place in all the world than Egypt for amateur and professional archaeologists? Anyone who thinks it is all dry bones and old stones has only to attend a lecture or go on a field trip with any of these organizations to be disabused of this notion: the American Research Center in Egypt (ARCE), the Egyptian Exploration Society, or the Netherlands Institute (**Organizations**). Certainly go hear Dr. Kent Weeks, Egyptologist and raconteur par excellence, the first chance you get. In early 1995, his excavations in the tomb known as KV5 in the Valley of the Kings at Luxor led to the discovery of the tomb of the children of Ramsis II after 3,100 years.

ARCHITECTURE

SPARE, the Society for the Preservation of the Architectural Resources of Egypt, organizes walks through the labyrinth of Cairo's history and is actively engaged in the preservation of many of the city's crumbling treasures in cooperation with ARCE (see Archaeology above).

ART CLASSES

Locally renowned artists Mansur and Jamila Yosri run classes at the Community Services Association (CSA). Classes in pottery, painting, and drawing are given at The

Workshop in Maadi and at al-Madyafa in Heliopolis.

AVIATION

For about $5,000 inclusive, you can get your pilot's license through EgyptAir's Flight School at Imbaba Airport. It includes 135 hours of classwork and theory plus twenty-five hours of flight time. For those who already have licenses, the airport also has small planes for rent, but their maintenance is questionable. Experienced pilots should also note that much of Egypt's airspace is a carefully monitored military zone.

BACKGAMMON

Men can pick up a game at any of the cafés all over town. The one opposite the entrance to the Windsor Hotel is particularly lively and, due to its location, might even tolerate the presence of women who enjoy this popular pastime.

BEAUTY SALONS

There seem to be surprisingly few really top-notch salons in Cairo. Our evidence for this is that a large number of expatriate residents of long standing routinely have their hair, facials, manicures, massages, and so on, done by beauticians and cosmetologists trained abroad who work out of their homes. Resistance to neighborhood salons seems to be based partly on language barriers, partly on concern about cleanliness and sterilization of equipment, and partly on a perceived lack of know-how. But by all means, check out a few for yourself, as a trip to a beauty salon is invariably a fascinating immersion into any country's feminine culture. At the upper end, three places are recommended: Mohammed Jr., Gharib, and Jimmy Beauty Salon in Heliopolis. Seasons Salon in Maadi has Color Me Beautiful products beauty ser-

vices, plus clothes and accessories. The Margaret Rose Salon in the Semiramis is not recommended except for the many Egyptian actresses and belly-dancers who patronize it. Surely they get star treatment, but others will find dirty towels, overflowing wastebaskets, and general sloppiness. Get recommendations from Egyptian friends, or ask for private practitioners at the Women's Association.

BIRDWATCHING

Egypt's plethora of native birds native and migrant, such as bee-eaters, ibis, egrets, and hoopoes, make it a great place to take up birdwatching. The north coast and the oases are uncluttered viewing locations for birds, as is Lake Qarun closer by. Larger birds such as white storks and pelicans, which have to migrate over land because of their size, can be spotted in Sinai or on the Suez coast. In spring, the cliffs at 'Ayn Sukhna provide a perfect view of thousands of birds of prey, like eagles and vultures, which spiral on the thermals there before heading north. Read Richard Hoath's monthly "Nature Notes" in *Egypt Today*.

BRIDGE

The Cairo bridge scene is hopping, if this can be said of such a sedentary pastime. The Annual International Bridge Tournament held in January in the Ramsis Hilton is opened by Omar Sharif and attracts an impressive entry list. There are games at all the sporting clubs, and local groups advertise regularly. An excellent way to expand your social circle.

CAR AND MOTORCYCLE RALLIES AND MOTOCROSS

The annual Pharaoh's Rally held every October is a grueling event for 4-wheel drives, trucks, and motorcycles through some of Egypt's toughest terrain. Motocross enthusiasts also have lots of organized company. The contacts given in the Directory, Rami Siag and Raed Baddar, can tell you all you need to know and more.

CLASSIC CARS

Since it is illegal to export antique cars, there are some real gems in Cairo. Beautifully preserved and worth a fortune anywhere else, these vehicles can only be polished and admired here. And talked about and shown, of course. The Muhammad Ali Club, headed by Maged Farag of the Max Group, is the place to meet fellow devotees, and to get the lowdown on repairs and maintenance.

CHURCH ACTIVITIES

Finding kindred souls to worship and socialize with can ease the settling-in period for many newcomers. The most active Western Christian churches are All Saints Cathedral in Zamalek, Saint Andrew's downtown, and the Community Church in Maadi, but there are many others of most denominations represented in Cairo (**Churches**).

COMPUTER COURSES

The British Council's courses (LE275 each) on the most popular software programs are said to be the best. Class size is limited so that each student gets a computer to work on. For more advanced or esoteric packages and programming courses, AUC's Computer Science Department, RITSEC, and Internet Egypt may be your best bets. Many of the computer companies (**Computers**) also offer group and private instruction.

COOKING CLASSES

The CSA in Maadi offers classes, mostly in Egyptian and Indian cookery, depending on demand and the supply of teachers. The Marriott in Zamalek runs occasional Teach and Taste sessions, as do some of the other hotels as part of their regular and advertised food promotions. For this kind of information, we have found it is best to contact the hotels' public relations officers, who invariably speak English and French at least, in addition to Arabic.

COUNSELING

CSA has its own counseling unit currently headed by Dr. Isis Badawi, a clinical psychologist. She can put you in touch with a wide range of resources for psychotherapy, clinical and educational evaluation, and support groups of various kinds, including Alcoholics Anonymous. Befrienders offers non-judgmental, anonymous telephone support and referral for anyone at all who feels in need of a sympathetic ear or a lifeline in times of crises great and small. Both organizations often seek volunteer and professional additions to their staffs.

CREATIVE WRITING

If the muse strikes in Cairo, you can entice her continued company by taking a creative writing course along with other budding authors at CSA or at AUC. The CSA courses are through the University of Maryland; undergraduate credits for them and for the AUC course are transferable to other American universities, as well they should be considering the per-credit fees, which are hefty. AUC also has an excellent journalism program.

CULTURAL CENTERS

Egyptian and foreign cultural centers (**Organizations**) are listed in the back of *Egypt Today*, as well as in the Directory, and exist to show the best of their countries' cultures. Depending on their size and budget they offer films, plays, dance troupes, art exhibitions, libraries, and language classes. Specific programs are listed weekly in *Al-Ahram Weekly* and the *Middle East Times*. The Opera House is a frequent venue for visiting performers on goodwill tours. Its programs overall provide an accessible, inexpensive opportunity to douse oneself in cultural offerings that are too costly or crowded in other major capitals.

DANCING

So far the Scots seem to have folk dancing all sewn up, as the American country–western or line dancing craze has not yet hit Cairo. There are two lively choices, the Cairo Scottish Country Dance Group and St. Andrews Church Scottish Country Dance Group. You do not have to be a Scot or own a kilt to join. Discotheques abound (see **Arts, Entertainment, & Nightlife**), and a few places have live music for slightly more staid dancing. Two good spots for dancing under the stars: the top decks of the Imperial boat hotel and Le Pacha 1901, next door to each other in Zamalek.

DIETING

Dieting is in vogue in Cairo. Exercise classes, hypnosis, herbs, slimming salons with vibrating tables and other exotic equipment, acupuncture, and liposuction; all can be—and are—utilized by foreigners and locals in pursuit of the perfect body or a reasonable approximation thereof. Beauty Essentials in Zamalek is a good source for the latest dieting information. You might consider fasting during Ramadan—but most people say that they add rather than subtract pounds then as a result of the lavish *ifTaar*s and *suHuur*s.

DRAMA GROUPS

Three groups are currently active: Maadi Community Players, Heliopolis Community Activities Association (HCAA) Drama Group, and the Cairo Players. The Maadi group has been around for over twenty-five years. It is heavily American in its membership and productions—lots of Cairo American College faculty members—and does professional workshops, plus readings, in addition to the normal theatrical fare. Cairo Players and the HCAA group are more British in their orientation, with Cairo Players drawing much of its talent from the British International School. HCAA particularly encourages amateurs and is very community-oriented.

FASHION SHOWS

Local and international designers hold shows throughout the year at the big hotels. Watch the press for details. Women's groups also frequently sponsor fashion shows; they are a good way to get a picture of the clothing and fashion scene in Cairo.

FLOWER ARRANGING

The bounty of beautiful, cheap flowers in Cairo make this an ideal place to learn the art of arranging them well. Salwa Fadil teaches ikebana. Call her or the Japanese Embassy to find out about classes.

An annual flower and plant show is held each March at the Fish Garden in Zamalek, where you will see everything you could possibly need to create your own Hanging Gardens of Babylon. Go with an Arabic speaker.

LANGUAGE CLASSES

This cannot be overemphasized: you must learn some Arabic if a) you are living in Cairo, b) you are not a hermit, c) you disdain to live in an exclusively expatriate world, and d) you certainly do not want to be taken for a tourist in Khan al-Khalili. Fortunately, opportunities abound. The British Council, CSA in Maadi, and the International Language Institute (ILI) all have excellent classes, both classical and colloquial. AUC has a year-long intensive program. Every foreign embassy has or arranges classes. Private tutors are plentiful and reasonable (LE20–LE40 per hour), and there are always ads in the *Middle East Times* for people seeking to barter Arabic-for-English lessons, so money is never a deterrent. Conversation usually precedes reading and writing in the learning process. Classes create a natural source for a social life, whereas semi-private or private tutoring works faster; most foreigners recommend starting with a class.

Because Cairo is such a cosmopolitan city, it is also the ideal place to learn or brush up on other languages as well. This is particularly true for French, which is widely spoken, but each country represented by an embassy can provide names of tutors or classes in its language.

LIBRARIES

Cairo has a glorious range of libraries esoteric and mundane. All those listed in the Directory are open to the public, and scholars can usually gain entrance easily to those that are not. For English readers, there are the British Council library in Agouza and the American Studies Library at the US Embassy in Garden City. Both carry periodicals and provide audiovisual services, CD-ROM searches, and interlibrary loan facilities. Two new libraries with wide selections in English have recently opened in renovated and palatial premises, namely the Great Cairo Library in Zamalek and the Mubarak library in Giza. The Music Library at the Opera House Complex has listening rooms with tapes and CDs plus a wide range of musicology publications.

MUSIC AND SINGING

The Cairo Choral Society, the Maadi Community Chorus, and the Cairo Symphony Orchestra are just three of the groups that offer musicians an outlet for their talents. Voice and instrumental lessons are offered by a number of reputable teachers. For others, check with the groups above and in the Directory or contact the music departments of any of the larger schools.

MEDITATION

Serenity in Cairo is a rare commodity, but regardless of what is going on around you, it is possible to create your own internal island of calm and maybe even bliss through meditation. Sufi and yoga are the two most commonly practiced forms of it here. Groups start and stop, but the listings in the Directory will put you in contact with current ones.

NEEDLEWORK

The Heliopolis Tuesday Knitters meet weekly to knit for charity, the Women's Association has a sewing group, and Hetty, a woman in Heliopolis, is starting a quilter's guild.

PHOTOGRAPHY

For the past four years, there has been an annual photographic exhibition by the Journalism and Mass Communication Darkroom Workshop at AUC. This would be the place to start finding out more about photography workshops and supplies. One place that comes well recommended for **Film Processing** with custom features is the Photo Center downtown.

POTTERY

Classes in pottery and many other arts and crafts are given at the Madyafa in Heliopolis (**Art Classes**). Modeling clay may be purchased from Samir al-Guindi at the Mud Factory on Sudan Street. The clay from Mar Girgis is not recommended, as it often contains impurities such as glass or wire.

REFLEXOLOGY

Reflexology treats the whole body through the feet using a form of acupressure massage. Regardless of its therapeutic value, it feels wonderful. The local expert is Rawya al-Gamma of SACHA in Zamalek.

WOMEN'S GROUPS

Not all are for women only, and they are the best places for newcomers to get firsthand information on life in Cairo (**Organizations**). Many of the groups have small weekly get-togethers as well as more formal monthly meetings with speakers or demonstrations. The groups vary in their purpose and composition, but all are very active, sponsoring a wealth of activities, a portion of which are invariably charitable. The Women's Association is the largest and has a very international composition including many Egyptians. The Maadi Women's Guild focuses heavily on Christian church-related charitable work. Cairo Petroleum Wives does not require either a petroleum connection or even a husband for membership. Middle East Wives is for non-Arab women married to Egyptians or Arabs. Many nationalities also have women's

groups that give members a chance to socialize in their native language. Most groups and clubs tend to go into hibernation during the long hot summer, then go into full swing again in September.

VOLUNTEER WORK

Endless opportunities exist, some of which we review in Chapter 4.

ARTS, ENTERTAINMENT, AND NIGHT LIFE

From high-brow to low-life, Cairo's arts and cultural scene can keep even the most dedicated aesthete busy for a lifetime. And for those with energy to burn, New York cannot hold a candle to Cairo, which is the real 'city that never sleeps.' Foreigners may well wonder about the seemingly indefatigable Cairenes: how do they do it? The secret: nap time, either in the hot afternoon or in the early evening anywhere from 5 to 10 pm, before real life begins.

ART GALLERIES AND THE ARTS IN CAIRO

The astounding volume and perfection of ancient Egypt's monuments, sculpture, and painting are unmatched anywhere in the world. Modern Egyptian artists are fortunate indeed in their heritage, less so in their patronage since the days of the pharaohs, caliphs, sultans, and kings. Nevertheless, Egypt does have a thriving arts community filled with people for whom creating is a passion. It is also home to, and inspiration for, a number of foreign artists.

If you are looking for a painting that will always remind you of Egypt, several painters portray the daily life in Cairo and the villages. Mansur Ahmad, who has a gallery in Maadi, captures the nuances of

Egyptian life. Elhamy Naguib's works at Graffiti have a more mythical, dreamlike quality. Margo Veillon, a superb Swiss–Egyptian painter, has not yet, at eighty-nine, exhausted her Egyptian muse. Magdi Abd al-Aziz, who shows at Extra, reflects Egypt in abstract forms. For fresh new talents, you might try the Helwan University Faculty of Fine Arts in Zamalek, which exhibits the works of students and faculty, or the Hanager Arts Center in the Opera complex. In the Directory is a long list, by neighborhood, of many of the major galleries in Cairo. We have kept it largely to the fine arts, listing those that show artistic handicrafts under **Arts & Crafts**.

Those who appreciate the more abstract in art may be pleased to know what Mena Sarofim, the owner of Extra, passed on to us: most Egyptians, like most other people, prefer representational art and traditional subjects. This might not lower the price of that particularly exquisite piece of . . . what is it, anyway?. . . that you cannot live without, but at least it is unlikely that it will disappear immediately while you ponder the status of your bank account.

A good place to meet artists is the Atelier du Caire, a sort of salon open to the public.

BALLS

Ballroom dancing is not a big thing in Cairo, but there are annual institutions like the St. Andrews Ball in the fall, the Queen's (Elizabeth II, that is) Birthday Ball in spring, the US Marine Ball, and a new one, the Viennese Waltz competition at the Nile Hilton. The ambassadors of the larger embassies usually also sponsor at least one big dance annually, as do many of the social clubs and some business organizations.

BARS

It was a dirty job, but someone had to do it. Our young researcher plumbed the depths and dives of bar life in Cairo for our readers' edification and came up with the observations, recommendations, and the few thumbs-downs found here. The coolness factor is highly fickle; what is really cool one night may become a wouldn't-be-caught-dead-there spot by the next. But some things never change, like the local 'cafeterias,' which look like every other café but also serve alcohol. Check a few of them out when you want your Stella served with no pretensions whatsoever. In the meantime, here are some of the hot and not-so-hot spots, Wednesdays and Thursdays being the hot nights:

Pub 28 is the closest thing we have found to a real neighborhood bar in Cairo. It is tiny, always busy but rarely packed, does not have music, attracts local and expatriate loyalists, treats women civilly, and is completely fad-resistant. What a relief!

Harry's Pub in the Marriott: your generic suburban New Jersey hotel bar right in the heart of Zamalek. It has it all—the ersatz pub atmosphere, the theme nights (Karaoke, Western, Ladies' Night), and Engelbert Humperdinck songs repeated ad nauseam. Everyone ends up there once in a while anyway. Just down the Saray al-Gezira in the bowels of Le Pacha 1901 is the far more appealing (quieter, cleaner, more comfortable) *Tycoons Bar*, a version of the same, with excellent imported beer on tap, but for a pretty outrageous LE20 a pint. Go anyway and insist on Stella instead. But note that this and many other bars catering to tourists have begun a no-Stella or Export-Stella-only policy. Talk to the managers, complain, and appeal to their national pride.

Deals, behind Maison Thomas in Zamalek, is new and therefore in among the younger set. Also does the pub theme, but with a more contemporary twist, and inconsistently serves decent burgers. The tall tables and stools are designed to make adults feel like they are sitting in high chairs, and the ventilation is so bad that it drives out even inveterate smokers.

La Charmerie just in front of Deals may have an identity problem (is it British, Aussie, Irish, American, Mexican, or mongrel?), but the space and location are great, food is pretty good, and the friendly, buxom barmaids—barmaids being a rarity in Cairo regardless—are building a loyal following.

The terrace bar on the roof of the *Odeon* Hotel downtown is the funkiest in Cairo, according to our researcher. This is the place where dedicated barflies of all stripes—including headscarved women having beers with their shisha—can be found at all hours: it is open all day, all night, every day. The view is fine, too.

Le Tabasco is noted for both bar and food, with exactly the right fluid barrier between the two in a setting that somehow successfully mixes elements of a pharaonic tomb and the Flintstones' cave. The back is for dining, the front for seeing, being seen, and being democratically crushed by the chic and the great unwashed. Ventilation is nearly as bad as at Deals. Complain to the owner.

The Taverne in the Nile Hilton hangs in as a convenient, comfortable meeting spot regardless of fashion. You can go there and feel comfortable with that special someone regardless of his, her, or your gender. *Whiskey's* in the Atlas Hotel remains popular with AUC graduates and pool sharks. *Los Amigos* in the Semiramis might run out of beer, but might have a decent band. *On the Rox* and *Piano Piano* at the World Trade Center attract young lovelies and their older sisters and their swains in appealingly decadent settings with live music that will not drive you nuts unless you are under thirty. If you are, there is *Upstairs* right in the same building. The *British Community Association* (BCA) bar in Mohandiseen requires membership in the BCA, but it is pretty cheap, has a nice outdoor garden, and is the best place in Cairo for the fish-and-chips and steak-and-kidney pie you occasionally pine for.

For something completely different, try these places: *Da Baffo's* before 1 am, and *Borsalino* and *Africana* after. For something completely ordinary, all the hotels have their lugubrious clubby-type bars that attract mostly businessmen, but they are better than nothing when you don't want to watch the tube.

BELLY-DANCING

What you will see on the Nile cruise boats, which is all most tourists see, ranges from the sublime to the silly, mostly falling closer to the latter. It is definitely worth the loss of a night's sleep while in Cairo to see both the Las Vegas-like productions of the big hotels, with Fifi Abdou at the Cairo Sheraton and Dina at the Nile Hilton, or the more . . . authentic? . . . heartfelt? . . . affairs at the nightclubs along the Pyramids and King Faisal roads, off 26th July Street downtown, or at the Cave des Rois in Zamalek. Salima at the Casino al-Nahr is also a must-see.

CAFÉS AND SHISHA

It is a man's world when it comes to cafés, and it is rare to see non-Egyptian men, let alone women, in any of them. The exceptions are to be found in Khan al-Khalili, on the terrace of the Nile Hilton, on the top deck of Le Pacha 1901, at the Odeon Bar, and at the Hurriya in Bab al-Luq under the footbridge. Order apple tobacco *(tuffaaH)* in your shisha—it is cool, delicious, heady in a harmless way, and smells divine.

CLASSICAL MUSIC— ARABIC AND WESTERN

Arabic and Western classical music is regularly performed at the Opera House complex, which is also home to the Cairo Opera and the Cairo Symphony. The Opera House's Main and Small Halls are terrific, by the way—comfortable, and aesthetically as well as acoustically delightful. Foreign cultural centers also regularly sponsor musical evenings, all to be found most reliably in the cultural listings of *Al-Ahram Weekly* and the *Middle East Times*.

CULTURAL CENTERS

The various Egyptian and foreign cultural centers (**Organizations**) enrich Cairo enormously. Lectures, films, performances, and exhibitions on a wide variety of topics, including political and economic, afford free or low-cost opportunities for everyone in Cairo to learn more about 'the other.' No excuses whatever for cultural illiteracy here.

DANCE PERFORMANCES (BALLET, CLASSICAL, MODERN, FOLK)

The Opera House is the main venue for international dance troupes, including the Bolshoi Ballet, which has come to Cairo annually in recent years. The various cultural centers also sponsor performances, as do the larger hotels now and then, usually in conjunction with international food promotions.

DISCOTHEQUES

To a large extent, we have covered this already, but for dedicated disco dancers, there are a few other resources besides those under Balls, Bars, and Restaurants. Try Tamango at the Atlas Hotel and al-Yotti in Mohandiseen, Downstairs at the World Trade Center, Jimmy's at the Pyramisa Hotel, and Windows on the World at the Ramsis Hilton. All late night, of course.

FELUCCA RIDES

The hourly price for feluccas now ranges from LE 15 to LE 20 depending on the size of the boat. It is worth it. The places near Felfela in Maadi allow for more varied and longer rides as no bridges obstruct the feluccas' cruising, but the ones in town near the Helnan Shepheard and the Meridien are fine, even though after your tenth trip the basin feels like a bathtub. Feluccas a perfect for catching the breeze on a hot summer night and for brisker sails the rest of the year. They are ideal for an impromptu party after work, a romantic evening, and for soothing the tots on the weekends. Mosquito repellent is vital in the marshy waters near Maadi.

FILMS AND FILM FESTIVALS

Cairo in its glory days was considered the Hollywood of the Middle East, but the film industry declined sadly from the 1950s on. However, in an attempt to reverse and recoup, a brand new mega-studio has been built on the outskirts of Cairo to produce films for distribution throughout the Arabic-speaking world. This is good news for the Egyptian film industry and its many internationally acclaimed professionals. In addition, Cairo and Alexandria have held international film festivals in recent years, but both have been universally panned by the critics for their lack of organization; let's hope 1997 sees an improvement for the sake of film buffs, Egyptian film-makers, and tourism dollars.

Quality foreign-language films are shown regularly, but for the briefest of runs, at the various cultural centers. They are often subtitled or dubbed in Arabic, not English, or neither. Check the *Middle East Times* for listings.

Current American films are shown at many of the cinemas around town. They lean toward the *Terminator*-type box-office smashes rather than the artsy, but there is lots in between. A number of the movie houses downtown such as the Metro and the Radio are gorgeous old remnants of the 1930s and well worth the price of admission (LE10 to LE15) regardless of what is showing. Egyptian movie audiences are a lively, talkative bunch who view film as an interactive experience, so don't expect reverential silence when the lights go down.

JAZZ AND LIVE MUSIC

The liveliest jazz spot in all Cairo back in late 1995 was in Maadi. This alone should tell you something: the place is now a pool hall and bar with canned music. It is a crying shame, but Cairo's many terrific musicians cannot support themselves except by going abroad or playing for the tourists in Sharm al-Sheikh and Hurghada. Main venues for Western and mixed-style jazz are the cultural centers, the Opera Complex, and once in a while, Katcho'z in the World Trade Center, Windows on the World at the Ramsis Hilton for Western jazz singers, and the Wikalat al-Ghuri near the Khan, where Fathy Salama and his band, Sharkiat, have played. Catch this group whenever you can. It is idiosyncratic and inconsistent, but when they're on, they're really on. Yehia Khalil sometimes plays at After Eight downtown. Heliopolis hotels may turn out to have the most interesting and mixed live music offerings, specifically Le 51 Bar at the Meridien Heliopolis, Pygmalion at the Swissôtel El-Salam, and the Terrace at the Baron Hotel. Note, though, that the live music scene is even more unpredictable than the bar scene.

MUSEUMS

A wonderful array of good, not so good, and deliciously odd museums graces Cairo. The ones devoted to the fine arts tend to be better maintained than the historical and natural history ones. Having reviewed the major museums (Egyptian, Islamic, and Coptic) plus a few minor ones (Postal, Manial Palace, Agricultural, and those in the Citadel complex) in Chapter 1, we give brief descriptions of a number of others here; all are listed together in the Directory.

The *Museum of Modern Art* is superb, devoted to Egyptian art of this century. The *Mr. and Mrs. Mohamed Khalil Museum* houses a fantastic collection of French Impressionists. The *Museum of Egyptian Civilization* at the Opera Complex traces the panorama of Egypt's history in dioramas and paintings. The *Mukhtar Museum* in the Hurriya Gardens on the southern tip of Gezira shows the sculpture of Mahmoud Mukhtar, whose monument to modern Egypt rises at the entrance of the boulevard to Cairo University. *Dr. Ragab's Papyrus Museum* is a Disneyesque place, good for kids because of the boat ride, good for adults because it shows some reasonably authentic papyrus art as opposed to the paint-by-numbers junk seen elsewhere.

Close by Midan al-Tahrir are a number of interesting museums. The *Bayt al-Umma Museum* is more notable for its neo-Egyptian architecture than for its contents devoted to the life of the nationalist hero Sa'd Zaghlul. The *Ethnological Museum* on Qasr al-'Aini displays artifacts of everyday life from all of Egypt. The Gallery of Contemporary *Artists* is housed in the Chamber of Commerce building just east of Midan al-Tahrir. The *Entomological Museum* near the train station is devoted to bugs and to the eradication of the ones that destroy crops; the *Agricultural Museum* in Dokki has a better setting, broader exhibits, and is more fun for kids, even budding entomologists, as is the *Manial Palace Museum*. The *Railway Museum* next to the train station also appeals to pint-sized and grown-up train buffs.

NILE DINNER CRUISES

If you are a tourist, this is obligatory. If you live here, you will have to take your mother and cousins when they visit. This is what the dinner cruise operators must count on at LE80 a head, as neither the bland buffet food nor the belly-dancing are up to snuff on any of them, even the Marriott's Nile Maxim, which is reputedly the best. The quality of the food does not change, but we suspect the entertainment is generally better on the late-night sailings, based on having seen an excellent belly-dancer and Sufi dancer one midnight on the Scheherezade.

OPERA

The very popular Cairo Opera season at the Opera House complex starts in October. This is one venue for which tickets do sell out, so reserve immediately if not sooner. The Cairo International Conference Center (CICC) in Nasr City also occasionally sponsors opera and other classical music productions. Some people put on the dog for these galas, and ties for men are always required at the Main Hall of the Opera House itself. The Ambassadors of Opera also show up annually and put on a potpourri of arias.

THEATER

There are a number of lovely theaters scattered around Cairo, most of which primarily mount Arabic-language performances. A particular favorite is the elegant, intimate Gumhuriya Theater downtown, which also occasionally features foreign-language productions of excellent quality sponsored by international cultural centers. Not speaking Arabic need not deter one from at least attempting to get the gist of an Arabic-language performance, particularly comedies or politically-charged dramas. Being part of a theatrical audience and absorbing more through osmosis than language can be a revelation in itself. Try it if and when you see an interesting review in *Al-Ahram Weekly* that is published before rather than after the play's run is concluded, and when you can get an Egyptian friend to translate during and after. Your reactions, perceptions, and misperceptions are bound to enlighten and entertain both of you.

VIDEO

English-language videos are very popular in Cairo, as you will notice by the video rental places on every corner. Libraries and cultural centers also rent videos in various languages, giving wider options to the non-fans of *Terminator VI*.

WALKING TOURS

Are these 'sports' or 'entertainment'? Both, but here they are. Most of the women's and cultural organizations regularly sponsor walking tours, except in summer, when no sane person would walk far. If you have reached the point where you are fussing and fuming about the Dust and Dirt and Disarray of Cairo, a walking tour with a knowledgeable guide and curious companions is the perfect antidote. It will awaken your imagination and refresh your eyes so that you can see the extraordinary beauty, history, and much intrigue that lie just under the surface of the three Ds.

SPORTS AND FITNESS

Cairenes are addicted to both spectator and participant sports of every kind. For foreigners from cold and/or expensive climes, Cairo and Egypt are a godsend, especially— but by no means only—for equestrians and divers. For practically every sport, there is a sports federation to keep things bureaucratic; these are good sources of information on events related to your sport, but it helps if you speak Arabic when contacting them. *Sports & Fitness* magazine has especially good listings of dive centers in Cairo, Hurghada, and Sinai and keeps readers informed about the latest in sporting equipment, manufacturers, techniques, and personalities.

Contact information for each sport is listed alphabetically under **Sports** in the Directory. Sports supply sources are under **Sporting Equipment**. If your sport is not mentioned below, check **Sports Federations** in the Directory, where you will probably find it. If you find it difficult to get through to any places on the telephone, and you most definitely will, just go in person, but not on Fridays.

AEROBICS

CSA in Maadi has good classes, as does the Gezira Sporting Club, SACHA in Zamalek, Eleanor Curtis in Dokki, and Samia Allouba's Creative Dance and Fitness Centers in Maadi and Dokki (**Sports—Exercise Classes**). Hotel health club classes tend to be irregular and not as good. Classes are between LE10 and LE15 each depending on how you pay. Stretch, step, Callanetics, high and low impact, cardio-funk, street dancing: take your pick and rock out. Classes tend to be late mornings or early–late evenings. Create a groundswell of demand for early morning classes and someone good is bound to oblige. Note that many health clubs

advertising classes directed to women, like aerobics, have limited women's hours; two examples are the American Fitness Center in Dokki and the Sports Palace in Zamalek.

BADMINTON

Newcomers and beginners as well as old pros are welcome to play on the court at the British International School Cairo (BISC) in Zamalek on Tuesday nights 7:30 to 10 pm.

BASEBALL

The Americans and anyone who wants to join them play serious league softball every Friday all day and every night from September to May, plus on Tuesday and Saturday evenings all summer at Victory College field in Maadi. They even send teams abroad for competitions. Just show up to see how to get involved.

BASKETBALL

Besides checking with the Basketball Federation, contact either Cairo American College's athletic department or Maadi House, both in Maadi, to find out how to pick up a game.

BELLY-DANCING

(Doing, not watching; for watching, see **Entertainment** above.) Egyptian belly-dancers understandably subscribe to the position that foreigners cannot get the moves down. No reason not to try; you might surprise yourself and them. Besides, it is great exercise, surprisingly strenuous— albeit subtle—and lots of fun. Lessons are given at the Creative Dance & Fitness Centers in Maadi and Dokki, or you might eventually find your own personal belly-dancing guru or *ma'allima* to learn as the Egyptian women do.

BOATING (SAIL AND MOTOR)

The Cairo Yachting Club on the Nile in Giza accepts memberships from sail and motorboat owners. For Egyptians and permanent residents, there is a lifetime membership fee of between LE10,000 and LE20,000. For foreigners here temporarily, the annual fee is $1,200. Reciprocal privileges are extended to members of other yachting clubs. Rowing, water-skiing, and windsurfing are also available from the marina. The Maadi Yacht Club also has a marina and will rent sail or motor boats. Membership is $630 per year for a family of three and $385 for half-year memberships.

Swedish-designed motor boats and cabin cruisers called Ocean Classics are made and sold in Egypt. Might be a good thing to check into for the boat of your dreams.

BODYBUILDING AND WEIGHT TRAINING

These seem to be the preferred sports of gilded Egyptian youth, at least the males among them. Gyms and health clubs devoted to musculature exist all over town, sometimes advertised by wonderfully campy posters. A few of them have special women's hours. Not all have well-qualified trainers or state-of-the-art safety features, so check them out carefully and get recommendations. The required belts, harnesses, weights, and whatnot are available at the Weider Fitness Centers or the Sports Mall (**Sports Equipment**). Elsewhere, unfortunately, steroids are freely available over the counter; while they may aid in producing that bulked up, Hulk-like look (ugh!), they are also linked to sterility. Make sure your fifteen-year-old 90-lb weakling aspiring to the Mr. Egypt title is aware of this.

CHESS

Contact the Arab Contractors Club and the Gezira Club to find out about chess-playing opportunities and competitions.

CROQUET

There are lovely pitches at the Gezira and Shooting Clubs.

CYCLING

Cairo Cyclists ride Fridays and Saturdays starting at Cairo American College in Maadi and also sponsor occasional special events rides. According to the Cairo Cyclists, the best place in town for **Bicycle Repairs** is Ghoukho Trading & Supply near St. Mark's Church in al-Azbakiya; hard to find, but worth it. Five or six other good shops are nearby. Most cyclists advise bringing in spare parts when coming from abroad, as they are very hard to find here.

DARTS

Where else but at the British Community Association's clubhouses in Heliopolis and Mohandiseen? Contact them or drop in to any of the overabundant pubs or quasi-pubs in town. And, for your very own superduper custom-made dartboard, contact Maher El-Sabagh in Shubra, surely one of Cairo's very best small businessmen (see **Cork Boards** in Directory). He delivers quality work on time at reasonable prices in a most professional and courteous manner. A miracle!

DIVING

The Red Sea is considered by many to be equal or superior to the Great Barrier Reef of Australia for diving and snorkeling. It is no wonder then that diving is big business in Egypt and that the social lives of its many devotees revolve around it. Through many of the diving schools and clubs in Cairo and at the resorts, one can get the PADI Open Water Diver certification in about a week, including a number of classroom sessions and in-pool practice held in the evenings, followed by four open-water dives at Sharm al-Sheikh or Hurghada on the weekend. At Scuba Plus in the World Trade Center, one of the places with a very good reputation, this costs $320 exclusive of accommodations in and transport to and from the resort. Instructor Wael Hamroush speaks English.

Various diving clubs like the British Sub-Aqua Club (highly recommended) and Cairo Divers Club sponsor exploration trips, underwater photography exhibits, and marine life lectures. Snorkelers are invariably welcome, and at Basata among other places they can just walk into a marine wonderland from the beach rather than having to take a boat. Serious divers rave about Marsa 'Alam; go only with a guide.

FISHING AND HUNTING

Lake, river, and deep-sea fishing are popular and accessible in Egypt. Hunting would seem to be confined to desert foxes and birds, with many areas like Lake Qarun thankfully now protected. There seems to be an alarmingly high number of ammunition and gun stores around Cairo. One of the best-stocked for both hunting and fishing gear is Abu Dief on Sharia al-Tahrir downtown. The owner and his family are knowledgeable on both sports. There is also the Anglers Federation downtown which even has a fax, but not a phone that works.

GOLF

The British Golf Society meets regularly at Mena House and sponsors local and international tournaments. It is open only to foreigners, apparently. Golf for women is organized by the Mena House Ladies. There is a nine-hole course at the Gezira Club, a nicer

one at the Saqqara Country Club, plus eighteen holes at the Nile Country Club. But golf is hitting Egypt big-time soon, with at least six serious resorts in the planning and even digging stages.

HEALTH CLUBS

These are mushrooming everywhere, but Heliopolis probably has the highest concentration of them anywhere in the city. Facilities and prices vary from basic to lavish. As with many other things in Cairo, but this in particular as it affects motivation through convenience, the best may be the closest to home or work. Facilities tend to be sex-segregated and more time-limited for women than men. Most of the hotels have memberships for residents; shop and bargain on these. One of the clubs that seems to be popular with movers and shakers in Cairo's business community and not usually advertised is at the World Trade Center. You have to visit and inspect any club to see how it is run and whether it is right for you.

HORSEBACK RIDING

Don't miss out on the many and varied opportunities related to the equestrian art in Cairo. So what if you are pushing forty and still have not lived out your *National Velvet* fantasies? Now you can. Most of the stables-cum-schools are out by the Pyramids and Saqqara, but there is also one in Zamalek (al-Furusiya) and a famous one near Heliopolis, the al-Zahraa Stud Farm, where Arabian horses are bred and sold. If you play polo (or aspire to), you may run into Dr. Farouk Younes, whose lovely farm on the outskirts of Cairo boasts the only private polo field in Egypt. The Saqqara Country Club nearby has excellent stables.

The numerous stables located just south of the parking lot entrance to the Giza Pyramids vary in amenities and quality of horses, most of them being simple but adequate affairs. Each one develops a loyal following among its patrons, so just ask a few people for recommendations. Horses can be leased long-term everywhere as well as rented by the hour for LE10. It is LE50 for the five-hour round-trip between Giza and Saqqara. We understand that long-term leases are preferable to renting because the lessee has fuller control over the care and feeding of his or her horse for the duration; leasing is also preferable to buying because it is very difficult for foreigners in Egypt to recoup the horse's price when sold. Boarding of one's own horse runs from about LE150 to LE350 per month depending on where you go and who you know.

Riding equipment, apparel, and horsefeed are available at the Alpha Market in Giza (upstairs from the supermarket) and from Equicare in Zamalek, but prices are high. You can have boots custom-made at El-Aziz in Zamalek (see **Shoemakers**) for LE300–LE350.

GYMNASTICS

The Gezira Club has an excellent after-school and summer program in gymnastics for kids.

MARTIAL ARTS

Boxing and the many Asian martial arts—judo, karate, kung fu, tae kwon do—are popular in Cairo. Each has its very own sports federation. Check the Sports Mall in Mohandiseen, which gives martial arts lessons (tae kwon do); they are very helpful and should be able to help you follow up on other types. Martial arts equipment is also well manufactured here by A-Sport, whose two owners, Amr Khairy and Nasser Shahata, are former tae kwon do champions; they may also be able to advise on competitions and teachers.

POOL AND SNOOKER

When the legendary Minnesota Fats went to heaven, it was probably to Cairo. There must be more pool halls here than there ever were in Chicago. Fats might be a bit disappointed, though, as many of them have a distinctly wholesome atmosphere, housed as they are in shopping malls and frequented by well-dressed teens. The BCA clubhouses in Mohandiseen and Heliopolis organize both British and American rules pool tournaments. The Ramsis Hilton Billiard Hall is a particularly soignée venue straight out of a movie set, and it does serve alcohol.

ROWING

The Nile is a great spot for sculling, which is also a superb, soothing, strenuous form of exercise, as you can tell by the young gods working out in their shells early in the morning (women can do it, too). Start to explore the possibilities for learning or joining a crew by contacting the rowing people at the al-Nil Sporting Club in Giza. The trick is getting the boats in the water; surprisingly, they are incredibly heavy.

RUGBY

The Cairo Rugby Club in Maadi, now ten years old, has a very active rugby and social program, and its own clubhouse. Kids', women's, and men's divisions play lively matches on the Victory College fields. The Club is part of the Gulf Rugby Union, which conducts the second largest rugby tournament in the world. Cairo Rugby also has darts, pool, and cricket leagues and plays Gaelic football when enough Irishmen are in town.

RUNNING

Cairo's branch of the international Hash

House Harriers, the drinking club for people with a running problem, has a long and cheerfully disreputable reputation reinforced by bizarre rites and rituals. Actually, they are a diverse, organized, and—dare we say it?—wholesome bunch. Runs are held every Friday afternoon two hours before sunset for runners (and even walkers) at every energy level. It is a very international and age-mixed group (from babies in backpacks up to octogenarians), occasional weekend-away running forays take place, and once in a blue moon it even deserves its accolade as one of the best places in Cairo to meet members of the opposite sex.

Independent-minded joggers run in Maadi's streets, at Merryland in Heliopolis, and at the Gezira Club's track. Very, very early in the morning before the traffic starts, it is also pleasant and perfectly safe to run the leafy streets of Zamalek, Dokki, and Mohandiseen. Just don't do it in shorts, girls.

SHOOTING

As in skeet shooting, not murder and mayhem, but at the Shooting Club (known by all as Nadi al-Seid) they use live, not clay pigeons. If this appeals to you, contact the club.

SNORKELING AND SCUBA

See Diving above.

SOCCER AKA FOOTBALL

The national obsession. The two most important words in Cairo are Ahli and Zamalek, for the rival soccer teams. All semblance of work stops when they play, and the streets are jammed with their frenzied supporters careening by in cars and buses after a match. You can play yourself or just watch at the CAC fields in Maadi.

SQUASH

Not the national obsession, but since it is President Mubarak's game (yes, that's how this 68-year-old keeps in such good shape) it is starting to become one. In mid-1996, al-Ahram sponsored a lavish international tournament at the foot of the Giza Pyramids in portable plexiglass courts. Many sporting clubs have excellent courts, particularly the Gezira Club.

SWIMMING, DIVING, AND WATER-SKIING

Hardy souls can enjoy these year-round in Cairo. All the big hotels have good pools, the Nile Hilton's and the Meridien's seeming to be the most popular. But a lot of the smaller neighborhood hotels, like the Kanzy Hotel in Dokki, also have decent pools that may be a far better bet for serious swimmers who do not want kids and beach toys in their lanes. Note that fees at many of the five-star hotels are becoming exorbitant to the point of exclusion (LE60–100 per day), a good way to guarantee lost business from residents. Gezira has a stupendously high diving tower where national champions train, and a number of the international schools have excellent pools that are open on weekends and evenings for parents. Though one is not supposed to swim in the Nile, water-skiing in the middle of it must be okay, as plenty of people, some of whom are not crazy teenaged boys, do it. The theory seems to be that the critters that cause bilharzia and giardia don't swim or survive in moving water, so as long as you stay in the middle where the current is swift, you are all right. Check with the Cairo Yachting Club Commodore on this and the arrangements that can be made for water-skiing.

TENNIS

Tennis is a good way for Egyptians and foreigners to meet as the sport is popular among both. We are told that at the sporting clubs you might have to sit around forlornly on the sidelines for quite a while before you are invited to join the regulars, but once asked, you are in, so be patient. Most courts in Cairo are clay. To play at a hotel like the Nile Hilton, it is LE40 for the court for an hour. If you play with the pro, add LE30, plus LE1–3 tips for the ball boys. The Maadi Ladies Tennis group meets weekly at the Maadi Club; all levels are welcome and lessons are available.

WALKING

If you are into power walking, don't feel weird even if you look weird. We have seen one Egyptian guy doing it.

WINDSURFING

It is impossible to get through to the Egyptian Windsurfers by phone, so just join them every second Monday of the month at 8 pm at the Cairo Yacht Club.

SPORTING AND COUNTRY CLUBS

Having touted the sporting clubs of Cairo in our discussion on sports, a few words devoted specifically to them are in order, particularly for ignorant foreigners. As near as we have been able to ascertain, the sporting clubs, with the sole exception of the Gezira Club, are not exactly foreigner-friendly unless one speaks Arabic or is married to an Egyptian member. The prices of new memberships at all the sporting clubs have skyrocketed recently: for Egyptians, it is now LE25,000 at the Gezira and the Shooting Club for lifetime (presumably family) memberships, plus small annual fees thereafter. For foreigners, a family of three will pay close to $1,400 all-in for the first year, about

$800 thereafter at Gezira; at the Shooting Club, which is not as pleasant, though more modern, it is $2,000 for the first year. The Heliopolis Sporting Club offers a July and August membership to Egyptian couples for LE1,000 and to foreigners for $1,000. One would have to do an awful lot of swimming in sixty days to make that worthwhile. And some clubs at least (Gezira for one) do not pro-rate membership fees depending on when one joins, so that if you join mid-year, you still pay for the whole year! You also pay additionally for every activity. The fees are not much, but it is a nuisance. These issues and oddities are raised in honor of our friend Caveat Emptor.

All the sporting clubs used to be very posh, particularly Gezira. But all are now government-owned, and it shows in the very spotty maintenance and extraordinarily poor service on the whole. Older Egyptian friends shake their heads in consternation and mourn the good old (grantedly elitist) days when locker rooms were clean, facilities were painted, grass was mowed, and waiters waited. The inflated membership fees seem to have a precisely inverse relationship to overall upkeep and management. Food, however, remains absurdly cheap, which, along with the range of activities available, partially offsets the fees in many members' eyes.

Anyone may enter most of the clubs for a LE10–20 fee without being a member, and use most of the facilities for small additional fees (swimming pools and tennis excepted at Gezira, although we are not sure how this is monitored). None of the clubs serves alcohol, and very few women feel comfortable in bathing suits except around the kiddie pools or very early in the morning. Nevertheless, families who can afford it join a sporting club for the sake of the children, tots through teens, for whom they provide quite superb sports facilities, playgrounds, and social centers.

An out-of-town alternative that is much more foreigner-friendly is the Saqqara Country Club—beer and bikinis allowed—with its particularly fine stables and setting. It is about a 45-minute drive from Cairo toward Saqqara and is privately owned. This is reflected in the generally superior upkeep and atmosphere, and in the considerably lower membership fees, at least short term. For Egyptians, they are LE6000 one-time registration fee per family plus LE600 annually; for foreign residents, $200 one-time registration fee per family plus $800 annually. Horseback riding is LE16 per hour and horses can be boarded for LE300 per month. Non-members are admitted only as guests of members for LE10.50 per day for adults with children free.

Every hotel offers summer pool memberships and health club memberships, depending on facilities. Check on them thoroughly regarding safety and sanitary conditions, especially with respect to children, and for hours and reliability of equipment and instructors before making any long-term commitment.

3 LIVING IN CAIRO

BASIC DECISIONS

If you are lucky, you have made a positive choice about moving to Cairo. If not, pretend you have. Positive thinking exerts highly beneficial effects on energy levels, physical well-being, and social opportunities, all of which help anyone to make the transition to a new life in a new place. This decision—to anticipate your move with enthusiasm rather than dread—is the first choice you can make, and will simplify all the others.

In the first two chapters, we have done our best to demonstrate that Cairo is an exciting, amazing, multicultural, and highly livable city. That said, it is also huge, complex, crowded, and confusing, especially (but not only) to foreigners, and even more so to those who do not speak Arabic. If you have any form of institutional support from the organization you or a spouse work for, obviously you take advantage of it. This chapter on living in Cairo is written largely on the assumption that you do not, either by choice or by destiny. In other words, we have assumed that you, the reader, are quite clueless and must rely basically on yourself and whatever hard-earned help we offer here to find a place to live, plan for children's schooling, make household purchases, and create a life. It is a challenge, it is exhausting, and as you may know if you have done it before, it is fun.

PRE-DEPARTURE CHORES AND CHOICES

Firstly, get the family's or your own medical basics taken care of the minute you know you are leaving. Cairo's medical care is generally excellent, but having to get rabies pre-exposure shots or find vaccination certificates or get that old root canal fixed is not what you will want to do first thing upon arrival. Secondly, if you are shipping household goods, find a good international mover. 'Good' is the operative word, and this chore is far easier said than done. Do not assume that the ones recommended or forced upon you by your government or company fit the bill. If you have a little time and any choice in the matter, contact people you know who have done international moves, preferably more than one, and get their advice and opinions on specific companies. Then interview a few places as to whom they have moved to Cairo and if possible, talk to, fax, or e-mail those references. (This is assuming the reader is a terribly organized person for whom information, good or bad, provides a modicum of control, however illusory.)

Once you have chosen a mover, buy a good-sized but portable notebook, on the first page of which should be all detailed contact information for everyone who is involved in your move, including the president of the moving company and all others involved, and the same for the shipping agent/receiver at the Egyptian end, both in Cairo and in Alexandria. Then begin making a polite but persistent nuisance of yourself to keep the move moving. This is obvious and standard to old pros, but not to novices. Other advice that may or may not be relevant follows.

Adopt a Zen-like attitude toward material possessions. In transit to anywhere, things can get lost, stolen, or damaged. Store or hand-carry rather than ship precious stuff. If you cannot conceive of life without Mother's heirloom silver, carry it. Bring one photo album but don't ship the five or ten that represent your family's history from time immemorial.

Get notarized copies of important documents (marriage license, birth certificates, divorce papers, passports, naturalization papers, insurance papers, wills), one set of which you leave at home in a safe but easily accessible place, the other you carry. You never know.

Back up computer files on diskettes and carry them. Get and carry the software programs (including installation disks) that you use or might use. Also carry hardware manuals and documentation.

Use air freight rather than sea freight for most clothing. Use sea freight for big toys, carrying only the portable, absolutely-can't-live-without items that represent comfort, love, and security to little ones. Cairo has loads of inexpensive toys.

Do all the horrible, boring, picayune things necessary to secure your home and finances in your absence, writing down everything as you think of it in your notebook and checking off as you accomplish each task.

Update your address book, including the fax and e-mail numbers you never used at home but well might in Egypt.

Give or send close friends and family who will stay behind some little Egypt-related memento before you leave. They will be touched, you will feel virtuous. We used sphinx paperweights in plexiglass pyramids—tacky, but amusing and appreciated.

If you are paying your own airfare, make reservations at the earliest possible date. Choice and economy loom large the larger your family. (Sorry, but in the departure flurry, this item often gets shelved for too long.)

BRING AND DON'T-BRING LISTS

You really can find almost anything in Cairo—eventually. But it can be exhausting, even maddening, to do so, especially for new householders. Hence, the odd-lot array of items listed below, which are rarely available, expensive, of poor quality, or inconvenient to locate on short notice. So stash or ship whichever of them you deem essential, depending on how long you will be here. Instead of making two lists, one for visitors and one for householders, we have made a comprehensive alphabetical one from which you can pick and choose. People with embassy purchasing privileges can probably shorten the list considerably. If you will have some sort of deal that allows you to purchase regularly at a duty-free shop here, don't count on it for anything except booze (not wine) and cigarettes.

BRING:

Answering machine

Appliances large and small, 220-volt only*

Baby wipes, small packets of which are invaluable for the fastidious

Baggies with ziplocks or twisties

Bath stoppers (the flat kind that fit most drains)

Bathrobe and slippers (flats are chilly Nov–March)

Bicycle spare parts, including lock and clincher-type tires

Books, books, books

Cat and Dog repellent for furniture and/or outdoors

Coffee filters

Computers, fax machines, modems, printers, all switchable to 220 volts or with correct transformers (but document everything and make sure you take it with you when you leave Egypt)**

Cosmetics (imports cost a bomb; hypoallergenics rarely available)

Decaffeinated tea and coffee (very expensive, very rare)

Eye drops

Eyeglass and contact lens prescriptions

Flashlights in different sizes (handy for tombs, stairwells, nighttime taxis, power outages)

Gerber Multi-Pliers or Leatherman (compact all-in-one tools)

Insect repellent

Kitty litter (it is le50 a sack here for imported, and Egyptian makes are no good)

Medications (only for unique medical conditions; all others are here)

Pantyhose

Roach motels

Sports equipment and clothing

Stationery and cards (just an initial supply)

Sweaters (Cairo is cold in winter)

Tampons (only Tampax brand available here and expensive)

Telephones

Transformers and multiplugs

Vitamins

Wine

For serious cooks: good knives, olive oil, wine vinegar, cream of tartar, ethnic foodstuffs like water chestnuts, lemon grass, dried shrimp, pickles and chutneys, olives, anchovies.

For serious fashion plates: the clothes, clothes hangers, and most of all shoes you love.

* Most flats come equipped with the basic—often very basic—large appliances. But if you will be here for years and you somehow know you will rent an unfurnished flat, and if you have a shipping allowance, consider buying and/or shipping your own 220-volt major appliances. Egyptian-made stoves (cookers) in gas and electric models are good and reasonable here, other appliances are not so by some European and American standards. You can buy 220-volt appliances in major cities in the United States, including at ABC Trading in New York (31 Canal St., New York, NY 10002, (212) 228 5080; fax (212) 529 5579; Rosetta knows all about shipping to the Middle East), which has better prices and better selection than places around Washington recommended by shippers or the State Department. The duty-free shop in Mohandiseen has imported appliances, but choice is limited, prices are very high, and the purchasing process is a major headache.

** Fax machines, photocopiers, and cellular phones are all supposed to be licensed or authorized or something very bureaucratic and complicated in order to enter Egypt. Insist that your company or shipper get you something official on the current status of these items or be prepared for major headaches, including their confiscation.

DON'T BRING:

Basic toiletries (all easily obtainable)

Excess men's clothing; good quality, selection, and prices are here

Fitted American sheets unless you bring the mattresses they fit, too

Short shorts, skimpy tops, miniskirts; you'll look and feel like an idiot in them

Small appliances in 110 voltage; transformers in the kitchen especially are a nuisance

Pets, unless they're child or spouse equivalents; you can adopt pets easily here (many Muslims consider dogs unclean and may feel uncomfortable around them)

Umbrellas

THE SHIPPING NEWS IN CAIRO

Sea shipments arrive at Alexandria in anywhere from two weeks to forever-never, a month being a good low, two months high-average, and three months not unheard of. Then the stuff must be trucked into Cairo after customs clearance in Alexandria. Customs clearance is a week- to a month-long affair, very much depending on the local expediter with whom you have been allied. You must have the originals of all shipping documents for the expediter. No substitutions whatever allowed. Egyptian friends swear that the right baksheesh to the right people can speed this process up, but we have not found anybody who has found anybody reliable in this category, so trust in your expediter. Express International in Dokki worked fine once; they seem generally competent, friendly, and reasonably accessible to the politely persistent. Cars are treated separately by us (see **Cars in Cairo**) and by the expediters.

Air shipments arrive and are cleared for customs at the Cairo Airport, which streamlines their processing somewhat. Some expediters advise their nervous clients to go to the port in Alexandria to help oversee the clearing of their sea shipment, but unless you have a lot of time on your hands—two or three days is not unusual—and a high tolerance for frustration, this undoubtedly educational experience might well be skipped. Large sea-shipped containers will arrive in Cairo at night, possibly very late at night, because trucks are not allowed in Cairo until after 10 pm. Therefore, get a good nap on moving day, and make sure to have plenty of LE5 and LE10 bills to tip each member of the moving army.

AS SOON AS YOU ARRIVE

Call CSA, the Community Services Association in Maadi, and sign up for their two-day orientation program. It is a soup-to-nuts smattering on life in Cairo from a wide range of experts. You meet other newcomers in the same boat right away, and come out armed with good information and maybe a few potential buddies. It costs a little too much but some companies and embassies pay for it, and virtually everyone says it is well worth the price.

HOUSING DECISIONS

How much to spend . . . the kids' schools . . . the commute . . . security . . . proximity to shopping. The same factors that limit housing everywhere limit them in Cairo. Many new arrivals have no choice whatsoever, as their housing is preselected for them by families or employers. If you do have some leeway, you are lucky, but it also means you have to educate yourself quickly on the confusing Cairo real estate market. Here, then, is a primer, by no means exhaustive.

BUYING VS. RENTING AND WHAT YOU WILL PAY EACH WAY

A great many changes are occurring in the laws surrounding real estate. Foreigners can now buy flats in their own names. Rent control, the bane of Egyptian landlords and one of the reasons for the nonexistent maintenance in many buildings, is being phased out for Egyptians, with unforeseeable implications on the market for all. On one hand, there is a very serious housing crunch for middle-class Cairenes. On the other, one sees literally tens of thousands of empty or incomplete flats all over Dokki, Mohandiseen, and Giza. This is partly due to the parental obligation we mentioned earlier to provide male offspring with homes for marriage. Hence parents start acquiring flats as soon as they can, completing them in fits and starts as financing allows.

Property acquisition is no easy task, as mortgages per se do not exist. Either you pay the whole cost up front, or you pay at least 50 percent, with remaining payments stretched out over six months to three years. And what you get is a shell most of the time unless you buy a finished flat. In other words, it will have walls and flooring (usually raw), but no plumbing, electric wiring, tile, kitchen, or even windows. The owner installs everything.

If you are considering buying, consider having close to LE1 million in the bank for a raw, good-sized three–five bedroom flat in a good building in a good area, no Nile view. For really lavish, presumably finished, fancy flats and villas, we have heard quotes of between LE20 million and LE60 million. Alternatively, you could buy a raw three-bedroom, 115 square meter flat in downtown Abdin, which is not fashionable or foreigner-infested, but is very safe, convenient, and lively, for about LE95,000 and finish it to Western standards for an additional LE30,000. Add in another LE20,00 for appliances and nice but basic furnishings and include about LE4,000 for lawyer's and procedural fees, and you are talking about LE150,000 all-in. Legal establishment of ownership can be a tricky business best not left to novices. The purchase must be registered at a government office, but one may also go to court to have ownership legally established. And you must be certain that you are buying from the real owner, as a few hapless buyers have learned too late.

Most foreigners rent at least initially, usually through a broker/real estate agent. Often the 'broker' is the *bawwaab* (doorkeeper)! If you know exactly where you want to live, the bawwaab broker is the way to go. Just wander around with an Arabic-speaking friend and ask the bawwaabs in likely-prospect buildings if anything is available. Of course, if a bawwaab finds you your dream flat, a very generous tip is in order, perhaps not on the scale of a month's rent, but at least a hundred pounds. Discuss this with the landlord.

If you do not have any idea where you want to live, check out areas and flats or villas under the wing of a broker. Except in extremely rare cases, no brokerage fee is paid by the tenant; the rare cases usually involve a broker who has an established relationship with a given client company that pays an additional separate commission to the broker. Normally, the agent-broker receives a commission of one month's rent from the landlord. Make this clear immediately before you start looking, to avoid uncomfortable misunderstandings later, and don't deal with anyone who hedges on this issue. Conserv, with offices in Zamalek and Maadi, is very good; you can look at good photos of what is available before going out to do some constructive eliminating, but it tends to have only high-end places available.

Here are some recent sample monthly rents for a range of properties, all rented to foreigners:

Simple, small two-bedroom flat in Abdin: LE600.

Decent two-bedroom, two-bathroom furnished flat in Maadi in an ugly building on a busy road: $300.

Funky, student-type digs on a quiet alley in a nice old Zamalek building, high ceilings, horrible bathroom: LE750.

Very nice smallish three-bedroom Zamalek flat, high floor, light, decent furniture, very iffy lift: LE1,500

Large, light three-bedroom furnished Mohandiseen flat, fourth-floor walk-up, big terrace, old kitchen and baths: LE2,000.

Top-notch Dokki duplex penthouse four-bedroom, three-bathroom, great kitchen, two big terraces, no furniture or appliances: $1,700.

Antique-filled three-bedroom flat overlooking US Embassy, high ceilings, great details, awful baths and kitchen: $2,500.

Huge three-story Maadi villa, big enclosed garden, furnished, undistinguished kitchen and baths: $3,750.

Lavish, large top-floor flat, elegant furnishings, the works, in Four Corners building, Zamalek: $5,000.

Seriously beautiful 1,000 square meter Maadi villa with pool: $8,000.

A few other miscellaneous price-related points: Rents in Maadi are skyrocketing because landlords think they can get the higher prices; a friend recently had to vacate her nice $1,500 flat because the landlady raised the rent to $2,300. Split-unit air conditioners cost landlords about $1,200 each, so their price is reflected in the rent; ditto reasonably state-of-the-art bathroom, which can cost $4,000. Buying all new furniture for a large flat can easily cost $20,000, which is one reason so many quote-unquote furnished flats seem to be warehouses for generations of cast-offs from the landlord's family. Flats on the Nile with views carry an asking price of $2,000–4,000. Landlords' initial asking prices are based largely on an uninformed what-the-market-will-bear notion and may have very little do with what they will ultimately take, but on the other hand, some seem quite willing to keep a flat unrented rather than lower the price. Heliopolis, Nasr City, Agouza, Abdin, and Giza Pyramids area rents are considerably lower than in others for reasons of proximity or fashion. And, at least until rent control really expires, some very wealthy Egyptians pay monthly rents of LE15 to LE50 for large, gorgeous, old flats that have been in the family for generations.

OLD VS. NEW, FURNISHED VS. UNFURNISHED

The stock of available old apartments is very small due to families hanging on to places because of rent control. If you have your heart set on one, the only places to look are in the heart of downtown, in Garden City, or along the Saray al-Gezira and the many beautiful older buildings in Zamalek. Dokki, Mohandiseen, and Giza Pyramids, being newer areas, have virtually none. Such flats, dating from the turn of the century through the 1940s, have enormous appeal—for their size, gorgeous architectural detail, and high ceilings. Kitchens, baths, plumbing, and wiring are usually pretty bad unless they have been redone.

Practically every place is rented to foreigners furnished, as unfurnished flats are at least theoretically subject to rent control. Except for a very few high-end flats, furnished—even 'furnished to Western tastes'—means crowded with odd assortments of stuff, often in what is affectionately referred to as the Louis Farouk style—lots of gilt, heavy patterned velvets, very ornate. Washing machines are almost always in the bathroom, clothes dryers are rare, and kitchens tend to be small and dark, as only servants used to enter them. Newer kitchens often have wonderful Egyptian granite countertops—a real luxury for many foreigners.

Large reception areas are rarely used by Egyptians except for entertaining; instead, a smaller television room is where the family normally spends time. Closets are custom-built cabinets often extending to the ceiling; all have keys rather than door knobs, and you will need a tall ladder to open, let alone reach into, the upper doors. Ideally, cupboard and closet doors have dust lips, which help somewhat to deter the dust. Leaking toilets, pipes, and faucets are the norm, even in new buildings. A shocking amount of water is wasted this way in this desert country, and a hue and cry is regularly raised about it in the newspapers, but little or nothing is done. Elevators are usually claustrophobically small and in most buildings it is forbidden to use them to transport anything but people and groceries. Hallways and stairwells are kept very dark, even in elegant buildings, so carry a small flashlight everywhere. On higher floors, an independent water pump (around LE700) may be a necessity to produce adequate water pressure; the landlord should pay for this.

All these fact-of-life points aside, foreign readers should know that with a little luck and a lot of persistence and flexibility, they will find a flat that well suits their needs and that the space they get will likely be far larger than what they could hope for in their home countries.

CHOOSING A NEIGHBORHOOD

"What choice?" as one friend said. "Where does he work? Where do the kids go to school? Yes, I guess we'll live here!" But if you do have some say in the matter, the brief descriptions of major neighborhoods below will help. You decide which elements of them are pros and which cons. One nice thing almost all have in common, except perhaps for the heart of the downtown commercial area, is a 'neighborhood' feel. Cairo is a city full of friendly street life, and as a resident you become part of it. Hence, all areas are wonderfully safe.

Agouza is cheaper than other neighborhoods, except along the Nile. It is fairly crowded, not too green, and generally lacks charm or atmosphere, but it is extremely convenient—you rarely need a car for errands. Rather few foreigners live here except in the high-rises along the river.

Downtown Cairo covers a lot of ground, and so is hard to characterize. While it is busy and noisy, there are many pockets of relative quiet to be found in the alleyways. And a lot of charm—art nouveau balconies, mashrabiya screens, little markets tucked away. You just have to look under the dust. Lots of galleries and restaurants, and in Abdin, a great local atmosphere.

Dokki is perhaps the greenest part of Cairo after Zamalek, and fewer foreigners live there compared to Zamalek, so rents are lower. It is getting crowded, too, but less so

than Mohandiseen. The Dokki market is fun, and the many small midans are lovely oases. Very few of the shopkeepers speak English and a car or taxi is required for shopping. A lot of hospitals are nearby. No Nile and rare Pyramid views.

Garden City is embassy country and a few of its streets are reminiscent of Paris. Lots of traffic, no parking, not convenient for shopping except for souvenirs. Quiet as a tomb at night, but very close to downtown nightlife. Not much of a neighborhood feel in comparison to others. Great old flats if you can find one.

Giza Pyramids area is booming. Lots of shopping, both Western and Egyptian. Quite a few mixed-marriage families live here, and there are a couple of excellent schools. It is a long way into town and not particularly green, edging the desert as it does. Good for avid horseback riders, convenient to the Alexandria desert road. Much cheaper than more upscale areas, but maybe not for long, and you spend a lot on taxis.

Heliopolis (*maSr ig-gidiida*, 'New Egypt') was the first suburb, laid out by three French engineers. The president lives here, as do loads of foreigners. There is a strong French influence, and there are street signs—in Arabic and English. Convenient shopping, but spread out, so a car is necessary. Arduous commute into town, but close to the airport. Good restaurants, hotels, sports facilities, and schools. Fairway is the best supermarket in Cairo by far, and almost reason in itself to live here.

Maadi is expat heaven, very suburban, very expensive, very American. Some people love it and never leave it, others would not be caught dead living there. Malls, ugly high-rises, and heavy traffic alternate with tree-lined streets and lovely villas. Excellent schools, good shopping, some decent restaurants, not much nightlife, very community- and family-oriented. Impossible street naming system involving the apparently random assignment of random numbers. The Metro into town is great.

Mohandiseen sort of overlaps with Dokki but is more fashionable and established, and hence in parts more expensive. There are lots of upscale shops, particularly around Sharia Shehab, and many good restaurants, as well as a number of pretty classy-looking new apartment buildings. No good schools, but convenient to those in Zamalek. A lot of nouveau-riche Cairenes live here, fewer foreigners.

Nasr City is a relatively new suburb-within-the-city composed almost exclusively of high-rises, and overlapping with Heliopolis. Rents are considerably cheaper here than elsewhere, and shopping is diverse and excellent. Foreigners may feel a bit isolated, as residents are largely middle- and upper-middle class Egyptians.

Zamalek is the in-town expat heaven, very cosmopolitan, lots of charm, the AUC dormitory, and completely walkable. For these attributes, you pay—a lot, in terms of both housing and shopping. It is also singles heaven for the well-heeled, with lots of bars and restaurants. And there is the Gezira Club, which is Cairo's rival to Central Park, but private. No parking to speak of, and very dense, but green.

WHAT TO LOOK FOR AND WHAT TO LOOK OUT FOR

Once you have chosen or been assigned to a neighborhood, start contacting agents and bawwaabs. A good agent will get a clear idea of your wants and needs after you have reacted to a few flats or villas. You can be relatively blunt about your feelings with a broker, and in fact it is far better than dealing directly with owners, which can be an awkward proposition. Much of life in Cairo is conducted on a word-of-mouth basis, including real estate, so tell everybody you know that you are looking. Agents often

expect the client to provide transportation.

Having finally found a place or two that have potential, give them a thorough going-over. Some items to check carefully and note down are:

Leaks: These are standard, but should be fixed, however temporarily, before you move in.

Water pressure: See the comments on water pumps above, but also note that low pressure can be a simple matter of cleaning out faucet filters, which regularly get clogged with sand and debris.

Electrical outlets: In many places, these are few and far between. Outlet plates are usually poorly installed. Will landlord add outlets and repair existing ones?

Voltage current, circuit breakers, type of wiring (two- or- three-phase), and grounding: Depending on appliances, air-conditioners, etc., these may need upgrading. When you are getting down to the wire, make sure the landlord demonstrates and gives you a clear list or label for each circuit breaker, as it might be time-consuming later to figure out what goes to what. Outlets in Cairo are not generally grounded, but there is something that can be done to them to prevent electric shocks. Ask about this, particularly in relation to major appliances.

Telephones: Don't only pick up the phone to see if it is connected. Actually call someone in Cairo to see if and how well the phones work. And make sure it is not a party-line. Go armed with the number of a hotel or person in another city to see if the local long-distance feature actually works. International lines are becoming something of a moot point, thanks to calling cards and call-back services. It can take ages to get phone problems sorted out later, so make this a deal-breaker.

Elevators: Breakdowns are not an uncommon occurrence, regardless of the building, so if this would drive you nuts, get a ground-floor flat.

Doors, windows, shutters, latches, drawers: Check and note down every little quirk of every single one, including the doors on closets. The year-round dust and the chill winds of winter, not to mention the badly hung door that screeches along the floor every single time you open and shut it, suggest that an ounce of prevention may ward off future insanity.

Water heaters: The size of these will definitely affect the length of your shower, especially in winter, and whether there is enough hot water to do a sinkful of dishes.

Fans: Ceiling fans are not common in Cairo homes, but they should be as they can keep air-conditioning bills way down. All-white Japanese models go for LE150–165; an elaborate wood-and-brass affair with Victorian light shades is about LE100. Negotiate these with the landlord, as standing and table fans are for some reason much more expensive and uglier.

Screens: These are not standard. Get as many installed as possible, as they keep out mosquitoes, flies, and some of the dust.

Bugs: These are not much of a problem in Cairo compared to, say, New York, but it might be wise to make sure the place is thoroughly fumigated before you move in.

Parking: At a premium everywhere in Cairo. Find out what, if any, provisions there are.

LEASE NEGOTIATIONS

Just as one has to haggle over the price of tomatoes in the suq, one has to negotiate several items in a lease contract and the price of the flat or villa. Good apartments go fast, so make offers on a few that fit the bill. The landlord or agent will likely have other prospective tenants bidding on desirable places.

There is a very standard, very simple one-page lease form to which the tenant makes addenda. These should be extremely precise in terms of dates, repairs, preexisting damages, and a penalty clause for lateness on agreed-upon repairs of LE100 per day. Do not make the mistake of moving in or paying rent before repairs are made. Make sure the lease or addendum specifies who pays the bawwaabs and security and trash men how much and when. Note that it is extremely easy to be taken in by the charm and friendliness of many agents and landlords, much to tenants' later dismay. Being friendly but firm and unsusceptible up front will save you both many hassles later on. Tenant and landlord both sign both lease and addendum, and for it to be worth the paper it is written on in a legal sense, the full document should be translated into Arabic and certified. In fact, the last thing you or the landlord wants to do is go anywhere near an Egyptian court, and so this formality is rarely observed.

The duration of the lease is negotiable. Rents can be paid either monthly or quarterly. Security deposits are flexible. Ten percent annual increases are common, but negotiable. Electrical, and if relevant, gas meter readings should be taken, noted, and signed on move-in day by tenant and landlord to avoid the tenant being billed for back utility charges. Meter readers normally show up at the door monthly and are paid in cash with a signed receipt.

FINDING A LOCAL MOVER

If, heaven forbid, you should have to move at some point while in Cairo, it is definitely worthwhile to explore options and get quotes from various sources. Official moving companies will charge foreigners an arm and a leg if they think it will fly, but labor is very cheap here, and a guy with a truck and a few helpers can do practically as good a job or better under careful supervision.

HOUSEBOAT LIVING

"The view is worth twice the rent —the Nile is my backyard." Some of the more fanciful among you might enjoy at least contemplating the notion of houseboat-living. Relics of a more exotic past, when they were scenes of passion and intrigue—especially during World War II—the twenty-five or so somewhat dilapidated houseboats moored at Kit-Kat near Imbaba still have a magic allure.

The atmosphere is an island of tranquillity far from the downtown bustle. The wooden, creaking, frequently rocking houseboats are convivial international abodes of mostly young bohemians. Most boats are divided into three or so apartments. They are hooked up to electricity, telephone, and water, and all are supposed to have sewage tanks that are emptied daily, by law, by the boat bawwaabs, presumably into holding tanks whose contents are then disposed of *not* into the Nile. The boats used to be moored on the Zamalek side of the river but were moved after the Revolution and exist under sufferance. Owners must register regularly with countless authorities.

Houseboats appeal chiefly to diehard romantics. They are unbelievably cold in the winter, but delightful in the hot summer months, although mosquitoes can be a problem. To buy a houseboat will cost around LE200,000, while a small, partly self-contained apartment will cost around LE1,000 a month to rent in a typical boat. Recently, however, houseboat-living has come back into vogue and some boats have been renovated and fitted with double glazing; obviously these come with a different price tag. Old-timers reckon that the bohemian atmosphere is changing as the boats' new inhabitants are better-heeled. Indeed, a couple have been turned into trendy restaurants. If you are curious, go talk to current residents.

SCHOOL DECISIONS

Cairo and environs offer a wide choice of schooling from preschool through the International Baccalaureate. Beyond that, there is the American University in Cairo (AUC) with its large international student body and American curriculum. We start with some general comments on education in Egypt, followed by a description of the schools that foreign and Egyptian parents recommend.

Egyptian parents and children take schooling very, very seriously. After-school and summer tutoring is a way of life, with public and private school teachers making far more money through tutoring than through classroom teaching. Tenured university professors may earn LE700 per month, and though moonlighting is technically illegal, many of them do it to supplement their incomes. Although public (state) school is free, books and uniforms are not, and the quality of education in the public system is regarded as abysmal by one and all. Hence, the deck is stacked against the poor, although poor bright children can be singled out and educated at the better schools, often producing enormous cultural gaps between parents and child.

The national curriculum controls Egyptian children's destinies very early on through a system of rigorous examinations. At the eighth-year level a major cutoff occurs: children who do not pass their exams with sufficiently high marks are relegated to a commercial–vocational track. At the end of secondary school, based on *thanawiya 'amma* exam scores, young people who are eligible for university are assigned to a particular faculty—science, arts, engineering, medicine, etc. Personal choice and parental control then are limited, a point that might help foreigners to sympathize with the great pressures that exist for Egyptian families regarding their kids' schooling.

FedEx®

The best way to ship it over there

EGYPT OFFICES

Garden City • Mohandiseen • Heliopolis • Maadi • Alexandria
Hurghada • Port Said • Sharm El-Sheikh • Luxor • Suez

CAIRO HOTLINE

357-1304

One decision that couples in mixed Egyptian-foreign marriages and living in Egypt have to consider is their offsprings' cultural identity. The children will have a dual heritage regardless, but where they attend school affects whether they will identify more with Egyptian or with expatriate companions and the very different worlds represented by the two. Not all parents who can afford to make the choice of one of the large and very expensive international schools here opt for it. Their rationale makes sense: their Egypt-resident children deserve the security of feeling Egyptian, of using Arabic in school, of having friends who are Egyptian rather than often-transient foreigners. Others intentionally educate their children in schools with a foreign-language medium and exposure to foreign schoolmates with the goal of sending them abroad for university.

Depending on the age of your children and on how long you will be in Egypt, different factors carry different weights. For preschool-aged children, the nurturing environment of a nursery school close to home may supersede the vaunted rigor of the curriculum. One nursery school, for example, prides itself on having homework, exams, and competitive sports for three-year-olds, which may or may not be in keeping with the parents' child-rearing views. Others are excellent babysitting establishments, but may not address cognitive development at all. Most fall somewhere between these two extremes. For older children, the decision is largely based on how well the medium of instruction and the curriculum dovetail with the ones they will eventually return to. There are American schools, British schools, French lycées, and language schools that are based on the Egyptian system but taught in English or French. Part of your decision will hinge on where you live. The American schools are in or near Maadi and Heliopolis. There are British schools in Zamalek and Maadi. There is a good English-language private school near the Pyramids called El-Alsson. If you are permanent residents of Cairo, a school with a strong Arabic program and with the curriculum leading to the Egyptian colleges is probably your best bet. Most English-language schools prefer children where at least one of the parents speaks English.

One thing Cairo does not have yet is a school that meets the needs of English-speaking children with severe learning disabilities. The Community Services Association has a superb educational specialist, Beth Nougaim, who can help you make educational decisions for your special needs child. If you have a child who needs extensive help, though, think carefully about moving here.

Below, we describe the most-highly recommended 'international' elementary and secondary schools whose instructional medium is English. (There are two other excellent schools: the German School in Dokki and St. Joseph's Lycée Français, with instruction in German and French respectively.) They all have native-language, foreign-trained faculty. There are many others, some of which we have also listed in the Directory (**Schools**). Talk to your embassy, to Egyptian and foreign friends, and to the school directors to make a decision you are comfortable with. Most of these schools can be classified as expensive to outrageously expensive, for four reasons: 1) good teachers cost a lot to attract and retain, 2) good facilities cost a lot to build and maintain, 3) wealthy Egyptians will pay anything for their children's education, and 4) most expatriates do not pay for their children's schooling here, as it is provided as part of many employment packages, thus giving little or no leverage to those who pay out-of-pocket.

ELEMENTARY AND SECONDARY SCHOOLS

American International School (AIS) in Nasr City has classes for children ages 4 to 18. It has a very good reputation. Tuition ranges per year: $4,400 for kindergarten, $5,500 for primary, $6,500 for grades 5–8, $6,700 for grades 9–12. Initiation fee: $1,500; bus: $800.

British International School Cairo (BISC) in Zamalek uses the British national curriculum and offers GCSE and IB programs. It has over 450 students aged 3–19 and a wide and creative curriculum, including sports and the arts, but no outdoor sports facilities on campus to speak of: the children use the nearby Gezira Club for these. The preschool is housed in a nearby villa. Annual tuition starts at £4,260 for grade P1, plus £700 for supplies, plus one-time primary admission fee of £1,420, plus £100 assessment fee, plus uniforms. It only goes up as the children grow up.

Cairo American College (CAC) in Maadi goes from kindergarten through twelfth grade and has an IB as well as AP high school curriculum. Currently there are 1,330 students enrolled, with 55 percent of the enrollment composed of American students, 13 percent Egyptian, and the rest a combination of over sixty other nationalities. In addition to a challenging curriculum, it has a good ESL program. Second-language study starts in third grade. All students are enrolled in Arab culture classes. Sports facilities are superb on the large suburban campus. Annual tuition plus bus (in Maadi only) plus fees comes to $13,415—even for kindergarten.

El-Alsson in Harraniya (out by the Pyramids). This school has a British curriculum and has programs for students from age 6 to 18. It has both the international track and the Egyptian government track for students going on to Egyptian universities. Most of the classes are taught in English, except for religion and of course Arabic or Arabic literature. Students in the upper grades can take either French or German.

Heliopolis British International School is for children from nursery school age to 11. It was established in 1978 and uses the British National Curriculum. Teachers are British-trained and -qualified.

Maadi British International School in New Maadi is for ages 2–11 and has around one hundred pupils, hence small classes. It follows the British National Curriculum. It is a school with a lot of parental support and is growing.

Modern English School in Heliopolis has a British curriculum. It is a popular school for those living in this part of the city and one advantage is that children can start at age 2 and go straight through until they are 18.

Schouiefat International School near Heliopolis is brand new—that is, in its embryonic stages. Many people are talking enthusiastically about this one. Its curriculum is a synthesis of the American and British. Currently it offers grades KG1 through tenth grade. When construction is finished, it may meet the standards of the CAC facilities. It is a school to consider if you want to be in on the ground floor and thereby benefit from the lower tuition rates than those prevailing at established schools. We were assured it will have a big library, six tennis courts, squash facilities, and two pools. Sounds like it will be great. Annual tuition is in the $6,000 range.

NURSERY SCHOOLS

Some of the schools listed above, including the British International Schools in Maadi and Heliopolis have excellent preschool programs. Following is a list of others with English as the primary language. Virtually all the schools provide lunch and snacks, some have bus transport, and most are open year-round Sunday through Thursday from approximately 8 am to 4 pm, with a few having Saturday hours as well. Tuition ranges from about LE250 to LE600 per month.

Alf Leila Wa Leila Preschool is the nursery for AUC staff, faculty, alumni, and, if there is space, others. This school does not emphasize academics but believes in letting the "child be a child." Serves vegetarian meals.

American Wonderland caters to those who are particularly oriented toward sports and/or music. The owner, Maha Arram, hires professional sports and music coaches. The school is selective, it says, and evaluates both children and parents. There are also different sections (English, French, or German), all taught by native speakers.

Busy Bees in Heliopolis comes highly recommended.

Charlie Chaplin Nursery and Preschool is British-managed with qualified teachers and assistants. It has a special-needs class, videos, puppet theater, small zoo, bus service, and more. Children can start at 3 months.

The Irish School in Dokki provides immersion in a language (English, French, or German). Children stay with their core group so that they develop fluency in the language. Sixty percent of the children are Egyptian, the rest a mix of foreigners. All teachers are native speakers of the language they teach.

Reiltin. Children start at age 2 and go through 6. It is academically oriented and children are taught reading readiness skills, some math and science, and art classes. One class is taught in German.

Schweizer Kinder Garten in Dokki. Children have a choice of three sections (English, French, or German). All teachers are university graduates who majored in one of the languages.

Sindbad al-Bashaer School in Maadi is a nursery, preschool, and primary school with programs in English, French, and German. A pediatric clinic is available.

Stepping Stones Nursery Schools (there are several in Cairo, all American-owned and -operated) offer Gymboree, music and dance classes, and monthly field trips.

Tom and Jerry Kids in Maadi accepts children from 6 months.

CARS IN CAIRO

Whether to buy a vehicle for use during your stay in Egypt is a decision that is best made prior to your arrival in the country. Different regulations for different folks allow diplomats and employees of certain companies with a government contract to bring in a vehicle duty-free during the first six months of their contract. Check your status with your employer.

A sliding scale of import duties depending on the options (power steering, central locking) and on the size of the engine can reach up to 200 percent of the purchase price, so this duty-free business is not one to be taken lightly. Duty free cars are 'temporarily' duty free, which means that they have to be driven out of Egypt every year, but company agents can make this relatively painless.

If you prefer to buy your vehicle here (and save on shipping costs), and if you have duty-free privileges, you will be able to buy it much more cheaply than everyone else in Egypt. The locally produced Opel Vectra or Jeep Cherokee, for example, are assembled from an imported kit but have to have 40 percent local content to encourage local feeder industries. Thus you will not have to pay tax on the 60 percent imported parts of such a car.

When you leave Egypt, you must sell your duty-free car to someone else with the same status or else pay the duty. You can of course ship it out, but bear in mind that regulations in your next posting may require expensive alterations.

If you do not have duty-free privileges, the situation is not hopeless, but it can be very expensive. The past few years have seen a dramatic improvement in the quality of vehicles plying Cairene streets. Where previously a shiny new car was the exception, the growing number of cars produced here has made it quite unremarkable. There are even new taxi cabs! Suzuki, Jeep, Peugeot, General Motors, Citroën, and Hyundai are already manufacturing limited ranges here and Mercedes is set to join them with a line of trucks very soon. Unfortunately, because of tax on their imported parts (see above) they are considerably more expensive than at home, but still cheaper than a fully imported duty-paid car. Recent GATT agreements are forcing a reduction in tariffs, so the situation may improve.

WHERE TO BUY NEW CARS

Check the listings in the Yellow Pages for dealers and agents. Major distributors are located in Mohandiseen and on Sharia Huda Sha'rawi downtown but local dealers are springing up thick and fast. These guys will send your head into a spin with their patter, so take a notebook and don't be shy. A big drawback to buying a car is that there is no facility for a test drive. Reasons given by salesmen include lack of insurance and the fact that the public are wary of a car with more than a few kilometers on the odometer.

USED CARS

There is no shortage of secondhand vehicles for sale. The Friday edition of *al-Ahram* carries a large classified section where private individuals advertise, and used-car markets are held in Basatin and Nasr City every Friday and Sunday. Many showrooms have used cars on their books, but no one can offer any guarantee as to their quality or durability. Egyptian mechanics, however, can fix anything. Take one with you and drive the car to a gas station to test shock absorbers and suspension and chassis length to check for accident damage.

LONG-TERM RENTAL

Several companies, such as Europcar Leasing and Elite, offer long-term rental, ideal if you are not sure how long you will be here and wish to avoid all the hassle of registration, insurance, and maintenance. But this route is far from cheap. The spring 1996 price for an Opel Vectra was $1,195 per month for a minimum of six months for a private individual. Smart Cars offer a Starlet for $600 per month under the same conditions.

REGISTRATION

Buying the car is the simplest part of the process. Ask someone from the showroom to lead you by the hand through the minefield of Egyptian bureaucracy surrounding registration of a new car. Foreigners must register their vehicles at the Ataba office. To obtain the car license you must produce ID (your passport) and proof of residential address in Egypt. Every vehicle must have a fire extinguisher and police insurance, which is third-party insurance; all can be purchased at the registration office. Police insurance costs LE30 and up, depending on engine size. The laminated computer printout license indicates when the car is next due for inspection (every three years) and when the document is due for renewal (normally after one year). In order to renew the license, any fines incurred in the interim must be paid. The total cost of license and plates is around LE100. Registering a used car in a new name involves a similar trip to the department. If the car was made in Egypt the fee is a small percentage of the price of the car, but an imported car may cost as much as LE1,000 to register.

INSURANCE

The Federal Insurance Association sets the tariffs, so all the insurance companies basically offer the same rates. The premium is calculated at 5 percent of the value of the car (assessed by the agent), a little more for Japanese and Korean cars. The companies compete by offering discounts based on no-claims bonuses. It is worth bringing your claims history with you as some companies will recognize it and it will significantly reduce your premium. The premium on a LE75,000 car with a five years no-claims bonus could be reduced from LE3,500 to LE1,250. Many Egyptian drivers do not bother with insurance—repairs are often cheaper than the premiums, and drivers are unfamiliar with the concept. In case of theft, insurance is essential, especially if your car is duty-free. If it is not insured and disappears, not only will you be car-less, but in a classic case of insult-added-to-injury, you will have to pay the duty when you leave.

LICENSES

You can drive on an international license issued outside Egypt for a year, or on your current foreign license for three months. An Egyptian license is obtained on production of a valid driver's license, a medical and an eye examination certificate, two photos, your passport showing proof of residence, and a nominal fee. You may have to take a test at the Traffic Department in Zamalek, which is usually quite simple; it involves driving around cones and identifying some international road signs.

FINES

Illegal parking will attract a sticker on the window indicative of a fine due. You pay this when you next re-register the car. Check that you were in the country and that you in fact owned the car when the alleged infringement took place; occasional inaccuracies have been known to occur. Serious illegal parking that obstructs the traffic will result in your vehicle being towed away. Speeding is monitored by radar on most major roads out of Cairo. The joy of being able to finally put your foot down will usually keep the speed cops busy. They may take your license and give you a receipt; they will tell you where to collect it and how much the fine is. If you get three speeding tickets you can lose your license.

ACCIDENTS

A scrape between two cars, however slight, will often result in much gesticulation and shouting, and is likely to attract a large audience. Often the argument will be settled with no money changing hands, but face will have been restored. Foreigners should not generally get out of the vehicle, and only pay up if they were clearly in the wrong.

In the case of a serious accident when someone or an animal has been wounded or worse, foreigners are advised to drive straight to their embassy or company headquarters and then to report to the police, taking along details from the other driver's license and registration plate.

DRIVING A CAR

If you will or you must drive in Cairo, you should understand two basic rules: 1) the car in front has right of way even if it is only in front by a headlight rim, and 2) in the case of a shunt, the fault lies with the shunter. These rules underline most behavior patterns.

Cairene drivers often pay scant attention to their rear-view mirrors—they are more concerned about edging forward, with a carefree disregard for what is going on directly behind them. They may pay more attention to side mirrors, if present, to check the proximity of vehicles sidling up beside them. In order to attract the attention of the driver in front, they will sound the horn. This can start quite a tooting conversation as the driver behind says "Move over, will you, I'm trying to pass," the driver in front hoots "OK," and the first driver toots back "Shukran" and passes. This makes for a lot of noise, but it is mostly cheerful, friendly noise.

Lane markings are largely ignored by local drivers. To move across several disorderly lines of traffic requires nerves of steel, a feel for the horn, and confidence that the other vehicles will let you through. Amazingly, they usually do. Turn signals should not be afforded too much significance. Some drivers signal to the right when they wish to turn to the right, others when they want to inform you that the road ahead is clear, others again have forgotten to turn the thing off. If you want to make a turn by all means signal, but nothing beats a hand out of the window or a toot to drive the message home.

Beware of buses, the undisputed bullies of the road. Make sure they know you are there before you try to slip past them. Also watch for the driver of a battered vehicle: what does another scrape matter anyway? Most of all, while ambulance and fire engine sirens are largely ignored, official motorcades should be shown the utmost respect. Never, ever, argue your turf or tarmac with ministerial police outriders or members of an embassy convoy.

Traffic lights are generally only observed if they are accompanied by a policeman, who has the authority to signal vehicles on—even when the light is red. Do not flout this authority: policemen on point duty carry little notebooks in which to record plate numbers and when you go to renew your registration, your fines will have to be paid.

While metropolitan Cairo positively buzzes at night, elsewhere the dark empty highways can be the scene of horrendous accidents. Many drivers do not believe in using their headlights until they realize that a vehicle is approaching, whereupon they flash on full beam. Also, since trucks are banned from the city during the day, at night they hurtle in from Suez and Alexandria in droves. Not the ideal fellow travelers, so avoid night-driving outside Cairo if you can.

You still want to do this? Well then, treat driving as the chance for a new adventure every day. It is full of surprises and unusual maneuvers that somehow, mostly, work. Generally drivers look out for each other and are remarkably tolerant. Mercedes and BMWs share crowded roadways with herds of sheep, bicycles, darting pedestrians, donkey carts, and a few brave wheelchair riders. Be tolerant too, and you will do fine with a little practice.

ALTERNATIVES TO DRIVING

For those who decide that driving is not for them, taxis are quite cheap and readily available. Their amenities vary widely, the ones with all handles and windows intact being the exception, not the rule. (Where do all those handles go, anyway? Is there a window-handle black market out there?) If you hit upon a good driver, get his number and call him regularly and he will be worth his weight in gold to you. Cairo taxis, by the way, do not know Maadi and vice versa, so always add at least twenty minutes to your schedule for getting lost either way.

فندق وبرج وكازينو الجزيرة شيراتون
El Gezirah Sheraton
HOTEL, TOWERS & CASINO
CAIRO

ITT Sheraton

1:29 11/5 / A Sat 10:30

Said al-Ahram

new bldg

11 th floor

If you do have a car and can afford the luxury, by all means consider hiring a driver for between LE300 and LE600 a month. He will run your errands, wash and maintain the car, deliver packages, take the kids to school, and generally simplify your life enormously. But take him for a few varied test runs and establish a clear trial period before hiring him permanently: if his road sense or twitches or lack of common sense alarm you, or if he seems even more clueless than you about directions, these characteristics will only get worse, not better, with time.

A last alternative is a bicycle. For short runs on quiet streets, they really work well here—much quicker than either driving or walking, good exercise, and non-polluting. Just exercise twice the caution you normally would, and you will be fine.

HOUSEHOLD HELP AND SERVICES

This is a complex and somewhat politically sensitive subject. The very high unemployment rates in Egypt do not translate into a large pool of willing and able domestic help. Nor do the inventive skills attributed to mechanics seem to extend to carpenters, painters, plumbers, electricians, and the like. Consequently, it is a constant battle to keep a home clean and in good repair. A very handy spouse with an excellent tool kit is the ideal solution to the latter, and doing it oneself is the horrible solution to the former. Handy spouses being in short supply and anything being better than cleaning in most householders' eyes, getting help is the normal route.

MAINTENANCE AND REPAIRS

People would rather give you their first-born child than the names of their good, reliable maintenance people. They are in such short supply and little things go wrong so frequently that they must be hidden away on some sort of family retainer basis. Landlords are supposed to be good sources of these valuable folks. Some are, some are not: many are more concerned with the price rather than the quality of the maintenance people they employ, and many others are in exactly the same boat you are—they cannot find good people either. Once you have become friendly with your neighbors or a reliable taxi driver, they can be good sources for maintenance and repair people. Other avenues to explore: for plumbers, stores that sell and install plumbing fixtures; for carpenters and housepainters, home furnishings shops and places that make kitchen cabinets; for electricians, lighting stores. Every once in a blue moon, you will luck out. Foreigners who have lived here a long time and/or are married to Egyptians, ideally to Egyptians who are architects or have construction companies, are probably your best hope. Not speaking Arabic is a big drawback when dealing with repair people, so this in itself may be sufficient motivation to learn the language.

Very close supervision of repair people is vital. It is far from certain that the plumber will have a wrench, the man who's come to install ceiling lights a ladder, the carpenter a tape measure, the painter drop cloths, or the man who's come to bore holes in your walls a drill. Well-meaning as they may be, it all makes for a situation that will alternately make you want to cry, laugh, or have a nice old-fashioned temper tantrum.

DOMESTIC HELP

The domestic help situation is better by a hair. Well-off Egyptians and a lot of foreigners hire foreign domestic helpers if they can afford them, usually Filipinos, Sri Lankans, Indians, or Ethiopians, most of whom are here illegally unless they work for diplomats. Lacking papers, people who are here illegally may be very hard to track down should anything go wrong, but these foreigners are nevertheless perceived by many to be more reliable and trustworthy than their Egyptian competition, particularly in the cooking and childcare departments.

In the old days, a person would go to their family's village and find a young girl to work for them in Cairo. Today more village girls are getting the rudiments of an education and prefer to work in factories. Many do not want to be 'plate lickers,' a derogatory term they use to mean someone who eats the leftovers. Hence, many experienced housekeepers and cooks are very old. It is also a fact that many women say they do not want to work for Egyptians because salaries are low and abuse levels can be high. Working for foreigners is perceived as preferable, but that does not mean you will have droves of good people showing up at the door.

Before hiring a housekeeper, cook, or nanny, check references very carefully and take copies of identity papers. No matter how sad the stories you may hear, particularly if you are a foreigner who is unfamiliar with the culture, think at least twice before hiring someone who cannot provide references. It is practically impossible to verify tales of abuse proffered as a reason for leaving a previous employer; every potential new employer is in the dark here. Make sure to raise the honesty issue up front so that the person understands you will prosecute for stealing. Make very clear what he or she may use and not use, take and not take. Employers are understandably perceived by household helpers as being rich as Croesus, so keep temptation at bay in whatever ways seem comfortable and reasonable to you. If you are generous, kind, and firm, the last at least initially, you will most likely be paid back with great devotion and loyalty. And once in a great while you will get a kick in the teeth.

The question of living in or out depends on your and your employee's needs and wishes. Some people hate having live-in help, others love it. Fewer and fewer flats have rooms for this purpose, and if they do, they are usually pretty dreadful. Living out seems to be more common than living in.

FINDING AND PAYING HOUSEHOLD HELP

An Egyptian housekeeper working full-time for a very generous Egyptian family makes LE200 per month; more often, it is closer to LE100 a month. An Egyptian housekeeper working for foreigners makes between LE350 and LE500—more than many professionals in Egypt earn. For this salary, you can expect them to work hard, to do heavy cleaning, babysitting, laundry, carrying groceries, and so on. They will also prove invaluable regarding the best prices and shops and service people. Normally they get their salary at the end of the month and bonuses—half a month's salary—at both 'Id al-Adha and Ramadan, plus gifts of food and clothing then and throughout the year. Make sure to find out their birthdays and give a nice personal gift then, too. Usually a full-time worker gets at least a day off a week, often two, plus vacation time of two to three weeks annually. Do not get into the habit of giving loans for family problems unless you are willing to perpetuate further requests.

Foreign domestic workers, particularly Filipinos and Sri Lankans, get much higher salaries, usually between $300 and $400 per month, plus round-trip airfare home for a visit after two years at most.

Of course, it is also possible to find someone to come and clean your apartment on a part-time basis—say once or twice a week at LE20 to LE30 a time.

Part-time Egyptian cooks can be a real treat and a real bargain. A foreign couple we know and some Egyptian friends have women who come one day a week and do all the shopping and cooking for a week's worth of meals, which are then frozen. The foreign couple pays LE70 per week for this—including the groceries!—and the Egyptians pay LE30 excluding the groceries. Both say their cooks prepare delicious, nutritious meals. If this interests you, ask your Egyptian housekeeper or a friend's, who will undoubtedly find you an aunt or sister of theirs who will do the same for you.

The *Maadi Messenger* newsletter has big listings of people looking for work as housekeepers, houseboys, drivers, and cooks. At CSA in Maadi and at the Women's Association office in Dokki, there are bulletin boards for seekers and offerers of jobs. The Heliopolis Community Association has an English newsletter that carries ads for maids. But mainly, ask around. Everyone is happy to help find you a maid, and often word-of-mouth is the best way. If you have a friend with a Filipino housekeeper, just tell her you are looking and the phone will start ringing.

BUILDING SERVICES AND PERSONNEL

Most buildings still have *bawwaabs,* who may serve as concierge, mailman, guard, sweeper-upper, cigarette-runner, real-estate agent, and busybody all rolled into one. Often they or their wives wash the cars and keep the front of the building clean. They get paid between LE10 and LE20 a month by each tenant, plus tips for extra personal tasks. More and more of the fancier buildings now have round-the-clock security guards, each of whom gets about LE10 per month from each tenant. You also give them food, money, and maybe clothing at the end of Ramadan and maybe on the Prophet's Birthday. Talk to Egyptian neighbors about all this so as to avoid ignorance and follow the customs of the building. The men who magically appear and haul away your trash daily generally get LE5 per month, which they usually augment by selling your trash for recycling. If they are very reliable and climb a lot of stairs on your behalf you might consider being more generous. You will rarely see a mailman, but he does deliver to the building, so some sort of baksheesh is in order one or twice a year if you have mail delivered to your home rather than your place of work. If you plan on getting important mail at home regularly, it is a good idea to establish a friendly, personal, and remunerative relationship with your mailman.

OTHER SERVICES AND CHEAP THRILLS

Here are some other wonderful aspects of living in Cairo. They may not be on the same plane as the myriad cultural diversions, but they sure are nice. We will have more to say on psychological adjustments later on, but in the meantime, any of these can lift your spirits:

Men called *makwagis* come and iron your clothes and sheets for you or take them away to iron.

You can have fresh-squeezed orange juice every day all year long.

Veterinarians make house calls for LE30; so do some human doctors for slightly more.

Many dry-cleaners pick up and deliver within a day or two.

The best croissants in town cost 50 piasters each at Etman Bakery on Muhammad Mahmud Street near AUC.

The *bawwaab*'s wife or son will do your neighborhood grocery shopping for LE1.

Mangoes, delicious mangoes, are in season from early summer through late fall.

Maison Thomas in Zamalek is open twenty-four hours a day for hot and cold sandwiches.

Possibly the world's best and richest chocolate cake, La Poire's Wolf Cake, can be splurged on for LE45.

MAKING YOUR HOUSE A HOME

Even if you rent a furnished flat or have shipped furniture from abroad, there are many things you will have to or want to acquire while you are here. Following is a discussion in alphabetical order of what some of those things might be and on how to spend your money wisely. In the Directory you will find the source information under each heading. If you do not find what you are looking for here, look at the listings in the **Shopping** section in Chapter 1. February and August are sales times for household furnishings, so then is when to look for bargains. At the end of this chapter, you will find a practical, reasonably comprehensive series of Shopping and Other Lists for the compleat householder, in Arabic and English.

AIR CONDITIONERS

Split rather than window models are preferable—more powerful and somewhat quieter. Both types are dual purpose for heating in winter and cooling in summer. Carrier is the major brand. Try hard to get servicing documents in English from the vendor or your landlord and find out where to get filters, as they have to be changed frequently. Note that bills for heating with air-conditioners in the coldest months can reach LE500 per month for relatively modest use of four to five hours a day, one or two rooms at most. For big air-conditioning users, summer could be as bad or worse.

APPLIANCES

All major appliances made in Egypt are rea-

sonably comparable to European models. Americans might find them somewhat below par, but they are serviceable—and they can be serviced (servicing may pose a problem with imports). Fresh is a good brand for stoves, National for other appliances. Their cost is comparable to middle-upper-middle-range American appliances. Imports are much more expensive. Refrigerators tend to be smaller than humongous American ones; many families have two to make up for this. The Omar Effendi department store in Mohandiseen has a very wide selection of large and small appliances of every description. FutureHome in Maadi does, too. Avoid Chinese imported small appliances like phones; quality is poor. Also avoid Egyptian phones. Counter-top and under-sink water filters and purifiers are available here.

BATHROOMS

Bathrooms are a big deal, a major part of the marriage contract in Egypt. Whether to have a modern toilet and what kind of bath and water heaters to have can be major bones of contention in less affluent marriages. Whether to have imported or Egyptian marble and tile is the issue among the more affluent. Many older Egyptian flats have squat toilets, but flats for foreigners have the usual modern amenities. What they rarely have is a linen cupboard for storing toiletries and towels, or enough towel racks; ask your landlord to have these installed. Very often a supremely elegant all-marble bathroom with gold-plated fixtures will also house the clothes washer, except in the few places that have laundry rooms. If you want thick skid-free bathroom rugs, get them from abroad, but thick terry bathmats are available here. Shower curtains can be found at major supermarkets such as Alpha or at Omar Effendi, but the designs leave much to be desired. At a few places downtown, Patti on Sharia Tal'at Harb being one, you can have unobtrusive shower curtains made in cloth or plastic with reinforced holes. One unique item you should have in your bathrooms is a *jirkin,* a large closed plastic container with a cap to fill with water for the frequent water stoppages—especially important for Maadi residents, who are suffering through major water and sewer line renovations. Integrated Interiors in Agouza and Netline in Mohandiseen are excellent places to look for state-of-the-art imported bathroom fixtures, but there are many others, less expensive, on Sharia al-Faggala off Midan Ramsis.

BEDS AND BEDDING

Good foam mattresses in various firmnesses are available in all standard metric sizes, which is why Americans should not bring fitted sheets. Taki is the major brand, available at Carpet City, Salon Vert, and other government department stores like Omar Effendi. Pillow variety is limited to lumpy cotton or so-so dacron fills. If you are fussy, bring from abroad. All-cotton sheets, embroidered and plain, are a treat. White is hard to come by, as Egyptians prefer lots of color in their bedding. You can get sheets embroidered and monogrammed to your specifications at many places along Qasr al-Nil. Acrylic blankets in garish prints abound, but you can have cotton-filled comforters *(laHaaf)* made by the tentmakers or at department stores in your fabric selection. You have to specify that the filling should be thin or you will end up with a very heavy quilt. Down-filled comforters are not available here to our knowledge, and they are perfect for cold winter nights, so consider bringing them from abroad.

CARPENTRY AND CABINETS

There is a high demand for and rather low supply of genuinely good carpenters in Egypt. Wood is very expensive as it is all imported. Carpenters seem to charge on a basis of about LE500 per square meter of wood for things like cupboards regardless of how simple or elaborate the work. Most furniture is custom-made; what you see in a showroom is not in stock but must be ordered, and it is usually an ordeal. Upholstered sofas and chairs rarely have canted backs, so they are rather uncomfortable, and having it done differently is not easy to explain or obtain. If you decide to embark on such a project, start with one piece and insist on seeing the piece at the frame stage, when changes can be made. Most carpenters want at least 50 percent of the item's cost up front to buy wood, but you can find ones who do not—they are better: they deliver faster to get their money. Despite what everyone tells you, you cannot have even the simplest thing like a four-legged wooden kitchen stool reliably replicated from a picture, except in rare and fortunate instances.

CHRISTMAS TREES AND ORNAMENTS

Trees fill the sidewalks of Muslim Egypt just as they do in Christian counties; they are there for the foreigners and for the few Egyptians who like to have a tree at New Year (often confusingly referred to as *il-krismas*). They are a rather scruffy lot, and asking prices are high (LE50–100) for foreigners until down-to-the-wire Christmas Eve. The 'live' trees planted in pots often are not. It might be better to consider a large native plant strung with lights instead. Muski glass Christmas balls can be found in the Khan, and other decorations are sold at the many annual Christmas bazaars. Tinsel and such is available, white light strings are not. Bring giftwrap from abroad unless you are not remotely fussy about this.

CLOTHING

A bit of a problem for the fashion-conscious. A lot of foreign and Egyptian women say they have given up on buying clothes here. This is somewhat extreme, but you have to be resourceful if you care about style, work quality, and fit and do not want to spend a small fortune. All recommended shops are listed in the Directory under their specific categories and by neighborhood where possible, except for the ubiquitous Benetton, Naf Naf, Mexx, On Safari, etc. At all you can find fairly reasonable casual clothes, although check details closely, particularly at Mexx—some things there seem to be seconds, and a nice blouse, not cheap, fell part after one washing. The new minimall at the Nile Hilton looks like a very good bet for a number of creative-looking women's shops plus a few of the chains. The World Trade Center so far offers surprisingly little in the way of interesting clothes shops, with a few exceptions.

Alterations and Tailoring: Ask oldtimers, particularly French-speaking Cairenes, for leads on dressmakers. Men's tailors seem to be more prevalent than women's. One recommended place for alterations is Chamade in Heliopolis.

Bathing Suits: The selection in Cairo is limited, less so at the resorts. Energy in Zamalek may be your best bet, or the Sports Mall. Women's suits are expensive, about LE200 up, for very so-so style, quality, choice, and size range.

Children's Clothes: Other than the places listed above, Bunny's, Bambi, and Gerard Darel have very cute kids' clothes, a bit pricey, but generally well made, with good fabrics, and not hopelessly frou-frou. Babycare in Zamalek is a small shop, also with some nice things on occasion.

Designer/Sophisticated Women's Clothes: There are a number of good spots, some extremely expensive. Queeny is unique and has Paris designer originals and some Egyptian-made knockoffs of high quality and absurdly high prices—for example, LE800 for a simple silk T-shirt tunic. It is a beautiful shop, though. The oddly-named Up 16 in Zamalek has very sophisticated Italian imports. Luciano di Nardo is a good and welcome addition to the scene, with prices below the stratospheric level and excellent quality. Selective and Fashion both have some wild fun-sexy stuff in the high chic category as does Pandora's Box at the World Trade Center, which is more teen-to-twenties oriented. Stephanie also has some amazing attire for men and women, custom- and ready-made.

Discount Clothes: Very cheap, very good selection of casual wear made for export at New York in Heliopolis.

Evening Clothes: Belles of the ball who actually go to balls and have a lot of money to spend have their every need catered to in Cairo. Three places in the Dokki-Mohandiseen area very close to each other, Manelia, Boutique Viola, and Melodies, have exquisite stuff, as does Fantastic in Zamalek, which leans heavily toward bangles and beads and is less expensive than the others. Donna is a very strange shop—Madonna-type gear in the window, headscarf-wearers' gear on the ground floor, and glamorous evening gear upstairs, some sexy, some mother-of-the-bridey.

Maternity Clothes: Half the clothes here look like maternity clothes even if they are not, which may be why we have not found any specialist shops. You will find an abundance of long, loose blouses and sweaters plus large-sized elastic-waistbanded skirts and pants.

Men's Clothes: New Man is good for casual stuff, Executive Club irregularly has decent suits, BTM has expensive imports. The Shirt Shops are great for—shirts. Only Ties doesn't have only ties, but a full range of men's wear. A tiny place near the Shooting Club, Arrogant, has gorgeous Italian imported everything, very expensive and tempting.

Sweaters: Men get a much better choice than women, so women should consider looking in men's shops for their sweaters, unless they like a lot of gewgaws, pompoms, crocheted edges, and what-not on them. Rimy & Riry in Zamalek does good hand-knit wool sweaters.

Women's Clothes, Smart Casual: It is hard to find unfrumpy stuff in this category. Clip has some, mostly black-grey, a bit unisex looking; it has men's clothes, too. Trendy is hit-or-miss, as is Elegante; both are worth a quick look when you are in their neighborhoods. One great shop for tailored, simple-but-sophisticated looks is Moods in Zamalek. The Marie Louis shops often have nice suits and dresses for office wear.

COMPUTERS

You will need a voltage stabilizer–transformer, dual-purpose gadgets that sell here for between LE300 and LE600. And a multiplug to connect all the pieces to the juice. As a private individual, it is somewhat difficult to get a competent engineer or technician to come to the house when something goes awry. The bigger companies have big-company clients to nurture. By hook or by crook, by eavesdropping, by begging, try to find a friendly nerd who will help you in your hour of need. AUC's computer science department and the Cyber Café may harbor the one you are looking for. Supply shops for computers are popping up everywhere, particularly in Heliopolis and Mohandiseen. A few helpful hints: have all documentation on hand; bring or buy a name-brand machine rather than the one your genius brother-in-law built in the basement; have copies of all software installation disks.

DESIGNERS AND DECORATORS

These exist (**Interior Designers**), but not in the same formal sense as abroad. A number of wealthy women do this work for fun and profit. For opulent advice, try Nermine Mokhtar at Atrium. For highly original and artistically quirky advice and ideas, Alef is the place to go. There are also a number of excellent architects in Cairo who might lead you to a design consultant.

FABRICS

The hardest thing about getting fabrics in Egypt is choosing what you want. There are exquisite upholstery fabrics in Cairo and good upholsterers (**munaggid**) are plentiful. Fabric shops will lead you to them. The same shops also carry lace panels, voile, and other curtain fabrics. They mostly carry the necessary hardware and will custom-make what you need.

There are many shops specializing in the up-scale market, several in the World Trade Center (Raytex and Texmar), in Maadi (El Patio, Everon, Texmar, or Carpet City), in Dokki , Zamalek, and, of course, Heliopolis. Tanis in the World Trade Center has hand-block printed cottons for a unique look. Omar Effendi, Carpet City, and Salon Vert have large selections at reasonable prices, as do the shops in the Wikalat al-Balah behind the World Trade Center. (See **Fabrics**, Chapter 1.)

FLOOR COVERINGS (CARPETS)

Imagine rich Bedouin carpets (see **Carpets & Rugs**, Chapter 1) on beautiful marble floors, or fresh cotton rag rugs on bleached wood parquet. Both are easily obtainable in Cairo. Oriental designs made in Egypt are most reasonably available at Oriental Weavers. With luck you start with good floors such as parquet or marble, but if it is a flat that you are doing from scratch you will need to make these choices. Wood is warmer and slightly more resilient to stand on than marble or terrazzo, but it is a matter of preference. A carpenter can do the wood flooring. Ask to see samples of his work and to see the wood and different designs. For marble *(rukhaam)* you will need a stonemason *(banna)*, or if you want tiles *(balaaT siramiik)* you will need a tilesetter *(muballaT)*.

Doormats are a necessity here because of the grime in the streets. Carpet stores carry the fancy ones with watermelons or cute animals or 'Welcome' emblazoned on them. The rustic jute doormats found in cafes and village homes are called *mashshaaya* and have dark green, rose, or purple and yellow stripes on a light brown background. You need to soak them in water first to make them more compact, then dry them in the sun. They are sold in Ataba or the Muski. Expect to pay about LE5 for them.

FLOWERS

Cut flowers for the house are a great bargain, especially roses, which can be had for LE10 for a big bouquet. The usual price is LE5 for a dozen, and one very persuasive bargainer charms fifty out of the guys outside of Sunny's for LE2.50 every week! Gladioli cost somewhat more, about LE15 for twenty, but they make a big splash. You can befriend a local florist, who will deliver regularly.

FURNITURE

Compared to the British, the French were only in Egypt a short time, but they made an enormous impact on the Egyptians as far as furniture goes. (Of course, ancient Egypt made a great impact on the tastes of the Napoleonic Empire, too.) The dream of most middle-class Egyptian brides is to have a salon in the French style with gold gilt chairs and sofas, tapestry upholstery featuring eighteenth-century ladies and their cavaliers cavorting, and heavy damask drapes. Comfy, contemporary, and casual are not the ideal.

In Cairo you can find some fine and beautiful furniture as well as a lot of schlock, the latter very often right in your own living room. If you like French reproductions, be aware that while they are somewhat cheaper than European reproductions, the quality is not as fine and the brass fittings are inferior. If you just want the look, a few pieces to add interest, shop carefully. Chairs are the best made of the French replicas. Also beware of authentic French 'antiques'; even in Paris there are Egyptian reproductions being passed off as French antiques to the unsuspecting. Good but very expensive places to look for antique European styling are Al Home, Gallery Mansour, Masterpiece, Mit Rehan, and Gallery Gaby.

More contemporary designs are gradually making progress against Louis Farouk. Furniture stores like the Design Centre in Heliopolis and the new Dimensione in Mohandiseen carry interesting contemporary pieces. Styler in Maadi is very contemporary and very reasonable (a glass-topped marble end table is about LE750). Al-Fostat, Animation, and Ultra also carry excellent modern pieces. Venezia in Roxy is another one.

Oriental furniture with its inlaid mother-of-pearl and exotic woods, intricate carvings, and turned legs can be found in the Khan, at brass shops such as Ahmed Goma in Maadi, and in some galleries like al-Ain and Asila. The Mashrabiya Institute (NADIM) specializes in this sort of furniture and will custom-make pieces for you. If you want reproductions of ancient Egyptian furniture such as was found in King Tutankhamun's tomb, look in Khan al-Khalili or at Dr. Ragab's Pharaonic Village, but pickings are slim. Ironically, foreigners go for it far more than do the Egyptians.

Much of the office furniture is imported, particularly desk chairs with adjustable features, and so is expensive. A nice and less costly alternative for a home-office desk top might be a slab of marble or granite on a wrought iron base or on pedestals. Animation does office design and sells good office furniture.

Simple, well-designed children's furniture is not abundant in Cairo. Much of it is fussy, brightly-colored, full of Western cartoon themes. An exception can be found at al-Fayoumi in Basateen Industrial Zone behind Maadi.

GARDENS—LARGE AND SMALL, INDOORS AND OUT

If you enjoy plants and gardening, Cairo is a delight, and the brilliant sunshine all year long is your ally. Although you can spend quite a lot of money on pots and plants if you go in for imports or shop at some of the Zamalek nurseries catering to foreigners, you do not have to. Everything you need to create your own personal oasis, whether on a handkerchief-sized balcony, in a corner of your living room, or on the larger canvas of a villa garden, is produced locally and reasonably.

Pots: Before buying plants, you will need pots to plant them in unless you have a real garden, in which case you will likely have a gardener who can be your adviser. Terracotta and earthenware pots in all sizes can most easily and cheaply be found in the pottery fields along the main road in Old Cairo. A lesser selection is available from some vendors along the Corniche on the way to Maadi. If you plan on bargaining, and you should, avoid doing so in the heat of the day; the sun will sap your skill and patience much faster than it does the vendor's. Remember that you will also need a vehicle

to transport the haul as the potters do not usually arrange for this. A pick-up truck, jeep, or van is best is if you plan on getting large pots, but a station wagon taxi also works, ideally one with a friendly driver who helps in the negotiations. Small pots are as little as LE1–2, medium–large LE5–10, and the largest, in which an agile adult could easily hide and good-sized trees can grow, can be had for as little as LE20. Outdoor candle-holders with pretty cut-out designs are also here; some have holes for the insertion of light bulbs and can be hung flat on walls.

If you want to go to the source for round water-jug–type pots, it is an ideal excuse for a morning in Fayyum, where a wide variety of baskets are also made and sold. To suspend clay pots from wrought-iron rings embedded in an outdoor wall, inquire of Madame Lise at al-Ain Gallery on Sharia Husayn in Mohandiseen (**Arts & Crafts**); their handyman–gardener, Husam, will be glad to oblige. And to preserve clay pots, we are told that coating the outside with a floor wax such as Flic works well.

If money is no object, the lightweight plastic imitation terra-cotta pots can be found too, but they are imported. You will also find rectangular planters in green or white plastic with hooks for hanging on balcony railings; they range from LE8 to LE15 each with hooks, depending on size and bargaining.

Soil: Next, dirt. For outdoor plants, the plain old soil from the ground is fine and available from wherever you buy plants, or from your bawwaab. For indoor plants, a cleaner potting soil mixture is required. This is rather expensive, as peat moss is imported. A less expensive alternative to pure peat moss is this home-made blend: 7 parts loam or plain soil, 3 parts peat moss, 2 parts washed, coarse sand. Remember the hauling problem: you may have to pay to have pots, soil, and plants carried up the stairs rather than by lift in your building. For sand and rocks, the place to go is where the sand trucks congregate in Ard al-Liwa across the railroad tracks in Mohandiseen.

Plants: And now for the fun part—buying the plants. For indoor plants, the very best, and wholesale, nurseries are in Mansuriya and Usim, about an hour northwest of Cairo on the Alexandria Desert Road. They include Egypt Green, Mahmoud Helmi, Nimos, and Forest Nurseries. For outdoor and indoor plants the many nurseries along the banks of the Nile on Roda Island and the Corniche toward Maadi and Helwan are fine, fun, and cool. The prices go down closer to Helwan, and in Giza along the road to Saqqara are also many less expensive nurseries. Closer in, another large one is Agami in Dokki, behind the small white mosque just west of Sharia Dokki off Sharia al-Tahrir. They have trees, dirt, cacti, and flowering plants. And an exception to high prices right in Zamalek can be found at Abu al-Ghayt inside the gate to the Furusiya horseback riding club just south of the Gezira Club. Every year in March, a weeks-long flower and garden show is held at the Fish Garden in Zamalek. It will intoxicate anyone with a remotely green thumb.

Many of the most popular summer plants in temperate climates (nasturtium, pansies, impatiens, begonias, petunias, salvia) do well in Cairo in winter. Bougainvillea, jasmine, gardenias, clematis, geraniums, wisteria, and roses fill summer gardens with color and scent. For lots of showy color, geraniums are cheap and grow beautifully outdoors; pay 50 piasters to LE1.50 depending on size. In early spring, you will see great clumps of seneraria in blue, purple, white, fuchsia, and pink, for about LE2 per pot; these provide a quick and cheap jolt of intense color, but they are short-lived. Vinca with its small blue flowers and *sabbaar isra'iili,* a succulent with small red or pink flowers, are both good choices for hanging

vine-like off balconies, as is the purple-leaved wandering Jew with its pale pink flowers. Another is morning glory, which self-seeds and produces clusters of deep royal purple flowers rather than the anemic-looking pale blues found in northern climes. For pale gray-green borders, ask for seneraria maritima, which comes in lacy and short-thick varieties.

If you have the room for larger bushes and trees, bougainvillea and hibiscus grow to gigantic proportions; the secret is to cut, cut, cut to keep them from getting spindly and forlorn-looking. The same is true of roses, both climbing and bush varieties, but neither do as well in the heat as the bougainvillea and hibiscus. Dracaena does well indoors and out, and you can sculpt its branches and nurture it to tree size by cutting regularly. Jacaranda and flamboyans, the fern-leaved trees that are carpeted with incandescent violet and red flowers respectively all spring and summer, can also be grown in large pots. Judicious watering and regular fertilizing keep the trees growing without the roots overgrowing the pot to seek water and food. A three- to four-meter jacaranda is only about LE20, but normally, the larger the plant, the more expensive, particularly in the case of cacti.

Some other advice on plant care: For indoor plants, water once weekly in winter and twice weekly in summer. Outdoor plants require two waterings a week in winter and once a day all summer. It is best to water outdoors in the early evening, as daytime temperatures in summer can literally boil the water on leaves. Although it is tempting, don't use manure as fertilizer; the flies it draws and the smell will prevent enjoyment of any garden. Instead, use slow-release chemical fertilizer, available from most nurseries and some supermarkets. Plants need rest, a period of dormancy, in order to grow, so don't fertilize from November through mid-February.

GARDEN SUPPLIES, SHADE, FURNITURE, AND DECOR

All sorts of gardening supplies are available from the Taht al-Rab'a market, which is in the street next to the big Security Police Administration building across from the Islamic Museum. Tools, fertilizers, garden hose, and Dutch and Egyptian flower and vegetable seeds are all here, but you should go with an Arabic speaker. You can also ask, but discreetly, for plants you see in pots at any of the municipal gardens in midans throughout Cairo, but especially in Dokki and Mohandiseen. Just point and say *Hilwa di . . . bikaam min faDlak?*—"This is pretty . . . how much, please?"

To enjoy a Cairo garden, some shade is a must. Balcony roofs provide it, but on larger open terraces, you need to think about awnings, trellises, umbrellas, or pergolas. One of the cheapest and most portable shade sources is a garden or beach umbrella. Large ones are made in the Wikalat al-Balah behind the World Trade Center off the Corniche for about LE60. In this crowded warren of alleys you will find all kinds of beautiful fabrics, often the same as in the posh shops, but for half the price. This is also the place to go for canvas (*'umaash khayamiyya*—the tentmakers' fabric) to cover outdoor or informal furniture; several stores carry it in bright stripes and rich solids, ranging from LE5.50 to LE10 per meter. Remember that the sun, and, according to some, even more so the moon, will instantly fade whatever you choose. Prices at Wikalat al-Balah go lower as you go to the interior of the area where tourists rarely venture; therefore, dress modestly, be aware of crowds, and ideally, drag along an Arabic-speaking friend.

Outdoor furniture (**Furniture**) can be as simple as woven date palm chairs for LE20 each, available at a few roadside stands on the way to Saqqara; ask for *kursi*—'chair'— in the village after crossing the canal bridge at the police station and turning left (south) towards Saqqara. With a cushion, they are very comfortable, certainly cheap, and will last a few years at least—and they can be delivered. Wrought-iron tables, chairs, and pergolas can be ordered hand-made from the ironmongers along Ramsis Street. Al-Fostat in the World Trade Center also has beautiful mass-produced metal furnishings. Prices there tend to be pretty high and complications on delivery and dates have been known to arise, but Madame Laila is very charming, with an excellent eye, and helps nurture orders through. An excellent place with factory and showroom in one is al-Fayoumi behind Maadi; they do a wide range of garden furniture in metal, plus bunk beds and office furniture, at quite reasonable prices, even promising two-week delivery for anything. Sample al-Fayoumi prices: LE430 for bunkbeds, LE375 for lounger with side tray, LE870 for covered garden swing-sofa, LE88 for garden armchair, all with cushions; contact Hazem or Tarek al-Fayoumi. Having garden furniture done in wood will be more expensive, but once you find a decent, reasonable carpenter, he can make trellises, slatted pergolas, and so on. NADIM in Dokki is another place to consider for more ornate carved and mashrabiya accents for your haven. Bamboo and cane, normally inexpensive and hence popular choices for outdoor furniture, are surprisingly expensive in Cairo because the raw material is imported, but you can check the many places along Sharia Ramsis past the train station.

For ornamental stoneware, columns, and fountains, look to your left along the Corniche heading south near the al-Salih Bridge. The craftsmen who display their wares there can often make anything you want from a picture or drawing if they do not already have what you want. Venus de Milo in bas-relief? No problem. An elaborate plaster medallion meant for a ceiling works well as a table when set on a column and topped with glass.

HARDWARE

Well-stocked all-in-one hardware stores seem not to exist in Cairo. You have to go to one for paint, another for wire, another for tools, and so on. Fortunately, one off-shoot of the Ataba market has a bunch of such places all in a row.

KITCHENS

Stocking up the kitchen and laying a nice table are pretty easy here. Supermarkets carry the basics, department stores much more, and arts and crafts galleries the interesting serving pieces and decorative tableware. For beautiful silver or copper serving pieces and trays, go to Khan al-Khalili. There you can find unique chafing dishes and bowls. Make sure anything that will carry food is tin-lined to avoid poisoning your guests. Wissa Wassef in Harraniya village has rustic glazed pottery. Tourists like the pottery camels with saddlebags that hold condiments. For everyday glassware like tumblers and pitchers, inexpensive Muski glass works well. Touch of Glass in Zamalek has very nice designs including wine glasses, beer steins, and the like, plus lovely vases.

Pots and Pans: Modern brides in Egypt like the same pans as foreigners, Teflon or stainless steel. You can find them at supermarkets, department stores, and houseware stores everywhere. To find the old-style conical aluminum pans used by their mothers means venturing into the markets at Ataba or in Giza across from Casino de Hammam, behind Tseppas bakery. They are sold by weight (LE10 per kilo) and do not have handles, but they are great for slow even distribution of heat and make nice

stews. Beautiful copper pots can be found in Khan al-Khalili for a fraction of what they cost in the States or Europe. There is also a very good Egyptian-made stainless steel line of cookware with brass fittings; good design and functionality at a pretty good price.

Kitchen Fittings: If you have to have kitchen cabinets and counters installed, there are many good places, but Contistahl, which has a high reputation and prices to match, is not one of them. You will get far more competent and professional service just about anywhere else.

LIGHTING

Good news for Americans: you can use your 110-volt lamps, even halogen ones, in Egypt—just have an electrician rewire them. If you need to buy new lamps and fixtures, there are a lot of beautiful ones on the market, more on the ornate than the modern end of the spectrum. Copper, brass, or ceramic vases can all be wired for use as lamps. Chandeliers, the bigger the better, are very popular; one place with an especially good selection is Asfour Crystal in Shubra. For modern lighting, two of the best places to go are Style Team and Pavillon right across the street from each other in the Zamalek Club alley off Sharia Gam'at al-Diwal al-'Arabiya in Mohandiseen. And, a useful bit of information: Mr. Sadoon El Rawy, Pavillon's owner, has a very good electrician!

MIRRORS AND WINDOWS

You only have to worry about windows if you are doing an apartment from scratch; then you would use a contractor such as Hassan Helmy and Company. Mirrors are very popular in Egypt. For mirrors try Golden Mirror, which has all kinds of decorative glass, including etched and stained, as well as mirrors. There are numerous other places listed in the directory.

CLEANING

High on the list of good things about Cairo is that housekeepers are inexpensive. Yes, it is decadent, but yes, it is also delightful. Cairo is very, make that *very*, dusty. Especially if you like your windows open now and then, you have a constant battle against dirt. It is one you cannot win, but with help, it can be kept from reaching intolerable levels.

Egyptian cleaning techniques differ considerably from Western ones. Tools for cleaning are old-fashioned and generally back-breaking. Vacuum cleaners are not standard equipment, though good ones are available. Teach housekeepers to clean the way you want them to clean. Otherwise, they will throw buckets of sudsy water on your parquet floor, then sponge it up with a towel leaving puddles under the sofa. Dishwashing is likely to be done with cold water and minimal rinsing. Bleach cleansers like Clorox are either not used or way overused. Rugs get beaten with a wooden swatter over the balcony rather than vacuumed.

If none of these things bothers you, you are a paragon of mental health and much to be envied. If they do, be patient and appreciate fully that you, not your housekeeper, are the oddball here.

A few housekeeping hints from an Egyptian mother-in-law:

Relax about dirt. You will live longer.

Area rugs are more practical in Cairo than wall-to-wall carpet—easier to shake out or vacuum up the sand.

Parquet, tile, and marbled floors need daily sweeping with a soft broom or duster mop and weekly washing with water and a little vinegar (about two or three tablespoons to a pail of water).

Parquet is often heavily varnished and needs a good professional paste-waxing about every six months; hire outsiders with the machines to do the job.

Wood railing on balconies need weekly washings with Murphy's Oil Soap or warm water with a little dish detergent and a tablespoon of vegetable oil.

To wash windows, use equal parts vinegar and water.

Setting out a bowl of ammonia and water (two tablespoons to one cup water) will get rid of stale odors and cigarette smoke.

A cut onion will get rid of the smell of fresh paint if left in a dish overnight.

Baking soda sprinkled on carpet and left for thirty minutes, then vacuumed up, will freshen the smell of carpets and rooms.

Open all windows in the early morning to let out stale odors.

In bedrooms, take off all the bedclothes and allow the mattress to air out.

Take advantage of the disinfecting and deodorizing powers of the sun. Hang bed linens and used towels outside to freshen for a few hours in the morning.

To keep the heat out, draw shutters or drapes during the afternoon. Spray screens with water when windows are open.

To keep the house unfriendly to bugs, spray screens if you are lucky enough to have them. Use mosquito netting if not. Spray for bugs, especially mosquitoes, under beds and dining table, and use electrical vapor repellents. Plug up ant holes by rubbing them with a bar of soap and sprinkle black pepper in their haunts. For cockroaches, sprinkle boric acid. It is easier and much safer than fumigating, harmless to tots and pets, and works like a charm; you have to be persistent with your local pharmacist to get the boric acid in powder form, though. Lastly, flies are said to be deterred by the hanging of water-filled bags or balloons, but the cure seems almost worse than the disease in this case.

When you feel that dirt has reached epic proportions beyond the capacities of you and a housekeeper to manage, hire an outside **Cleaning Service** to give everything a real going-over. You may have to watch them like a hawk, but it is worth it. After the *khamsiin* is over is a good time.

FOOD AND FOOD SHOPPING

EGYPTIAN HOME COOKING

In Chapter 1 we touched upon the Egyptian and Middle Eastern foods tourists and newcomers are likely to run into. For foreigners setting up their own homes here, a little elaboration and historical background may be of interest.

Egyptian cuisine seems to be almost the same today as it was in pharaonic times. Bread has always been a vital part of the diet. In ancient times it was made of barley, millet, and wheat, making hard, chewy loaves—perhaps like *'eesh shamsi*. Eventually, a new strain of wheat was developed which did not require heat to remove the husk for threshing; thus flour with the glutinous quality necessary for the production of a light loaf became available. Either by accident or design, the ancient Egyptians learned how to leaven their bread. Today, fully 60 percent of Egyptian caloric intake is from bread products (85 percent of which comes from wheat imported from the United States).

Grilled fish, pigeons, and other fowl were also mentioned in the ancient papyrus texts and are still an important part of the cuisine. (Casino de Hammam on the Giza Corniche specializes in pigeons.). Other meats were less common and usually found only in the diets of the very rich or royal families. The peasants ate vegetables and bread and drank water from the Nile stored in porous clay jars, or milk. Their favorite drink was beer,

which was invented in ancient Egypt.

The poor still eat vegetables, especially beans. *Ta'miya* (fried bean croquettes) and *fuul midammis* (fava beans slowly simmered in a big pot until tender, then seasoned) are native Egyptian dishes. Dishes with lentils such as *kushari* and lentil soup are also traditional staples. Other vegetables common in particular to Egyptian cuisine are *qulqaas* (taro root) and *mulukhiyya*. (*Qulqaas* becomes nearly as slimy as *mulukhiyya* if not prepared correctly.) Both are used in meat stews or soups. Okra and eggplant are also popular in Egypt.

Many of the most common dishes in Egypt are not originally Egyptian. The grilled kebabs are of Turkish origin, as are the stuffed vegetables and vine-leaves. The macaroni with béchamel is the Egyptian form of the *pastitsio* of the Greeks. *TaHiina* and *babaghannuug* come from the Lebanese. The difference in the Egyptian versions of many of these regional specialties is in the flavoring used. Egyptians use garlic, cumin, coriander, dried mint, and dill. Hot pepper is also popular, as is lots of salt. The extensive use of spices (cinnamon, cardamom, turmeric, allspice, cloves) as in the Gulf countries and the Levant is not common. Nor do Egyptians mix meats with fruit as the Iranians, Moroccans, and Iraqis do.

The Egyptians have many dishes that are connected with certain holidays. At 'Id al-Adha they serve *fatta*, a soup of boiled lamb served over rice with pieces of bread in a piquant garlicky vinegar sauce. At Shamm al-Nesiim they eat salty dried fish called *fisiikh* and spring onions. During Ramadan feasting, a special sweet is often served called *'aTaayif*, which is a filled sweet crepe deep-fried and then dipped in syrup.

OUTDOOR FOOD MARKETS

Most Egyptians do the majority of their food shopping at the outdoor markets. They are cheaper. Here you can find mounds of strawberries, carts full of eggplants, tomatoes, and zucchini, crates of live chickens and rabbits, and bundles of fresh herbs piled on mats. Fresh fish is sold in boxes of ice. Grains and pulses are sold from huge sacks. It all makes for a crowded, colorful scene.

All areas of Cairo have sections that cater to the local clientele. If you live close to a *suq*, by all means try buying your fresh produce there at least a few times. In the *suq* is where Egyptians haggle for their cucumbers and potatoes, where they choose a chicken for dinner and then have it slaughtered and plucked. To shop here, you need a basic command of Arabic, a knowledge of the prices and numbers in Arabic, and a will to bargain. Watch that the vendors do not slip in any rotten tomatoes or give you less than the whole kilo. Different prices among different vendors in the same *suq* may have some valid reasons. All the vendors go to a special wholesale market outside of Cairo in the early hours of the morning to choose their produce. Some, depending upon their clientele, will buy B or C quality tomatoes or apples because they are cheaper and they know their customers are looking for price over quality. Others will look for the best because their customers are quality-conscious. The best time for produce in any market is very early in the morning, but not so early that no one is awake.

These markets have not changed in decades, even centuries. Ataba and Bab al-Luq are still the main ones. If you are going in order to save money, take your cost of transportation and time into consideration to see if it is really worth your while. If just for the sheer joy of the sights, smells, and social scene, do it!

SUPER- AND NOT-SO-SUPERMARKETS

There is one place in Heliopolis worthy of waving the supermarket banner, the new and terrific Fairway. Next comes Alpha in Giza and its better-equipped Maadi branch, which even has a Baskin Robbins on site. The Sunny supermarkets in Zamalek and Mohandiseen, the old expatriate standbys, are something of a disgrace; the Maadi branch recently succumbed to shame in the face of the competition, and the others may follow suit as soon as convenient alternatives are available. For more budget-minded shoppers, there are a few small wholesale-like places, Abu Zakry in Dokki and 3S and al-Hawari in Mohandiseen, plus a popular Cash and Carry nearby. The government supermarkets called al-Ahram are scattered around town. Selection is limited, but prices are very good. The two Gomas in Maadi are reliable and cater particularly to their many American customers. Imported foods are very expensive in Egypt, naturally (Cheerios: LE34 a box); learn to live off the land. All markets, except for Fairway the last time we checked, deliver and will take orders by phone, but Arabic is a must for this.

BREADS AND BAKERIES

The major breads—*'eesh shami* and *'eesh baladi*—plus a few sweet pastries like *fiTiir*—were touched on in Chapter 1. Bread bakeries are called *furn;* some also carry cumin- or sesame-flavored bread sticks called *batusaleeh* (French: *batons salés*). Another Egyptian bread is *simiit,* crusty wreaths of bread covered with sesame. In Upper Egypt, besides *'eesh shamsi*, there is *ru'aa',* a crisp unleavened loaf made in huge rounds in a special oven. In addition you can get baguette-like breads, hamburger-buns called *kayzar,* small rolls, and even sliced bread for sandwiches at all the supermarkets and most of the *furn*s in better neighborhoods. Mouginis is a commercial bakery that has good-quality Western-style breads and baked goods; their milk bread is good for American-type sandwiches. Mirabelle in Maadi has the best real French baguettes in Cairo plus authentic French baked goods.

In addition to the *furns*, there is an abundance of pastry shops. Many of the old ones were owned by Greeks (Tseppas, for instance). Most have a variety of French-style pastries called *bitifuur (petits fours)* and *gatooh (gateaux)*, plus the Oriental pastries like *baqlaawa, kunaafa,* and *basbuusa.* They also normally carry a variety of what the French call *bouchés* or little savory hors d'oeuvres. La Poire is one that gets raves throughout Cairo as being one of the best, but there are many others that have their specialties. Khoudier in Maadi has great *kaHk* (the traditional holiday cookies) and their European-style ice cream is made into beautiful layered desserts. St. Moritz is popular in Zamalek and has outlets in the Alpha markets. A shop specializing in decadent imported cheesecake called the Cheesecake Factory has opened in Heliopolis, but it clearly epitomizes the sins of gluttony and conspicuous consumption with its LE250 per cake price tag!

MILK AND DAIRY PRODUCTS

There are many safe dairy products to enjoy, including cottage cheese, heavy cream, milk, and yogurt. Make sure you buy your items in a reputable supermarket and that the packages are properly sealed. We have found Juhayna brand yogurts to be wonderful and the Subaniyah butter is great. Processed cheeses are available for hamburgers or quick sandwiches for the children.

Though the most popular cheeses are the *ruumi* and *gibna beeDa*, most delis carry cheddar (*sheedar*) and a selection of European cheeses such as Emmentaler, Gouda, or Brie. You can have them cut the cheese in slices (*transhaat*); this is especially great with the ruumi, which a hard cheese. The feta-type buffalo cheeses called *gibna beeDa* come in a wide range of grades or types. Some are saltier, or more dry and pungent, some are creamy and mild. Try a variety until you find one that suits you. The creamy mild ones are good in quiches. These cheeses tend to spoil fast. Make sure you store them in a salty brine or rinse if they are too salty and put in a plastic container with olive oil and some oregano or basil.

BUTCHERS (MEAT, POULTRY, AND PORK)

Egyptian meat is very fresh: you can go to market and buy live chickens, ducks, lambs, occasionally cows (and, if you are inclined, pigs) and have them slaughtered. Many Egyptians prefer their meat never to touch a freezer or plastic wrap. But foreigners who are finicky about carnivorous realities can also go to a store where the meat is fresh but plastic wrapped. The butchers in the more affluent sections of Cairo are similar to the best butchers in Europe or the United States. They can cut you a crown rib roast or bone your chicken. It is normal to tip a pound for these special services. The veal is superb, but not milk-fed. Lamb is excellent. Chickens are flavorful and tender if you freeze them a few days prior to cooking. In fact, most of the meat benefits from a few days in the freezer, which tenderizes it. One acquaintance just in from four years in Paris avers that Egyptian meat is better than French.

For ground meat, it is best to have the butcher grind a piece of meat before your eyes to ascertain that you are not getting old scraps of who knows what. Remember that most ground meat dishes are more tender if there is a bit of fat in the meat, so ask the butcher to include some fat. Also tell the butcher how you want to cook the meat and he will suggest the best cuts.

Poultry sellers, who also sell rabbits, are usually separate establishments from beef and lamb butchers. Pork, of course, is separate from everything else. Good vendors of all meats are listed under **Butchers** in the Directory.

FISHMONGERS

The fish markets have a variety of fish and shrimp. It is safest, especially at restaurants, to eat fish and seafood in the cooler months, unless you are at the source in Alexandria. Follow the adage to eat fish only in months with an R in them. If the eyes are still glossy and there is no objectionable odor, the fish is fresh. One can find fish in the outdoor markets; there is one on the Corniche near the Nilometer that has fish piled high in boxes. One can also buy it cooked from a fish restaurant (such as Samak Mahmud downtown or Samak Hurriya in Maadi) very reasonably. For the names of your favorite fish, look in the shopping vocabulary section at the end of this chapter.

Another unusual fish option (besides *baT-Taarikh,* the pressed dry salmon roe), is the dried fish called *ringa.* Don't try eating it straight from the store. It is incredibly salty and some people get very ill from the salt concentration. Egyptian housewives wash it in cool running water to get rid of some of the salt, then they marinate it in a combination of olive oil and lemon and onions for a few days in the refrigerator.

FROZEN FOODS

Supermarkets carry an array of frozen foods that can save you a lot of time. Many of the prepared foods are Egyptian favorites such a ground beef *kufta* (little meat logs for grilling) or stuffed grape leaves, and they are delicious. Try *sambuusak* as a snack for the children and quick meals on the weekend. Frozen moussaka and the grape leaves are a good meal for those 'I don't want to cook' days. Hamburgers, hot dogs, and philo-and-egg roll wrappers are also available.

FRUITS AND VEGETABLES

Cairo's fresh-produce carts and shops, found everywhere in great profusion, are a feast for all the senses. Most local produce is safe if washed properly or peeled. Real fanatics or people with jumpy stomachs can sterilize produce by first washing it in a mild soapy solution, then rinsing thoroughly, then soaking for fifteen minutes in a gallon of water to which two tablespoons of bleach have been added, then rinsing again in purified water. The whole prospect kills any appetite for the food along with the germs! A gentle quick wash with maybe a touch of dish detergent followed by a short soak in Cairo's already heavily-chlorinated water is what most philosophical types do with no ill effects.

Some fruits are the special delights of the Middle East: fabulous fresh figs, the fresh red dates that look like chili peppers and have a sort of nutty, astringent quality, and tamarind. Broccoli is considered a foreigner's vegetable, and though not much eaten by Egyptians, it is increasingly available. Here is a rough guide to what you will find when; many items, like oranges, are available more or less year-round, but we indicate their high and overlapping seasons, when they are at their finest.

Winter (Dec–Feb): apples, artichokes, broccoli, carrots, cauliflower, chili pepper, green pepper, lemons/limes, pears, peas, potatoes, sweet potatoes.

Spring (Mar–May): cantaloupe, chili pepper, garlic, ogen melon, onion, oranges, potatoes, strawberries, watermelon.

Summer (Jun–Sep): apricots (a few fleeting weeks in early June), avocado, cherries, corn, cucumber, grapes, guava, honeydew melon, mangoes, *mulukhiyya,* ogen melon, peaches (Sinai peaches are the best), prickly pears, plums (May–June), watermelon.

Fall (Oct–Nov): cabbage, dates, lemons/limes, pears, sweet potatoes.

SPICES AND HERBS

Fresh herbs are often sold at vegetable stands. Selection is limited because Egyptians generally use only fresh parsley, dill, mint, and coriander. Basil for pesto and oregano, thyme, and sage are unheard of except dried and imported at the major supermarkets. The most popular spices are cumin and cinnamon. Liquid vanilla is impossible to find. To substitute with the local dried packets, use half a teaspoon of the dried for one teaspoon of the liquid in your recipe.

CATERING AND TAKE-AWAY

There are excellent private caterers, foreign and Egyptian, who work by word-of-mouth only and who are more flexible than the hotels, who also do catering, as do many restaurants. There are also a few **Party Planners**; one is Suzy Damati who worked for many years at the American Embassy coordinating all kinds of social events and outings. An excellent choice for solid professional catering with some superb Egyptian food is Care Service, which does catering for and outside of AUC. Bon Appetit in Mohandiseen and Zamalek have an excellent reputation and do things on a less grand scale than some of the hotels, although they are also capable of a lot of panache with their ganache. These by no means exhaust the possibilities. Ask your favorite hosts how they do it and whom they use.

Everybody and his brother is scooting around town on motorcycles delivering every imaginable foodstuff to the hungry hordes of Cairo who cannot or will not cook. The demise of dishes in favor of tin pie plates and cardboard cartons is not far behind. Is this good? Well, it's modern, it's successful, it's fast and cheap: it's life in Cairo.

DINNER PARTIES

You can jump right in and host your first dinner party for a convivial crowd of foreigners and Cairenes as long as you keep a few things in mind: 1) have plenty of soft drinks as well as alcohol if you serve it; 2) worry more about the quantity than the originality of the food; 3) don't expect anyone to show up on time; and 4) figure out ahead of time what in the world you're going to do with all the pastry gifts!

The host and hostess are not supposed to leave their guests, so have the kitchen covered, perhaps with the help of a caterer or reliable assistant. Hire someone to do drinks if you have more than twelve people. Do a buffet so people, including you, can circulate until you get to know each other better. Westerners tend to forget how eclectic their palates are. Laden your table with several familiar, reasonably sure-fire casseroles, meats, and salads, and give guests something more than carrot sticks to nibble on before dinner. 'Salad,' by the way, is the term used in referring to dips like *TaHiina*, *labna*, and *babaghannuugh* as well as to Western salads. A reasonable compromise on when to serve dinner is 10 pm, not beyond the late pale for other foreigners, nor beyond the early one for Egyptians, assuming you have invited people for 8 pm. Everyone but a few foreign die-hards will leave very shortly after dessert.

PARTIES FOR CHILDREN

Now that you have launched yourself socially, consider the kids. The Western rule of thumb is never to have more children than the age of your child. Not so in Egypt, where 'the more the merrier' prevails. Once your child is in school, he or she can end up being invited to a birthday party a week. For small children, it is the rule to invite the whole class to a birthday do, often held in a kids' restaurant, a hotel, a bowling alley, or maybe a pool. Quite a lot of parental vying for originality and excess can go on in the fancier schools. Which does not mean you have to join the fray or risk little Fauntleroy's becoming a social outcast at age six. Party hats and a french-fries-and ketchup birthday cake at Arby's or some equivalent suit the kids just fine, and these places are professionals at their business. It is cheap, easy, and there is no mess to clean up afterwards.

PSYCHOLOGICAL ADJUSTMENTS

"People are rude. They can't drive. They don't stand in line. They smell bad. The pollution is awful and houses are filled with soot. The metro is disgustingly dirty."— Cairo? No, Paris! Paris from the perspective of an unsettled, disgruntled, and maybe scared American who found herself uprooted and unwillingly transplanted to the City of Light. (You knew it wasn't Cairo because the people and the Metro here are clean!)

Earlier on we suggested that even if you did not have a choice about moving to Cairo, you can pretend that you did—that is also a choice. Some newcomers immediately find Cairo fascinating: the haggling and joking in the streets, downtown pulsing with light and life at 2 am, the muezzin's mournful-joyous calls to prayer punctuating the silent dawn, the mystery and history lurking in the alleyways. Others find a filthy city with raucous people who yell rather than speak, honk their horns like maniacs, and cheat their customers at every turn. Cairo is both, and everything in between. Its 16-plus million people, the bulk of them very poor, endure a lot of pressures and frustrations, yet are for the most part astoundingly good-humored and gregarious in the face of it all.

For Westerners, differences regarding psychological space and privacy stand out between our cultures. Cairenes sit, stand, and talk together at closer range than Londoners, to make a broad contrast. You, the foreigner, are not being crowded; you are

just—here. Yet no physical contact between the sexes in public is allowed (two men, however, are likely to walk holding hands, rest their heads on each other's shoulders, and even kiss, with no speculation as to sexual preference being warranted). Casual Westerners should note the sanctity of the private areas of the Egyptian home. The reception room—not the kitchen or closed doors or hallways—is the place for guests, period. The house is private, but finances, specifically yours, are not. You may feel a bit flustered when bluntly asked what you pay in rent; your Egyptian inquisitor may find this a little weird (we are a little weird this way, no?), but he or she certainly will not feel flustered. Related to privacy and space is the different perception of solitude. Most Egyptians prefer company to solitude and noise to silence. Westerners' apparent desire for the opposites at times must seem quite odd to the sociable, noise-tolerant Egyptians. Why would anyone want to take a ride in a taxi without the radio blaring? Or gaze at the Pyramids without being chatted up?

What can you do for yourself to aid and abet a smooth rather than a rocky transition to Cairo? Work is the saving grace for those who have it. But if you have free time on your hands, first take that CSA Newcomers' Orientation as soon as possible if you can afford it. Then start something regular that involves other people, be it tennis, a book club, Arabic class, church, or hanging out at the neighborhood pub. Don't wait around like a wallflower to be invited. You will have to check out a few options before finding your niche. And don't spend all your socializing time with people who constantly bitch about Cairo; it is boring, catching, and extraordinarily rude and unattractive, as these insensitive idiots frequently do it within earshot of Cairenes. You will want to crawl under the table in mortification when you find yourself with them. Keep your kids away from them and make sure you do not become one of them for their sakes. In general, but with exceptions, children who are not adapting have parents who are not adapting.

The same old euphoria–crash–balance phases that accompany any move will accompany you in Cairo. The unlucky among us might skip the entire first step, but most people are at least somewhat susceptible to the excitement of change if they give it a chance (another choice). Euphoria lasts perhaps three months. Then you lose your doubles match or see a man with no legs begging or the shower head falls out of the wall again or your two-year-old has a tantrum and pees on the floor at Sunny's and—Crrraaashh! So you mope around for a few days in total despair reciting the 'I-hate-this-place' mantra. Try to pull yourself out of it with whatever works best: a good book? a pedicure? giving the guy with no legs LE10? Occasional short forays out of town also work wonders. When you finally laugh again, at yourself, you know the worst is over. And life begins again, not way up, not way down, but balanced. If you are not going anywhere but down after the crash (staying alone, not eating or eating too much, overimbibing, sleeping too much, crying uncontrollably) for any more than two to three weeks maximum, get help. Having read this far, you know it is available.

If you DO feel uprooted and transplanted, here is one final thought: Bloom where you're planted! Cairo is a rich and wonderful city in which to grow, no matter what your age.

SHOPPING AND OTHER LISTS

FOOD

EGYPTIAN SPECIALTIES

babaghannuug	smoked mashed eggplant / oil / garlic dip
baTaarikh	semi-dry, pressed Egyptian salmon-roe caviar; an acquired taste
fuul	stewed broad beans; the Egyptian breakfast of champions
kufta	spiced, grilled meatball fingers
kushari	lentils, macaroni, and rice topped with dry-fried onion and spicy tomato sauce—delicious
'ul'aas	taro-like starchy root vegetable used alone or in soup
mazza	mixed appetizers
mulukhiyya	Jew's mallow, a slightly bitter, spinach-like green used in soup of the same name
umm 'ali	(lit. 'Ali's mom') rich bread pudding with coconut, cream, nuts (for dessert or breakfast)
TaHiina	dip of ground sesame seed paste with mild spices

Ta'miyya	felafel: fried patties of ground chickpeas, onion, herbs, and (sometimes) egg
wara' 'inab	stuffed vine leaves

BREADS AND PASTRIES

'eesh	bread in general
'eesh baladi	wholewheat pita-like bread
'eesh shaami	white-flour version of *'eesh baladi*
'eesh shamsi	Egypt's answer to *pain poilane*; superb, but so far available only in Upper Egypt
[pastries]	all sweeter than sweet; try *kunaafa* (thread-like cake), *ba'laawa*
fiTiir	a versatile puff-pastry; great for home-made pizza crust, or top with sweet fruit topping
[baguettes, croissants, etc.]	use the same words for these and other *khawaaga* (foreigner) foods

DAIRY PRODUCTS

butter	zibda
eggs	beeD
ghee	samna
milk	laban; Haliib
sour cream	ishTa fallaaHi; ishTa miziz
whipping cream	ishTa; ishTa shaantii
yogurt	zabaadi
yogurt, Middle Eastern	labna (used to make dips with lemon and olive oil)

CHEESE (gibna)

Egyptian cheeses are listed by their very approximate English equivalents.

cheddar	sheedar; much less sharp than foreign brands; a good all-purpose cheese
feta	gibna beeDa; available hard or soft, spiced or plain, dry or runny
mozzarella	mutsarilla; look for wet plastic bags marked "for pizza"
parmesan	barmizaan (gibna ruumi will do)
ricotta	rikutta; sold in plastic bags
romano	gibna ruumi
Swiss	gibna swisri; usually imported

FRUIT (fakha)

For ripe fruit, say *mistiwi;* for juice, ask for *'aSiir* ('juice') followed by the fruit's name; for dried fruit, add *naashif* ('dried') after the fruit.

apples	tuffaaH
apricots	mishmish; dried in sheets: 'amar id-diin

avocado	abukaadu
bananas	mooz
cantaloupe	kantalubb
cherries	kireez
coconut	gooz il-hind ('India nut')
dates	balaH
figs	tiin
gooseberries	Harankash
grapefruit	gribfruut
grapes	'inab
guavas	gawaafa
kiwi	kiiwi
limes, lemons	lamuun
mango	manga
mulberries	tuut
*olives, black	zatun iswid
*olives, green	zatun akhDar
oranges	burtu'aan
peaches	khookh
pears	kummitra
persimmon	kaaka
pineapple	ananaas
pomegranates	rummaan
prickly pear	tiin shooki
raisins	zibiib
strawberries	farawla
sweet melons	shammaam
tamarind	tamr hindi
tangerines	yustafandi
watermelon	baTTiikh

*The best cured olives seem to be available only from monasteries and are rarely sold in Cairo

VEGETABLES (khuDaar)

artichoke	karshuuf
asparagus	kishkalmaaz
aubergine	bidingaan
beets (beetroot)	bangar
broad beans	fuul
broccoli	brakli
carrots	gazar
cauliflower	'arnabiiT
celery	karafs
corn (maize)	dura
courgettes	koosa
cucumber	khiyaar

eggplant	bidingaan
fennel	shamar
fenugreek	Hilba
french beans	lubya
green beens	fuSuulya beeDa
Jew's mallow	mulukhiyya
leeks	kurraaT
lentils, brown	'ads bi-gibba
lentils, yellow	'ads aSfar
lettuce	khass; salata (greens in general)
lupine	tirmis
mushrooms	'ish ghuraab; shampinyoon
okra	bamya
onions	baSal
onions, pearl	'awirma
peas	bisilla
peas, sweet	bisillit iz-zuhuur
peas, black-eyed	lubya
peppers, sweet	filfil ruumi
potatoes, sweet	baTaaTa
potatoes, white	baTaaTis
pumpkin	'ar' 'asali
radish, red	figl ruumi
radish, white	figl abyaD
scallions	baSal akhDar
spinach	sabaanikh
taro	'ul'aas
tomatoes	'uuTa; TamaaTim
turnips	lift
zucchini	koosa

POULTRY (Tuyuur)

breast	Sidr
chicken	firaakh
duck	baTT
gizzards	'awaaniS
goose	wizz
leg	wirk
pigeon	Hamaam
quail	simmaan
rabbit	arnab
turkey	diik ruumi

MEAT (laHma)

bacon	beekan
beef	kanduuz

brains	mukhkh
chitterlings	mumbaar
feet	ruguul
filet	filittu
ham	jamboon
heart	'alb
kidney	kalaawi
lamb	Daani; 'uuzi
liver	kibda
pastrami	bastirma (not always beef)
pork	khanziir
roast beef	ruzbiif
roast	rustu
sausage	sugu''
scallops	iskalubb
shanks	kawaari'
steak	bufteek
tongue	lisaan
tripe	kirsha
veal	bitillu

FISH (samak) AND SEAFOOD

anchovies	anshuuga
calamari; squid	kalamari; SubeeT
clams	gandufli
crabs	kaburya
grouper (sea bass)	wa'aar
mullet, grey	buuri
mullet, red	barbuuni; murgaan
mussels	balaH il-baHr
herring	ringa
lobster	istakooza
salmon	salamun
sardines	sardiin
shrimp / prawns	gambari
sole	muusa
tuna	tuuna

NUTS, SEEDS, AND GRAINS

almonds	looz
barley	shi'iir
bulghur	burghul
carob	kharruub
chickpeas	Hummus
couscous	kuskusi
filberts (hazelnuts)	bundu'

lentils	'ads
peanuts	fuul sudaani
pecans	bikaan
pinenuts	sineebar
pistachios	fuzdu'
popcorn	fishaar
pumpkin seeds	libb abyaD
sunflower seeds	libb suuri
walnuts	'een gamal

HERBS (a'shaab) AND SPICES (tawaabil; buharaat)

ground	maTHuun
whole	SiHiiH
allspice	buharaat
anise seed	yansuun
basil	riHaan
bayleaf	wara' lawra
capers	abu khangar
caraway	karawya
cardamom	Habbahaan
cayenne	shaTTa
celery seeds	bizz karafs
chard (leaves)	sal'
chicory	shikurya
chili powder	filfil aHmar amrikaani
spring onion	baSal akhDar
cinnamon	'irfa
cloves	'urunfil
coriander	kuzbara
coriander, fresh	kuzbara khaDra
cumin	kammuun
curry powder	kaari
dill	shabat
fennel	shamar
fennel seeds	Habbit il-baraka
fenugreek	Hilba
garlic	toom
ginger	ganzabiil
green mixed spices	khuDra (dill, parsley, coriander, and/or chard)
horseradish	figl baladi
mace	bisbaasa
mint	na'naa'
mixed spices	buharaat (nutmeg, cinnamon, sweet pepper)
nutmeg	guzt it-tiib

oregano	za'tar
paprika	paprika; filfil ruumi
parsley	ba'duunis
pepper	filfil
pepper, black	filfil iswid
pepper, hot	shaTTa
pepper, white	filfil abyaD
peppercorns	'arn filfil
rosemary	HaSa libaan
saffron	'uSfur; za'faraan (usually not genuine)
sage	maryamiyya
salt	malH
savory	stoorya
sesame seeds	simsim
tarragon	Tarkhuun
thyme	za'tar
turmeric	kurkum
vanilla	vanilya

FOOD STAPLES

baking powder	bakinbawdar
baking soda	bikarbunaat
candy	bunboon
chocolate	shukalaaTa
cookies (biscuits)	baskoot
cornstarch	nisha
flour	di'ii'
gelatin	jelatiin
honey	'asal abyaD
hot sauce	hut soos; shaTTa
ketchup	katshab
mayonnaise	mayuneez
molasses	'asal iswid
mustard	mustarda
oil	zeet
oil, corn	zeet dura
oil, olive	zeet zatuun
oil, safflower	zeet 'uSfur
oil, sunflower	zeet suuri
pasta	makaroona
rice	ruzz
salt	malH
sugar	sukkar
sugar, icing	sukkar budra
vinegar	khall
wine vinegar	khall 'inab

Worcestershire sauce	lii an birinz
yeast	khamiira

BEVERAGES

alcohol	kuHuul; khamra
alcoholic beverages	khumuur
beer	biira; stilla
cocoa	kakaw
coffee	'awha
hibiscus tea	karkadeeh
juice	'aSiir
soft drinks	[use brand name]; haaga sa''a
tea	shayy
water	mayya
water, mineral	mayya ma'daniyya
wine	nibiit

CLOTHING (huduum)

do you have — —?	'andak/ik — —?
my size	ma'aasi
I need size — —	'ayz/a ma'aas — —
medium	mutawassiT
large, larger	kibiir/a, akbar
small, smaller	Sughayyar/a, aSghar
same style, different color	nafs il-stayl bass loon taani
bathing suit	mayooh
bathrobe	burnuus
blouse	biluuza
brassiere	sutyaan
cardigan	biluuvar maftuuH
coat	balTu
dress	fustaan
jacket	jaakit
nightgown	'amiiS noom
pajamas	bijaama
panties	kilutt
pantihose	kuloon
pants (trousers)	bantaloon
scarf	isharb
scarf, wool	kufiyya
shawl	shaal
shirt	'amiiS
shoes	gazma
shoelaces	rubaaT

skirt	jiiba; juup
slip / underskirt	'amiiS taHtaani
slippers	shibshib
socks	shuraab
suit	badla
suit jacket	jakitta
suit, women's	tayiir
sweater	swiitar; biluuvar
undershirt	fanilla
underwear, men's	slibb

COLORS

light	faatiH
dark	ghaami'
plain	saada
patterned	man'uush
striped	mi'allim
beige	beej
black	iswid
blue	azra'
blue, pale	labani
blue, navy	kuHli
brown	bunni
gray	rumaadi
gold	dahabi
green	akhDar
maroon	nibiiti
orange	burtu'aani
pink	bamba
purple	moov
purple, violet	banafsigi
purple, royal	bidingaani
red	aHmar
white	abyaD
silver	faDDi
violet	banafsigi
yellow	aSfar

FABRICS ('umaash)

canvas	kheesh; 'umaash khiyam
cotton	'uTn
corduroy	'aTiifa
leather	gild
linen	tiil; kittaan

silk	Hariir
suede	shamwaa
wool	Suuf

VERY IMPORTANT PEOPLE

I need a/an — — who is excellent, honest, and reasonably priced
'ayz/a — — mumtaaz, shariif, wa mish ghaali

barber	hallaa'
cabinetmaker	naggaar
carpenter	naggaar
doorkeeper	bawwaab
dressmaker	khayaaT/a
driver	sawwaa'
drycleaner	tanturleeh
dyer	maSbagha
electrician	kahrabaa'i
exterminator	raagil yurushsh il-beet
gardener	gineeni
hairdresser	kwafeer
laundryman	makwagi
maid	shaghghaala
mailman	bustagi
nanny	naani
painter	na''aash; mibayyaD
plumber	sabbaak
servant	Sufragi
tailor (men's)	tarzi rigaali
tailor (women's)	tarzi Hariimi
translator	mutargim

FURNISHINGS (farsh) AND FURNITURE (mubiliya)

used furniture	mubliliya musta'mal
awning	tanda
bed	siriir
blanket	baTTaniyya
bookcase	maktaba
chair	kursi
crib / cradle	mahd
cupboard	dulaab
curtain	sitaara
desk	maktab
file cabinet	shaanun
lamp	abajuura
lampshade	burneetit abajuura

mirror	miraaya
picture frame	birwaaz
pillow (bed)	makhadda
pillow (floor)	shalta
pillow (sofa)	khudadiyya
sheet	milaaya
shelf	raff
sofa	kanaba
shutters	shiish
table	tarabeeza
table, dining	Sufra
tent	khiima
tentmaker	khayyaam
towel	fuuTa
towel, large	bashkiir
toys	li'b aTfal

HANDY HOUSEHOLD TERMS AND ITEMS

this — — doesn't work / is broken	il- — — da / di bayZ/a
this chair is broken	il-kursi da bayZ
this table is broken	il-tarabeeza di bayZa
clean (adj.)	niDiif/a
dirty	mish niDiif/a
air conditioner	mukayyif
air filter	filtar hawa
bathroom	Hammaam
bathtub	banyu
batteries	Higaara
bedroom	oodit noom
bucket	gardal
butagaz tank	anbuuba
candles	sham'
dining room	oodit Sufra
door	baab
drawer	durg
drill	shanyuur
electrical switch	muftaaH nuur
electrical outlet	bariiza
elevator (lift)	asanseer
extension cord	waSla; silk
faucet (tap)	Hanafiyya
flashlight (torch)	baTTariyya
floor	arD
flowerpot	'aSriyya
flowers	ward

freezer	friizar
garden hose	kharTuum gineena
hammer	shakuush
heater	daffaaya
ice	talg
key	muftaaH
kitchen	maTbakh
living room	oodit saloon
lock	kaloon
mop	mamsaHa
multiplug socket	mushtarak
newspaper	gurnaal
oven	furn
padlock	'ifl
rat(s)	faar (firaan)
receipt	faTuura
recipe	waSfa
refrigerator	tallaaga
roaches	SaraSiir
scissors	ma'aSS
screwdriver	mifakk
shower	dushsh
sink	HooD
sponge	safinga
stairs	sillim
stove / cooker (butane)	butagaaz
subscription	ishtiraak
toilet	twalitt
towel rack	fawwaaTa
transformer	tarans
voltage stabilizer	stibilayzar
washing machine	ghassaala
water heater	sakhkhaan
water pressure	DaghT il-mayya
window	shibbaak
window screen	silk shibbaak

CARS AND CAR TROUBLE

fill it up	imlaaha
I'm having trouble with my car	fii mushkila ma' 'arabiiti
I think it's the — —	aftikir hiyya fi-l-— —
battery	baTTariyya
car	'arabiyya
carburetor	karbiriteer
engine	mutoor

fuel line	sikkit il-banziin
gas (petrol)	banziin
gas (petrol) station	maHattit banziin
gasket	juwaan
headlight	fanuus
ignition	marsh kuntakt
oil	zeet
shock absorber	musaa'id
spark plugs	bujihaat
steering	diriksyoon
tire	kawitsh
wheel	'agala

4 WORK AND RESEARCH IN CAIRO

Work is the driving force behind the presence of almost all the foreigners in Egypt. For a small but considerable number of them, that was not the original intention at all, but for whatever reasons, they just 'fell into' Egypt, falling in love with the country or one of its citizens, with its history, with its tempo and/or its exoticism. Others, mostly (but not only) young people, come to study, either at al-Azhar or at AUC. A great many more foreigners are here living off the direct or indirect bounty of a foreign-assistance related job, trailing their reluctant or eager dependents behind them, and the whole international diplomatic community is a veritable industry in itself. Finally, there are the entrepreneurs, both individual and corporate, large and small, and yes, even legal and illegal, all banking on Egypt to put money in their pockets. Now add to these the incalculable number of Egyptians whose livelihood flows from this foreign presence—armies of bureaucrats high and low, a huge service-sector industry, and a good chunk of the business communities of Heliopolis, Maadi, and Zamalek at the very least. The sum total of connections and interdependencies is dizzying.

CHANGES IN THE ECONOMIC CLIMATE

The last few years have seen relatively dramatic changes in the Egyptian business climate as the country opened up to foreign investment and private companies challenged the state monopolies. Under Nasser the country was a socialist state, under Sadat the 'Open-Door' policy theoretically reversed its position, and under Mubarak the Investment Law 230 of 1989 has encouraged foreign direct investment.

On the street, evidence of these changes is glaring. The local Sport Cola has been pushed aside by giants Coca-Cola and Pepsi-Cola, and many of the fast-food franchises familiar abroad (McDonalds, Baskin Robbins) have opened up shop. Fully imported clothes are still relatively rare and expensive, but companies such as Naf Naf and Benetton are producing Western-style clothing designed in Europe but manufactured in Egypt. As Egyptian produce entered the seasonal fruit and vegetable markets of cooler lands to the north, the local *suqs* have been able to offer home-grown apples, sweet corn, and asparagus among other new varieties originally grown for export.

But as the marketplace has developed apace, it has become increasingly difficult to keep up with the latest rules and regulations governing business in Egypt. It is therefore essential to hire a consultant or expediter and to use the services of a reputable law firm to cut through the red tape of business as usual to accomplish anything here. Egyptian bureaucracy is still caught in a 1960s socialist time warp, with a welter of paperwork to slice through before licenses can be granted. Good advisors will know the right procedures and have friends in the right places.

In recognition of the time-consuming legal processes, temporary permits are often granted in the meantime that are quite valid until all the i's have been dotted, the papers prepared in triplicate and translated, and the whole lot stamped upside-down, inside-out, and back to front by any number of important officials.

Official hours for government offices are 8 am to 2 pm from Saturday through Thursday. It is always better to present yourself early in the day, yet not unduly early in view of the fact that these hours are, after all, official. Banks are open 8:30 am to 2 pm Sunday through Thursday. Many shops close on Sunday.

Doing business in Egypt is very much a matter of timing, as in taking enough of it to exchange the vital pleasantries and formal courtesies early on that will save hours later. Don't expect to rush people into doing as you demand; you will create a wall of hostility and leaden feet to do your bidding.

Thoughtful foreigners working here understand and appreciate that they are foreign, that their ways are different rather than necessarily better, and that they have more to learn than to teach.

WORK PERMITS AND OTHER PAPERWORK

As an employee coming to work in Cairo, your company will arrange for you to have a work permit, which happily allows you to avoid a personal visit to the Mugamma. Your company or the Mugamma will need your passport and seven photographs for a work permit; academics will likely need their academic qualifications notarized by their embassy. Work permits are valid for one year from date of issue, renewable for an additional year at a time. You must apply for a renewal one month prior to the expiry date. Issue of the permit depends on reciprocal treatment being granted to Egypt by your home country and the permit is issued in accordance with certain conditions laid down by the Ministry of Manpower and Training. These conditions are: the foreigner must not take work away from an Egyptian; consideration must be given to the economic needs of the country; the foreigner must have the qualifications and experience required for the position; enterprises permitted to employ foreign experts and techni-

cians are required to appoint an Egyptian assistant with the appropriate qualifications who is to be trained to replace the expatriate; and foreigners born in Egypt and who reside there permanently shall have priority over non–Egyptian-born and non–permanent-resident expatriates.

A work permit grants automatic residency for the duration of the permit, but you still have to apply for the residency stamp in your passport. Submit your request along with applications for your spouse and children as appropriate; they also have right of residence based on your work permit. Everyone needs to hand in two passport photos and a passport valid for at least two months longer than the residency period requested. Armed with a residency visa, you will not have to pay for a tourist visa (currently $15) at the airport when you enter the country and, far more significantly, you will reap the benefits of cheaper foreign-resident hotel rates and of internal airline tickets at a third of the tourist rate. These are not, by the way, economies than can easily be extended to your friends and relatives visiting from abroad, but discuss options with a travel agent or bargain with the hotel.

TAXATION FOR INDIVIDUALS AND BUSINESSES

TAX ON YOUR SHIPMENT

The government continues to amend laws regarding import and export of goods, so seek and take current advice. Normally individuals can import electrical and household goods as part of their shipment and not pay import duty if their company can submit a letter of guarantee. This means that if the objects in question do not leave the country with the individual who brought them in, then the company guarantees to pay the taxes due. Thus, even if your vacuum cleaner is irretrievably broken you must take it out with you, or you will be charged the full price for a new one, with duty.

However, import duty must be paid on air-freight shipments. This bill may be picked up by your company, but do get clarification, in writing, before you ship; the dues are very high, even on audio cassettes. If you are in Egypt only for a short stay, electrical items such as video cameras and computers can be entered in your passport on arrival at the airport. This ensures against their resale in the country and you may have to show the items again when you leave.

INDIVIDUAL TAXES

Depending on your company, you may be required to pay Egyptian taxes. Inquire at your payroll office. Check with your consulate about the tax requirements in your home country while you are working in Egypt.

Egyptian but not foreign employees are required to pay social insurance to provide for old age, injuries, sickness, unemployment, and retirement, and their employer must also contribute to this.

COMPANY TAXATION

The law governing corporate income tax is Law No 157 of 1981 and is applied to joint stock companies, limited liability companies, and partnerships limited by shares. The tax rate is 40 percent except in the case of a) industrial enterprises in respect to their industrial and exporting activities, for which the rate is 32 percent; and b) oil exploration and production companies, for which the rate is 40.55 percent. The tax is paid on the net profits of the company in question as established by duly audited financial statements. Losses may be carried forward for a period of five years. There is no special tax treatment for capital gains.

However, since certain activities are exempted from this law, it is very important to seek expert legal advice.

ENTREPRENEURSHIP: STARTING YOUR OWN BUSINESS

Once again, since the laws, decrees, and regulations of Egypt are more complicated than those in Europe and North America, and often amended, it is essential to seek professional advice. This guide cannot hope to offer more than an outline. However, the **Law Firms** in the Directory are well recognized and established as the most reputable firms in the city. We have allowed more leeway with respect to individual **Lawyers**, as this is a more subjective question, but as far as law firms go, no quarter was given.

There are a number of forms of business organization in the Egyptian private sector. The usual vehicle for foreign investment is the joint stock company or the limited liability company. There are two regimes under which a foreign company may incorporate one of these companies: Law 230 of 1989 (the Investment Law) and Law 159 of 1981, known as the Companies' Law. Generally foreign companies prefer to form companies under the Investment Law to be eligible for the benefits and privileges available under that law.

JOINT STOCK COMPANY (JSC)

The joint stock company requires a minimum of three shareholders and a minimum issued share capital of LE250,000 if the shares are not offered to the public. If shares are offered to the public, the minimum of the share capital is LE500,000. The issued capital must be fully subscribed with 25 percent being paid up at the incorporation and the balance within the period of ten years as determined by the Board of Directors. Any capital contributed in kind must be fully paid at incorporation and the founder's valuation of such capital in kind must be ratified by a special committee set up within the Capital Markets Authority. At least 49 percent of the share capital must be offered to the Egyptian public via registration with the Stock Exchange. There is no restriction on transfer of shares and preference shares are permitted. The company is managed by a board of directors, the majority of which should be Egyptian nationals (unless the company is formed under the Investment Law). Employees must be allowed to participate in the management of the company and the law requires a share of the profits to be distributed to the employees, which must not be less than 10 percent of the net profits, and which must not exceed the total payroll.

LIMITED LIABILITY COMPANY (LLC)

A limited liability company may not carry out the activities of insurance, banking, savings, deposit-taking, or investment of funds on account of third parties. The minimum issued share capital is LE50,000, which must be fully paid up at incorporation. Capital contributed in kind does not require valuation by a committee as in the case of the JSC; an LLC may have this valuation done by an expert, but the shareholder in question may then be held liable for the excess if the capital contribution is overvalued. At least one of three managers of a limited liability company must be of Egyptian nationality. There is no requirement for employee participation in management as for the JSC nor for the distribution of profits to employees unless capital exceeds LE250,000. There is no public subscription, stock exchange registration, or preference share issue.

After you have come to grips with the laws governing the formation and activities permitted by your would-be company, you must familiarize yourself with the country's labor laws. A written employment contract must be drawn up, in Arabic, in triplicate, with a copy for the employee, the employer, and the Social Insurance Office. The Company Law 159 of 1981 provides that 90 percent of all employees must be Egyptian and that they must receive at least 80 percent of the wages paid. Similarly, at least 75 percent of technical and administrative staff of joint stock companies must be Egyptian and must receive 70 percent of the wages paid to employees in that category. An employee may be engaged for a definite (that is, limited) or an indefinite (that is, possibly interminable) period. However—and this is a big however—once a contract for a definite period is renewed, it becomes a contract for an indefinite period. One consequence of this is that it is extremely difficult to fire an incompetent worker, who may claim unfair dismissal and engage in a protracted legal procedure. Again, seek advice!

PREMISES

Companies investing directly in Egypt in the industrial sector are likely to need manufacturing premises—most probably in one of the new industrial cities such as 6th October City (southwest of the capital), 10th Ramadan City (northeast), or the Burg al-'Arab area west of Alexandria, complemented by an administrative office in Cairo. Foreign investors can also carry out projects in the Egyptian free zones, which are considered as being located offshore, and are free from the usual customs duties and from income tax obligations.

The areas most favored for corporate offices in Cairo are Garden City, Zamalek, Mohandiseen, and Heliopolis. Since luxury accommodation in downtown Cairo is expensive (smart apartments can be $2000-plus a month before utilities) and rooms at the top hotels complete with business centers can be around $100 a night, executives on a shorter stay may consider having a hotel address rather than taking up a lease on a property. There are a number of other **Business Service Centers**, whose rates and range and quality of services may compare favorably with those in hotels. For example, most of them can locate a more economical place to rest your weary head than on a hotel pillow while using their business address, services, and personnel.

PRIVATIZATION: THE CURRENT CLIMATE

In May 1991 Egypt agreed to sign an economic stabilization program supported by the IMF. As part of this program, trade has been freed up somewhat by selective tariff reductions and by the elimination or reduction of import and export quotas. Another important component has been the liberalization of the banking industry and the rejuvenation of Egypt's capital market. The most important part of the reform process has been the encouragement of private-sector development, activity, and investment in Egypt.

A first move in the major drive toward privatization in the public sector was simply to expose it to more competitive influences. The government created new organizational structures for public-sector companies aimed at allowing them to enjoy greater autonomy and to compete among themselves and with the private sector. Managers were also introduced to the concept of accountability for their results and made subject to the same financial disciplines as the managers of private-sector companies, including the risks of liquidation and bankruptcy. Banks were instructed to break with tradition and lend only on commercial terms. The sale of 125 public enterprises over a five-year period was planned along with the divestiture of the government's

shares in over 250 public joint-venture companies and twenty-three public joint-venture banks. An independent advisory body, the Public Enterprise Office, was established in November 1991, funded by the government of Egypt and international agencies. Additionally, a series of holding companies assumed responsibility for the future sale of other state companies, which encompass almost every sector of the Egyptian economy except the public utilities.

The first wave of privatization included the sale of al-Nasr Bottling with assets of LE187 million and about 5,600 employees, which was sold by the Holding Company for Food Industries to a consortium made up of two local companies and Coca-Cola International for LE325 million. Under the deal, the investors were obliged to retain the company's workforce for at least three years and to invest LE500 million over a ten-year period—a reflection of government concern about the potential social upheaval that may accompany the privatization program.

However, the path to privatization has been far from smooth. What was to have been the opening of the flood gates has turned out to be a leaky faucet.

The leisurely pace of the 'Behemoths' Auction'—the sale of the large wholly state-owned public-sector units—has left room for the expression of much frustration on all sides of the issue. There is a perception that only the successful slices (tranches) of the unprofitable state monoliths are being offered for sale and that the whole process is going much too slowly. Meanwhile, a suit has been brought against the government challenging privatization on the grounds that it is unconstitutional. In another related corner, impassioned unionists raise their membership's consciousness with patriotic speeches about the threat privatization poses to its jobs and its very patrimony. Newspaper accounts of these issues make for instructive reading.

From potential investors comes a cry for a freer flow of financial information at all levels to increase confidence among local and international investors. The government has been slow to release reliable macro-economic data, nor do all companies publish full annual reports. However, the situation is improving: the Ministers' Cabinet Information Office in Zamalek and the Central Bank of Egypt now publish reports covering macro-economic issues, and companies quoted on the stock exchange must provide annual reports.

Also on the positive side for those who support it is the fact that economic reform, specifically privatization, is now regarded as irreversible. Hopes are high that the large number of expatriate Egyptians who formed part of the massive brain drain during the Nasser years will now be willing to invest their considerable financial assets in their homeland, given the right economic climate and incentives—and that they may indeed return themselves, bringing with them other valuable assets for investment: their skills and expertise.

NETWORKING AND FINDING MORE INFORMATION

Before you go any further, make sure you have a good supply of suitably impressive business cards to hand. This essential tool is much used in Egypt and is quick and easy to acquire. It is a culturally sensitive touch to have these cards done up in English on one side and Arabic on the other.

Businessmen will find the American Chamber of Commerce based in the Marriott Hotel in Zamalek a good source of information. The chamber issues occasional reports on specific aspects of the Egyptian economy and a magazine, *Business Monthly*. Their regular luncheon meeting is definitely a place to network and they have very interesting speakers.

The new *Business Today* magazine carries not only business stories but also an invaluable mini-directory of government agencies, accountancy firms, aid agencies operating in Cairo, and so on.

There is a well-stocked commercial library at the USAID office in the Cairo Center Building near the Semiramis Intercontinental Hotel, open to members of the public.

For laws, decrees and regulations in English contact the Middle East Library for Economic Services (MELES). They produce the *MELES List* and the *MELES Bulletin* covering Egyptian law to date with the latest amendments in English, at reasonable prices. The library can provide its subscribers with certain economic studies.

An invaluable source of information is the book *Egypt: Investment and Growth*, published by Euromoney Publications. It is revised every six months.

Finally, do not forget the commercial section of your embassy for advice and suggestions regarding useful connections.

SCHOLARLY RESEARCH

It is relatively easy to study in Cairo provided you have a letter of reference from your alma mater or current university back home. Many of the English-speaking students coming to do research for their doctorate of philosophy in, for example, ninth-century Arabic literature or archeology have been impressed by their welcome into local intellectual circles.

Take your introduction letter to the dean of the faculty for your subject at the American University in Cairo. You can become a 'fellow without stipend' and for under $500 a year can attend a class per semester of your choice. This allows you to use the AUC library, probably the best one in Cairo. If you already have your Ph.D. you

The American University in Cairo Press

Cairo Papers in Social Science

Cairo Papers in Social Science is a unique English-language journal that for the past eighteen years has published the results of local research on social, economic, and political development in the Middle East. Cairo Papers was founded by the three social science departments at the American University in Cairo and has grown to include people from other institutions. The objectives have been to demonstrate the relevance of Middle Eastern social science and disseminate the results of research on issues and problems of development in the Middle East. To date, 70 monographs in eighteen volumes have been published on a wide range of subjects and Cairo Papers has proven invaluable to Middle East specialist, scholars, international libraries, and research centers.

New and forthcoming titles:

Volume 18

3 The Development of Social Science in Egypt: Economics, History, and Sociology. *Fifth Annual Symposium.*

4 Structural Adjustment, Stabilization Policies, and the Poor in Egypt. *Karima Korayem.*

Volume 19

1 Nilopolitics: A Hydrological Regime, 1870–1990. *Mohammed Hatem El-Atawy.*

2 Images of the Other: Europe and the Muslim World Before 1700. *David R. Blanks, ed.*

Subscriptions — one year, four monographs:

Individuals	Institutions	Single issues
$25 / LE20	$35 / LE25	$7.50 / LE7.50

The American University in Cairo Press
113 Sharia Kasr el Aini, Cairo, Egypt.
Tel: 357-6891/4/5/6; fax: 354-1440

can become a 'scholar without stipend,' and similarly avail yourself of the AUC facilities. Indeed, anyone can read books at the AUC library on production of an appropriately authorized ID, but not everyone is allowed to borrow them.

Seek out public lectures in your subject (advertised in *Egypt Today*) and you will soon find a group of people with similar interests and knowledge to yours. There are weekly or monthly talks at ARCE (the American Research Center), often on Egyptology but also on literature and the legal system, while the talks at the Netherlands Institute tend to focus on Classical Arabic and Egyptology. The French CEDEJ covers more modern subjects such as sociology and politics. L'Atelier du Caire holds weekly talks in Arabic on modern poetry and drama. There are frequent lectures at the British Council. The major institutes have resources you can use for a modest membership fee and your colleagues will pleased to help you with your research.

For more information from other **Organizations**, **Business & Scholarly**, check with the British Council and other cultural centers. For funding and alternative sources, contact:

Amideast, which provides information on all aspects of American education and training at post–secondary school level and material about graduate studies.

The Council for the International Exchange of Scholars, which has programs for senior scholars.

The European Commission, which provides some funding for research projects. You must apply on a form issued by the Cairo office by May for the following year. They have a documentation center and library on the premises open to the public.

The Ford Foundation, which sponsors projects rather than individuals.

The Fulbright Commission, which administers exchange of scholars between Egypt and the United States through a variety of programs. The core program oversees an exchange of post-doctoral professors for lectures or research in all fields. The commission administers other educational and cultural exchange programs for Egyptians to study in the States. For Americans wishing to study in Egypt Fulbright has two programs, the Senior and the Student Scholar prorams.

The Hubert H. Humphrey North–South Fellowship Program, Eisenhower Fellowships, Fulbright-Hays Foreign Curriculum Consultant Program, Salzburg Seminar: Apply to the Fullbright Commission for more information on these.

The Institute of International Education, which organizes student scholar programs in the United States for Egyptians (contact the IIE in the United States and/or Amideast in Cairo).

Two others:

ICARDA (International Center for Agricultural Research in the Dry Areas) is the local branch of the main office situated in Aleppo, Syria, and supports applied agricultural research in the Nile Valley. It aids Egyptian scientists and workers in planning and conducting research and produces reports in English that are available to the public.

IDRC (International Development Research Center, Canada) opened a regional office in 1977 to fund research projects of an applied nature. It accepts proposals from institutions only and publishes a quarterly newsletter in French and English and an annual journal in Arabic.

TEACHING

Professional teachers for schools in Cairo are generally hired direct from overseas. They may tutor in their spare time — the going rate is $20 an hour — although some contracts prohibit this practice. If you would like to tutor privately, register yourself with the CAC or BISC schools, or substitute teach until a suitable vacancy occurs. Salaries in local language schools can fall far short of those offered in the foreign schools; classes are bigger and less disciplined but the rewards from teaching may be greater. Local language schools are always keen to recruit native English speakers qualified overseas, as these fee-paying schools recognize their marketing potential to the parents. Teachers report that the administrative side of local schools can leave a lot to be desired; it is a question of going with the flow.

Teachers of English as a Foreign Language (EFL) are imported and home-grown, for there are a number of centers that offer the RSA CTEFLA certificate. This training program takes between four and five weeks and is very intensive. It costs around $900. There is an entry test to complete before acceptance into the course, which examines your command of the English language and your grammatical knowledge. The British Council runs its training course in the summer months and generally some employment opportunities for qualified teachers follow.

The International Language Institute (ILI) is part of the International House group based in London. Some people come especially to Cairo to take the ILI course, as it is cheaper here than in Britain, as are living expenses. There are two ILIs, in Mohandiseen and in Heliopolis, which both run courses several times a year. AUC offers the course three times a year.

The advantage of these center-based courses is that you become familiar with their resource library and so do not have to reinvent the wheel every time you teach a new concept to your class. The possible disadvantage is that teaching hours are often in the late afternoon or evening, as that is when the regularly employed are free: you may prefer to devote such time to your family or socializing.

There is a considerable demand in Cairo for teachers of English. Everyone, it seems, wants to learn and practice English, as evidenced by the number of small boys whose opening line on the street is "What time is it?" or "What is your name?" Forward-looking businesses have approached the British Council to ask them to provide a series of classes to teach anything from technical English to how to answer the telephone in the language.

WORKING FOR EGYPTIAN COMPANIES

It is essential to know that if you are employed as a 'foreigner' from overseas, you will be paid the sort of salary you are used to. If, however, you accompany your spouse to Egypt with the idea that, with your professional qualifications, you will be able to find work and receive adequate payment for it, you will be sadly disappointed. 'Local hire' rates are very low by Western standards. A good salary here is LE1000 a month. You can, however, get quite a bit more, depending on the perceived value of you and/or your qualifications to the given company.

A few observations from foreign friends working for Egyptian firms—schools, law firms, Egyptian NGOs (Non-Governmental Organizations): document every initiative you might ever want credit for; get an advance if you have been promised reimbursement for out-of-pocket money; make sure your employment contract is in a certified Arabic translation as well as in English; determine how best to assure receipt of your last paycheck particularly if you are working freelance; don't alienate yourself in the comfort and isolation of workaholism; and don't gossip, a most difficult rule to follow in Egypt's chatty and conspiracy-theory-prone corporate culture.

And now, a bouquet of comments and advice—and a few expressions of frustration—culled from a wide range of people in the world of work—an Egyptian woman who runs a large information technology company, a foreign engineer managing a large Egyptian labor force, a few boutique owners foreign and Egyptian, temporary consultants, and so on. We have mixed them kaleidoscope-fashion, because this reflects well the range and diversity of their experiences:

"Egyptian laborers can make anything with their hands." . . . "It's very hard to delegate; you have to be on top of eveything yourself." . . . "One easy aspect of doing business in Egypt is that it's in an infantile stage—there's no competiton." . . . "Teaching someone with a dirt floor how to keep the floor clean is hard." . . . "There's no management training here—people are given responsibility but no authority." . . . "Mine information like gold!" . . . "Where are the opportunities? Career development training, distribution franchises, technical education for adults, public relations/marketing/advertising, and entertainment for Egyptians and foreigners." . . . "Why do they want to cheat me instead of getting a good customer?" . . . "I got my job through the English Language Institute (AUC) bulletin board." . . . "They don't manage their time right. . . . It's constant phone calls and interruptions." . . . "A patchwork work background can work really well here." . . . "The good things about doing business as a woman here is that Egyptian women get a natural respect, plus sympathy, curiosity, and interest beause they're a minority; the bad thing is that at the top, it's a real old boys' club." . . . "How to make life easy? Smile. How to make it difficult? Be the arrogant foreigner."

VOLUNTEER WORK

There are many opportunities to give of yourself in Cairo, depending on where your interests or talents lie and how much time you have. Below is a brief listing. If you have a particular skill or training, ask around—your help will be much appreciated.

Al-Nur wa-l-Amal ('light and hope') Association is founded and run entirely by volunteers and depends on donations to keep going. It is a boarding center for blind girls that educates and trains them to be self-sufficient, integrated members of society. By transcribing sheet music into Braille, the institute has taught the girls to master musical scores, and this professional orchestra is world famous.

Friends of Children with Cancer is a fundraising organization that helps children in Egypt to receive the best medical care possible. Eighty percent of children with leukemia in Europe are cured while only 30 or 40 percent of children in Egypt recover, mostly due to the high cost of the treatment required. To make a donation or volunteer, telephone Liz Naylor at 340-8619 or Marguerite Kelly at 353-1390.

Awladi Orphanage in Digla looks after up to 220 boys and girls. (Remember, formal adoption is illegal in Egypt.) The girls can stay until they are married, the boys are transferred to another orphanage at age twelve. Volunteers are needed to supervise the children and it is better if they can be familiar faces: encouragement, love, and hope are essential to all children, and security is even more important to children in Egypt without a home. Telephone Shadia Salem at 350-5694.

The Thrift Shop under All Saints' Cathedral in Zamalek accepts used clothing and household goods, which it sells in order to raise money for a number of Egyptian charities. Recently, for example, they were able to buy braces for child victims of polio. The shop often welcomes help. Telephone Inge Osborne at 242-2212.

The Deaf School, run by the Episcopal Church in Egypt, needs volunteers to help deaf and hearing-impaired children with their afterschool activities. Contact Clair Malik, 362-6022 or 340-9464.

'Ayn Shams Hospital's Clinic (contact Mary Gurguis, 290-1759) in Heliopolis welcomes volunteer staff with or without medical backgrounds.

St. Andrew's Church Refugee Relief needs people to teach English, basic computing skills and accounting, arts and crafts, and carpentry. Telephone James Ward, 575-9451.

Shubra Evangelical Church needs native English speakers to teach adults. Telephone Maher al-Sabagh at 574-0023.

Befrienders Cairo, the local equivalent of the Samaritans, is a community service for the depressed and suicidal. Arabic speakers are particularly needed. Contact Karim Gohar at 303-6035.

The following opportunities to help out are offered by the Maadi Women's Guild:

The Baby Wash program is part of the Caritas effort to help Egypt's poor. At its clinic near the Pyramids mothers are encouraged to bring their new-born babies for a bath and general medical check up. Volunteers do the bathing and bring anything unusual in the baby's appearance to the attention of the clinic staff.

The Home of Love and Compassion in Muqattam has babies and toddlers in need of a hug and old people whose families cannot care for them and need someone to talk with.

The National Tumor Institute needs volunteers to visit ninety children with cancer every week, and welcomes donations of crayons, coloring books, soap, and milk—indeed, anything to brighten these children's lives.

The local free newsletter in Maadi, the *Maadi Messenger*, lists other opportunities to help as the need arises—and itself (because of the transient nature of most expatriates) is always looking for volunteers to take ads, type, or help distribute.

Finally, you can always volunteer to help out at your local school and get to know other parents at the same time. **Volunteering** is a well-know cure for many ills, and a tried-and-true avenue to successful networking as well.

5 CAIRO ARABIC: THE BASICS

Macabre (*maqaabir:* tombs), cipher (*Sifr:* zero), admiral (*amir al-maa':* commander of the sea), camel (*gamal*), algebra (*al-jabr:* reduction), assassin (*hashshashiin:* hashish-smokers), cotton (*quTn*). These are just a few of the hundreds of words from the Arabic that color and enrich everyday English.

Short-term visitors limiting themselves to upscale hotels and tourist haunts can get by with no Arabic whatsoever in Cairo. But for foreign residents dealing with 'real life,' a minimal vocabulary is vital. Upper-class and professional Egyptians speak English, and often French as well, as do tourist-oriented shopkeepers, but the vast mass of Cairenes do not. So if you plan to travel independently, shop, and meet your neighbors, you can sally forth with this very brief introduction. We hope it will whet your appetite for more.

There are hundreds of Arabic classes and tutors in Cairo (see **Language Classes** in the Directory). You're bound to find one that suits your needs and interests. Learning Classical Arabic, the language of literature, newspapers, and formal discourse, requires a serious commitment. But picking up a useful vocabulary of colloquial, spoken Arabic, is relatively easy. The various guttural sounds may throw off native English speakers initially, but the pronunciation guide below will help demystify these. To expand upon the brief vocabulary given here, check the **Shopping and Other Lists** at the end of Chapter 3 for all sorts of shopping and household terminology. Next, try Stevens and Salib's *A Pocket Dictionary of the Spoken Arabic of Cairo* (The American University in Cairo Press, 1992; LE 25); if you are put off by phonetic transcription symbols, though, use *Say It In Arabic (Egyptian)* by Farouk al-Baz from Dover Publications.

So plunge in. Ask questions, make mistakes, and use this great tip from our Research Editor: label everything in the house as you learn its name, using whatever unique transcription works best for you. Then photocopy the lists in Chapter 3 and post them in the kitchen; using these words will earn you much kudos with your local shopkeepers.

1) For gender variants, we use male version / female version
2) Alternatives and explanations are preceded by a semicolon

CONSONANTS

Distinctly lengthen any consonant that is doubled, e.g., pronounce "kk" as the "k" sound in bookcase, and don't ignore the oft-cited difference between *Hamaam* (pigeon) and *Hammaam* (toilet).

Capital letters anywhere in a word indicate a stronger emphasis on the sound than their lower-case counterparts; **D, S, T, Z, H** require a Heavier, Harder Hit than **d, s, t, z, h**.

g   is always pronounced hard, as in English 'go.'
j   is pronounced "zh," as in the English 'measure.'
kh   is equivalant to "ch" in the Scottish 'loch' or the German 'echt.'
gh   is similar to "kh," but with the vocal chords vibrating.
q   sounds like a softer English "k" uttered from further back in the mouth.
r   is a trilled r, as in Italian and Spanish.
s   is pronounced as in 'its,' never as in 'his' or 'hers.'
'   (apostrophe): glottal stop, like "tt" in American 'Manhattan' or Cockney 'matter'
'   (reversed apostrophe): the *'ain,* a forcing of the air through a constriction in the throat, a kind of backward gulp. If you find it impossible, substitute "a" as in 'cat.'

VOWELS

a   as in 'back'
aa   as in 'car' if near an emphatic consonant (S, T, D, Z), otherwise as in 'care'
ee   as in 'cane'
i   as in 'win'
ii   as in 'clean'
oo   as in 'bowl'
u   as in 'put'
uu   as in 'cool'

MINIMALIST'S GRAMMAR

The Arabic verb 'to be' is rarely used in the present tense; instead, one uses the personal pronoun plus the adjective for statements which describe a condition, e.g., *ana 'ayyaan/a,* meaning 'I [am] sick.'

Nouns have gender, as in French and Spanish. Those ending in *-a* are usually feminine; the rest are masculine, with a few exceptions.

Sex further complicates matters as follows: In speaking to males, *-ak* is added to certain phrases; to females, *-ik* is added, e.g., *min faDlak* ('please') to a male, *min faDlik* to a female. We indicate this by showing *-ak/ik* where appropriate. Another version of this same general principal is the addition of -i to a verb, e.g., *law samaHt* ('if you please') to a male, but *law samaHti* to a female.

There are also linguistic differences between male and female speakers: in referring to themselves, men use the masculine (m) adjective form and women the feminine (f), e.g., *ana aasif* (m) and *ana asfa* (f) ('I [am] sorry'). We indicate this with a slash, with the masculine first, the feminine following.

Adjectives generally follow the noun they modify and agree in gender and number.

Verb conjugations are less irregular than in English; nevertheless, we're skipping the whole subject here.

Mish in front of a word negates it, e.g., *mish mumkin:* 'impossible.'

VOCABULARY

COURTESY

hi/hello	ahlan; ahlan wa sahlan
goodbye	salaamu 'aleekum; ma'a-s-salaama; salaam
how are you?	izzayak/ik
fine, thanks	kwayyis/a il-Hamdulillaah
my name is ____	ismi ____
thank you	shukran
please	law samaHt/i; min faDlak/ik
excuse me, pardon me	'an iznak/ik
I'm sorry	ana aasif / asfa
I don't know Arabic	ana mish 'aarif / 'arfa 'arabi
I don't understand	mish faahim / fahma
I understand	faahim / fahma
to your health	fi SaHHitak/ik

QUESTIONS

what's your name?	ismak/ik eeh?
do you speak English?/French?	bititkallim/i ingiliizi / faransaawi?
who is that?	miin da / di?
what is this?	eeh da / di?
what are these / those?	eeh dool?
where (is) ——?	feen ——?
when?	imta?
how?	izzaay?
how much (money)?	bi kaam?
how many?	kaam?
why?	leeh?
which (one)?	anhi?
who knows?	miin 'aarif?

URGENCIES AND EMERGENCIES

where is the toilet?	feen il-Hammaam?
now	dilwa'ti
it's not working	'aTlaan/a; bayZ/a
help me! (emergency)	ilHa'uuni!
help me (less urgent)	saa'idni
emergency	Taari'
police	shurTa; buliis
fire	Harii'a
water	mayya
hospital	mustashfa

call a doctor	'ayziin duktuur ('we want a doctor')
help! thief!	ilHa'uuni! Haraami!

COMMON EXPRESSIONS

Given in the approximate descending order in which you will hear them.

thanks be to God	il-Hamdulillaah
God willing	insha'allah
yes	aywa; aah
no	la'; la'a (more emphatic)
and	wa; u
don't worry; no problem	ma'lish
I mean	ya'ni
so / then	fa
again	kamaan
also	barDu
don't	balaash
okay, can do	maashi (lit. 'it goes')
sure, no problem	mish mushkila
can do, possible	mumkin
finished, done, okay	khalaaS
isn't it? n'est ce pas?	mish kida?
impossible	mish mumkin
not bad, okay, so-so	mish baTaal
okay, fine	Tayyib; Tab
connections, influence	wasTa; koosa
nonsense, empty talk	kalaam faaDi
exactly	miyya miyya, (lit. 'a hundred percent'); biZZabt
so-so, okay	nuSS u nuSS (lit. 'half and half')
only, quit it, enough	bass
bit by bit	shwaya shwaya
"in the time of apricots"	fil-mishmish (meaning 'almost never')

DIRECTIONS

Especially handy with taxi drivers.

straight ahead	'ala Tuul
right	yamiin
left	shimaal
next to	gamb
across from, in front of	'uddaam
facing	fil-wishsh
behind	wara
before	'abl
after	ba'd

near, close to	'urayyib min
far from	ba'iid min
corner (of a street)	naSya; this corner: in-naSya di
between — — and — —	been — — wa — —
at — —	fi — —
stop here	hina kwayyis
go slowly	bi-shweesh
go quickly	bi-sur'a
how many kilometers?	kaam kiilu? (better by far than 'How far?')

PLACES

Just say the word, and add *law samaHt/i* for 'please.'

airport	maTaar
bridge	kubri
cathedral	ik-katidra'iyya
church	kiniisa
embassy	sifaara
floating restaurant	resturan 'aayim
home	beet
hotel	fundu'
market	suu'
— — mosque	gaama' — —; masgid — —, e.g., gaama' SulTaan Hasan
museum	matHaf
office	maktab
post office	busta
school	madrasa
square	midaan
street	shaari'
train station	maHattit il-'atr
university	gam'a

For names of **Landmarks**, see the chart at the front of the book.

MONEY (AND POLITE BARGAINING)

pounds	gineeh
piasters	'irsh
and a half	nuSS, e.g., itneen gineeh u nuSS: two and a half pounds
and a quarter	rub', e.g., talaata gineeh u rub': three and a quarter pounds
small change	fakka
change (back from transaction)	baa'i (literally 'the rest')
do you have change?	ma'ak fakka?
no change	mafiish fakka

I'm broke	ána mifallis
how much?	bi kaam; kaam?
too much / unreasonable	kitiir; mish ma'ʿuul
my last word / offer	aakhir kalaam
congratulations	mabruuk; response: allah yibaarik fiik/i; depending on tone of voice, this exchange concluding a bargaining session indicates genuine or sarcastic admiration of the opponent's bargaining skill

FAMILY, FRIENDS, AND OTHER PEOPLE

people	naas
(my) mother	umm(i); waldit(i) (formal)
(my) father	abu(ya); waalid (waldi) (formal)
(my) brother	akhu(ya)
(my) sister	ukht(i)
(my) son	ibn(i)
(my) daughter	bint(i)
(my) children	awlaad(i)
(my) husband	gooz(i)
(my) wife	maraat(i), il-madaam (formal)
man	raagil
woman	sitt
child	Tifl
children, kids	aTfaal; 'iyaal (slang)
baby	beebi; Tifl
boy	walad
girl	bint
my friend	SaHbi (m) / SaHbiti (f)
my sweetheart	Habiibi (m) / Habiibti (f)
my fiancé/e	khaTiibi (m) /khaTibti (f)
stranger	ghariib/a
foreigner	agnabi (m) / agnabiyya (f)
Westerner	khawaaga (m) / khawagaaya (f) (can be friendly, derogatory, or deferential)

TIME (WA'T)

now	dilwa'ti
later	ba'deen
today	innaharda
tonight	innaharda bil-leel
tomorrow	bukra
day after tomorrow	ba'da bukra
yesterday	imbaariH

morning	iS-Subh
afternoon / evening	ba'd iD-Duhr
evening / night	bil-leel
on time	fi-l-ma'aad
(five) o'clock	is-saa'a (khamsa)
half past five	khamsa u nuSS
five fifteen	khamsa u rub'
five forty-five (quarter to six)	sitta illa rub'
Sunday	il-Hadd
Monday	il-itneen
Tuesday	it-talaat
Wednesday	il-arba'
Thursday	il-khamiis
Friday	il-gum'a
Saturday	is-sabt

PERSONAL PRONOUNS AND DEMONSTRATIVE ADJECTIVES

I	ana
you (s)	inta (m) / inti (f)
he	huwwa
she	hiyya
we	iHna
you (pl)	intu
they	humma
this, that	da (m) / di (f)
those	dool

ADJECTIVES

To add emphasis indicating 'very' or 'too,' add *'awi* after the adjective; to negate, precede it with *mish*. Feminine endings are shown as /a; if not shown, the adjective is invariant.

big	kibiir/a
small	Sughayyar/a
more	aktar
less	a'all
nice / good / fine	kwayyis/a, Tayyib/a
beautiful / pretty	gamiil/a; Hilw/a (sweet)
ugly	wiHish/wiHsha
bad	wiHish/wiHsha; mish kwayyis/a
broken, not working	bayZ/a
interesting	kwayyis/a
boring	mumill/a
important	muhimm/a
crowded, busy	zaHma
tall	Tawiil/a

short	'uSayyar/a
fat	tikhiin/a
thin	rufayya'/a
funny	muDHik/a
generous	kariim/a
greedy	Tammaa'/a
happy	mabsuuT/a
honest	amiin/a; shariif/a
hot; cold	Harr; bard (for weather)
hot; cold	sukhn/a; saa'i' / sa''a (for temperature of things and food)
polite	mu'addab/a
sick	'ayaan/a
spicy	bi-shaTTa; Haami/Hamya
strange	ghariib/a
terrible	faaZii'/a
tired	Ta'baan/a
wonderful	haayil/hayla

ADVERBS

slowly	bi-shweesh
quickly	bi-sur'a
immediately	Haalan
later / next	ba'deen
soon	'urayyib
often / a lot	kitiir
here	hina
there	hinaak

PREPOSITIONS

in	fi
inside	guwwa
outside	barra
up / on top of	foo'
down / under	taHt
around / about	ta'riiban; Hawaali
after	ba'd
before	'abl
with	ma'
without	bi-duun; min gheer

DETERRENTS

Women may experience unwanted attention from men in the street—from polite attempts at conversation to coarse language or gestures to physical assault. Depending on what the situation demands, some of the following deterrents may be useful. And remember that if you raise your voice (in any language) you will immediately attract a crowd, who will probably deal swiftly and efficiently with your aggressor.

ana mitgawwiza	I'm married
'eeb	shame on you, for shame!
iHtirim nafsak	have respect! (lit. 'respect yourself')
inta magnuun?	are you crazy?
bass kifaaya	enough! leave me alone!

Numbers: see the chart at the front of the book.
Colors: see **Shopping and Other Lists**, Chapter 3.

The American University in Cairo Press

Womens' Studies

**Doria Shafik, Egyptian Feminist
A Woman Apart
Cynthia Nelson**
14.5x23cm. 14 illus. 345 pp. Paperback.
ISBN 977 424 413 3
For sale only in the Middle East
LE65 / $29.50

**Feminists, Islam, and Nation
Gender and the Making of Modern Egypt
Margot Badran**
14.5x23cm. 368pp. Paperback.
ISBN 977 424 385 4
Not for sale outside Egypt
LE60 / $24.50

**Gender and Development
Raana Haider**
14.5x23cm. 184pp. Paperback.
ISBN 977 424 379 X
LE40 / $19.95

The American University in Cairo Press
113 Sharia Kasr el Aini, Cairo, Egypt.
Tel: 357-6891/4/5/6; fax: 354-1440

DIRECTORY

Note: Entries are largely recommendation-based, except for categories such as Airlines, Banks, Embassies, Theaters, etc. The Arabic for 'street,' *shaari'*, is not included; use it in front of the street name when giving addresses.

ABBREVIATIONS

AG: Agouza
CA: Cairo International Airport
DT: Downtown Cairo
DK: Dokki
GC: Garden City
GZ: Giza
HE: Heliopolis
KK: Khan al-Khalili
MA: Maadi
MN: Manial
MO: Mohandiseen
NC: Nasr City
PY: Pyramids
WTC: World Trade Center
ZA: Zamalek

EMERGENCY AND OTHER IMPORTANT NUMBERS

DOCTORS

Central beeper dispatch telephones: 777-474; 575-1851; and 575-9010. Dial and give dispatcher your doctor's beeper number in English, French, or Arabic.
With real touch-tone phone only: Dial 010, then doctor's beeper number. Wait for tone, then enter your own telephone number followed by two pound signs (# #).

HOSPITAL EMERGENCY AND AMBULANCE

As-Salam Int'l Hospital, Corniche al-Nil, 363-8050; emergency 362-3300
Nil Badrawi Hospital, Corniche al-Nil, 363-8684/8688; ambulance 363-8168

DIRECTORY INFORMATION

140 or 141

TELEPHONE COMPLAINTS

Dial 188 or your Centrale

TELEPHONE CENTRALE NUMBERS (FOR SERVICE, REPAIRS, COMPLAINTS)

Bab al-Luq, 356-1717
Dokki, 337-4259
Garden City, 354-8390
Giza, 570-0701
Heliopolis, 249-0002
Maadi 1, 350-9805
Maadi 2, 352-1695
Mohandiseen, 346-4466
Zamalek, 341-1519

LOCAL NUMBERS FOR INTERNATIONAL LONG-DISTANCE SERVICE

AT&T, 510-0200
MCI, 355-5770
Sprint, 356-4777

LOST/STOLEN CREDIT CARDS

American Express, 570-3147/ 3152/3153
Diners Club, 341-6006
Mastercard, 357-1148/ 1149/ 1249
Visa, 357-1148/1149/1249

IMPORTANT NUMBERS

Alcoholics Anonymous (AA). Meetings in HE, GC, MA, 348-7692 or contact CSA below
Al-Anon: contact AA or CSA (below)
Befrienders Cairo: 344-8200; 303-6025; 303-6035
British Community Association (BCA), 2 'Abd al-Rahman al-Rifa'i, MO, 348-1358
Community Services Association (CSA), 4 Rd. 21, MA, 376-8232; 350-5284
Nadim Center for Victims of Violence (abuse, torture), 337-6186, director Dr. Suzanne Fayad
Tourist Police, 391-9144
Western Union Money Transfer, Cairo Hotline, 357-1300 (9am–10pm)
Women's Association of Cairo, 21 Bulus Hanna, DK, 360-3475

TRAVEL INFORMATION

EgyptAir, 390-0999; 390-2444; 759-9806
Cairo International Airport (new airport), 291-4255/ 4266
Cairo International Airport (old airport), 244-8977/3249
TWA, 574-9904/9914/9916
Ramsis Train Station, 147 or 575-3555

ACCOUNTING FIRMS

Allied Accountants (Arthur
Andersen), Mobica Tower,
37 al-Ahrar, MO, 336-2000,
fax 360-0813
Farid S. Mansour (Coopers &
Lybrand), Tiba 2000 Center,
Rab' al-'Adawiya, NC,
260-8500, fax 261-3204
KPMG Hazem Hassan,
72 Muhi al-Din Abu al-'Izz,
MO, 336-9094/8, fax
349-7224/348-7819
Nawar & Co., International
Chartered Accountants,
21 Tal'at Harb, DT,
391-6987, fax 392-1615
Price Waterhouse P.W., 4 Rd.
261, MA, 353-0914/0837,
fax 353-0915
BDO Saleh Barsoum, Abd
al-Aziz & Co., 95c
al-Mirghani, HE, 290-3278,
fax 290-4038
Shawki & Co., Deloitte
Touche, Tohmatsu
International, Banque Misr
Tower, 153 Muhammad
Farid, 19th-20th fl., DT,
392-6000/6111/6400,
391-7299, fax 393-9430
Youssef Nabih & Co., 22 Qasr
al-Nil, DT, 393-7801/2/3,
fax 393-7804

AEROBICS

See Sports

AIR CONDITIONERS AND
REPAIR

Adel Serour, 16 'Abd al-Hamid
Lutfi, MO, 335-2965, fax
335-2781 (also heating,
ventilators)

Al Tawheed Co., 7th Area
15/13 al-'Uruba, MA,
353-6242
Hany Nagy, Ain Shams,
251-3212, freelance repair
Spring Air Co., 94 Musaddaq,
DK, 335-0362, 335-52071,
fax 336-0728
Seven Engineers, 32 Gaziret
Badran, Shubra, 776-077,
765-656, fax 765656

AIRLINES

Aeroflot, 18 al-Bustan, Bab
al-Luq, DT, 390-0429/
393-7409, fax 390-0407, CA
291-4602
Air Algeria, 13 Qasr al-Nil,
DT, 574-0686/8,
fax 574-0686,
CA 2911-0409
Air Canada, c/o Imperial
Travel, 26 Mahmud
Basyuni, 575-8939/8402,
761-769, 760-071, fax
773-056
Air France, 2 Midan Tal'at
Harb, DT, 575-8899, admin.
394-3939, fax 771-744, CA
417-5306/7
Air India, 1 Tal'at Harb, DT,
393-4873/75, 393-4864/
0165, 392-2592/7467
Air Malta, c/o Emeco Travel,
2 Tal'at Harb, DT,
574-9360, 390-7045, fax
574-4212/ 9369
Air Sinai, Nile Hilton Hotel,
Midan al-Tahrir, DT,
760-948/9, 750-777,
fax 772-947
Alitalia, Nile Hilton Hotel,
Midan al-Tahrir, DT,
574-0984/3488, CA
418-8168/9, fax 779-907

American Airlines,
20 al-Gihad, MO, 345-5707,
347-0033, c/o Emeco Travel,
1 Tal'at Harb, DT,
574-9360, 390-7045
Austrian Airlines, 22 Qasr
al-Nil, DT, 392-1522/8838,
fax 392-8857/4799
Aviation Int'l Scorpiol
(charters only), 17 Midan
Aswan, MO, 346-1287,
fax 346-1287
Belgian Airlines (Sabena),
2 Mariette Pasha, Midan
al-Tahrir, DT, 575-1194,
577-7125, Airport: 669-144
British Airways, 1 'Abd
al-Salam 'Arif, off Midan
al-Tahrir, DT, 752-852,
759-977, 777-045, 772-612/
981, fax 772526;
3502264/2265, MA;
671-741, 673-038, CA
Bulgarian Airlines, 17 Qasr
al-Nil, DT, 393-1152/1211/
9119
Cathay Pacific, 20 al-Gihad,
MO, 302-9627/8, fax
303-0593
China Airlines, Nile Hilton
Hotel, Midan al-Tahrir, DT,
578-0322, 578-0329
Continental Airlines, c/o
Imperial Travel, 26 Mahmud
Basyuni, DT, 575-8939,
575- 8402, 761-769,
760-071, fax 773-055
Cyprus Airways, 16 'Adli, DT,
390-8099/7669/391-8874,
fax 391-1104
Czechoslovak Airlines (CSA),
9 Tal'at Harb, DT,
393-0416/0395/392-0463,
fax 390-0463
Delta Airlines, c/o Five
Continents, Jeddah Tower,
17 Isma'il Muhammad, ZA,
341-9498/9770, 342-0981,
341-2039

EgyptAir, 9 Tal'at Harb, DT,
392-7444/7205, 390-0554,
fax 390-1557; Nile Hilton
Hotel, 765-200, 759-703/
806; Mövenpick Hotel,
697-268, 245-5793; Cairo
Sheraton, 348-8630/8600;
26th July, MO, 347-2027,
346-4501; 22 Ibrahim
al-Laqqani, HE, 664-305,
668-552; CA, 245-4400, fax
245-9316

El Al Airlines, 5 Maqrizi, ZA,
341-1795, 340-5912, fax
341-9629, CA ext: 3821

Emirates Airlines, Marriott
Hotel, ZA, 340-6492/1102/
1142, fax 340-6568, CA
291-9039

Ethiopian Airlines, Nile Hilton
Hotel, Midan al-Tahrir, DT,
574-0911/0603/ 0852

Finnair, 15 Midan al-Tahrir,
DT, 763-771, 776-895,
769-571, fax 769-571

Gulf Air, 64 Gam'at al-Duwal
al-'Arabiya, MO, 348-4116/
7781, fax 349-0955;
21 Mahmud Basyuni, DT,
575-8391/0852, fax 773-055

Iberia Airlines, 15 Midan
al-Tahrir, 574-9955/9716,
fax 575-6856; 78 al-Hegaz,
HE, 245-6993/7299;
62 al-Nasr, MA, 352-5871,
353-2344; GZ, 384-2989/
5452; CA 483-3165,
482-9160

Japan Airlines (JAL), Nile
Hilton Hotel, Midan
al-Tahrir, DT, 574-7233, fax
574-7232, CA 660-843

KLM, 11 Qasr al-Nil, DT,
574-7004/5/6/7/8, freight:
662-256, fax 574-7330; CA,
418-2386/7

Kenya Airlines, Nile Hilton
Hotel, Midan al-Tahrir, DT,
762494, 776771, fax
578-0475/6, CA ext 3638

Korean Airlines, c/o Emeco
Travel, 2 Tal'at Harb, DT,
574-9360, 390-7045, fax
574-4212

Kuwait Airlines, 4 Tal'at Harb,
DT, 574-2135/2747, fax
764408; 24 Ibrahim
al-Laqqani, HE, 660-006,
291-6495, MO, 344-0471;
CA 291-9591

Lufthansa, 6 al-Sheikh
al-Marsafi, ZA, 342-0471,
fax 340-7981; CA, 666-975

Malaysian Airlines, c/o
Imperial Travel, 26 Mahmud
Basyuni, DT, 575-8939/
8402, 761-769, 760-071, fax
773-055

Malev-Hungarian Airlines,
12 Tal'at Harb, DT,
574-4959, fax 575-3111;
CA, 666-688, ext. 3783

Middle East Airlines (MEA),
12 Qasr al-Nil, DT,
574-3151/3422/575-0888,
fax 574-2157; CA 663-670

Olympic Airways, 23 Qasr
al-Nil, DT, 393-1277/1459/
1318, fax 391-0574; CA,
664503

Pakistan International Airlines
(PIA), 22 Qasr al-Nil, DT,
392-4055/4134/4213, fax
393-1604; CA, 674154

Philippine Airlines, 17 Isma'il
Muhammad, ZA, 342-0453/
0861/340-1948/341-9409,
fax 341-9626

Polish Airlines (LOT), 1 Qasr
al-Nil, DT, 575-7403, fax
574-7312

Pyramid Airlines, 52 al-Sawra,
HE, 290-0168/0335, fax
290-2553, CA ext.3838/4554

Qatar Airlines, Nile Hilton
Hotel, Midan al-Tahrir, DT,
578-0322

Royal Air Maroc, 9 Tal'at
Harb, DT, 392-2956/0378

Royal Brunei, Nile Hilton
Hotel, Midan al-Tahrir, DT,
578-0321/2/3/4/5/6, fax
574-4536

Royal Jordanian, 6 Qasr al-Nil,
DT, 575-0875; CA, 668-903

Sabena, see Belgian Airlines

Saudia, 5 Qasr al-Nil, DT,
574-7388l7392; CA,
290-7038l7036, fax 766-271

Shorouk Air, 2 al-Shahid
Isma'il Fahmi, HE,
417-2313, fax 417-2308

Singapore Airlines, Nile Hilton
Hotel, Midan al-Tahrir, DT,
575-0276, fax 769-681; CA,
291-5242

South African Airlines, Nile
Hilton, Midan al-Tahrir, DT,
578-0323/574-4536

Sudan Airways, 1 'Abd
al-Salam 'Arif, off Midan
al-Tahrir, DT, 574-7145/
7398/7299; CA, 660049

Swissair, 22 Qasr al-Nil, DT,
reservations 392-1522,
information 393-7955/7856;
CA, 291-0283/9/291-8095

Syrian Arab Airlines, 25 Tal'at
Harb, DT, 392-8284/5, fax
391-0588; CA, ext. 4890

Thai Airways, c/o United
Airlines, 16 Adly, DT,
390-8099/7669, fax
391-1104

Tunis Air, 14 Tal'at Harb, DT,
574-3420/67, fax 574-0677;
CA, ext. 3725/26

Turkish Airlines, 26 Mahmud
Basyuni, DT, 760-071,
758-939/402, fax 773-096

TWA, 1 Qasr al-Nil, Midan
al-Tahrir, DT, 574-9904/5/6/
7/8, fax 574-9909; CA,
244-1050

Uganda Airlines, 1 'Abd
al-Hamid Badawi, HE,
245-3779/8110, fax
245-6535

United Airlines, 16 'Adli, DT, 390-5090/2344, fax 391-1104; CA, 417-0589

Varig (Brazilian Airways), 37 'Abd al-Khaliq Sarwat, DT, 391-3979

Yemenia Airways, 7 Zamalek Club, 26th July, MO, 346-6499/9854/344-6965; CA, 669-356/670-599

Zas Airlines of Egypt, 61 'Uruba, HE, 290-7840/7836, fax 672-045

AIRPORTS

Cairo International, 417-4776 or switchboard 291-4255/66/77

Alexandria, (03) 420-2021

Aswan, (097) 322970

Luxor, (095) 383294

Hurghada, (065) 442831/3976

Sharm al-Sheikh, (062) 600-314/664/302

AIRPORT MEET & ASSIST

American Express, CA: 417-6577; 567-2217; internal: ext. 2127; GZ, 570-3411/19; 573-8465/3685; MO, 361-3660

ALCOHOLIC BEVERAGES

Ambrogio, 12 Brazil, ZA, 340-9239

King Soliman, 3 Midan Sulayman Guhar, DK, 335-9942

ALTERNATIVE THERAPIES

ACUPUNCTURE

Dr. Adel Badr, 22 'Abd al-Mun'im Riyad, MO, 337-4350

Dr. Amgad al-Zoghbi, 11 Latif Mansur, al-Qiyada al-Mushtaraka, HE, 290-1624; 59A 'Abd al-Mun'im Riyad, MO, 345-3064

AROMATHERAPIST

Ashling Badrawi, 340-0813

AROMATHERAPIST AND REFLEXOLOGIST

Rawya al-Gammal, SACHA, 29 Ahmad Hishmat, 7th fl., 340-6167

CHI KUNG PRACTITIONER

Chanmin Yang, contact CSA, 376-8232; 350-5284

CHIROPRACTOR

Shamil Fahmy, 350-4470; 350-1685

FELDENKRAIS MOVEMENT METHOD

Carol Ann Clouston, 341-1769

HERBS

Harraz Herb Shop, Bab al-Khalq

HYPNOTHERAPIST

Polly Cunningham 361-6899

MASSAGE

Pam Rizk, 341-2927

REFLEXOLOGY

Jan Argo, 353-2265

REIKI PRACTICTIONER

Betty Brody, 352-6612

WOMEN HEALERS GROUP

340-1373, Leslie Zehr

YOGA

See Meditation

AMUSEMENT PARKS

Aqua Park, Ismailia Rd., 32 km out of Cairo after al-'Ubur market, 477-0088/99

Cooky Park, behind Mövenpick Jolie Ville near Pyramids

Sindbad Amusement Park, Ismailia Road, near Airport

ANTIQUES & ANTIQUE REPRODUCTIONS

DOWNTOWN CAIRO

Ahmed Zeinhoum, Huda Sha'rawi

Galleries Tony, 4 Tal'at Harb

Hassan & Ali, Huda Sha'rawi

Louvre Meuble, 14 Huda Sha'rawi

Mahrous, Huda Sha'rawi

Philippe Devlay, 9 'Urabi, DT, 574-6349

HELIOPOLIS

Ashraf & Khalid, Midan al-Gami', 241-8417 (brass beds)

Hamdi Fayek, 49 Hurriya, 241-8417

Poupi Interiors, 5 Siti (off Baghdad), 679-991

Sucash, 12 'Abd al-Mun'im Hafez, 660-077

KHAN AL-KHALILI

Old Shoppe, 7 Khan al-Khalili, 924-976; 926-050

MAADI

Bric-a-Brac, 43 Misr Helwan Rd. near Bukara Restaurant

El Safa, 41 Rd. 7, 350-7948

Morgana, 57 Rd. 9, 375-1089
Patu Antiques, El Karnak
   Tower behind Military
   Hospital, 364-8835
Nelly Essawy, 353-3559

MOHANDISEEN

Clarine, 11 Sulayman Abaza,
   360-8393
Samia Imports, 42 'Abd
   al-Halim Husayn, MO

ZAMALEK

Atrium, 4 Muhammad Mazhar,
   340-6869; Owner: Nermine
   Mokhtar
Avenue 30, 30 al-Gezira
   al-Wusta, 340-6058
Galerie Odeon, 110 26th July,
   340-2172/5
Noubi Antiquaire, 157 26th
   July, 340-1385, 345-2331
Nostalgia, 6 Zakaria Rizk,
   342-0880; contact:
   Mr. Marwan

ANTIQUES, RESTORATION & REPAIR

Ahmed Seif, Samia Imports, 42
   Abd al-Halim Husayn, MO
Ayman El-Azabawi, Morgana,
   57 Rd. 9, MA, 375-1089
Guido Leone, 5 Sulayman
   al-Halabi (off Ramsis), DT,
   574-2771

APPLIANCES

All Omar Effendi stores
Shops on 'Abd al-'Aziz, DT,
   for near-wholesale prices on
   all kinds of appliances and
   electronics
Electric House, 3 Wahib Doss,
   MA, 350-7029 (local &
   imported, also satellite
   dishes); contact: Nasr

FutureHome, 23 al-Nadha at
   Rd. 6, MA, 375-8555; fax
   375-8444
Genedy, 51 Ahmad 'Urabi,
   MO, 347-0095-6 and
   52 Shihab, MO, 303-3001,
   344-1018 (large appliances)
Helwagi Electric, 60 Sulayman
   Guhar, DK, 349-3242
Maison Khedr, 14 Baghdad,
   HE, 290-7314 (small
   appliances)
Ogeil, 134 26th July, ZA,
   340-4368

APPLIANCES REPAIRS

Mohsen Gomaa, office
   561-755, home 561-3741
Osman's Repair, Rd. 205, MA,
   352-9020 (also new/used
   appliances)

ARCHAEOLOGY

American Research Center in
   Egypt (ARCE), 2 Midan
   Qasr al-Dubara, GC,
   354-8239, 355-8683, fax
   355-3052; email: arce@
   brainy1.ie-eg.com
Egyptian Antiquities Project,
   2 Midan Qasr al-Dubara,
   GC, 344-8622 (phone/fax);
   email: arceeap@brainy1.
   ie-eg.com
Egyptian Exploration Society,
   at the British Council, 192
   al-Nil, AG, 301-0319;
   contact: Rosalind Phipps
Netherlands Institute,
   Dr. Mahmud Azmi, ZA,
   340-0076

ARCHITECTS

Markus El Katcha, 301-5402
Rami El Dehan and Soheir
   Farid Assoc., 344-2481
Dr. Mona Zakaria, 360-3191

Ibrahim Nagi, 335-6576

ARCHITECTURE

SPARE (Society for the
   Preservation of the
   Architectural Resources of
   Egypt); contact ARCE,
   2 Midan Qasr al-Dubara,
   GC, 354-8239, 355-8683,
   fax 355-3052; email: arce@
   brainy1.ie-eg.com

ART CLASSES

HELIOPOLIS

El Madyafa, 34 Nabil
   al-Wakkad, Golf area next to
   Bon Appetit, 418-7809;
   678-111, Shaheera Fawzi

MAADI

Community Services
   Association (CSA) , 4 Rd.
   21, 376-8232, 350-5284
The Workshop, 38 Rd. 6 (next
   to Conserv by the flyover),
   350-6473

ART GALLERIES

DOKKI

Atelier Palette, 25 Rifaa, Midan
   al-Misaha
Atelier 87, Marwat al-Zahraa,
   702-553/ 361-3668
Bashayer, 58 Musaddaq
   (upstairs), 713-233
Orman Gallery, 48 al-Giza,
   349-8627

DOWNTOWN, GARDEN CITY, AND OTHER

Arabesque, 6 Qasr al-Nil,
   574-7898
Atelier du Caire, 2 Karim
   al-Dawla, DT, 574-6730

British Council, 192 al-Nil,
AG, 354-3281
Cairo-Berlin Art Gallery,
17 Yusuf al-Gindi,
Bab-al-Luq, 393-1764
Duroub Gallery, 4 Amrika
al-Latiniya, 354-7951
Espace Karim Francis,
1 al-Sharifein (off Qasr
al-Nil), 393-1699
Mashrabia, 8 Champollion,
Midan al-Tahrir (Stephania
Angarano), 578-4494
Musafirkhana, near Khan
Khalili, co-op atelier
(Khedive Ismail's
birthplace)
Sony Gallery at Adham Center,
AUC, Midan al-Tahrir,
354-2964

HELIOPOLIS

Hend Shalabi, 38 Sheikh 'Ali
Mahmud, 245-8234
Kharamana, 32 Ishaq Ya'qub,
290-4644
Mesteka Art Gallery, 83
al-Hurriya, 290-1143
Noun Gallery, 4 Mahmud Abu
al-'Uyun (off Hegaz),
248-0082
Oasis, 3 Mahmud Nashed (off
Harun al-Rashid), 245-5634

MAADI

Graffiti, 28 Nerco Bldg. off Rd.
213, 353-1426
Haddouta Amir, New Maadi,
352-4352
Al-Shomou Art Gallery, 12 Rd.
150, Midan el-Hurriya,
350-2073/3142
Le Touche, Midan al-Ittihad
and Rd. 106
Mansour, 116 Rd. 9, 350-3707

MOHANDISEEN

Al Nuqfa, 67 Hussein, 3rd fl.,
349-5604

ZAMALEK

Akhnaton Gallery V (Center of
Arts), 1 al-Ma'had al-Swisri,
340-8211
Alef, 14 Muhammad Anis,
340-3690
Anas al-Wagoud, 23B Isma'il
Muhammad, 6th fl., flat 40,
341-8189
El Mustardia, 1 Mahmud
Mukhtar, 341-8005
El Nil, Gezira Exhibition
Grounds, 341-8796
Extra, 3 al-Nasim, 341-4534
Fine Arts Gallery, 173 26th
July, 342-0904
Faculty of Fine Arts,
4 Muhammad Ibn Thaqeb,
340-7570
Four Seasons, 11 Hasan Sabri,
341-3601
Hanager Arts Center, Opera
House Complex, 340-6861
Mervat Masoud Gallery,
6 Gezira, 341-2493
Museum of Egyptian Modern
Art, Opera Complex,
341-6665
Nostalgia, 6 Zakaria Rizq,
342-0880
Riyash, 6 al-Gezira al-Wusta,
340-9994
Safar Khan, 6 Brazil, 340-3314

ARTISTS

Ahmed Mansour, 54 al-Nadi
Golf and 116 Rd. 9, MA,
351-5588; 350-3707
Elhamy Naguib, 28D Rd. 232,
Nerco Complex, Digla, MA,
352-1644
Hend Shalabi, 38 Sheikh Ali
Mahmud, 245-8234
Jemila Yosri, 2 Amr, New MA,
352-6047
Mohammed Allam, Saqqara
Rd. across from Sabil Umm
Hashem

ARTS & CRAFTS

DOKKI

Al Ain Gallery, 73 Husayn,
349-3940
Assila, 98 Muhi al-Din Abu
al-'Izz, 709-719
Bashayer, 58 Musaddaq,
713-233
Shahira Mehrez &
Companions, 3rd fl., 12 Abi
Emama (left-hand entrance
between Omar Effendi and
Cairo Sheraton), 348-7814

HELIOPOLIS

Association for the Protection
of the Environment,
7 Sulayman al-Sayyed,
510-2723
Sahara-El Souk, 34 Nabil
al-Wakkad next to Bon
Appetit, 418-7809
Oasis, 3 Mahmud Nashed (off
Harun al-Rashid), 245-5634

MAADI

Bedouin Market 15 Rd. 231,
Digla
El Patio, 4 Rd. 77, Golf Area,
351-6654
Morgana, 57 Rd. 9, 375-1089
Per Nefer, Maadi Grand Mall,
353-8261
Spiro Arts, Rd. 77, Golf Area
The Workshop, 38 Rd. 6,
350-6473

MISCELLANEOUS

Beit al-Sinnari Workshop,
Haret Monge (off Port Said
towards Sayyida Zaynab)
Marisa & Ismail, 17 Ahmad
Tulun, opp. Ibn Tulun
Mosque, 982-863; 257-9422
Nabil Darwish Studio, Saqqara
Road, Harraniya 385-5894
(Pottery)
Senouhi, 54 'Abd al-Khaliq
Sarwat, 5th fl., DT,
391-0955.

Wikalat al-Ghuri Workshop,
 near al-Azhar
Wissa Wassef Studios, Saqqara
 Road, Harraniya, 385-0746;
 contact: Suzanne Wissa
 Wassef

MOHANDISEEN

Samir El Guindi (The Mud
 Factory), 261 Sudan,
 347-3445/7032 (Pottery)

ZAMALEK

Nomad, Cairo Marriott,
 341-2132; 14 Saray
 al-Gezira, 1st fl., 341-1917;
 Owner: Carol Sidky
North Sinai Women's Projects,
 27 Yahya Ibrahim, Apt. 8.
 340-1045; fax 340-0387;
 contact: Manal Bayad

ASSOCIATIONS

See Organizations

ATTORNEYS

See Law Firms; Lawyers

AUCTIONS

Osiris, 15 Sharif, DT, 392-6609

AVIATION

EgyptAir Flight School,
 Imbaba Airport, 346-5990

BABY SUPPLIES

Taki, 285-4422, bedding,
 furniture, etc.
Baby Admiral, 349-4195, cloth
 diapers made in Egypt

La Leche League, contact CSA,
 350-5284/376-8283

BAKERIES

DOKKI
Abu Higazi, 1 Wizarat
 al-Zira'a, DK (for fiTiir)
La Parisienne, al-Hussein and
 al-Tahrir Streets.

DOWNTOWN
Etman, 17 Muhammad
 Mahmud past AUC Library,
 DT, 354-9160 (croissants)

HELIOPOLIS
The Cheesecake Factory,
 Merryland Commercial
 Center, Roxy, HE, 452-6690
La Palma, 3 al-Qubba, Roxy,
 HE, 258-3998/2743; open
 24 hrs.

MAADI
Mirabelle,71 Rd. 9, MA,
 378-4288

MISCELLANEOUS
La Poire, at least 12 branches
 in Cairo and suburbs; contact
 Mr. Hesham Gamal,
 Musaddaq branch, 349-6931,
 for closest branch
Le Bec Sucré, Midan Sheikh
 Yusuf, GC, 355-6792;
 105 al-Mirghani, HE,
 290-4165; 14 Rd. 218, MA,
 352-5908; 6A Dr.
 al-Mahruqi, MO, 345-7282;
 22 Taha Husayn, ZA,
 340-0652/0718;

MOHANDISEEN
Bon Appetit, 21 Wadi al-Nil,
 MO, 342-4815; 2 Isma'il
 Muhammad, ZA, 340-4382.
La Brioche, 7 'Abd al-Mun'im
 Riyad, MO, 360-6121 (pain
 au chocolat)

ZAMALEK
Rigoletto, Yamama Ctr.,
 3 Taha Husayn, ZA,
 340-8684
Soufflé, Hasan Sabri, ZA,
 340-2833

BALLS

Viennese Ball, Nile Hilton,
 578-0444/0666 (March
 1997)

BANKS

Al-Watany Bank of Egypt,
 Head Office, Midan Muhi
 al-Din (off Gam'at al-Duwal
 al-'Arabiya), MO, 337-9134/
 287, 336-0115, fax 337-9302
Alexandria Kuwait
 International Bank,
 Evergreen Tower, 10 Tal'at
 Harb, DT, 779-766,
 764-644, 778-933, fax
 764-844
American Express, head office
 4 Syria, MO, 360-5256/
 5258/8228, 349-2458, fax
 360-8227; 72 'Umar Ibn
 al-Khattab, HE, 290-9528,
 fax 290-9527; 21–23 Giza,
 Nile Tower, GZ, 571-2948,
 fax 571-2947
Arab American International
 Bank, 5 Midan al-Saray
 al-Kubra, GC, 354-5094/5/6,
 fax 355-8493
Arab Bank PLC, 50 Gezirat
 al-'Arab, MO, 302-9069/70,
 fax 302-9068
Arab International Bank,
 35 'Abd al-Khaliq Sarwat,
 DT, 391-2140/6120/8794,
 fax 391-6233
Arab Investment Bank, 8 'Abd
 al-Khaliq Sarwat, DT,
 766-716, fax 766916

Bank of Alexandria, 49 Qasr
al-Nil, DT, 391-822/079/
796, fax 392-1479, 391-0481
Bank of Commerce &
Development (al-Tegaryoon)
13 26th July, Midan Sphinx,
MO, 347-6461/5584/2056/
63, international div.
344-7537, fax 345-0581,
international div. 344-7537
Bank of Nova Scotia, 3 Ahmad
Nasim, GZ, 336-5728,
336-5731/4/5; fax 336-5730;
Mgr: Mr. Mohamed Jayangir
Bank of Oman Ltd., 21 Giza,
Nile Tower, GZ, 735-124,
730-732, fax 736-614
Bank of Tokyo, Ltd.,
Representative Office, Nile
Hilton Annex, Rm. 247,
Midan al-Tahrir, 766-318,
fax 762-833
Bank Saderat Iran, 28 Sharif,
DT, 393-1147
Bankers Trust Company,
17 Qasr al-Nil, DT,
392-3427/898, fax 392-0628
Banque de L'Union European,
3 Ahmad Nasim, GZ,
727-504/729-508
Banque du Caire et de Paris,
3 Amrika al-Latiniya, GC,
354-8323/4/5, fax 350616
Banque du Caire, 20 Rushdi,
'Abdin, DT, P.O. Box 1495,
390-4554, fax 393-5478
(numerous branches all over
Egypt)
Banque Francaise du
Commerce Exterieur,
Representative Office,
48/50 'Abd al-Khaliq
Sarwat, DT, 390-4667/5173,
fax 391-5705
Banque Indosuez, 9 Mariette
Pasha, Midan al-Tahrir, DT,
575-5960/770-871, fax
771011

Banque Misr, 151 Muhammad
Farid, DT, 391-2711/106/
150/0709, fax 391-9779
(branches all over Egypt)
Banque Nationale de Paris,
Representative Office,
al-Sabbah Tower, third fl.,
Apt. 306, 8 Ibrahim Nagib,
GC, 354-7805, 355-7080,
fax 3548296
Banque Paribas, 6A Ghandi,
GC, 354-0391/7323,
355-7278, fax 355-5081/2
Barclays International S.A.E.,
12 Midan al-Sheikh Yusuf,
GC, 354-9415/2195/9422/
1408, fax 355-2746
Central Bank of Egypt, 31 Qasr
al-Nil, DT, 392-6211, fax
3926361
Chemical Bank, 3 Ahmad
Nasim, GZ, 361-0393, fax
361-0498, 349-0321
Citibank, 4 Ahmad Pasha, GC,
355-1873/4/5/6/7, 354-9523/
7246, fax 355-7743
Commerzbank AG, Banque
Misr Tower, 22nd fl.,
153 Muhammad Farid, DT,
393-1661, 390-7242, fax
392-3718
Commercial International Bank
(CIB), Nile Tower,
21–23 Giza, GZ, 570-3043,
fax 570-2691/3172
Credit Commercial De France,
26 Mahmud Basyuni, 4th fl.,
DT, 574-0441, fax 777-603
Credit International D'Egypte,
46 al-Batal Ahmad 'Abd
al-'Aziz, MO, 336-1573, fax
360-8673
Credit Lyonnaise, 3 al-Yaman,
GZ, 709608/609/10/12, fax
705637
Credit Suisse, 33 Harun,
349-9760, 348-4333/4777,
fax 361-5136
Credito Italiano, 10B Bahgat
Ali, ZA, 341-0774

Delta International,
1113 Corniche al-Nil,
574-0831, fax 750-904,
574-2892
Dresdner Bank AG, Nile
Tower, 12th fl., 21/23 Giza,
GZ, 572-3451, 572-8168,
fax 572-3782
Egyptian American Bank,
4–6 Hasan Sabri, ZA,
340-0063, fax 340-9430
Egyptian British Bank, 3 Abu
al-Fida, ZA, 341-0797,
340-4849/9186/9286, fax
341-4010
Egyptian Gulf Bank, al-Urman
Plaza Bldg., 8, 10 Ahmad
Nasim, GZ, 360-6580/43/
6457/67, fax 356-6512
Egyptian Saudi Finance Bank
(former Pyramids Bank),
12 Ittihad al-Muhamiyin
al-Arab, GC, 354-7112/
9641/4512, 355-5464, fax
355-5914
Egyptian Workers Bank, 90
Galaa, Midan Ramsis,
763-622/4, 778-368,
760-109, fax 768-903
Export Development Bank of
Egypt, Evergreen Building,
10 Tal'at Harb, DT,
574-9653/4/5, fax 774553
Faisal Islamic Bank of Egypt,
1113 Corniche al-Nil,
753-109/165/389, 750-998,
fax 777-301
Housing & Development Bank,
12 Surya, MO, 349-2013/4/5
Industrial Development Bank
of Egypt, 110 Galaa, DT,
779-188/087/247, 772-468,
771-509, fax 777324,
765470, 763026
Lloyd's Bank PLC, 44
Muhammad Mazhar, ZA,
341-8366/5929, 340-6437/
6508, fax 340-5356

MIBank (Misr International
Bank), 54 al-Batal Ahmad
'Abd al-'Aziz, MO,
349-4424/7091, fax
348-9796
Middle East Bank, 25 Yehia
Ibrahim, ZA, 340-3672,
341-9008, fax 340-3592
Misr America International
Bank, 12 Nadi al-Seid, DK,
361-6613/23/4/5, fax
361-6610
Misr Exterior Bank, Cairo
Plaza Bldg., Corniche al-Nil,
778-619/701/380, 766-410,
fax 578-0238, 762-806
Misr International Bank,
54 al-Batal Ahmad 'Abd
al-'Aziz, MO, 349-4424/
7091, fax 348-9796,
349-8072
Misr Iran Development Bank,
Nile Tower, 21 Giza, GZ,
572-7311, fax 570-1185
Mohandes Bank, 30 Ramsis,
DT, 748-659, 751-973/708,
fax 750-922; 3, 5 Mossadak
DK, 336-2760, 337-3107/10,
fax 336-2741
National Bank for
Development, 5A Bursa,
392-3528/245
National Bank of Abu Dhabi,
21 Giza, GZ, 735-342/62,
fax 724640
National Bank of Egypt,
24 Sharif, DT, 392-4022/
4177/7977/9855/4143, fax
393-6481
National Bank of Greece,
2 'Aziz 'Usman, ZA,
340-6610, 341-1772, fax
341-8530
National Bank of Pakistan,
64 Gam'at al-Duwal
al-'Arabiya, MO, 349-8955/
8307, fax 349-8955

National Bank of Sudan,
1 Behler Passage (off Qasr
al-Nil), DT, 393-1691,
392-1945/7208, fax
393-7208
National Societe Generale
Bank SAE, Evergreen
Building, 10 Tal'at Harb,
DT, 574-9376, fax 776249
Nile Bank, 35 Ramsis, Midan
'Abd al-Mun'im Riyad,
751-105,574-1417/ 3502,
760470/75, fax 575-6296,
574-5577
Rafedein Bank, 114 al-Tahrir,
DK, 715-728, 711-473,
715-608, 349-6858, fax
715-608
Societe Arabe International De
Banque, 56 Gam'at
al-Duwal al-'Arabiya, MO,
349-9460/64/97
Societe Generale, 3 Abu
al-Fida, ZA, 341-1636/27,
fax 392-4654
Suez Canal Bank, 11 Sabri Abu
'Alam, DT, 393-1048/66/33,
fax 391-3522
Sumitomo Bank Ltd.,
21/23 Giza, GZ, 736-126,
fax 734-656
Swiss Bank Corporation,
3 Ahmad Nasim, GZ,
729-384, 726-603
Union de Banques Arabes et
Francaises, 4 Behler Passage
(off Qasr al-Nil), DT,
393-3678, fax 392-4654
United Bank Ltd., 8 al-Sadd
al-'Ali, DK, 709-935

BARS

Africana, al-Haram, GZ
After Eight, 6 Qasr al-Nil, DT,
574-0855
Cairo Cellar, President Hotel,
22 Taha Husayn, ZA,
340-0718

Casanova, in Arc en Ciel Hotel,
GZ
Da Baffo, 15 al-Batal Ahmad
'Abd al-'Aziz, MO,
344-8468
Downstairs, WTC
Harry's Pub, Cairo Marriott,
ZA, 340-8888
Johnny's Pub, Le Pacha 1901
boat, ZA, 340-6730
Katcho'z, WTC, 578-6324
Le 51 Bar, Meridien
Heliopolis, HE, 290-5055
ext. 8151
Le Tabasco, Midan 'Amman,
DK, 336-5583
Odeon, Odeon Hotel,
6 Dr. 'Abd al-Hamid Sa'id,
DT, 776-637, 767-971
Piano Piano, WTC, 762-810
Rive Gauche, 21 Ma'had
al-Swisri, ZA, 341-6874
Sevilla, Flamenco Hotel,
2 al-Gezira al-Wusta, ZA,
340-0815/16
Taverne, Nile Hilton Hotel,
Midan al-Tahrir, 578-0444
Tycoons, Le Pacha 1901, Saray
al-Gezira, ZA, 340-6730
Versailles Palace, Cave des
Rois, 10 Muhammad Ibn
Thaqeb, ZA, 341-8980
Whiskies Pub, Atlas Zamalek
Hotel, 20 Gam'at al-Duwal
al-'Arabiya, MO, 346-4175/
6569/7230

BASEBALL / BASKETBALL

See Sports

BATH ACCESSORIES

Abu Nil, 41 Sulayman Pasha,
DT (next to Group
Americain)
Patti, 33 Tal'at Harb, DT,
393-7796

Sidi, 159 26th July, ZA,
340-9142

BATHROOM FIXTURES

Faggala, near Midan Ramsis,
many shops
Netline, 13 al-Hikma, Midan
al-'Ataba, MO, 360-6533
Integrated Interiors, 134 al-Nil,
AG, 349-0479 (Kohler,
Gaggenau)

BEAUTY SALONS

Beauty Essentials, 14 Ahmad
Hishmat, ZA, 341-2927
Centre Carita, Sonesta Hotel,
4 al-Tayaran, NC, 262-8111;
261-7100 ext 261,
Madame Veronique.
Color Me Beautiful,
8 al-Sharifa Dina, MA,
375-1830
Gharib (men & women).
Meridien Heliopolis,
290-6617 or 290-5055 ext
8075; 15 Qasr al-Nil, DT,
575-0950
Lily Beauty Recreation Center,
23 Surya, MO, 345-0432,
347-3164, Dr. Nagwa
Mustafa
Mohammed Jr., 20 Sawra, MO,
361-4046/0369 and
Semiramis Hotel, 355-7171/
5920
Santé Sport Beauté, 67 'Abd
al-'Aziz al-Sa'ud, MN,
365-2300, Sharon Rooney

BEAUTY SUPPLIES

Digla Center, Benetton Bldg.,
ZA
La Beauté, 13 Sulayman
Abaza, MO

Morgana, Taha Husayn St,
al-Nil Towers, ZA,
341-4703; Yamama Center,
3rd fl., ZA, 341-1592

BICYCLE REPAIRS

Ghouko Trading & Supply Co.,
99 Gumhuriya, al-Azbakiya
near St. Mark's Church,
935-880.

BICYCLES

Azkalany Bicycle Shop, 12 Rd.
15 and 54 Rd. 77, MA

BICYCLING

See Sports

BILLIARDS

Cheers, 22 Gam'at al-Duwal
al-'Arabiya, MO, 347-6292
Rules, 16 Muhammad Kamel
Mursi, MO, 337-9079

BILLIARD TABLES

Alamein Recreation Products
Co., 13 Mar'ashly, ZA,
340-9987

BOATS & BOATING

Cairo Yachting Club, al-Nil,
Giza, 348-9415, Commodore
Nabil Sirghany
Maadi Yacht Club, Corniche,
Maadi, 375-2066
Ocean Classics, 582-0766; fax
582-0632

BOOKBINDING

Hisham Ragab, L'Orientaliste,
15 Qasr al-Nil, DT,
575-3418
NADIM, al-Mazaniya (off
Sudan behind Coca-Cola
plant), DK, 348-1075

BOOKSTORES

DOKKI

Academic Bookshop,
121 al-Tahrir, DK

DOWNTOWN

Al-Ahram Bookshop, Nile
Hilton front courtyard;
Semiramis Intercontinental
lobby
Anglo-Egyptian Bookshop,
165 Muhammad Farid,
391-4337 (academic/
medical/psychology,
literature)
AUC Bookstore, Main
Campus, Midan al-Tahrir,
357-5377, 354-2964
Dar al-Bustani, 29 Faqqala,
590-8025
El Shorouk, 1 Midan Tal'at
Harb, 391-2480
General Egyptian Book
Organization, 18 26th July
Lehnert and Landrock
44 Sharif, 393-5324
Livres de France, 36 Qasr
al-Nil, 393-5512
L'Orientaliste, 15 Qasr al-Nil,
575-3418; fax 391-1104
(rare/used/new)
Madbouli, 6 Midan Tal'at Harb
Reader's Corner, 33 'Abd
al-Khaliq Sarwat, 392-8801
(rare/new/used)

HELIOPOLIS

Baron Bookshop, Le Meridien
Heliopolis hotel, 290-5055
ext. 8040

Everyman's Bookstore,
12 Baghdad, 417-6064 (good
children's section)
Horus Stationery,
72B Granada, Roxy
International Language
Bookshop, 2 Muhammad
Bayumi (off al-Mirghani),
670-420
Oxford Books, 5 Ibrahim
al-Laqqani, 259-6771

KHAN AL-KHALIL

Seif El Nasr Megahed

MAADI

D & S Bookshop, Maadi Grand
Mall, underground fl.,
518-2112
IPL, 95 Rd. 9, 351-6244
Isis, 88 Rd. 9, 350-6034
Volume I, 17 Rd. 216,
353-8557

MOHANDISEEN

Dar al-Nashr Hatier,
20 al-Sawra, 361-5835
International Language
Bookshop, 3 Mahmud 'Azmi
(off Ahmad 'Urabi),
Sahafiyin, 344-0996
Madbuli, 45 al-Batal Ahmad
'Abd al-'Aziz, 347-7410

ZAMALEK

Aly Masoud, 159 26th July
(entrance from Behler)
AUC Bookstore, 16
Muhammad Ibn Thaqeb,
339-7045
Dar al-Shark, Brazil
Maktabit Hishmat, Ahmad
Hishmat
Shady, 26th July
Zamalek Bookstore, 19
Shagarat al-Durr, 341-9197

BOWLING

Bowling Kingly, Maadi Grand
Mall, 5th fl., 518-1468/1614
El Bustan Bowling Center,
Bustan Commercial Center,
9th fl., Bab al-Luq, DT,
392-8420; 391-8597
Nile Bowling, al-Nil, Agouza

BRASS

See also Khan Khalili
Essam Brass & Copper, 5 Rab'
al-Silahdar, upstairs, KK,
591-8774

BRASS REPAIRS

Sadek Gayed & Sons, 7 Talkha
(at Midan al-Gami'), HE,
241-8417

BREASTFEEDING

La Leche League, contact
Community Services Assoc.,
376-8232; 350-5284 or
Leslie at 340-1373.

BRICKS

The Arab Brick Co., 3 Ahmad
'Urabi, MO, 346-0762

BRIDGE

Bridge Club, Gezirah Sporting
Club; contact Rhoda Boraie,
669-629
Heliopolis Sporting Club, Mon
6pm

Maadi Duplicate Bridge Group,
Tues 6:45 Sofitel Maadi;
contacts: Mrs. Cressaty,
375-3304; Mrs. Issa,
350-3526
Ramses Hilton, Sun. afternoons

BROKERAGE HOUSES

Arab Investment Bank
(Financial Securities),
8 'Abd al-Khaliq Sarwat,
DT, 766-716, fax 766-916
Cairo Stock Exchange, 4A
al-Sharifein, 392-1402/1447,
fax 392-8526
Capital Market Authority,
20 'Imad al-Din, 6th fl., DT,
777-774, 762-626, 755-339
Egyptian Financial Group,
55 Giza, GZ, 628-455,
627-764, fax 571-0849
Egyptians Abroad Investment,
21 Giza, GZ, 729-062, fax
729-106
Hermes Financial, 65 Gam'at
al-Duwal al-'Arabiya, MO,
336-0101/0102/0103, fax
336-0104
El-Eman Co. for Brokerage and
Dealing in Securities (SAE),
105 'Umar Ibn al-Khattab,
HE, 417-8910/2/417-2294/7/
8, fax 417-2295
El-Rashad, al-Bustan Trade
Center, 393-7580
Investment & Securities Group
(ISG), Nile Tower, 21 Giza,
19th fl., GZ, 571-0844/1845,
fax 570-3100
Hussein Shukri & Co., WTC,
13th fl., 1191 Corniche
al-Nil, 779-723
Megavest International, WTC,
19th fl., 1191 Corniche
al-Nil, 574-9662/3/4, fax
574-9665

Misr Financial Investment Co.,
56 Gam'at al-Duwal
al-'Arabiya, MO, 349-8537/
8538, fax 349-3394

Mondial Expatriate Services
Ltd., 5A Rd. 208, Digla,
MA, 353-0626, 517-0090/1,
fax 517-1115

Okaz, 35 'Imad al-Din,
591-8955

Omnia International, 8 Rd. 258,
MA, 352-9526

Triple A Securities,
45A Shambulyun, 3rd fl.,
DT, 578-1302/3

BUSINESS SERVICES CENTERS

CBC (Computer & Business
Center). NC, 275-2256/
2258; Midan al-Tahrir,
354-6311/6152; HE,
418-1167 and 290-8234.

IBA (Int'l Business
Associates), 1079 Corniche
al-Nil, GC, 357-1300 and
354-7475; 21 Muhammad
Ghunaym, HE, 291-3410;
24 Surya, MO, 349-0986 and
360-1276; 31 Gulf, MA,
351-6070; 19 Rd. 151, MA,
351-9917

ISS (Int'l. Service Systems,
19 al-Shahid Hilmi al-Misri,
Almaza, HE, 291-2218, fax
418-7273

Markenz Services, 81 'Abd
al-Hamid Badawi, HE,
241-8269; 248-7216; fax
244-0115

Premeir Recruitment, 16A
Ma'mal al-Sukkar, GC,
355-0776

BUSINESS EQUIPMENT

See also Computers

Xerox, 2 Lebnan, MO,
344-4918; for servicing,
347-7735

Systel, 2A Shafiq Mansur, ZA,
341-1800; al-Sheikh Gadd
al-Haqq, NC, 401-8892;
Maadi Grand Mall, MA,
517-1218 (pagers/beepers)

BUTCHERS

Boucherie de la Republique
Bolbol, 122 26th July, ZA,
340-2330; 341-1940

Maison Thomas, 157 26th July,
ZA, 340-7057 (pork)

Miro Protein Market, 84 Rd. 9,
MA (pork)

Morcos, Ataba Market Grand
Bazaar, 390-5477, DT (pork)

Omarah, 13 Chiribini at
Sulayman Gohar, DK
337-4068

Sobkey Protein (larger),
al-Tahrir at Dokki, DK,
348-3522/3

Sobkey Protein (smaller),
103 al-Tahrir, DK, 335-8291

Viennoise Meat Market,
3 Midan Tal'at Harb (across
from Sednaoui), DT,
393-6294 (pork)

CABINET-MAKER

Nabil, 440-4248; furniture,
cabinets; will come to your
home

CAFÉS

Coffee Roastery, 3 Makka (off
Sulayman Abaza), MO,
361-0995

CyberCafé, 2 Midan Qasr
al-Dubara, 6th fl., GC,
356-2882, fax 354-9611,
email: info@brainy1.ie-eg.
com

Maison Thomas, 157 26th July,
ZA, 340-7057

Simonds, 112 26th July, ZA,
340-9436

CALL-BACK SERVICES

Cross Communications,
202 al-Higaz, HE, 241-1141,
244-4123, 249-2496/3186

Kallback (USA) 206-284-8600;
fax: 206-282-6666; email:
care@kallback.com

New World
Telecommunications (USA)
201-996-1670; fax: 201-996-
1870. email: newworld@
newworldtele.com.

CAR & MOTORCYCLE RALLEYS

Pharoah's Rally, contact Rami
Siag at Siag Travel,
385-2626, fax 384-0874

Motocross, contact Raed
Baddar, 290-0989

CAR RENTAL

Alex Limousine, 33 al-Tawfiq,
NC, 401-7251, 401-7350

Avis, 16A Ma'mal al-Sukkar,
GC, 354-7400/7081/8698,
fax 356-2464

Bita Car Rental, 73 al-Nuzha,
Manshiet al-Bakri,
454-2620, 23 Dr. Ahmad
Zaki, al-Nuzha al-Gadida,
299-1527, 1628, fax
299-1799

Budget Rent-A-Car,
5 al-Maqrizi, ZA, 340-0070/
9474/2565, fax 341-3790,
Marriott Hotel (24 hours),
340-8888, CA, 291-4288/99,
85 Rd. 9, MA, 350-2724;
1 Muhammad 'Ibid, HE,
291-8244, 667-711

Egytrav, (24 hours), Nile
Hilton Hotel, DT, 576-7444/
5666, fax 577-8861

Elite Rent-A-Car, 2 Tahran (off
Musaddaq), DK, 360-9976,
337-6050, fax 337-6050

Europcar/InterRent, Egypt,
Max Bldg., 27 Libnan, MO,
347-4712/3, 345-1022, fax
303-6123

Fast Car Rental, 7 Yanbu', DK,
361-3743, fax 348-3937

Hepton Limousine (buses
only), al-Nuzha, HE,
417-7800/7900

Hertz Rent-A-Car, 195, 26th
July, AG, 303-4241,
347-4172/2238, fax
344-6627

Iveco (bus & coach),
22 Mahmud Basyuni, DT,
759-061, 747-006, 747-377

Limousine Misr Touristic
Company, Misr Travel
Tower, 13th fl., Midan
al-'Abbasiya, DT, 285-6721,
fax 285-6124

Mohammed Hafez Co. (car &
limousine), 4A Harun, DK,
360-0542, 348-6652, fax
348-1105

Rawas Car & Limousine
Rental, 4 Tahran (off
Musaddaq), DK, 349-9831,
710- 477, 349-5313, fax
349-9831; Gezirah Sheraton
341-1333/1555 ext. 8341/2;
Ramses Hilton 777-444; CA
291-4255/77/88/99 ext:
2207/8

Smart Limo, 151 Corniche
al-Nil, DT, 365-4321/2/3,
fax 363-7231

Sunshine Car & Bus Rentals,
106 Muhammad Farid, DT,
392-2559/6326

Top Car, 11 al-Misaha, DK,
349-9585/9363

CARPET CLEANING & REPAIR

Ali Kazrouni, 14 Sarwat
(across from U. Cairo
Faculty of Commerce), DK,
349-3011

El Assiouty, 118 26th July, ZA,
341-6732

El Kabbany, 11 Khan
al-Khalili, KK, 914-236

Mohammed Rahmy, 5 Rab'
al-Silahdar, 907-873,
591-2282

Nasr Ahmed Mohammed,
7 Isma'il Muhammad, ZA,
342-0852

CARPETS

Classic Carpet, 10 al-'Ubur
Bldgs., Salah Salem, HE,
263-3097

El-Assiouty, 7 al-Batal Ahmad
'Abd al-'Aziz, MO,
345-1499

El-Assiouty, 118 26th July,
ZA, 341-6732, 342-1609

Mamdouh El-Assiouty, Sofitel,
MA, 351-6777

Medhat El-Assiouty, 31 Muhi
al-Din Abu al-'Izz, MO,
336-0305, 337-4975

Oriental Weavers, Airport Rd,
HE, and off Gam'at
al-Duwal al-'Arabiya, MO

CARS, CLASSIC --- REPAIRS

Club Mohammed Aly
(pre-1950 car club); contact:
Maged Farag, Max Group,
246-5233

Ramadan Mohsen, behind City
of the Dead, Fustat,
352-7319

Safwat Saleh, 3 Yusuf
al-Digwi, MN, 364-4014
(mechanical)

Samayo Car & Part Co.,
25 al-Lasilki (behind
satellite station), MA,
352-1384

CARS, NEW

Daewoo Motor, 195 26th July,
AG,303-1583/1595

KIA Motors, 69 al-Nasr Rd,
New Maadi, MA, 518-1782/
5/fax 518-1786 (Duty-free
available)

Modern Free Zone, 11 'Uqba,
DK, 348-8500/1; 349-2930
(Suzuki & Nissan)

CATERING

Amelia's Kitchen, 585-2301
(Brazilian specialities)

Bon Appetit, 21 Wadi al-Nil,
MO, 342-4815; 2 Isma'il
Muhammad, ZA, 340-4382

CARE Service, 339-7109

Samy, 10 Bahr al-Ghazal (off
Ahmad 'Urabi), Sahafiyin,
MO, 346-6393 (ice cream,
dairy products, etc.)

CHEMICALS, AGRICULTURAL

Ismail Ahmed al-Hadidi and
Co., 17 al-Higaz, MO,
346-0521, fax 346-4930

CHILDREN'S ENTERTAINMENT

See also Amusement Parks
Young Star Club, Forte Grand
Hotel, Alexandria Desert
Road, Pyramids, 383-0383/
0772
ZASSY Puppets, 346-8705

CHURCHES

DOKKI

German Evangelical Church
Community (Lutheran).
6 Gaber Ibn Hayyan,
361-4398; contact: Rev.
Gunter Selbach.

DOWNTOWN

Christian Science Society.
3 Midan Mustafa Kamel,
DT.
Church of God: St Andrew's
United Church Hall, 26th
July and Ramsis 759-451/
360-3527.
Eglise Evangelique du Caire,
services in MA and DT;
contact Pasteur Martin,
392-8199.
Friends Meeting (Quaker).
Meetings move from home
to home; contact Ray at
357-6969 or Johanna at
357-3653.
St. Andrew's United Church,
38 26th July (between Galaa
& Ramsis); contact: Rev.
Michael Shelley, 759-451/
360-3527.

St. Joseph's Roman Catholic
Church, Muhammad Farid;
contact: Father Mamdouh
Shehab Bassilios, 393-6677.
Daily mass in French at
7:30am and 6:30pm;
Saturday rosary 6:10pm (Fr);
Sunday masses: 7:30am (Fr),
8:30am (Arabic), 10am
(Ital), 12n (Fr), 4:30pm
(Eng), and 6:30pm (Fr).
Mailing address: PO Box 4,
Sharia Muhammad Farid,
11111 Ataba, Cairo; fax
392-0859

HELIOPOLIS

Heliopolis Community Church
(at St. Michael's, below);
contact: Rev. Bill Grossman,
418-6828.
St. Anthony's Coptic Orthodox
Church, 'Ali 'Abd al-Razik
(off al-Higaz); contact:
Father Antonius, 246-4962
St. Clare's Convent, Isna,
290-7188
St. Michael's Episcopal
Church, 10 Siti (off
Baghdad)

MAADI

Church of Christ Fellowship,
Rd. 11, Bldg 18, Apt 38;
376-8376
Church of Jesus Christ of
Latter Day Saints, 21 Rd. 17,
350-1676 or 350-8746.
German Evangelical Church (at
St. John's, below); contact:
Rev. Selbach, 347-8549.
Holy Family Church (Roman
Catholic), 55 Rd. 15;
contact: Father Abel,
350-2004.
Korean Church (at St. John's,
below); contact: Rev.
Joon-Kyo Lee, 350-4620.

Maadi Community Church (at
St. John's, below); contact:
Dave Petrescue, Senior
Pastor, 351-2755
St. John the Baptist
(Episcopal/Anglican), Rd. 17
& Port Said; contact: Rev.
Robin Lee, 351-5459/
340-7032 or Cy Reed,
Church Warden, 353-1453.

ZAMALEK

All Saints' Cathedral
(Episcopal/Anglican),
5 Mishil Lutfallah,
341-8391. Jim Doust,
provost & chaplain,
340-2074
St. Joseph's Roman Catholic
Church, 4 Ahmad Sabri;
contact: Father Pio,
340-8902.

CIGARS

La Casa Del Hubano,
Semiramis Hotel, 355-7171

CINEMAS

Al Haram, al-Haram, GZ,
385-8358
Al Horreya 1 and 2, al-Ahram,
HE, 452-9980
Al Tahrir, 112 al-Tahrir, DK,
335-4726
Cairo, Saray al-Azbakiyya, DT,
574-5350
Cairo Sheraton, Giza, DK,
336-9700/9800
Cosmos 1 and 2, 'Imad al-Din,
DT, 574-2177
Diana, 17 Alfi, DT, 924-727
Faten Hamama, MN, 364-9767
Karim 1 and 2, 15 'Imad
al-Din, DT, 591-6095
Qasr al-Nil, Qasr al-Nil, DT,
575-0761

Lido, 23 'Imad al-Din, DT,
934-284
Metro, 35 Tal'at Harb, DT,
393-7566
MGM, Maadi Grand Mall,
MA, 352-3066
Miami, 38 Tal'at Harb, DT,
574-5656
Normandy, 31 al-Ahram, HE,
258-0254
Odeon, 4 'Abd al-Hamid Sa'id,
DT, 575-8797
Radio, Tal'at Harb, DT,
575-6562
Ramses Hilton 1 & 2, top floor
of Annex, 574-7436
Rivoli 1 and 2, 26th July, DT,
575-5053
Roxy, Midan Roxy, HE,
258-0344
Sphinx, Midan Sphinx, MO,
346-4017
Swissôtel Cairo al-Salam
Hotel, 65 'Abd al-Hamid
Badawi, HE, 297-4000/6000
Tiba 1 and 2, Nasr, NC,
262-9407

CLEANING SERVICES

First Inter-City, 390-9103
Makram Cleaning Service,
Digla, MA, 353-3212

CLINICS

MAADI
Cairo Cancer Clinic,
33 Corniche al-Nil,
378-3774
Family Healthcare Clinic,
71 Rd. 9 (above Baskin
Robbins), 375-6766;
Dr. Mahmud Shirbini and
Jaqueline Shirbini, RN;
family medicine, general and
critical care, anesthesiology
and cardiology

MOHANDISEEN
Cairo Breast Clinic,
2 al-Fakawih (above
Chili's), 336-6645
Cairo Medical Tower, 55 'Abd
al-Mun'im Riyad, 344-5717
CairoScan & Cairo Radiology
Centre, 35 Sulayman Abaza,
704263; 717480; 361-3736
Shaalan Clinic, 11 al-'Anab,
348-3807/5479 and
360-3293; director:
Dr. Karim Shaalan,
360-5180.
Shaalan Surgicenter, 10 'Abd
al-Hamid Lutfi, 360-3920;
fax 360-3124

ZAMALEK
BCA (British Community
Association) Clinic,
Anglo-American Hospital,
ZA, 341-8630 (direct),
340-6162/3/4/5 ext. 315

CLOCK & WATCH REPAIR (ANTIQUE)

Francis Papazian, Midan
Ataba, 390-5616
Tewfik Goma, near Flower
Market, Muski

CLOTHING

ACCESSORIES
Tumuh, 63 al-Sayed al-Bakri,
ZA, 341-5243 (scarves)

ALTERATIONS
Chamade, 96 al-Mirghani, HE,
290-9995

CASUAL & SPORTSWEAR
Elegante, 1A al-Sayed al-Bakri,
ZA, 340-3425 (women's)

Mix and Match, branches
everywhere (WTC, Ramses
and Nile Hiltons, DT, MA,
HE, ZA), 340-1182,
303-8666, 303-9555
Naf Naf, branches everywhere
(MO, HE, DT, MA, WTC,
ZA), 360-1023
Rimy & Riry, 8 Brazil, ZA,
340-9633 (handmade
sweaters)
On Safari, branches
everywhere (46 Nuzha, HE,
666-680; 20 Sharifa Dina,
MA, 375-9194; 10 Mishil
Lutfallah, ZA, 340-1901;
WTC, 774-261; Nile Hilton,
578-0444

CHILDREN'S
Babycare, 17 Hasan Sabri, ZA,
340-4661 and al-Batal
Ahmad 'Abd al-'Aziz, MO
Bambi, Qambiz, DK, 337-8325
Bunny's, 12 Sulayman Abaza,
MO, 361-0156; call for other
new locations (MA, Nile
Hilton)
Gerard Darel Kids, 6 'Abd
al-Hamid Lutfi, MO,

DISCOUNT
New York, 48 Silim al-Awal,
Zeitun, and 44 Ramsis,
Roxy, HE, 259-1769

ETHNIC
Ed-Dukkan, Yamama Center,
ZA, 341-6500 ext 216 and
Ramses Hilton
Ethno, 38 Rd. 6, MA, 350-6473
Hazem Hafez, 35 Nazih
Khalifa, HE, 258-1376

LINGERIE
Elle, Fayrouz Center, 140 26th
July, ZA, 341-0147
Frivole, 38 al-Kawthar St, MO,
360-4868
Jolie Jolie (Valisere)
33 'Amman, DK, 360-3819

La Beauté, 13 Sulayman
Abaza, MO

MEN'S

Arrogant, Midan Ibn al-Walid
near Shooting Club,
335-1470

Only Ties, 2nd fl., WTC,
764-424 ext 4274;
41 al-Batal Ahmad 'Abd
al-'Aziz, MO, 344-0442

The Shirt Shop, Cairo Marriott,
Ramses Hilton, Semiramis;
also 9 Sulayman Abaza, MO
and 39 Syria, MO

MISCELLANEOUS

Sharia Shawarbi, DT, for every
kind of clothing

WOMEN'S DESIGNER & HIGH FASHION

Boutique Up 16, 114 26th July
St, ZA, 341-8459

De Luca, 4 al-Gezira, ZA,
340-4434

Fashion, 39 'Abd al-Mun'im
Riyad, MO, 348-3373;
360-7774

Luciano di Nardo, 215 Sudan,
MO, 344-8375 and 1 Brazil,
ZA, 341-2428

Moods, 27 Abu al-Fida, ZA,
341-3634

Pandora's Box, WTC,
578-8729

Queeny, 17 Sulayman Abaza,
MO, 349-6638

Selective, 42 Musaddaq, DK,
335-2893

Stephanie, 10 Mahmud 'Azmi,
ZA, 341-3926; 49 Dr. Hasan
Aflatun, Nuzha, HE,
257-2903

WOMEN'S-EVENING

Bekhita, Cairo Marriott, ZA,
340-1094

Boutique Viola, 20 al-Sawra,
MO, 360-0540

Cocktails, 2 Bahgat 'Ali, ZA,
341-8043

Donna, 25 Makka at Muhi
al-Din Abu al-'Izz, MO,
337-0928

Fantastic, 5 Brazil, ZA,
340-9930; Owner: Taheni

Manelia, 18 al-Quds al-Sharif,
MO, 344-8488 (also dressy
sportswear)

Melodies, 24 al-Sawra, MO,
336-7424 (also dressy
sportswear)

CLUBS

See Organizations

COFFEE

Café do Brasil, 1 al-Qadi Abu
Seif, DK, 349-7375

Coffee Roastery, 3 Makka (off
Sulayman Abaza), MO,
361-0995, fax 352-5789

El Oruba, 103 al-Tahrir, DK

TCBY, 14 Sur Nadi
al-Zamalek (off Gam'at
al-Duwal al-'Arabiya), MO,
302-8690

COMMUNITY ASSOCIATIONS

See Organizations

COMPACT DISKS

Jukebox, WTC, 578-2980

COMPUTER CLASSES

British Council, 192 al-Nil,
AG, 303-1514; 347-6118;
fax 344-3076

COMPUTERS

SALES, REPAIRS, MAINTENANCE, SUPPLIES, TRAINING

Note: All recommended by
users and/or computer
professionals

Alpha Omega Group,
102A al-Nil, DK, 360-3350;
349-2652

Amr Aboul Dahab, Midan Fini,
DK, 361-4189, 336-0217

AppleLine Computer, 75 Qasr
al-Aini, GC, 355-1200/1356
(IBM & Apple, new & used)

Aptec Egypt, 3 Mahmud
Nashed, HE, 245-5634; fax
247-5255 (Epson, Microsoft,
Fujitsu, Borland)

CBC (Computer & Business
Center) NC, 275-2256/2258;
Midan al-Tahrir, 354-6311/
6152; HE, 418-1167 and
290-8234 (hard/software for
IBM, Microsoft, Apple,
Xerox, HP)

CITE, Suite 77, 7th fl., 68 Qasr
al-Aini, GC, 354-5626;
356-0531 (indiv. & instit.,
mainly Apple)

Computek, 23 'Amer, DK,
360-2234; 154 al-'Uruba,
HE, 418-2264 & 417-4297

Diamond, 126 al-Nil, DK,
360-0857 (Parts)

Egos, 14 Mustafa Mafarasha
(off Mirghani), HE,
418-8196/3138; contact:
Alaa El Shimmy.

Egyptian Advanced
Technologies, 3 'Usman Ibn
'Affan, MO, 344-3001

El Nekhely Bros.,
176 al-Tahrir, Bab al-Luq,
DT, 392-7529; 393-6301;
fax 392-8612; contacts:
Emad or Wagid

ETS, 193 Sudan, MO,
303-7512/9151; Maadi
Town Center, Rd. 151, MA,
375-3457

Gateway 2000/Blue Max,
10A 'Umar Tusun (off
Ahmad 'Urabi at Midan
Sphinx), MO, 303-5473;
contacts: Mustafa Abu Bakr
& Selim Gamal (Gateway,
Fountain)

Giza Systems Engineering,
2 Midan al-Misaha, DK,
349-0140; fax 349-9253

Kolaly Engineering, 15 Nadi
al-Seid, MO, 335-6499; fax
348-2732 (IBM, instiutional)

Logitek, 336 al-Haram, GZ,
868-888.

Micom, 7 Dr. Hussein Kamel,
Nuzha, HE, 244-0466

Ofis, Badr al-Din, MO,
303-1221, 346-0705/0712;
contact: Engineer
Muhammad

Pyramids Computer Center,
54 'Abbas al-'Aqqad, NC,
260-6004

CONSULTANTS

Center for Quality Assurance,
21 Yusuf al-Gindy, 3rd fl.,
Bab al-Luq, 395-0952/3,
393-2996, fax 395-0954

International Executive
Services Corporation,
Bustan Commercial Center,
Suite 1, 390-3232, fax
390-2929

TerraConsult, 32 'Abd
al-Khaliq Sarwat, 392-6497/
33, fax 390-8600

CONFERENCE CENTER

Cairo International Conference
Center (CICC), NC,
263-4631/2

CONTACT LENSES

See Opticians

COOKWARE

See Kitchenware

COPPER

See Khan Khalili

CORK BOARDS & DART BOARDS

Maher El Sabagh, Shubra,
574-0023

COSMETICS

See Beauty Supplies

COUNTRY CLUBS

See Sporting & Country Clubs

COURIERS

DHL, 34 'Abd al-Khaliq
Sarwat, DT, 393-8988/5322;
20 Gamal al-Din Abu
al-Mahasen, GC, 355-7118/
7301; 35 Isma'il Ramzi, HE,
246-0324/3751; 43 Rd. 6,
MA, 375-8900; 16 Libnan,
MO, 302-9801, fax
302-9810

Express Mail Service, Midan
al-'Ataba, 390-5874/69 and
most post offices

Federal Express,
sales/advertising/new
accounts: 290-7337,
357-1300; 1073 Corniche
al-Nil, 1st fl., GC, 357-1300;
hotline 290-7337; 21
Muhammad Ghunaym, HE,
290-3773/ 291-6996; 31
Gulf, New Maadi, MA,
351-6070 and Midan
Hurriya, 350-7172; 24
Surya, MO, 349-0986,
361-5653

IML Air Couriers, 2 Mustafa
Kamel, MA, 350-1160/1240/
1241, 375-1598, fax
350-1240

Middle East Couriers,
1 Mahmud Hafez, Midan
Safir, HE, 245-9281,
243-6328

SOS Sky International,
45 Shihab, MO, 346-0028/
2503

TNT Skypak, 33 Dokki, DK,
348-8204/7228; fax
346-0028

World Courier Egypt, 17 Qasr
al-Nil, DT, 777-678,
741-313, 753-611, 390-587/
69

CRANE RENTALS

Target, 2 Sulayman Abaza,
MO, 360-3052

Triangle, 30 Nadi al-Seid, MO,
349-7875, 348-3664

CREDIT CARDS, LOST

See front of Directory

CRUISES

See Travel Agents

CULTURAL CENTERS

See Organizations

CURTAINS

See Fabrics

CUSTOMS CLEARING AGENTS

See Movers (int'l)

DANCE CLASSES

See Sports

DAYCARE

See Schools

DENTISTS

See Doctors

DANCE GROUPS

Cairo Scottish Country Dance Group; contacts: Lilian Clephane, 340-4692; Peter Stogden, 341-8347

St. Andrew's Church Scottish Country Dance Group; contacts: Nelle Evenhouse, 247-1445; David Davies, 352-7376

DEPARTMENT STORES

Omar Effendi, branches everywhere; one of the best is on Ahmad 'Urabi, MO

Salon Vert, 28 Qasr al-Nil, DT, 393-1937/1866

Sednaoui, 17 Qasr al-Nil, DT, 393-7990

DESERT AND/OR DIVING SAFARIS

Abercrombie & Kent (Trailmasters), Bustan Commercial Center, 10th fl., Bab al-Luq, DT, 393-6272

Isis Travel, 48 Giza, GZ, 348-7761/5592

Maadi Adventures, 14 al-Naser, HE, 244-5147; contact: Diaa Shawki

Maadi Divers, 18 Rd. 218, Digla, MA, 353-7144

Max Travel, 27 Libnan, MO, 347-4713

Red Sea Yacht Safari, 202-4924, fax 575-7864, Dr. Mounir Phillips

Saad Ali, 345-8524

Siag Travel, Siag Pyramids Hotel, Saqqara Rd., PY, 385-1444/2626

DIRECTORIES

American Chamber of Commerce Membership Directory, Cairo Marriott, ZA, 340-8888 ext. 1541, fax 340-9482

Egypt Trade, ABC Business Service Ltd. Head Office: 6 al-Ma'had al-Sahari, HE. 417-8428; 418-3445; fax 417-8428

Focus Area Guides, ABC Business Service Ltd. Head Office: 6 al-Ma'had al-Sahari, HE. 417-8428; 418-3445; fax 417-8428

Kompass Directories, Fiani & Partners, 143 al-Tahrir, DK, 348-7353; fax 348-5204.

Maadi Women's Guild Telephone Directory. Available through American Chamber of Commerce (340-8888 ext. 1541); Community Services Association (350-5284); Maadi Community Church (351-2755); Women's Association (360-3475); Heliopolis Community Church (66-0146)

Resorts of Egypt, Misr Institution for Advertising, 262-6066

DISCOTHEQUES

See also Bars

Atlantis, Shepheard Hotel, Corniche al-Nil, GC, 355-3800

Casanova, al-Burg Hotel, Saray al-Gezira, near Opera House, 341-4746, 340-6176

Jackie's. Nile Hilton Hotel, Midan al-Tahrir, DT, 767-444, 765-666

Tamango, Atlas Zamalek Hotel, 20 Gam'at al-Duwal al-'Arabiya, MO, 346-4157/5782/6569

Upstairs, WTC

DOCTORS

HOSPITAL/CLINIC CONTACT TELEPHONE NUMBERS:

Anglo-American Hospital, ZA, 340-6162/3/4/5; BCA Clinic, ext 315

As-Salam Hospital, MO, 302-9091/5

As-Salam Hospital, MA: 363-8050; outpatient clinic, 362-0644

Cairo Tower Hospital, Cairo Medical Tower, CairoScan, MO, 303-0810/0815

Nil Badrawi Hospital, MA:
363-8684/8688
Shaalan Surgicenters, MO:
348-3807/5479, 360-3293

ALLERGIST

Dr. Hisham Taraf, Nil Badrawi
Hospital and Cairo Tower
Hospital lab, 350-9781

CANCER SPECIALISTS

Dr. Reda Hamza, National
Cancer Institute, 989-531/
711; also contact Director of
Nursing: Dr. Nagwa
El-Khasib, 362-8199.

CARDIOLOGISTS

Dr. 'Abd al-Hakim Mahmud,
2 Sharif, DT, 392-1576
Dr. Ayman Aboul Meguid,
As-Salam and Shalaan
Surgicenter
Dr. Galal el Sayid,
121 Muhammad Farid St,
Bab al-Luq, DT, 391-1333,
As-Salam Hospital, & home
350-1807
Dr. Emad Awad, Anglo
American Hospital, ZA,
340-6162/3/4/5

CHILD PSYCHOLOGY/PSYCHIATRY

Dr. Emad Ismail, HE, h:
291-4006

DENTISTS

Dr. Aida Bastawi (General &
Cosmetic), 183 al-Tahrir
(Strand Building), DT,
354-7554
Dr. Ibrahim Hanna, Mirghani,
HE, 291-5668
Dr. Wafik Mahrous, 87 Rd. 9,
MA, 351-4067/350-2323, h:
351-1158/350-3660
Dr. Rawy Barsoum, 1 Rd. 217,
Digla, MA, 353-1510
Dr. Ihab Korra, 60 Libnan, 1st
fl., 346-8004

Dr. Raouf Abbassy,
9 Gabalaya, Tonsi Bldg.,
ZA, 340-1133/1144

DERMATOLOGISTS

Dr. Medhat el Mufti, As-Salam
Hospital
Dr. Ramzi Onsy,
Anglo-American Hospital

EAR NOSE THROAT

Dr. Abu Bakr Shannon, 73 Rd.
9, MA, 351-5631
Dr. Ayman Daoud,
Anglo-American

GENERAL PRACTITIONERS

Dr. Magdy Wissa, 662-198,
672-444, 384-2022/2024
Dr. Sherif Zakher,
Anglo-American and
340-9836, h: 417-9396;
beeper: 777-474 + 911741

HEMATOLOGIST

Dr. Sabry Megally, 32 Gulf,
MA, 375-9275

INTERNAL MEDICINE

Dr. Akil Youssef, BCA Clinic,
Anglo-American Hospital,
ZA, 341-8630 (direct),
340-6162/3/4/5 ext. 315

MAMMOGRAPHY

Dr. Hanan Gweifel, CairoScan,
MO

NEUROLOGIST

Dr. Akil Youssef, BCA Clinic
at Anglo-American,
341-8630 (direct)
Dr. Hassan Hosny, Shaalan
Surgicenter and Cairo
Medical Tower

NEUROSURGEONS

Dr. Ahmed Naguid, As-Salam
Hospital and 47 'Abd
al-'Aziz al-Sa'ud, MN,
362-3300, h: 375-1315

Dr. Ahmed Zokhdi,
Anglo-American Hospital

OBSTETRICS/GYNECOLOGY

Dr. Hossam Badrawi, h:
344-2260 & Nil Badrawi
Hospital
Dr. Mahmud Sobeih, Family
Health Care Clinic, MA,
375-6766
Dr. Salah Zaki, above
Aberdeen Steak, Rd. 9, MA,
351-2844 (infertility
specialist)
Dr. Sameh Zaki, 66 al-Manial,
MN, and As-Salam Hospital
outpatient, 362-0644
Dr. Salah Bassili, Anglo
American Hospital
Dr. Claude Mehreb, HE,
244-0848
Dr. Ahmed Menaoui, Shaalan
Surgicenter
Dr. May Hobrouk, Shaalan
Surgicenter and Family
Health Care Clinic, MA,
375-6766; h: 337-4383
Dr. Nevine Hafnawi, Cairo
Motherhood Center,
360-1605
Dr. Sherif Hamza,
53 al-Zahraa, MO, 348-3424
and al-Fayrouz & Damascus
Hospitals

OPTHAMOLOGISTS

Dr. 'Abdel Hassouna,
Anglo-American Hospital
Dr. Samia Sabry, 3 Rd. 79,
Delta Bank Building, MA,
350-8503

ORAL DENTAL AND MAXILLOFACIAL SURGEONS

Dr. Hatem Abdel Rahman, 17
Gam'at al-Duwal al-
'Arabiya, MO, 347-8282

Dr. Mahmud Hosny, 40 Tal'at
Harb, Apt. 31, 575-7910; fax
575-6276; 24-hr. beeper:
575-1851, then request
906-953 or 903-401; email:
dsmc@ritsec1.com.eg.

ORTHOPEDISTS

Dr. Atef Hanna, Anglo-
American Hospital
Dr. Samir Fanous, Shaalan
Surgicenter (348-5479) and
18 Mahmud Basyuni,
575-4623
Dr. Sherif Zaghloul, 6 Rd.
162A, MA, 378-7208,
351-5806

PLASTIC & RECONSTRUCTIVE SURGEONS

Dr. Fathi Khodeir, Cairo Tower
and 574-3747, 772-586; h:
572-6372
Dr. Hassan Abou Elsoud, Cairo
Medical Center, Midan
Roxy, HE, 258-1206/0566
Dr. Ibrahim Naguib, Shaalan
Surgicenters
Dr. Karim Massaoud,
Anglo-American and Ain
Shams
Dr. Nabil Elsahy, Cairo Tower
Hospital

PEDIATRICIANS

Dr. Adel Reyad, 10 Abu Bakr
al-Siddiq, HE, 249-6373
(off.), 243-0842, 247-8788
(home)
Dr. Fawzan Shaltout, 87 Rd. 9,
MA, 351-5323
Dr. Ibrahim Shoukry, Cairo
Tower and h: 351-1342,
evenings, 302-4577
Dr. Nasr Gamril, 344-8055 and
h: 302-2255
Dr. Lamas Ragab, Shaalan
Surgicenter

Dr. Sandra (aka Hayatt)
Tabbara, Shaalan
Surgicenter
Dr. Sherif Ibaa Faltaous, 43 Rd.
9, MA, 350-5196
Prof Elhamy Rifky, 8 Rd. 78,
MA, 351-5347

PSYCHOLOGISTS/ PSYCHIATRISTS

Dr. Isis Badrawi, Community
Services Association,
340-5284, 376-8283
Dr. Nasser Loza, Behman
Hospital, Helwan,
350-0711/229-2821

SURGEONS, GENERAL

Dr. Adel Hosny, 3 Rd. 79,
Delta Bank Blg, MA, Tel:
378-7525, ,
Dr. Galil Greis, Anglo-
American, As-Salam, and
31 Wizarat al-Zira'a, DK,
335-9334
Dr. Samir Massaoud,
Anglo-American

UROLOGIST

Dr. Hossam Mustafa, As-Salam
and Shaalan Surgicenter

DOORKNOBS

Modern Metals, 1 Qattawi,
Ataba

DRAMA GROUPS

Cairo Players; contacts:
Andrew Austin, 340-0137;
Matthew Kleinosky,
350-7183
HCAA Drama Group; contact:
Penny Thorpe, 669-535
Maadi Community Players;
contacts: Dave Torgerson,
375-2420; Ann Leibner,
351-4840

DRAPERIES

See Fabrics

DRESSMAKERS/DESIGNERS

Dafna Edwards, DK, 337-9597
Women's Association (for
referrals), 360-3475

DRYCLEANERS

Select, 50 Muhammad
Hishmat, ZA (specialist in
leather)

DUTY FREE SHOPS

106 Gam'at al-Duwal
al-'Arabiya, MO, 335-8258.
349-7092/4; manager:
Mme. Sanaa
Cairo Sheraton, GZ, 348-8600

EDUCATIONAL EVALUATIONS

Beth Nougaim, CSA, 350-5284

EMBASSIES AND CONSULATES

Afghanistan, 59 'Uruba, HE,
666-653, 662262,
fax 662-262
Albania, 29 Isma'il
Muhammad, ZA, 341-5651,
341-1064, fax 341-3732
Algeria, 14 Brazil, ZA,
340-7671/2466, 341-8527,
fax 3414158
Angola, 12 Fuad Muhi al-Din,
MO, 707-683, fax 3498259

Argentina, 8 al-Saleh Ayub,
Apt. 2, ZA, 340-1501/5243,
341-7765/6862, fax
341-4355
Australia, Cairo Plaza, South
Bldg., 5th and 6th floors,
Corniche al-Nil, Boulaq,
777-900/357/273/495, fax
768220
Austria, al-Nil (corner of Wisa
Wasef), 5th fl., GZ, 570-
2974, fax 570-2979
Azerbijan, 22 Hasan 'Asem,
ZA, 340-1230, fax 341-1228
Bahrain, 15 Brazil, ZA,
341-6604/6605/6609, fax
341-6609
Bangladesh, 47 Ahmad
Hishmat, ZA, 340-2401,
341-2645, fax 341-2631
Belgium, 20 Kamel
al-Shinnawi, GC, 354-7494/
95/96, fax 354-3147
Bolivia, 2 Hud al-Labban, GC,
354-6390
Bosnia/Herzogovinia, 15B
Taha Husayn, ZA, 340-0600
Brazil, 1125 Corniche al-Nil,
Maspero, 756-938, 773-013,
fax 761040
Brunei, 11 'Amer, Midan
al-Misaha, DK, 360-9735,
fax 361-5739
Burkina Faso, 9 Fawakih, MO,
360-8480, 709-098, fax
349-5310
Burundi, 22 Nakhil Madinet
al-Zubbat, DK, 337-8346,
337-3078, fax 337-8431
Cambodia, 2 Tahawia, GZ,
348-8934
Cameroon, 15 al-Israa, MO,
344-1114, 344-1101, fax
345-9208
Canada, 6 Muhammad Fahmi
al-Sayed, GC, 354-3110, fax
356-3548
Central African Republic,
41 Muhammad 'Azmi,
Sahafiyin, MO, 344-6873

Chad, 12 Midan al-Rifa'i, DK,
703-232, 703-379,
349-4461, fax 704-726
Chile, 5 Shagarat al-Durr, ZA,
340-8446/8711, fax
340-3716
China, 22 Bahgat Ali, ZA,
341-6561/7423, fax
341-7691
Colombia, 20A Gamal al-Din
Abu al-Mahasin, GC,
354-6152/3402, fax
355-7087
Commission of the European
Community, 6 Ibn Zanki,
ZA, 341-9393
Comoros, 4 Sa'id 'Abd
al-Wahed, MO, 344-4108,
fax 346-6698
Croatia, 3 Abu al-Fida, 10th fl.,
ZA, 340-5815/9802, fax
340-5812
Cuba, 6 al-Fawakih, MO,
710-525/564, fax 704298
Cyprus, 23A Isma'il
Muhammad, ZA, 341-1288/
0327, fax 341-5299
Czech Republic, 4 al-Duqqi,
GZ, 348-5469/5531, fax
360-8089
Denmark, 12 Hasan Sabri, ZA,
340-7411/2502/8673, fax
341-1780
Djibouti, 11 Muhammad Abu
al-Sa'id, DK, 345-6546/7,
fax 345-65 49
Ecuador, 4/6 Ibn Kawthar,
Suez Canal Bldg., GZ,
349-6782, 702-385, fax
360-9327
El Salvador, 20 al-Sadd al-'Ali,
DK, 700-834,
Eritrea, 13 Muhammad Shafiq,
MO, 344-7093, 303-0517
Ethiopia, 3 Ibrahim 'Usman,
MO, 347-7805, fax
347-9002
Finland, 3 Abu al-Fida, 13th fl.,
ZA, 341-1487/3722/7786,
340-2801, fax 340-5170

France, 29 al-Nil, GZ,
570-3920/19, fax 571-0276
Gabon, 17 Makka
al-Mukarrama, DK,
348-1395, 709-699
Germany, 8 Hasan Sabri, ZA,
341-0015, 340-5017/6017,
fax 341-0530
Ghana, 1 26th July, MO,
303-2295/4, 344-4000/455,
fax 303-2292
Great Britain, 7 Ahmad
Ragheb, GC, 354-0850/51/
52/58, fax 354-0859
Greece, 18 'Aysha
al-Taymuriya, GC,
355-5915/1074/0443, fax
356-3903
Guatemala, 8 Muhammad
Fahmi al-Muhdar, NC,
261-1813, fax 261-1814
Guinea, 46 Muhammad
Mazhar, ZA, 340-8408,
340-8109, fax 341-1446
Hungary, 29 Muhammad
Mazhar, ZA, 340-8634/
8659, fax 340-8648
India, 5 'Aziz Abaza, ZA,
341-3051/0052, 340-6053,
fax 341-4038
Indonesia, 13 'Aysha
al-Taymuriya, GC,
354-7209/7200/7356, fax
356-2495
Iran interests section, 12 Rifa'a,
Midan Misaha, DK,
348-6492/7641
Iraq, 9 Muhammad Mazhar,
ZA, 340-
8087/7964/8659/9815, fax
341-5075
Ireland, 3 Abu al-Fida, ZA,
340-8547, fax 341-2863
Israel, 5 Maqrizi, GZ,
361-0545/0528/0433, fax
361-0414
Italy, 15 'Abd al-Rahman
Fahmi, GC, 354-0658/3195,
fax 354-0657

Ivory Coast, 39 al-Quds
al-Sharif, MO, 346-4952/
0109

Japan, Cairo Center Bldg., 106
Qasr al-Aini, DT, 355-7553,
fax 356-3540

Jordan, 6 al-Guhayni, DK,
348-5566/6169/7543, fax
360-1027

Kazakhistan, 256 al-Ma'adi
al-Gadida, MA, 352-1900,
fax 352-1900

Kenya, 7 al-Muhandis Galal,
MO, 345-3628

Korea. 6 al-Saleh Ayub, ZA,
340-8219, 341-9532, fax
341-4615

Kuwait, 12 Nabil al-Wakkad,
DK, 360-2661/2/3, fax
360-2657

Lebanon (French Embassy,
Lebanon Interests Section),
5 Ahmad Nasim, GZ,
361-0623/0392, fax
361-0463

Lesotho, 10 Bahr al-Ghazal,
Sahafiyin, MO, 344-7025

Liberia, 11 Brazil, ZA,
341-9864/5, 345-6767, fax
347-3074

Libya, 7 al-Saleh Ayub, ZA,
340-8216/5506

Malaysia, 7 Wadi al-Nil, MO,
347-2868/0958, fax
346-0982

Mali, 3 al-Kawthar, MO,
701-641, 701-895, fax
701-841

Malta, 7 Rd. 20, MA,
350-3014, fax 375-4452

Marshall Islands, 8 Muhammad
Basyuni, al-Gulf, HE,
417-4246, fax 291-8828

Mauritania, 114 Muhi al-Din
Abu al-'Izz, DK, 349-0671,
349-1048, 349-0699, fax
348-9060

Mauritius, 72 'Abd al-Mun'im
Riyad, AG, 347-0929,
346-7642

Mexico, 5 Dar al-Shifa, GC,
3548622, fax 355-7953

Mongolia 3 Midan al-Nasr,
DK, 346-0670, fax 346-0670

Morocco, 10 Salah al-Din, ZA,
340-9849/677, 341-4718, fax
341-1937

Myanmar (Burma), 24
Muhammad Mazhar, ZA,
340-4176, 341-6793, fax
341-6793

Nepal, 9 Tiba, Madinat
al-Awqaf (off Gam'at
al-Duwal al-'Arabiya), MO,
361-1590/3426, fax 704447

Netherlands, 18 Hasan Sabri,
ZA, 340-
1936/6434/6872/8744, fax
3415249

Niger, 1010 al-Haram, GZ,
386-5607, 386-5617

Nigeria, 13 al-Gabalaya, ZA,
341-7894, fax 340-8311

North Korea, 6 al-Saleh Ayub,
ZA, 34~8219,341-9532, fax
341-4615

Norway, 8 al-Gezira, ZA,
341-3955, fax 342-0709

Oman, 30 al-Muntaza, ZA,
303-6011

Pakistan, 8 al-Saluli, DK,
348-7677/7806, fax
348-0310

Panama, 4A Ibn Zanki, ZA,
341-1093/94, 340-0784, fax
341-1092

Peru, 8 Kamel al-Shinnawi,
GC, 356-2974, fax 355-7985

Philippines, 5 Ibn al-Walid,
DK, 348-0396/0398, fax
348-0393

Poland, 5 'Aziz 'Usman, ZA,
340-5416/9583, fax
340-5427

Portugal, 15A al-Mansur
Muhammad, ZA, 340-5583/
5907, fax 341-5483

Qatar, 10 al-Thimar, DK,
360-4693/4697, fax
360-3618

Romania, 6 al-Kamel
Muhammad, ZA, 341-0107,
340-9546

Russia, 95 al-Giza, GZ,
348-9353/4/5/6

Rwanda, 23 Babel, DK,
337-9947/8

San Marino, 5 Ramez, MO,
360-2718, fax 393-9362

Saudi Arabia, 2 Ahmad Nasim,
GZ, 349-0797, 360-4560,
fax 349-4590

Senegal, 46 'Abd al-Mun'im
Riyad, MO, 346-0946,
346-0896, fax 346- 1039

Singapore, 40 Babel, Dokki,
703772, 349-0468, fax
348-1682

Slovakia, 3 'Adel Hasim
Rustum, DK, 718-2240

Slovenia, 5 Midan al-Saray
al-Kubra, GC, 355-5798, fax
355-8781

Somalia, 27 Iran, DK,
337-4577/4038

South Africa, Nile Tower, 21
Giza, 18th fl., GZ, 571-6234/
5/8/9, fax 571-7241

South Korea, 3 Bulus Hanna,
DK, 361-1234/5/6/7/8, fax
361-1234

Spain, 9 Hud al-Laban, GC,
3547069/7359, 3555018, fax
354-7259

Sri Lanka, 8 Sri Lanka, ZA,
340-4966, 340-0047, fax
341-7138

Sudan, 3 al-Ibrahimi, GC,
354-5043/5658, fax
354-2693

Sweden, 13 Muhammad
Mazhar, ZA, 341-1484/
4132, fax 340-4357

Switzerland, 10 'Abd al-Khaliq
Sarwat, DT, 765719,
758284, 770545, fax
5745236

Syria, 18 'Abd al-Rahim Sabri,
DK, 707020, 718320, fax
718232

Tanzania, 9 'Abd al-Hamid Lutfi, MO, 704286/155, fax 704286

Thailand, 2 al-Malik al-Afdal, ZA, 340-8356/0299, fax 340-0340

Tunisia, 26 al-Gezira, ZA, 341-8962, fax 341-2479

Turkey, 25 al-Falaki, Bab al-Luq, 354-8885, fax 355-8110

Uganda, 9 Midan al-Misaha, DK, 348-6070, 348-5544, fax 348-5980

Ukraine, 9 al-Saraya, 3rd fl. DK, 349-1030, 718-932, fax 3491030

United Arab Emirates, 4 Ibn Sina, GZ, 360-9722, 726266, 620278

United States of America, 5 Amrika al-Latiniya, GC, 355-7371

Uruguay, 6 Lutfallah, ZA, 340-3589, 341-5137, fax 341-8123

Uzbekistan, 2 Nawal, DK, 361-5070

Vatican, 5 Muhammad Mazhar, ZA, 340-2250, 340-6152, fax 340-6152

Venezuela, 15A Mansur Muhammad, ZA, 341-4332/ 3517, fax 341-7373

Vietnam, 39 Qambiz, DK, 701-494, fax 349-6597

Yemen, 28 Amin al-Rifa'i, DK, 360-4805/4806, fax 360-4815

Yugoslavia, 33 al-Mansur Muhammad, ZA, 341-1069/ 7954, 340-3622, fax 340-3913

Zaire, 5 al-Mansur Muhammad, ZA, 340-3662, 341-6855

Zambia, 2 al-Nakhil, Dokki, 360-7496, 361-0283

EMBROIDERY

See Sewing Supplies & Notions

ENVIRONMENTALISM

Arab Office for Youth and Environment (AOYE), 302-8391/2/4/5; fax 304-1635; email: aoye@ritsec1.com.eg

Association for the Protection of Services in Zamalek, 1 al-Kamel Muhammad, ZA, 340-6256, fax 337-6001; contact: Ennas Omar

Association for the Protection of the Environment, PO Box 32, Qalaa, Cairo, 510-2723, fax 417-2923

Egyptian Environmental Affairs Agency, 340-2665, 341-6019, 349-6458, 360-1243

EXERCISE CLASSES

See Sports

EXTERMINATORS

Bestox, 16 Huda Sha'rawi, DT, 243-0657/3156, 392-0021

Sayonara Cleaning Service, 4 Bahgat Sharara, Shubra, DT, 203-5592

EYE GLASSES

See Opticians

FABRICS

CLOTHING

Ahmed & Mahmud, Qasr al-Nil, DT

Chalons, Qasr al-Nil, DT, 393-1026

Champs Elysées, 32 Qasr al-Nil, DT

Chanzelleza, Qasr al-Nil, DT

Chez Elle, 32 Makka, MO, 365-7605

Lamour, Qasr al-Nil, DT

Madame, Qasr al-Nil, DT

Miss Paris, 19 Qasr al-Nil, DT, 393-8818/1492

Salem, 18 al-Quds al-Sharif, MO, 302-8357/8356

Sayyidati al-Gamila, Qasr al-Nil, DT

HOME FURNISHING

Bayan Palace, 9 al-Sawra, HE, 244-3177; also Ramses Hilton 5th fl.

Carpet City, branches everywhere

Etoffe Texmar, 29 Yathrib (at Husayn), DK, 361-0250, 349-5817; WTC

Etoile Mardini, 33 'Amman St, DK, 360-0936 & 361-0695; 13 al-Khalifa al-Ma'mun, HE, 291-5199/2126; WTC

Everon, 19 Abu al-Fida, ZA, 340-9575/3488; 19 Rd. 231, Digla, MA, 352-6652

Ouf, al-Azhar, KK

Raytex, 15 Nadi al-Seid, DK, 335-0715; 13 'Ubur Center, HE, 402-5190; WTC

Salon Vert, 28 Qasr al-Nil, DT

Tanis, WTC, 777972; fax 340-4611

FAX MACHINES

See Business Equipment

FILM PROCESSING

Alpha Market, Riyadh Tower, al-Nil, GZ, 572-6203

Photo Center, 3 al-Mahrani, off
Sharifein between Qasr
al-Nil and Sabri Abu 'Alam
DT, 392-0031 (professional
quality)

FISH

See Pet Shops

FLAGS AND BANNERS

El Banna, 53 al-Gumhuriya,
DT, 934-951
Seif Nasr Flags, 22 Qasr al-Nil,
DT, 392-1581

FLORISTS

AGOUZA
Fessel A. Shaib, next to British
Council, 192 al-Nil,
347-8800, 303-1114

DOKKI
Dina Flor, 143 al-Tahrir,
348-4417 (wholesale)
Rika, 1 Midan Ibn Affan and
Gamal Salem (near Feyrouz
Hospital), 360-0769

MAADI
Orchide Flower, 85 Rd. 9,
351-3446
Flower Center, 6 Rd. 205,
Digla
Pharonic Flowers, 70 Rd. 9
(across from Pizza Hut)

ZAMALEK
Gardenia Flowers, 5 al-Sayyid
al-Bakri, 340-9586

FLOWER ARRANGING, CLASSES

Salwa Fadil, 340-4976

Japanese Embassy, 355-7553

FOOTBALL

See Sports

FRAMING

Espace Karim Francis, Cairo
City Center, 1 Sharifein, 2nd
fl. off Midan Tal'at Harb,
DT, 393-1699
Framco, 26th July (near High
Court), DT, 575-2456,
762-418, contact: Mrs. Iman
Reader's Corner, 33 'Abd
al-Khaliq Sarwat, DT,
392-8801

FREIGHT FORWARDERS

See Movers

FUNERAL SERVICES (CHRISTIAN)

Antoine George Tawaf,
127 Ramsis, DT, 591-3275

FURNITURE

AGOUZA
Integrated Interiors, 134 al-Nil,
349-0479 (office & home
furnishings)

DOKKI
Asala, 8 Midan Ibn al-Walid,
361-4418 (all furnishings
including custom kitchens)
Collection, 87 Musaddaq,
349-4157 (traditional);
contact: Said Moharam

Jadis, 38 Qambiz (off Nadi
al-Seid) (excellent
traditional); contact: May
Rehim
NADIM, al-Mazaniya (behind
Coca-Cola plant), 348-1075,
335-4219/5927 (mashrabiya)

HELIOPOLIS
Belmondo, 3A Salah Salem,
HE, fax 349-1266 (rustic)
Design Center Cairo,
7 Baghdad, 669-752
(modern Italian and
Egyptian copies)
Sucash, 12 'Abd al-Mun'im
Hafez, Almaza, 290-3695
(interior design, antiques,
reporductions)

MAADI
Ahmed Gomaa, 73 Rd. 9,
375-4870 (Islamic-style
inlaid furniture & antique
metal work)
Artex Decorating and
Contracting, 21A Rd. 275,
352-2634.
Benzaion, Rd. 153, 350-4573
(furniture and housewares)
Carpet City, 19 Rd. 151,
351-4625 (all household
needs); also branches
everywhere
El Fayoumi, Basateen
Industrial Zone, 352-0458/
0403; fax 353-3814; contact:
Hazem or Tarek Fayoumi
(outdoor, office, and other
metal furniture)
Styler, 3 Wahib Doss,
378-3198 (high fashion
contemporary furniture)

MISCELLANEOUS
Alfostat, WTC, 776-531,
580-4542 (high-style
wrought-iron furniture);
contacts: Owner Nadim
Ayoub, Manager Mme. Laila

Cane, bamboo, rattan: Ramsis
past railroad station
Fagnoon, WTC, 1st fl., 776-180
(metal garden & other
furnishings)
Gallery Mansour, WTC and
64 al-Maryutiya, PY,
383-5349 (very expensive,
high quality)
Manasra District, 1k down
Sharia Muhammad 'Ali:
many shops, prices a third of
showrooms; also
upholstering
Nabil, 440-4248. Makes any
and all furniture/cabinets;
will come to your home
Rustic, 91A al-Mirghani, GC,
601-286 (solid country-style
furniture)

MOHANDISEEN

Animation, 28 Libnan,
344-0958; contact: Walid
Gohar (modern & traditional
home/office furniture; design
service)
Arcadia, 7 'Abd al-Mun'im
Riyad, 348-7579
Bon Bon, 25 Dimishq, MO
(children's)
Dimensione, 17 al-Higaz,
346-1237/0198, 347-0737;
showroom, 2 al-Fawalik,
336-4326
Le Style de Paris, 13 'Abd
al-Mun'im Riyad, MO,
360-3206, 364-4136
Masterpiece, 17 Gezirat
al-'Arab, 344-6919 (French
and English style)
Mffco, 3 Libnan, 345-3071
(lots of bedroom suites)
Wood Mark, 32 'Abd
al-Mun'im Riyad, 337-4100
(modern & traditional)

ZAMALEK

Al Home, 177 26th July,
340-0246 (all types furniture
& furnishings)

Alef, 14 Muhammad Anis,
342-0848, fax 342-0849
(eclectic; the best)
Ebony, 27 Abu al-Fida,
340-1823, 341-3634
(traditional)
Mit Rehan, 13 Mar'ashli,
340-4073, fax 340-4378
Ultra, 3 Mishil Lutfallah,
341-4507 (modern high-style
furniture; branch in WTC)

USED/SECONDHAND

Noshiner, 14 Gawad Husni,
DT, 392-4371
Osman Furniture, 213 Ramsis,
DT, 924-223
Sandy Trading, 1165 Corniche
al-Nil, Bulaq, 762-402

GALLEBEYAS

See Clothing, Ethnic

GALLERIES

See Art Galleries

GAMBLING CASINOS

Note: Foreign passport required
for entry; foreign currency
only
Casino Semiramis, Semiramis
Intercontinental Hotel, GC,
355-7171
Cairo Sheraton Casino, Cairo
Sheraton Hotel, GZ,
336-9700/800
Casino Las Vegas, Shepheard
Hotel, GC, 355-3800
Casino Libnan, al-Salam
Swissôtel Cairo, 297-4000 /
297-6000
Casino Ramses Hilton, Ramses
Hilton Hotel, DT, 574-4400 /
575-8000/768-888

Le Casino, al-Gezirah Sheraton
Hotel, ZA, 341-1333
Mövenpick Casino, Cairo
Heliopolis Mövenpick Hotel,
HE, 291-9400/247-0077
Nile Hilton Casino, Nile Hilton
Hotel, Midan al-Tahrir, DT,
578-0444/666
Omar Khayyam Casino, Cairo
Marriot Hotel, ZA, 340-8888
Sheherazade, Mena House
Oberoi Hotel, Pyramids
Road, GZ, 383-3222/444

GARDENING SUPPLIES

See also Plant Nurseries
Taht al-Rab' market next to
Security Police
Administration Building
opposite Islamic Museum,
DT

GIFTS

See Arts & Crafts

GLASS

El Nasr Glass & Crystal Co.,
11 al-Sherfein, DT,
392-1675, 393-1711
National Company for Glass &
Crystal, 16 'Abd al-Khaliq
Sarwat, DT, 392-6615
Stained Glass, 95 al-Mirghani,
HE, 418-3235, 263-9376,
Hazem Shoukry

GLASS BLOCKS

Buildmore Installation
Services, 17 'Ali Shalabi,
HE, 246-7821, 242-9609
Nassib Torcom, 15 'Imad
al-Din, DT, 591-1800/1102

GLASSWARE

See also Khan Khalili
A Touch of Glass, 8 Sheikh
al-Marsafi, ZA, 341-2392

GOLDSMITH

See Jewelers

GOLF

See Sports

GROCERIES

See Supermarkets

GRANITE

See Tile

GREETING CARDS

See Stationery

GUNS

See Hunting & Fishing

GYMNASTICS

See Sports

HAIRDRESSERS

See Beauty Salons

HANDICRAFTS

see Arts & Crafts

HARDWARE

Khatib Co., 45 al-Azhar (near
Bur Sa'id), Ataba

HEALTH CLUBS

DOKKI

American Fitness Center, 14
Iran, 336-5134
New Silhouette Figure Shapers,
10 Midan al-Misaha,
349-7958

DOWNTOWN

SheriNile Health Club, Ramses
Hilton, 777-113
SheriNile Health Club, WTC,
768-030
WTC Health Club, WTC,
764-425

HELIOPOLIS

Royal Health Club, 4A
al-Khalifa al-Ma'mun, Roxy,
454-6700, 455-0001/11
SheriNile Health Club,
Meridien Heliopolis,
290-5055
The Studio, 26 Muhammad
'Abd al-Hadi, Ard al-Gulf,
417-0445
Valentines, 70 al-Mirghani,
417-3321 (women only)

MAADI

Maadi Health Club, Maadi
Hotel, 350-5050 ext. 333

MOHANDISEEN

Al Nabila Hotel Health Club,
4 Gam'at al-Duwal
al-'Arabiya, MO, 346-1131,
347-3384, fax 347-5661

ZAMALEK

Mervat Beauty, Yamama
Center, 3 Taha Hussein,
341-3371

Silhouette, 4B Muhammad
Mazhar, 340-5039

HEARING AIDS

El Nahar Commercial Co., 6A
Gawad Husni, DT, 393-
0247, fax 392-5839

HEATERS

See Appliances

HENNA

Sudanese Trading Co.,
1 Gawad Husni, DT,
393-7121

HERBS

Harraz Herb Shop, Ahmad
Mahir, Bab al-Khalq

HOBBIES

See Bridge, Needlework, etc.,
and Sports

HOBBY SUPPLIES

Hobby Shop, 9 Mukhtar
al-Misri, Ard al-Gulf, HE,
418-8950, 679-258

HORSES &
HORSEBACK RIDING

See Sports

HOSES

See Gardening Supplies

HOSPITALS

DOKKI

El Fayrouz Hospital, 25 Gamal Salem, 360-0025, 360-0015/16/17/18/19, 360-0001/0002
Misr Int'l Hospital, 12 al-Saraya, Midan Fini, 349-4005; 716-555/004; 360-8261/70

DOWNTOWN

Italian Hospital in Cairo, 17 Bayn al-Sarayat, 'Abbasiya, 282-1581/1582/2397

GARDEN CITY AND SOUTH

Qasr al-Aini Teaching Hospital, Corniche al-Nil
National Cancer Institute, Qasr al-'Aini at Corniche and Fumm al-Khalig (Aqueduct); Director: Dr. Reda Hamza, 989-531/711; Director of Nursing: Dr. Nagwa El-Khasib, 362-8199

HELIOPOLIS

Arab Contractors Medical Center, Autostrade, NC, 280-0000/282-5768
Cleopatra Hospital, Cleopatra, Midan Salah al-Din, 291-5531/5532; 291-4590
Hayatt Medical Center, 6 Minis, 290-7017/7027
Nozha Int'l Hospital, behind Sheraton buildings, 269-655

MAADI

As-Salam International Hospital, Corniche al-Nil, 363-8050; emergency 362-3300
Nil Badrawi Hospital, Corniche al-Nil, 363-8684/8688; ambulance 363-8168

MOHANDISEEN

As-Salam Hospital, 3 Syria, 302-9091/9095
Damascus Hospital, 1 Dimishq, 347-0198/0208/0194/0206
El Safa Hospital, 4 al-'Iraq off Shihab, 349-1848/1884
Shalaan SurgiCenter, 10 'Abd al-Hamid Lutfi, 360-3920

ZAMALEK

Anglo-American Hospital, al-Burg (just west of Cairo Tower), 340-6162/6165

HOTELS IN CAIRO

DOKKI

Cairo Sheraton, Midan al-Galaa, 336-9700/9800
Pyramisa, 60 Giza, 336-7000/8000/9000, fax 360-5347
Safir Cairo, 4 Midan al-Misaha, 348-2424, fax 360-8453

DOWNTOWN AND GARDEN CITY

Cosmopolitan, 1 Ibn Tha'lab, DT, 392-3845/3663/3956; fax 393-3531
Garden City House, 23 Kamal al-Din Salah, GC, 354-4969/8126
Helnan Shepheard, Corniche al-Nil, GC, 355-3900/3800
Le Meridien Cairo, Corniche al-Nil, 362-1717, . fax 362-1927
Nile Hilton, Corniche al-Nil, 587-0444, fax 578-0475
Ramses Hilton, 1115 Corniche al-Nil, 777-444, 574-4400, fax 575-7152
Semiramis Intercontinental, Corniche al-Nil, GC, 355-7171, fax 356-3020
Windsor, 19 Alfi Bey, DT, 591-5277/5180; fax 921-621

HELIOPOLIS

Baron, 8 Ma'had al-Sahari, off al-'Uruba, 291-5757, fax 290-7077
Le Meridien Heliopolis, 51 al-'Uruba, 290-5055/1819, fax 290-8533
Mövenpick Heliopolis, Cairo Airport, 247-0077, fax 418-0761
Novotel, Cairo Airport, 291-8577, fax 291-4794
Sheraton Heliopolis, al-'Uruba, 290-2027/2037, fax 290-4061
Swissôtel al-Salam, 69 'Abd al-Hamid Badawi, 297-4000/6000, fax 297-6037

MAADI

Sofitel, Corniche al-Nil, Maadi Towers, 350-6092/93, fax 351-8449

MOHANDISEEN

Atlas Zamalek, 20 Gam'at al-Duwal al-'Arabiya, 346-6569, fax 437-6958
Jasmin, 29 Gezirat al-'Arab, MO, 346-3621, 347-2278, fax 344-5906
Al Nabila, 4 Gam'at al-Duwal al-'Arabiya, 346-1131, 347-3384, fax 347-5661

PYRAMIDS

Forte Grand Sphinx, Cairo–Alexandria Desert Road, 383-0827, fax 383-1730
Jolie Ville, Cairo–Alexandria Desert Road, 385-2555, fax 383-5006
Le Sphinx Sofitel, Cairo–Alexandria Desert Road, 383-7444, fax 383-4930
Mena House Oberoi, al-Haram, 383-3222/3444, fax 383-7777

ZAMALEK

Flamenco, 2 al-Gezira al-
Wusta, 340-0815/6;
fax 340-0819
Cairo Marriott, Saray al-Gezira,
340-8888; fax 340-7777
Gezirah Sheraton, 341-1333/
1555, fax 340-5056
Imperial, Saray al-Gezira,
341-4290, fax 341-4541
Pension Zamalek, Salah al-Din,
340-9318
President, 22 Taha Husayn,
340-0652/0718,
fax 341-1752
Safir Zamalek, 21 Muhammad
Mazhar, 342-0055/1203,
fax 342-1202

HOUSING AGENTS

See Real Estate Agents

HUNTING & FISHING EQUIPMENT

Abu Dief, 168 al-Tahrir, DT,
392-2634/5244
Alpha Market (upstairs) 5 Wisa
Wasef, Riyadh Tower, GZ,
572-6203

HYPNOSIS

See Alternative Therapies

IMPORT-EXPORT

Consult directories

INSURANCE, MEDICAL

BCA (British Community
Association) Medical
Scheme; contact BCA
Clubhouse, MO, 348-1358
or BCA Clinic,
Anglo-American Hospital,
341-8630 or 340-6162/3/4/5
ext 315

INTERIOR DESIGNERS

Dibaj, 54 al-Zahraa, MO,
336-3219
Nermine Moktar, Atrium,
4 Muhammad Mazhar, ZA,
340-6869
Dimensione, 2 Simar, MO,
336-4326/6864; contact:
Mohamed Hafez
Mona Hussein, 403-9237/9284
Zachy Sherif, 393-7485

INTERNET SERVICE PROVIDERS

AT&T, 31 al-Giza, al-Nil Tower
Bldg, GZ, 570-3266
Datum, 51 Bayrut, HE,
290-3501
Egypt Online, 24 'Adli, DT,
348-1801
EIS/MASH, 11 al-Thimar, MO,
336-2335
ENSTINET, 101 Qasr al-'Aini,
DT, 355-7253
Internet Egypt, 2 Midan Qasr
al-Dubara, 6th fl., GC, 356-
2882, fax 354-9611, email:
info@brainy1.ie-eg.com
Intouch, 3 Musaddaq, DK, 337-
6407, fax: 337-6480
Link Egypt, 3 Musaddaq, DK,
336-7710
MIST, 9 al-Gaza'ir, MO, 345-
2379
NileNet, 11 Abu-al-Mahasen al-
Shazli, AG, 332-8841
RITE, 10 al-Kamel
Muhammad, ZA,
341-4345/6, fax 341-4347
RITSEC, Muhammad Mansur,
ZA, 341-2918
Soficom, 30 Bahgat Ali, ZA,
342-1952
St@rNet, 2 Sharif, DT,
390-3923
Video On Line, 3 Musaddaq,
DK, 337-2041, 336-4910;
email: mlabs@vol.it

INTERPRETERS

See Business Services Centers

IRON, WROUGHT

See Furniture

INVESTMENT COMPANIES

See also & consult Directories
Cairo Capital Group, 4 Amrika
al-Latiniya, GC, 354-2049/
8018, fax 355-7479;
Managing Director: Dr.
Khalil Nougaim

JAZZ & LIVE MUSIC

See also Bars
After Eight, 6 Qasr al-Nil
(off Midan al-Tahrir),
574-0855
Fathy Salama & Sharkiat—
whenever and wherever
advertised; for information,
call 403-8289
Katcho'z, WTC, 578-6324
Le 51 Bar, Meridien Heliopolis
Hotel, 15 'Uruba, HE,
290-1819/5055
Lebanon Corner, Gezirah
Sheraton, 341-1333 (Arabic)
On the Rox, WTC, 578-4437,
580-4220
Piano Piano, WTC, 762-810
Starlight Bar Restaurant and
Terrace Restaurant, Baron
Hotel, 8 Ma'had al-Sahari,
HE, 291-2467/5757
Swissôtel al-Salam Hotel,
'Abd al-Hamid Badawi, HE,
297-4000/6000

JEWELRY

See also Khan Khalili
Hassan Elaish: WTC, 773-920;
3 Sur Nadi al-Zamalek, MO,
302-4440, 303-4767; 28
Gam'at al-Duwal
al-'Arabiya, MO, 302-2938,
303-4997; 10 Harun
al-Rashid, HE, 258-1845,
258-0227
Qasr El Shouk, 11 Brazil, ZA,
342-2111/2666 (silver)
Lalik, 49 'Amman (corner of
Qambiz), DK, 360-5295,
335-0807 and 2 Maspero,
HE, 257-9535
Saad of Egypt (I. A. Ibrahim):
KK, 589-3992/3; Ramses
Hilton, 574-6980; Mirghani,
al-Hurriya, HE, 290-9466
(silver)
Sirgany, many branches
including: KK; 'Abd
al-Khaliq Sarwat, DT,
391-7780; Sulayman Abaza,
MO
Song for Silver, 1 Ahmad
Hishmat, ZA, 340-8714

JEWELRY, ETHNIC

See also Khan al-Khalili
Al Ain Gallery, 73 Husayn,
349-3940
Bashayer, 58 Musaddaq, DK,
713-233
Katr El Nada, 18 Ibn al-Walid
(off main entrance to
Shooting Club), DK,
360-0290
Marie Louise Ibrahim,
337-1655
Nomad, 14 Saray al-Gezira, 1st
fl., ZA, 341-1917 and Cairo
Marriott, 341-2132
Shahira Fawzi, 3 Nabil
al-Wakkad, HE, 669-880,
678-111

Shahira Mehrez &
Companions, 3rd fl., 12 Abi
Emama (left-hand entrance
between Omar Effendi and
Cairo Sheraton), 348-7814

JUDO

See Sports (Martial Arts)

KARATE

See Sports (Martial Arts)

KHAN AL-KHALILI

(all recommended)

ALABASTER
Ali Hassan Ali, 8 Wikalat
al-Makwa, 933-463.

ANTIQUES
Handy El Dabb, 5 Sikkat
al-Badistan, 590-7823

BEADS & BEDOUIN JEWELRY
Emeil Sif Falamon, near
Naguib Mahfouz Café,
678-372; Turquoise,
19 Khan al-Khalili (see
Emad, "Mr. Beads"),
932-843; Bedouin Shop,
7 Khan al-Khalili, 589-6155;
Saad Artisans, 8 Wikalat
al-Makwa (upstairs),
591-7466

COPPER & BRASS
Noppein Copper, 6 Khan
al-Khalili; Muhammad
al-Mostafa, Mu'izz li-Din
Allah (al-Sagha); Said Ali
Abu Tahoun, 8 Wikalat
al-Makwa, 589-3635; Sayed
Mustafa, 8 Wikalat
al-Makwa, 588-0552;
Ahmad Goma, 5 Rab
' al-Silahdar (upstairs);
Sayed Hearrche or Ashraf,
5 Rab' al-Silahdar (upstairs),
589-6423; Essam Copper &
Engraving, 5 Rab
' al-Silahdar (upstairs); Adel
M. Aly, 5 Rab' al-Silahdar
(upstairs), 591-2282

GALLABIYAS
Abbas Higazi, 924-730; Atlas
Silks, 590-6139.

JEWELRY
Mihran & Garbis Yazejian,
near Naguib Mahfouz Café,
591-2321 (gold, cartouches);
Nassar Bros., 12 Khan
al-Khalili, 590-7210 (gold);
Saad of Egypt, 10 Shuwikar
Bldg., 589-3993 (Mr. I.A.
Ibrahim; silver)

LEATHER
Lutfi Rashid Co., 591-2748,
920-023 (upstairs, has toilet)

MUSKI GLASS
Sayed 'Abd El-Raouf, 8 Khan
al-Khalili, 933-463 (red
glass); Mosque Glass House,
8 Wikalat al-Makwa
(upstairs; Said Masheest)

PAPYRUS
Old Papyrus House, 8 Wikalat
al-Makwa (upstairs; Mohsen
Saad), 589-7077.

PERFUMES

'Abd al-Hady, 73 Gawhar
al-Qa'id (off al-Husayn),
590-9223.

RESTAURANTS

Hotel al-Hussein top fl.;
Naguib Mahfouz Café,
5 al-Badistan, 903-788,
932-262.

T-SHIRTS

El Safa Bazaar, 12 Khan
al-Khalili, 936-934 (made to
order)

KINDERGARDENS

See Schools

KITCHENWARE
(POTS & PANS)

See also Khan al-Khalili
Bazaar Zamalek, 107 26th July,
ZA, 341-0346 (crockery &
good oven-proof casseroles)
Zahran, 5 'Abd al-Rahman
al-Rifa'i (behind Makka),
MO, 348-5828, 349-7460
(good brand also sold
elsewhere)

KNITTING

See also Sewing Supplies
Rimy & Riry, 8 Brazil, ZA,
340-9633 (handmade
sweaters)

LABORATORIES, MEDICAL

Cairo Institute of Radiology,
23 Wadi al-Nil, MO,
347-3274, 344-4763
Cairo Tower Hospital
Laboratory, 350-9781

Technolab, 75 Muhi al-Din
Abu al-'Izz, MO, 360-0965

LAMPS

See Lighting

LANDSCAPE DESIGN

Ennas Omar, Forest Nurseries,
29 'Abd al-Mun'im Riyad,
MO, 335-3875; h: 340-6256
Fiorissima, 7 Ahmad 'Urabi,
MO, 346-0416/4811
Hydroscapes Egypt (Fatma &
Adel Niazi), 375-2817,
350-5968

LANGUAGE CLASSES

Community Services
Association, 4 Rd. 21,
350-5284, 376-8232 (Arabic,
English, French)

ARABIC

Arabic Language Institute
(AUC), 28 al-Falaki, DT,
354-2964 ext 5055, fax
355-7565
Egyptian American Center,
349-6934
Egyptian Center for Cultural
Cooperation, 11 Shagarat
al-Durr, ZA, 341-5419
International British Institute
(IBI), 47 Misr Helwan, MA,
350-6272, 351-2646
International Language
Institute (ILI), 2 Muhammad
Bayumi (off Mirghani), HE,
418-9212, 291-9295, fax
671-399, 291-2218; 3
Mahmud 'Azmi, Sahafiyin,
MO, 346-3087/8597

International Living Language
Institute (ILLl), Arabic
Language Department,
34 Tal'at Harb, DT,
574-8355, 392-7244,
354-8964
Maadi/Mohandiseen School for
Teaching Arabic (MSTA),
MA, 350-2671 (private or
group classes year-round)
The British Council, 192 al-Nil,
AG, 345-3281/2/3, fax
344-3076

ENGLISH

American University in Cairo
(AUC), 28 al-Falaki, DT,
354-2964, fax 355-7565
International Language
Institute (ILI), 2 Muhammad
Bayumi (off Mirghani), HE,
418-9212, 291-9295, fax
671-399, 291-2218; 3
Mahmud 'Azmi, Sahafiyin,
MO, 346-3087/8597
The British Council, 192 al-Nil,
AG, 345-3281/2/3, fax
344-3076

FRENCH

French Cultural Center,
1 Madrasat al-Huquq
al-Faransiya, Munira, fax
354-1012; 27 Sabri Abu
'Alam, Midan Isma'iliya,
HE, 663-241
Lycée Francais, 10 Rd. 14,
MA, 350-3574, fax
351-9514

GERMAN

Goethe Institute, 6 al-Sharifein,
DT, 759-877, 779-479, fax
771-140

ITALIAN

Italian Cultural Institute, 3
Sheikh al-Marsafi, ZA,
340-8791, fax 341-5723

JAPANESE

Japanese Cultural Center,
106 Qasr al-'Aini, DT,
355-3962/3/4, fax 356-3540

SPANISH

Spanish Cultural Center,
20 'Adli, DT, 360-1746/43,
fax 360-1743

LAW FIRMS

Baker & McKenzie, in assoc.
with Hamza & Helmy,
WTC, 18th fl., 579-1801–6;
fax 579-1808; partners:
Samir M. Hamza, M. Taher
Helmy
Fox & Gibbons, 126 Muhi
al-Din Abu al-'Izz, MO,
348-5955; fax 349-2210;
contacts: managing partner
Robert Sprawson; resident
manager Bridget McKinney;
asst. solicitor Jonathan
Taylor
Hassouna & Abou Ali, Cairo
Center, 5th fl., 2 'Abd
al-Qader Hamza, GC,
355-7188; 356-0852; fax
355-6140; contacts:
Muhammad A.K. Hassouna,
Ahmad G. Abou Ali
Kamel Law Office, 4 al-Shahid
Ahmad Yahya Ibrahim, MO,
347-4102/9453/3597/7179;
fax 345-2009; contact: Dr.
Muhammad Kamel
Shalakany Law Office, 12
Mar'ashli, ZA, 340-3331/
4214/3760; fax 342-0661;
email: shalakan@intouch.
com; Partners: Ali
El-Shalakany, Salah Morsi;
Mona Zulficar, Saleh Hafez,
Khaled El-Shalakany
Sherif Saad Law Office, Maadi
Palace Tower, MA,
378-6201/2/3

Veil Armfelt Jourde, 4 Gaber
Ibn Hayan, DK, 349-2217/
2498/8678; Partners:
Andrew P. Armfelt, Nigel
Hartridge

LAWYERS

Ahmed El-Shabini,
1 Muhammad Dawud, MA,
375-3064
Medhat Abu El Fadl, 8 Nakhla
al-Muti'i, HE, 242-0934, fax
244-0742

LEATHER GOODS

Choice, 7 'Ubur Buidlings,
Salah Salem, HE, 263-5148;
61 Canal, MA, 375-6455;
'Abd al-Hamid Lutfi and
al-'Anab, MO, 348-0760;
Ramses Hilton, 575-2752 ext
622; WTC, 575-5087
Leather Corner, 171 26th July,
ZA, 341-2110 and 10 Midan
al-Misaha, DK, 337-6989;
contact: Khaled 'Abd
al-Wahed
Montagna, 340-9987, 342-3375
Seven K, 46 Syria, MO,
361-4743 and 3 Wahib Doss,
MA

LIBRARIES

All Saints Cathedral Library,
5 Mishil Lutfallah, ZA,
341-8391
American Research Center in
Egypt (ARCE) Library,
2 Qasr al-Dubara, GC,
354-8239, 355-8683; head
librarian: Mr. Hammam
Fawzi

American Studies Library, US
Embassy, 5 Amrika
al-Latiniya, DT, 357-3124/
3133/3295
American University in Cairo
Library, 113 Qasr al-Nil,
DT, 357-6903; head
librarian: Shahira El-Sawy
American University in Cairo
Rare Books and Special
Collections Library,
22 Sheikh Rihan, DT,
357-5060
AMIDEAST Educational
Research Center, 6 Kamel
al-Shinnawi, GC, 354-1300
British Council Library,
192 al-Nil, AG, 344-8445;
345-3281/347-6118; head
librarian: Cathy Costain
Cairo American College
Library, Rd. 253, Digla,
MA, 352-9393/5244 ext 140
Egyptian Museum Library,
Midan al-Tahrir, DT,
772-352 (direct), 574-4267;
head librarian: Dr. Adel
Farid
Egyptian National Library (Dar
al-Kutub), Corniche al-Nil,
DT, 575-3254
Geographic Society of Egypt
Library, 109 Qasr al-'Aini,
GC, 354-5450
Goethe Institute, 5 'Abd
al-Salam 'Arif, DT,575-9877
Great Cairo Library,
15 Muhammad Mazhar, ZA,
341-2280
Music Library, Opera House
Complex, ZA, 342-0601,
339-8061 (direct); head
librarian: Mr. Galal Fouad
Mubarak Library,
4 al-Tahawiya, GZ,
336-0291-4
Netherlands Institute of
Archaeology & Arabic
Studies, 1 Dr. Mahmud
'Azmi, ZA, 340-4376

Pro Helvetica, 10 'Abd
al-Khaled Sarwat, DT,
575-8733
Spanish Cultural Center
Library, 20 Bulus Hanna,
DK, 337-1962, 360-1746;
head librarian: Belen
Fernandez Del Pino
UNESCO Library, 8 'Abd
al-Rahman Fahmi, GC,
354-3066/5599
US Agency for International
Development Information
Center, Cairo Center, 6th fl.,
106 Qasr al-'Aini, GC,
357-3225/3325/3357; head
librarian: Soad Saada

LIGHTING

Asfour Crystal, Shubra
al-Khima, Cairo, 220-1670
or 220-1032 (lamps,
chandeliers)
Atelier, 18 Gadda, MO,
361-3668
Pavillon, Sur Nadi Zamalek
(off Gam'at al-Duwal
al-'Arabiya), MO, 303-2766
(modern high style); contact:
Mr. Sadoon El Rawy
Style Team, Sur Nadi Zamalek
(off Gam'at al-Duwal
al-'Arabiya), MO, 303-2721
(modern & traditional)
Ultra, 3 Mishil Lutfallah, ZA,
341-4507 (modern high-
style)
WTC: Le Prince, 769-489
(traditional); Ultra, 764-424
(modern), Temple of Light,
619-237

LINGERIE

See Clothing

LINENS

Caresse, Yamama Center,
3 Taha Husayn, ZA,
341-0696
Salon Vert, 28 Qasr al-Nil, DT

LOCKS & SECURITY SYSTEMS

Sidi, 159 26th July, ZA,
340-9142

LUMBER

G.T.S., 6 Brazil, ZA, 340-6364
W.S., 206 Sudan, MO,
345-7679

MAGAZINES

British Community Association
(BCA) Monthly Magazine;
contact BCA Clubhouse,
MO, 348-1358, or Ann
Owen, 360-9812
Business Today, 1097 Corniche
al-Nil, GC, 357-1301, fax
357-1318.
Business Monthly, American
Chamber of Commerce in
Egypt, Cairo Marriott, Saray
al-Gezira, ZA, 340-8888 ext
264; senior editor Amira
Shahd
Cairo's (Culture &
Entertainment Guide),
19 Dimishq, MO, 302-1416/
2828, 344-6381; managing
editor Raef F. Nadda
Egypt Today, 24 Syria, MO,
349-0986, 360-1276,
361-5625/5653; editor-in-
chief Mursi Saad al-Din;
managing editor Lyla Allam;
senior editor Mary Kelly

Heliopolis Magazine,
Heliopolis Publishing
House, PO Box 2016,
Hurriya, HE, 290-2603;
editor–publishers Hamida
Moafi & 'Abdelmenem Ziko
KidMix, Egress Int'l, 6 Rd. 9B,
MA, 351-6105; editor-in-
chief Guinar Esmat; free
parents' magazine;
English/Arabic
Mother-to-Be, Link Int'l.,
71 Rd. 9, Apt. 11, MA,
351-5029; free; editor-in-
chief Rania Badr al-Din.
Pose, 2 Ghazl wa Nasig, MO,
346-7555, 303-5833;
director Goya Gallagher
RA: Residents Abroad,
Financial Times, London.
PO Box 461 Bromley, BR2
9WP, United Kingdom. Fax
44-181-402-8490.
Sports and Fitness, 3 'Abd
al-Hamid Lutfi, MO
336-9256; fax 336-4157

MAPS

Cairo A to Z, Palm Press, 34
Mansur Muhammad, 4th fl.,
Apt. 10, ZA, 341-5458, fax
341-3658
Lehnert & Landrock, 44 Sharif,
DT, 393-5324; director Dr.
Edward Lambelet

MARBLE & GRANITE

Sharia Ahmad Maher, Bab
al-Khalq (numerous dealers)

MARKET RESEARCH

AMER, 9 al-Shahid Hilmi
al-Misri, HE, 291-1585, fax
672399

Artoc Suez Trading Co.,
15 Giza, GZ, fax: 570-1780/
1803
Dyad (marketing consultants),
6 Dar al-Shifa, GC,
355-4482, 354-1781, fax
355-2388
Financial and Management
Consultants, the Office for
Studies & Finance—OSAF,
13 al-Khalifa al-Ma'mun,
HE, 291-2731/2733, email
osaf@ritsec1.com.eg, fax
291-3878
Kompass Egypt, Fiani &
Partners, 143 al-Tahrir, DK,
348-7353, fax 348-5204
Middle East Marketing
Research Bureau, 21 Dr.
Muhammad Gum'a, HE,
240-1799, 249-7099, fax
242-1685
RAC, Dr. Samy 'Abd al-Aziz,
39 Gam'at al-Duwal
al-'Arabiya, MO, 360-4851,
fax 360-8439
Rada Research & Public
Relations, 1 Mustafa
al-Wakil, HE, 291-2077/
7956, fax 671399, 291-7563
Wafai & Associates, 6
Dimishq, MO, 346 0601,
303-9289, fax 347-0118

MASHRABIYA

NADIM (National Art
Development Institute of
Mashrabeya), al-Mazaniya
(off Sudan behind Coca Cola
bottling plant), DK,
348-1075, 335-5927/4219

MASSAGE

See Beauty Salons, Health
Clubs

MEDITATION

See also Yoga
Sufi: Dr. 'Abdul Hay, AUC,
354-2964

MINISTRIES

Prime Minister, 1 Maglis
al-Sha'b, Midan Lazughli,
355-0164, 355-8025,
354-7370/76/77, fax
355-8016
Council of Ministers, 1 Maglis
al-Sha'b, Midan Lazughli,
355-0164/8020, 354-7370/
76/77, fax 355-8048
Agriculture & Land
Reclamation, Wizarat
al-Zira'a, DK, 702-677/596/
758, fax 349-8128
Awqaf (Waqfs), 5 Sabri Abu
'Alam, DT, 392-6022,
393-6163/6613
Culture, 2 Shagarat al-Durr,
ZA, 340-2195/6469,
342-0359, fax 340-644
Defense & Military Production,
23rd July, Kubri al-Qubba,
838-738
Economy & Foreign Trade,
8 'Adli, DT, 390-6796/6804,
391-9661/9278, fax
390-3029
Education, 12 al-Falaki, DT,
354-9479, 356-4065, fax
356-2952
Electricity & Energy,
Extension of Ramsis,
'Abbasiya, 260-2777/2888,
261-6299/6514/6317, fax
261-6302
Finance, 1 Maglis al-Sha'b,
2nd fl., Midan Lazughli,
355-7027, 354-1055/0601,
fax 354-5433
Foreign Affairs, Corniche al-
Nil, Maspero, 574-6862/71,
574-7490/1/2/3, 574-6903/
4574/6914, fax 574-9533

Health, 1 Maglis al-Sha'b,
Midan Lazughli, 354-1076/
1277/0426/8227, 355-7445,
fax 354-0526
Higher Education, 4 Ibrahim
Nagib, GC, 355-2155/6962,
354-8210
Housing & Utilities, 1 Isma'il
Abaza, DT, 355-3468/7014,
354-5638/4009, fax
355-7836
Industry, 2 Amrika al-Latiniya,
GC, 354-3600, 355-7048,
354-4261, fax 355-7507
Information, Television Bldg.,
Corniche al-Nil, Maspero,
759-570, 749-394, fax
757-144
Interior, al-Sheikh Rihan, DT,
354-5897/8307/8, 355-7500,
fax 355-7792
International Cooperation
(Ministry of State), 8 'Adli,
DT, 391-0008, 390-2945,
fax 390-9707
Irrigation & Water Resources,
3 al-Sheikh Rihan, DT,
312-3752/8103, fax
355-8008
Justice, Midan Lazughli,
355-1176/8103, fax
355-8103
Local Government, al-Islah
al-Zira'i Bldg., 10th fl.,
4 Nadi al-Seid, DK,
349-7470/7656, fax
349-7788
Manpower, 3 Yusuf 'Abbas,
NC, 260-617/8/9, 260-9359
New Urban Communities
(Ministry of State), 1 Isma'il
Abaza, off Qasr al-'Aini,
DT, 355-3885/3468/7836,
fax 355-7836
Parliamentary Affairs, Press
Office, Maglis al-Sha'b,
Midan Lazughli,
354-3116/30

Petroleum & Mineral
Resources,
16 al-Mukhayyam al-Da'im,
NC, 263-1000, 262-2268/
37/8, fax 263-6060
Planning, Salah Salem, NC,
263-4040/4747, fax
263-44747
Population & Family Welfare,
Corniche al-Nil, (next to
As-Salam International
Hospital), MA, 363-8137/
8786/8093/9818/8207, fax
363-8207/9818
Public Enterprises Sector &
Administrative Development
(Ministry of State),
2 Amrika al-Latiniya, GC,
355-9288 fax 355-3606/9233
Public Works and Water
Resources, 1 Gamal 'Abd
al-Nasser, Corniche al-Nil,
al-Warraq, 312-3315/3248/
8215, fax 312-7083
Scientific Research, 101 Qasr
al-'Aini, DT, 354-5205/6/9,
354-7642/0804, fax
355-8609
Social Affairs & Insurance,
Social Affairs: al-Sheikh
Rihan, DT, 354-2900/3873;
Social Insurance: 3 al-Alfi,
DT, 922-717, fax 917-799
Supply & Internal Trade,
99 Qasr al-'Aini, DT,
355-7613, 354-7832, fax
354-4973
Tourism, Misr Travel Tower,
Midan al-'Abbasiya,
285-9371, 285-9463, fax
285-9551
Transport, Communications &
Civil Aviation, 104 Qasr
al-'Aini, DT, 354-3623,
355-5566/5567/5568, fax
355-5564

MIRRORS

Golden Mirror, 7 Abu
al-Mahasen al-Shazli, AG,
347-1330 (mirrors & stained
glass)
Misr El Gedida for Glass and
Mirrors, 14 Aswan, HE,
666-246.
Stained Glass Designs,
95 al-Mirghani, HE,
418-3235

MOTHERS' GROUPS

Mom's Morning Out, Maadi
Community Church, MA,
352-5707

MOVERS

Danzas, 360-1710 (local &
international)
Express International,
60 al-Tahrir, DK, 349-0521,
361-6850
Four Winds, 11A Corniche
al-Nil, MA, 350-0113/0146
(local & int'l)
Global Movers, 258-7509,
256-2317 (local & int'l)
T.G. General Services, 22 Rd.
205, Digla, MA, 353-1353
(local & misc. services)
Trans-Express Worldwide Inc.,
15 Khurshed, New MA,
353-4915; email:
texp@wtca.geis.com (local
& int'l)

MOVIE THEATERS

See Cinemas

MUSEUMS

Agricultural and Cotton
Museums, al-Islah al-Zira'i,
DK, 702-933, 360-8682
Coptic Museum, Old Cairo,
Mar Girgis Metro station,
362-8766
Dr. Ragab's Pharaonic Village
& Papyrus Institute, 3 al-Nil,
GZ, 729-053/186, 348-8676/
9035
Egyptian Antiquities Museum,
Midan al-Tahrir, DT,
757-035
Ethnological Museum,
109 Qasr al-'Aini, GC,
354-5450
Folklore Museum, 18 Bursa,
DT, 752-460
Gayer Anderson House,
4 Midan Ahmad Ibn Tulun,
847-822
Islamic Art Museum, Bur
Sa'id, Bab al-Khalq,
390-9930
Mahmud Mukhtar Museum,
Tahrir, Gezira
Mr. & Mrs. Mohamed
Mahmoud Khalil Museum,
1 Kafur al-Ikhshid, DK,
336-2376
Manial Museum, Gezirat
al-Roda, Roda, 987-495
Military Museum, Citadel,
927-094
Muhammad Nagi Museum,
9 Mahmud al-Gindi, GZ
Museum of Modern Egyptian
Art, Opera Complex, Gezira,
340-6861
Railway Museum, Midan
Ramsis, DT, 763-793
Solar Boat Museum, Pyramids,
857-928

MUSIC AND SINGING, GROUPS & LESSONS

Cairo Choral Society, director
Larry Catlin, 340-4197
Cairo Music Center, HE;
contact: Mr Tobgy,
266-7544 /8649.
Carol Ann Clouston, voice,
speech, drama, &
Feldenkrais method;
341-1769.
Maadi Community Choir,
director Barbara Comar;
contact Cairo American
College, 352-9393

INSTRUMENTAL LESSONS
Guitar, Hamdy, 266-7195
Contact BISC (360-6674, 341-
5959) or CAC (352-
9393/9244) for the
following:
Woodwinds: Mr. Samir
Oboe: Mr. Ivan
Violin: Mr. Osman
Piano: Greig Martin, Jane
Hassan, Brian Kelly

MUSICAL INSTRUMENTS

The 'Abdel Ghafar Group,
39 al-Bustan, 1st. fl.
354-4948, manager Mr.
Hatem 'Abdel Ghafar; by
appt. only

MUSKI GLASS

See also Khan Khalili
Maryse and Ismail Borhan,
17 Midan Ahmad Ibn Tulun
(opposite Ibn Tulun
Mosque), 982-863, 257-9422

NATURAL FOODS

Sekem Farm, contact
Communitiy Services
Association, 350-5284,
376-8232

NEEDLEWORK

Heliopolis Tuesday Knitters;
contact Jenny, 291-0343
Quilter's Guild; contact Hetty,
418-5748
Women's Association,
360-3475

NEWS AGENCIES

MENA (Middle East News
Agency), 17 Huda Sha'rawi,
DT, 393-3000; chairman
Mustafa Naguib, 392-8888
Reuters, 153 Muhammad Farid,
21st fl., DT, 578-3290/1,
777-150, fax 777-107 &
771-807; bureau chief Rawhi
Abeidoh

NEWSPAPERS & NEWSLETTERS

Egyptian Gazette (daily) and
Egyptian Mail (Sat), 24
Zakaria Ahmad, DT,
578-3333/1515; fax
578-1110; ads: 578-1290/
1010
El-Wekalah, CIP, 19 Dimishq,
MO, 344-6381; 347-9104;
302-1416
Maadi Messenger (Maadi
Community Church),
378-5562; editor Jan
Learmonth (good classifieds)

Middle East Times, 2 al-Malik
al-Afdal, ZA, 341-3726;
341-9930; 342-4357/9; fax
341-3725; email: met@
ritsec1.com.eg
The Niler, U.S. Embassy,
357-2342 (embassy-related
personnel only; classifieds)

NIGHTCLUBS

See Bars, Jazz & Live Music

NOTIONS & BRIDAL

La Poupée, 21 Qasr al-Nil, DT,
393-3734 (bows, veils,
barrettes)

NURSE-MIDWIVES & OBSTETRICAL NURSES

Karen Betts (Brit. reg.
midwife), 244-6943

NURSERY SCHOOLS

See Schools

NURSES

Arylis Milligan, RN, Shaalan
Surgicenter, 360-3920
Jaqueline Sutton Shirbini, RN,
375-6766
International Nurses Group;
contact Lorea Ytterberg, RN,
351-0385

OPTICIANS

Baraka Optics, WTC,
574-8989; 159 26th July,
ZA, 342-0343; 10 Midan
Misaha, DK, 360-6790

Instant Center for Contact
Lenses, 25 al-Bustan, DT,
355-6566 and 180 Tahrir,
DT, 356-2686
Jean Greish, 33 Tal'at Harb,
DT, 392-7897
Maghraby Eye Center,
112 Muhi al-Din Abu
al-'Izz, MO, 361-0878/0891;
fax 361-0269

ORGANIZATIONS, BUSINESS & SCHOLARLY

American Chamber of
Commerce in Egypt, Suite
1541, Marriott Hotel, ZA,
340-8888 ext. 1541, fax
340-9482
American Research Center in
Egypt (ARCE), 2 Midan
Qasr al-Dubara, GC,
354-8239, 355-8683, fax
355-3052; email: arce@
brainy1.ie-eg.com; director
Mark Easton
Amideast, 6 Kamel
al-Shinnawi, GC, 354-1300,
355-2946; email:
103656.1253@compuserv.c
om; country director
Elizabeth Khalifa
Cairo Chamber of Commerce,
4 Midan al-Falaki, DT,
355-8261/2
CEDEJ, 14 Gam'iyat al-Nasr,
MO, 361-3147
Council for the International
Exchange of Scholars, 3007
Tilden NW, Suite 5M,
Washington, DC 20008-
3009, USA, 202-686-4019,
fax 202-362-3442.
Egyptian Antiquities Project,
2 Midan Qasr al-Dubara,
GC, 344-8622, fax same;
email: arceeap@brainy1.ie-
eg.com; director Robert K.
Vincent

Egyptian Businessmen's
Association, Nile Tower,
16th fl., 21 al-Giza, GZ,
572-3855/3020, fax
573-7258
Egyptian Exploration Society,
British Council, 192 al-Nil,
AG, 301 0319; contact
Rosalind Phipps
Egyptian Financial Group
(Euromoney Publications),
55 al-Giza, GZ, 568-8455/
7764, 573-0382, fax
571-0849; contact Ahmad
Marwan
Egyptian-American
Businessmen's Association,
Nile Tower, 21 al-Giza, GZ,
737-258/736-030/733-020
European Commission, 6 Ibn
Zanki, ZA, 340-8388,
341-9393, fax 340-0385;
director Michael McGeever
Federation of Egyptian
Chambers of Commerce,
4 Midan al-Falaki, DT,
354-2943, fax 355-7940
Federation of Egyptian
Industries, Immobilia Bldg.,
26A Sharif, DT, 392-8319/
7/8266, fax 392-8075
Ford Foundation, 1 Uziris, 7th
fl., GC, 354-9635/4450,
355-2121/4521, fax
355-4018; email: hdavies@
fordfound.org; representative
Humphrey Davies
French Commercial Section,
10 'Aziz 'Usman, ZA,
341-5701/2, fax 341-4955
Fulbright Commission,
20 Gamal al-Din Abu
al-Mahasen, GC, 354-4799/
8679, 357-2216/2258; fax
355-7893; email: aradwan@
bfce.eun.eg; executive
director Dr. Ann B. Radwan
German-Arab Chamber of
Commerce in Egypt, 3 Abu
al-Fida, ZA, 341-3664/2, fax
341-3663

Greek-Arab Chamber of
Commerce in Egypt,
17 Sulayman al-Halabi, DT,
741-190, fax 754-970
ICARDA (International Center
for Agricultural Research in
the Dry Areas) 15G Radwan
Ibn al-Tabib, 11th fl., PO
Box 2416 GZ, 572-5785/
4358, 573-5829, fax
572-8099; director general
Dr. Adel El Beltagy
(Aleppo); regional
coordinator Dr. Mahmud
Sohl (Cairo)
IDRC (International
Development Research
Center, Canada), 3 Midan
'Amman, 5th fl., DK
336-7051/2/3/4, fax
336-7056; email: fkishk@
idrc.ca; Director: Dr. Fawzi
Kishk.
Institute of International
Education (IIE), 809 UN
Plaza NY, NY 10017-3580,
212-9845329, fax
212-9845325
International Executive
Services Corporation,
Commercial Center, Bustan
Street, Suite 1, 390-3232,
fax 390-2929
Italian-Arab Chamber of
Commerce in Egypt,
33 'Abd al-Khaliq Sarwat,
Downtown, 392-2275, fax
391-2503
Japanese Foreign Trade
Organization, 56 Gam'at
al-Duwal al-'Arabiya, MO,
574-1111, fax 756966
Middle East Library for
Economic Services,
(MELES), 6 Sulayman 'Abd
al-'Aziz (off Duktur Shahin),
AG, 335-1141, 360-6804,
fax 360-6804; director Mr.
Nabil Foda

Netherlands Institute for
Archeology and Arabic
Studies, 1 Dr. Mahmud
'Azmi, ZA, 340-0076
Sixth of October Investors
Union, Sixth of October,
011-231-590/1/2, fax 011
231593
Tenth of Ramadan Investors
Union, 10th Ramadan City,
015-364-570-2586/11, fax
570-2565

ORGANIZATIONS, CULTURAL

American Center for Press and
Cultural Affairs, US
Embassy, 5 Amrika
al-Latiniya, GC, 354-9601
Austrian Cultural Section,
Austrian Embassy, Riyadh
Tower, 5th fl., al-Nil and
Wisa Wasef, GZ, 570-2975
British Council, 192 al-Nil,
AG, 303-1514; 344-8445;
347-6818
Cairo Art Guild, 350-2330;
contact Ola Seif
Canadian Cultural Information
Center, Canadian Embassy,
5 al-Saray al-Kubra, GC,
354-3110
Canadian Institute, 4 Rd. 4,
MA, 351-6980
Centre Français de Culture et
de Coopération, 1 Madrasat
el-Huquq al-Faransiya,
Mounira, DT, 354-1012/
1057/7679, 355-3725; 27
Sabri Abu 'Alam, Midan
al-Isma'iliya, HE,
417-4824/51
Egyptian Center for Int'l
Cultural Cooperation,
11 Shagarat al-Durr, ZA,
341-5419; director Nabila
Sayed
Goethe Institute, 5 'Abd
al-Salam 'Arif, DT,
575-9877

Greek Cultural Center,
14 'Imad al-Din, DT,
753-962/833
Indian Cultural Center,
23 Tal'at Harb, DT,
393-3396
Indonesian Cultural Center,
63 Musaddaq, DK,
337-4471, 348-8634
Israeli Academic Center in
Cairo, 92 al-Nil, DK,
348-8995, 349-6232
Italian Cultural Institute,
3 Shaykh al-Marsafi, ZA,
340-8791
Japanese Cultural Center, Cairo
Center, 2 'Abd al-Qader
Hamza, GC, 355-3962/3/4
Jordanian Cultural Center,
24 Gamal Salem (off
Musaddaq), DK, 349-5660
Korean Cultural Center,
56 Gam'at al-Duwal
al-'Arabiya, MO
Middle Eastern Cultural
Center, 17 Mar'ashli, ZA,
341-4053
Netherlands Institute, 1 Duktur
Mahmud 'Azmi, ZA,
340-0076
Spanish Cultural Center,
6 'Abdallah al-Katib (off
Midan Fini), DK, 335-5097,
337-1962, 360-1746
Swiss Cultural Center, 10 'Abd
al-Khaliq Sarwat, DT,
575-8133/8284
United Arab Emirates Cultural
Center, 9 Qambiz (off
Musaddaq), DK, 349-9166/
9669

ORGANIZATIONS, INTERNATIONAL

CIDA (Canadian International
Development Agency), Head
Office: Canadian Embassy,
5 al-Saraya, GC, 354-3110;
head of aid John Sinclair;
Program Support Unit,
7 al-Birgaz, GC, 354-5901/
2012; 356-4148, fax
354-2012; manager Suzy
Greiss
Care al-Salamlek, 10 al-'Ubur
Bldgs., Salah Salem, HE,
260-0467, fax 263-6963
Commission of the European
Community, 6 Ibn Zanki,
ZA, 341-9393/340-1184, fax
340-0385
French Commercial Attaché,
French Embassy, 29 al-Nil,
GZ, 341-5701/2, fax
341-8238
German Technical Cooperation
(GTZ), 4D al-Gezira, ZA,
342-0714, fax 3341-2445
Great Britain International
Cooperation Office, British
Embassy, 355-6904/8208,
fax 355-6904
Italian Trade Center, 3 Abu
al-Fida, ZA, 340-1734,
340-0540, 340-7218,
340-7219, fax 3400501
Italy International Economic
Cooperation Section, Italian
Embassy, 15 'Abd
al-Rahman Fahmi, GC,
354-0658/3195, fax
354-0657
Japanese International
Cooperation Assistance
(JICA), WTC, 10th fl.,
574-8240/1/2
US Agency for International
Development (USAID),
Cairo Center Bldg., 10th fl.,
106 Qasr al-'Aini, DT,
354-8211, fax 357-2233

UNITED NATIONS AGENCIES

Food and Agricultural
Organization (FAO),
11 al-Islah al-Zira'i, DK,
337-2789, 337-3475,
337-5979, fax 349-5981

Internaional Civil Aviation
Organization (ICAO),
9 Shagarat al-Durr, ZA,
340-1463/340-1532, fax
340-5344

International Finance
Corporation (IFC), WTC,
12th fl.,579-5353/6565, fax
579-2211

International Labor
Organization (IL0 Egypt),
9 Taha Husayn, ZA,
341-9290, 340-0123, fax
341-0889

International Monetary Fund
(IMF), 31 Qasr al-Nil, DT,
392-4257, fax 351-7137

UN Children's Fund
(UNICEF), 8 'Adnan 'Umar
Sidqi, MO, 361-6346

UN Development Program
(UNDP), WTC, 768-487,
768-672, fax 779-145

UN Educational, Scientific and
Cultural Organization
(UNESCO), 8 'Abd
al-Rahman Fahmi, GC,
453-3036, 354-5599, fax
3545296

UN High Commissioner for
Refugees (UNHCR),
13 al-Falah (off Shihab),
MO, 346-0618, 303-1751/2,
fax 303-1753

UN Information Center (UNIC
Cairo/UNDP), WTC,
769-595, 768-393, fax
779145

UN Population Fund, WTC,
772-253, fax 770-115

UN Relief & Work Agency for
Palestinian Refugees
(UNRWA), 2 Dar al-Shifa,
GC, 354-8502, fax 354-8504

UN Truce Supervision
Organization (UNTSO),
Observer Group Egypt
(OGE) Headquarters, 41511
Box 247, Ismailia, (064)
329-305, fax (064) 329-250

UNIC LIbrary, 1 Uziris, GC,
354-6288/355-3705, fax
355-0682

Universal Postal Union, Postal
Center, Midan Ramsis,
770-500

World Bank (Resident Cairo
Mission), 574-1670,
574-1671, fax 574-1676

World Food Program, WTC,
778-690, fax 779145

World Health Organization
(WHO), Sultan 'Abd
al-'Aziz, Alexandria, (03)
483-0090/6/7/9, fax (03)
483-8916; Cairo 341-2156,
fax 342-3300

ORGANIZATIONS, SOCIAL AND MISCELLANEOUS

British Community
Association, HE, 417-9775

British Community
Association, MA, 378-6729;
contact Sue Collins

British Community
Association, MO, 348-1358

Cairo 41 Club; contact Mike
Farnham, 350-0322

Cairo Petroleum Wives;
contact Gwen 352-7238

Community Services
Association, 4 Rd. 21, MA,
350-5284; 376-8232

Heliopolis Community
Activities Association;
contacts: Linda Coe,
418-2712; Richard Costin,
291-7299; Peg Grossman,
660-146; Ann Megallah,
290-9885

Hungarian Women's Club,
Hungarian Cultural Center,
13 Gawad Husni, DT,
392-6692

Latin American Circle in
Egypt; contact Argentina
Yassin, 346-2977

Maadi Women's Guild; contact
Cynthia Lydecker, 350-6685

Middle East Wives; contact
Carole Addas, 418-3091

North Sinai Women's Projects,
27 Yahya Ibrahim, Apt. 8,
ZA, 340-1045, fax
340-0387; contact Manal
Bayad

Republicans Abroad Egypt, c/o
Semiramis Business Center,
PO Box 60, Corniche al-Nil,
Cairo, 356-3020; or contact
Priscilla del Bosque,
340-5490 (evenings)

Rotary and Inner Wheel
Heliopolis; contact Hussein
Hashad, 291-8822

Spanish-Speaking Ladies Club;
contacts: Monica, 261-8113;
Sandra, 341-1224

The Swiss Club, al-Salam,
Imbaba, 314-2811; contact
Tessie El Gabi, 349-1116

Tree Lovers' Association,
contacts: Eng. Ahmed
Kamel, 352-9365; Salah
Samaha, 350-4266; Dr.
Ibrahim Kelany, 353-0621

Women's Association of Cairo,
' 21 Bulus Hanna, DK,
360-3457

ORGANIZATIONS, SPORTS

See Sporting & Country Clubs,
Sports Federations

ORPHANAGES

See Volunteering

PARKS

See Chapter 1, "Green Cairo"

PARQUET FLOORING

El Tawfik Parquet, 23 al-Qal'a,
DT, 512-9108
Eng. Tarek Fouad, 3 al-Batal
Ahmad 'Abd al-'Aziz, MO,
303-4019

PARTY PLANNERS

Suzi Damati, AG, 344-1650,
fax 344-6644

PERFUMES & ESSENTIAL OILS

See also Khan Khalili
G. Fleur Essential Oils,
53 al-Zahraa 5th fl., apt. 23,
DK, 349-0902/3049, Mme.
Nagat
International Perfumes &
Cosmetics, 5 al-Zahraa (at
Musaddaq), DK, 361-1624

PEST CONTROL

See Exterminators

PET ADOPTION

Brooke Hospital for Animals,
2 Bayram al-Tunsi, Sayyida
Zaynab, 364-9312
People's Dispensary for Sick
Animals (PDSA),
60 al-Sikka al-Bayda,
'Abbasiya, 482-2294, Dr.
Farouk, Dr. Osama Safar,
Dr. Ahmed Obeida

PET BOARDING

Dr. Rafik Nashed, Sharif
Mansur at Sri Lanka, ZA,
341-2402
People's Dispensary for Sick
Animals (PDSA),
60 al-Sikka al-Bayda,
'Abbasiya, 482-2294, Dr.
Farouk

PET SHOPS & SUPPLIES

(Reputable)
Anton Aziz, 229 & 191
Ramsis, DT, 591-2833
Mr. Amr's Pets, Heliopolis
Flower Shop, Meniz (behind
Baghdad), HE, 291-7812
Karim Pets, 18 Rd. 82, MA,
351-6881
Momen Azam's Pet Shop,
corner of Rds 9 & 82
Sami's Farm, 134 26th July,
ZA, 340-5173, George
Girgis

PETROLEUM COMPANIES

consult directories, esp. Maadi
Women's Guild Directory

PHARMACIES

DOKKI
Amman Pharmacy, 'Amman
and Qambiz, 349-2889
Sherif Pharmacy, 16 Qambiz
(off Musaddaq), 349-9122

DOWNTOWN
Gezira Pharmacy, 157 26th
July, 340-0809
Isaaf, Ramsis and 26th July,
743-369 (24hr.)
Seif, 76 Qasr al-'Aini,
354-2678 (24hr.)

HELIOPOLIS
Al Ezaby, 1 Ahmad Taysir,
Kulliyat al-Banat, 418-0838,
663-409 (24hr.)
Maqsoud, 29 Mahmud Shafik,
245-3918 (24hr.)
El Marwa, 82B 'Abd al-'Aziz
Fahmi, 247-7293 (24hr.)
Roxy Pharmacy, Subki,
290-5946

MAADI
Essam, 101 Rd. 9, 350-4126
(24hr.)
Hindam, Rd. 9, Midan
al-Mahatta, 378-5695/5194
(24hr.)
El Rahma, 35 Rd. 276, New
Maadi, 352-1568 (24hr.)

MOHANDISEEN
Aly & Aly Pharmacy,
37 Sulayman Abaza (9am-
12m)
El Ezaby Pharmacy, 11 Surya,
MO, 304-1647

ZAMALEK
Myra Pharmacy, 3 al-Gezira
al-Wusta (opp. Flamenco
Hotel), 342-0645
New Universal Pharmacy,
12 Brazil, 340-4896
Pharmacy Zamalek, 3 Shagarat
al-Durr, 340-2406 (24hr.)

PHILATELISTS

Cafe Muktallat, 14 'Ataba
Khadra, Ataba, DT
Postal Museum, off Midan
Ataba

PHOTOGRAPHERS (FASHION, COMMERCIAL, PORTRAITS)

Ahmed Mokhtar, 335-9391
Sherine El Semary, 290-0158

197

Thomas Hartwell, 340-7113,
fax 340-5661

PHOTOGRAPHY

See also Film Processing
AUC's Sony Gallery, al-Sheikh
Rihan, DT, 354-2964,
Darkroom Workshop

PHYSICIANS

See Doctors

PIANO LESSONS

See Music and Singing

PIANO RENTAL

Essam, 233-9282
Mustafa the Piano Man,
266-5029, 267-8987,
259-3138

PICTURE FRAMES

See Framing

PLANT NURSERIES (WHOLESALE)

See also Gardening Supplies
Egypt Green, 6 Zakariya Rizq,
ZA, 342-0374/5
Egypt Green Land, 27 Tal'at
Harb, DT, 392-9987,
393-0975; contact Nabil
Abdel Razik
Fiorissima, 7 Ahmad 'Urabi,
MO, 346-0416/4811; owner
Piero Donato
Forest, 29 'Abd al-Mun'im
Riyad, MO, 335-3875;
contact Inas Omar

Mahmud Helmi, (018)
400-346, 401-221
Nimos farm, 128 Immobilia
Bldg., Sharif, DT, 392-5714/
5822, fax 393-1101; contact
Nadia Niazi

PLANTS

See Gardening Supplies, Plant
Nurseries

POTTERY

See also Arts & Crafts
Nabil Darwish, Saqqara Road,
Harraniya, 385-5894
Samir El Guindi (The Mud
Factory) 261 Sudan, DK,
347-3445/7032
Suzanne Wissa Wassef, Wissa
Wassef Studios, Saqqara,
Harraniya, 385-0746

POTTERY CLASSES

See Art Classes

PRINTSHOPS

AUC Printshop, 113 Qasr
al-'Aini, 357-6936
Concorde Press, 52 Ratib,
Shubra, DT, 205-7902/3, fax
205-7901
Elias Modern Publishing
House, 1 Kanisat al-Rum
al-Kathulik, PO Box 954,
al-Daher, 590-3756, fax
588-0091
International Press, 5 Gamal
al-Shahed, Sahafiyin, MO,
345-8412

Masters Press, near Coptic
Hospital in Daher (off
Ramsis), 920-189, fax same;
contact: Fouad Lobbos
(business cards & stationery)
Modern Egyptian Press,
75 'Amman (off Mustafa
Hafez), Ain Shams East,
298-1735/5715, fax
298-0736; contact: Manal
Nubar, Madrasat al-
Mu'allimin, Shubra,
648-316, fax 640-643 (good
basic workhorse printers)

COLOR SEPARATION

JC Center, HE, 245-8797
Peak Image, 104 Gam'at
al-Duwal al-'Arabiya, MO,
349-8117, fax 247-3900
Style, 3 Abu Saber (off Ahmad
'Ismat), Ain Shams,
250-1580

PUBLICATIONS

See Newspapers & Newsletters,
Magazines

PUBLISHERS

See also Newspapers &
Newsletters, Magazines
The American University in
Cairo Press, 113 Qasr
al-'Aini, 357-6889, fax
355-7565, email
aucpress@auc-acs.eun.eg
A. A. Gaddis & Sons, Khalid
Ibn Walid, Luxor, (095)
382-838, fax (095) 382-837
Hoopoe Books, 13 Rashdan,
337-8164, 348-0050, fax:
347-3323
Lehnert & Landrock, 44 Sharif,
DT, 393-5324 (maps, art
prints)

Egyptian International
Publishing Co. – Longman,
10A Husayn Wasif, Midan
al-Misaha, DK, 349-7946/7
The Palm Press, 34 Mansur
Muhammad, 4th fl., apt. 10,
ZA, 341-5458, fax 341-3658

PUPPETS

See Children's Entertainment

QUILTING

See Needlework

REAL ESTATE AGENTS

Alfi Doss Services (apartment
rentals), 63 'Usman Ibn
'Affan, HE, 678-772/230
Arabian American Real Estate
Co., 71 Rd. 9 and 19 Rd.
151, 350-1022/6209/7897,
351-4571
Arabian American Real Estate
Co., 71 Rd.9 and 19 Rd.151,
6th fl., MA, 351-4571,
350-0122, fax 350-6209
Belanger and Issa, 354-5563/
1524
Bigger Builds Contracting Co.,
7 'Abd al-Latif Hamza, NC,
272-7961, fax 418-9352
Conserv, 17A Muhammad
Mazhar, ZA, 340-1811; 38
Nahda, MA, 350-3131,
351-8428
Diamond, 346-7366/5005
Excel Services, 69 'Umar Ibn
al-Khattab, HE, 290-7882,
679-339, fax 616805
Foresight, 7 al-Shahid Mahmud
Husayn al-'Ashri, HE,
418-5684, fax 418-9352
Maadi Today, 23 al-Gulf, MA,
351-7562

Nile Services, 26 Rd. 81 and
Mustafa, MA, 350-3130
Sourya 'Abd El-Wahab, 12
Midan al-Misaha, DK,
348-2713
Suburban, 43 Surya, MO,
303-4035/2567
Sunny Home, 35 Rd. 13, MA,
350-2278

REPAIRS, HOUSEHOLD

Mohsen Gomaa, office
561-755, home 561-3741
(general, electrical, TV,
video, etc.)

RESTAURANTS

NA= No Alcohol;
BYO = Bring Your Own

DOKKI

Ciao, 10 Midan al-Misaha,
335-2482
El Greco, 1 Midan 'Amman,
336-1183/4
El Tekia, 12 Midan Ibn
al-Walid, 349-6673, NA
Il Cortigiano, 44 Mishil
Bakhum, 336-0620,
337-4838, NA
La Casetta, 32 Qambiz,
348-7970, NA
La Parisienne, Husayn &
al-Tahrir
Le Sandwicherie, 33 'Amman,
361-3389
Le Tabasco, 8 Midan 'Amman,
336-5583
Scoozi, 16 Midan al-Misaha,
DK, 348-2393/8668,
349-9765
Susana, 7 Iran, 337-6028;
360-5088

DOWNTOWN

Abu Shaqra, 69 Road Qasr
al-'Aini, 364-8602/8811, NA

After Eight, 6 Qasr al-Nil,
574-0855
Alfi Bey, 3 al-Alfi, 771-888,
774-999
Aly Hassan El-Haty and Aly
'Abdou, 3 Midan Halim
Pasha, 591-6055
Arabesque, 6 Qasr al-Nil,
574-7898, NA, BYO
Carroll's, near Felfela on Tal'at
Harb
Chili's Too, al-Bustan Center,
9th fl., 392-8518/8420, NA
Estoril, 12 Tal'at Harb (near
Qasr al-Nil), 574-3102
Felfela, 15 Huda Sha'rawi,
392-2751/2833
Kowloon, Cleopatra Hotel,
Midan al-Tahrir
La Chesa (Swissair), 21 'Adli,
393-9360/5768
Le Bistro, 8 Huda Sha'rawi,
392-7694
Paprika, 1129 Corniche al-Nil,
Maspero, 578-7887
Peking, 14 Saray al-Azbakiya,
591-2381

GARDEN CITY

Champollion, Meridien Le
Caire Hotel, Corniche al-Nil

GIZA AND AGOUZA

Al Fanous, Oman Center,
Riyadh Tower, 5 Wisa
Wasef, NA
Flying Fish, 166 al-Nil,
349-3234
La Mama, Cairo Sheraton,
336-9700
Pharaohs, 31 al-Nil, 570-1000,
fax 570-3737 (floating
restaurant)
Swissair Restaurants, al-Nil,
348-5321/6720

HELIOPOLIS

Chantilly (Swissair),
11 Baghdad, 669-026,
665-620

Chili's, 18 al-Sawra,
417-5299/7419
Peking, 115 'Usman Ibn
'Affan, 418-5612.
Rossini, 66 'Umar Ibn
al-Khattab, 291-8282,
417-1401

KHAN AL-KHALILI

El Halwagi, Harat al-Busta
(between al-Azhar and Khan
al-Khalili) (best *ta'miyya*)
Naguib Mahfouz,
5 al-Badistan, 590-3788,
932-262
Hotel El Hussein, top floor

MAADI

Andrea, 45 Rd. 7, 351-1369
Bua Khao, 9 Rd. 151, 350-0126
Bukhara, 43 Misr Helwan,
375-7599
Gladiola, Rd. 257 and al-Nasr
518-1117
La Casetta, 11 Rd. 18,
350-7276, 351-9076
Lan Yuan, 84 Rd. 9, 378-2702
Lola and Lolita, 15 Rd. 9B,
351-5587
Maxie's Long Feng, Ghadat
al-Maadi Towers, 350-3964
Peking, 29 Rd. 257, al-Nasr,
MA, 352-3450.
Sea Horse, Corniche (opposite
As-Salam Hospital),
363-8830, 355-6856
Miscellaneous
Mamoura Torz, 1 Qasr
al-Manial, Roda, 364-4091
The Virginian, Corniche,
Muqattam Hills

MOHANDISEEN

Abu Shaqra, 17 Gam'at
al-Duwal al-'Arabiya,
344-2299/4509, NA
Bint Sultan, Midan al-Sawra
and Sulayman Abaza
Bon Appetit, 21 Wadi al-Nil,
303-5815

Chili's, Midan Gami' Mustafa
Mahmud, 361-7004/5/6, NA
Creeks, 15 Ahmad Sami
al-Sa'id (off Sawra),
360-7326, NA
El Omda, 6 Gaza'ir (behind
Atlas Hotel), 346-2247, NA
El Yotti, 44 Muhi al-Din Abu
al-'Izz, 349-4944
Kandahar, 3 Gam'at al-Duwal
al-'Arabiya, 344-3773,
345-5100
Maroush, 64 Midan Libnan,
346-6891/5350, 345-0972,
NA
Papillon, 26th July, Tersana
Center, 347-1672
Peking, 26 al-'Ataba, 349-9086
Peking, 9 al-Kawsar, 349-9860
Prestige Corner Pizzeria,
43 Gezirat al-'Arab,
347-0383, NA
Taj Mahal, 5 Midan Libnan,
302-5669
Tia Maria, 32 Gadda, 335-3273
Tirol, 38 Gezirat al-'Arab,
344-9725

PYRAMIDS

Andrea, 59-60 Maryutiya,
383-1133, 385-4441
Christo's Vue des Pyramides,
10 al-Haram, 383-3582,
386-0086
Moghul Room, Mena House
Hotel, 383-3222/3444

ZAMALEK

Al Dente, 26 Bahgat 'Ali,
340-9117, NA
Angus Grill, 34 Yahya Ibrahim,
340-1865
Casino Cleopatra,
3 al-Gabalaya, 341-4630/
2921
Chin Chin, 4 Hasan Sabri,
341-2961, 340-7510
Deals, al-Sayyid al-Bakri
(behind Maison Thomas)
Don Quichotte, 9A Ahmad
Hishmat, 340-6415

Five Bells, 13 Isma'il
Muhammad, 340-8980/8635
Florencia, Hotel Flamenco,
10th fl., 2 al-Gezira al-Wusta
(at Abu al-Fida), 340-0815
Gezira Grill, Marriott Hotel,
340-8888
Hana Restaurant, Nile Zamalek
Hotel, 21 Ma'had al-Swisri
(at Muhammad Mazhar),
340-1846, 341-3197
Justine's, 4 Hasan Sabri,
341-2961
L'Oasis, Le Pacha 1901, Saray
al-Gezira, 340-6730
La Charmerie, 157 26th July
(behind Maison Thomas),
340-9640
Le Steak, Le Pacha 1901, Saray
al-Gezira, ZA, 340-6730, fax
340-7905
Le Tarbouche, Le Pacha 1901,
Saray al-Gezira, ZA,
340-6730, fax 340-7905
Mandarin, President Hotel,
22 Taha Husayn, ZA,
340-5282, 341-3195,
341-6751 ext. 233, fax
341-1752
Piccolo Mondo, Le Pacha
1901, Saray al-Gezira, ZA,
340-6730, fax 340-7905
Pub 28, 28 Shagarat al-Durr,
340-0972
River Boat, Le Pacha 1901,
Saray al-Gezira, ZA,
340-6730, fax 340-7905
The Cellar, President Hotel,
340-0652, 340-0718

RESTAURANTS, DELIVERY AND FAST FOOD

Al Dente, 28 Bahgat 'Ali, ZA,
340-9117, fax 341-9730
Bon Appetit, 340-4382,
340-9108, GZ, MO, ZA;
418-8287, 418-8286, HE
Chesa Lino, 21 'Adli, DT,
393-9360, 393-5768

Chili's, Midan Gami' Mustafa
Mahmud, MO, 361-7004/5/6
Creeks, 360-7326
Ghanam, 26th July, ZA,
340-6671/1185
Hot 'n Tender, 118 26th July,
(entrance from 'Aziz
'Usman), ZA, 340-2655
KFC: 349-0306, 360-2169,
348-5909, 710-329, MO,
DK; 247-0599, 240-3230,
679-123, 677-423, HE;
350-4714, 351-7604, MA;
622-811, 864-606,
585-1478, 572-8307, GZ;
355-1144, 354-0480, DT,
GC; 303-7894, 303-7884,
303-7859, ZA; complaints
302-6459
Maison Thomas, 157 26th July,
ZA, 340-7057
Mandarin, President Hotel,
22 Taha Husayn, ZA,
340-5282, 341-3195,
341-6751 ext. 233, fax
341-1752
Maroush, 64 Midan Libnan,
MO, 346-6891/5350,
345-0972
McDonald's: 337-2226,
337-2189, DK; 337-5923,
337-5932, MO; 246-2632,
246-2518, HE; 355-8131,
355-8105, 355-8129, DT,
GC, ZA; 402-3899,
402-3860, NC; 585-3849,
585-1079, PY
Papillon, 26th July St, Tersana
Center, MO, 347-1672
Peking: 14 Saray al-Azbakiya,
591-2381, DT; 26 al-'Ataba,
349-9086, and 9 al-Kawsar,
349-9860, MO; 29 Rd. 257,
MA, 352-3450; 115 'Usman
Ibn 'Affan, 418-5612, HE;
fax 353-1517

Pizza Hut: 356-2628,
356-2755, DT, GC;
360-8048, 349-7609,
337-6899, 361-1347, DK,
MO; 622-911, 572-8397,
GZ; 256-4571, 256-9495,
454-0202, HE; 340-2069,
340-2057, ZA; 375-9362,
351-7619, 378-6651, MA;
384-2339, 385-4280, PY;
complaints 302-6459
Sandwicherie, 33 'Amman,
DK, 361-3389
Scoozi, 16 Midan al-Misaha,
DK, 348-2393/8668,
349-9765
Winchell's, Nile Bowling
Center, al-Nil, GZ,
336-1637, 336-1638; 3
Wahib Doss, MA, 378-5034,
378-5032; 13 Baghdad,
Kurba, HE, 291-9299

SCHOOLS, ELEMENTARY &
SECONDARY

American International School,
NC, 262-3147,
477-0044/0055
British International School
Cairo (BISC), 5 Mishil
Lutfallah, ZA, 340-6674,
341-5959, fax 341-4168
Cairo American College
(CAC), 1 Midan Digla, MA,
352-9393/9244, fax
352-3057
El Alsson, Harraniya, GZ,
385-0661
Heliopolis British International
School, 51 al-Shahid 'Abd
al-Mun'im Hafez, Almaza,
HE, 290-8424
Maadi British International
School, 9 Rd. 278, MA,
352-8211/8124
Modern English School, 8
Midan Saray al-Qubba, HE,
258-3961/3005, fax
258-3110

Schouiefat International
School, Qattamiya,
517-3279/3334, fax
517-3334

SCHOOLS, NURSERY AND
PRE-SCHOOL

AGOUZA

Reiltin, 16 Disuqi, 347-7152

DOKKI

American Wonderland,
9 Babel, 360-9667
Schweizer Kinder Garten,
65 Musaddaq, 337-2578
The Irish School, 64 al-Zahraa,
337-0399

DOWNTOWN

Alf Leila Wa Leila Preschool
(AUC Nursery), 24 Falaki,
357-5315

HELIOPOLIS

Busy Bees, 37 al-Shahid 'Abd
al-Mun'im Hafez, Almaza,
663-710

MAADI

Charlie Chaplin Nursery and
Preschool, 13 Filistin, New
Maadi, 352-4742
Maadi British International
Nursery School, 10 Rd. 77,
350-5911
Maadi Nursery British School,
9 Wahib Doss, 352-8124
One World Childcare Center,
Digla, 353-2467
Sindbad Al Bashaer School,
350-6803
Start Right Nursery, 9 Wahib
Doss, 350-0626
Stepping Stones Nursery
School, 352-3880
Tom and Jerry Kids, 21 Rd.
209, MA, 352-8896

MOHANDISEEN

Prince & Queen, 52 al-Quds
al-Sharif (off Shehab),
347-3310
Stepping Stones Nursery
School, 344-3044

NASR CITY

Stepping Stones Nursery
School, 401-0092

ZAMALEK

Stepping Stones Nursery
School, 340-2054

SCHOOLS, UNIVERSITY-LEVEL

Ain Shams University, Qasr
al-Za'farani, 'Abbasiya,
284-7818, fax 282-6107
al-Azhar University, Midan
al-Husayn, NC, 262-3284/
78, fax 261-1404
The American University in
Cairo, 113 Qasr al-'Aini, PO
Box 2511, 11511 Cairo,
354-2964; fax 355-7565
Cairo University, Orman, GZ,
572-7175/7066, fax 628884
Helwan University, Mudiriat
al-Tahrir, Helwan,
344-6441, fax 345-5461

SEAFOOD

Asmak Wadi El Nil, 88 Wadi
al-Nil, MO, 304-4188

SEWING SUPPLIES & NOTIONS

Aseel, KK, 590-6847; 56
'Ammar Ibn Yasir, HE,
248-1858 (dressmaker &
embroidery supplies)

Nomrossy Sons, 14 Muski,
KK, 907-220 (buttons,
beads, braid)

SHISHA SUPPLIES

Mahmud Eid El-Qalamawy &
Sons, 92 al-Mu'izz li-Din
Allah (opposite Qasr
Bishtaq), KK, 932-215

SHOEMAKERS, CUSTOM AND REPAIRS

'Abdel Mun'im Abu Zeid, 8
Brazil, ZA, 341-8263
El Aziz Shoes, 3 Isma'il
Muhammad, ZA, 340-0911

SHOES

Al Baraem Co., 9 Libnan, MO,
303-5990; Yamama Center,
ZA, 340-6631
Atlas, Khan al-Khalili,
590-6139 (embroidered silk
slippers)
Antonio, 41 Gezirat al-'Arab,
MO. 347-7137.
La Scarpa, 10 Rd. 218, Digla,
MA, 352-7159
T.A. Egypt, WTC; corner of
Qambiz and Midan Ibn
al-Walid, DK, 580-4176
Santana, 112 Commercial Ctr.,
Ramses Hilton, 575-2399;
Yamama Ctr., ZA

SHOES, MEN'S

Bally, 33 Ahmad Hishmat, ZA

SHOPPING PLAZAS

Bustan Center, DT

Digla Arcade, 11 Hasan Sabri,
ZA
Maadi Grand Mall, MA
Nile Hilton Annex, DT
Ramses Hilton Annex, DT
Sultan Center, 77 'Usman Ibn
'Affan, Midan Safir, HE
Tersana Center, 26th July, MO
WTC, 1191 Corniche al-Nil,
Bulaq; shopping center,
580-4000; business center,
578-8054
Yamama Center, 3 Taha
Husayn, ZA

SOFTBALL

See Sports

SOUND & LIGHT

Schedule for Pyramids,
385-2880/7320

SPORTING AND COUNTRY CLUBS

Ahli Sporting Club,
al-Gabalaya, ZA, 340-2112/
3
Cairo Sporting Club, al-Nil,
GZ, 348-9415
Gezira Sporting Club, ZA,
341-5270; 340-6000/6
Heliopolis Sporting Club,
al-Mirghani, HE,
291-0065/75
Maadi Sporting Club, MA,
350-5455, 375-2066
Maadi Yacht Club, 8 Palmer,
MA, 350-5169/5455/5693/
5405
Nasr City Sporting Club, NC,
263-331
El Nil Sporting Club, Manial
side of Abbas Bridge,
847-626

Nile Country Club, 374-2211/
3334
Saqqara Country Club,
Saqqara, PO Box 72,
al-Haram, GZ, 384-6115/
7893, 385-2282, fax
385-0571, email: scch@
rite.com
Shams Sporting Club, HE,
244-00941278, 243-3501
Shooting Club (Nadi al-Seid),
Nadi al-Seid, DK, 337-3337/
4535/4678/6747
Tawfiqiya Tennis Club, off
Ahmad 'Urabi, MO,
346-1930
Zamalek Sporting Club, Mit
'Uqba, MO, 263-3001

SPORTS

See also Health Clubs

AEROBICS
See Exercise Classes below

BADMINTON,
contact Steven Dale, 536-2378

BILLIARDS/SNOOKER/POOL
British Communty Association,
MO, 348-1358
Andrew Rees, 337-5227 (h)
Harry Dingomal, 352-9526

BOATING
Cairo Yachting Club, al-Nil,
GZ, 348-9415
Maadi Yacht Club, Corniche
al-Nil, MAd, 375-2066
Ocean Classics, 582-0766, fax
582-0632

CHESS
Arab Contractors Club,
283-2391
Gezira Sporting Club,
341-5270, 340-6000/6

DIVING
See also Desert & Diving
Safaris
British Sub Aqua Club;
contacts: Neil Cooper,
290-4111; Steve Devereux,
291-7892
Cairo Divers Group; contacts:
Mohammed Mabrouk,
340-0889; Amira Zeitoun,
360-8976
Diaa Shawki, 14 al-Nasser, HE,
244-5147
SCUBA Plus, WTC, 574-7988/
580-4165

EXERCISE CLASSES (AND AEROBICS)
See also Health Clubs
Creative Dance & Fitness
Center, 60 Musaddaq, DK,
361-2613
Eleanor Curtis, 8 Midan Ibn
al-Walid, DK, 349-8119.
Community Services
Association, 4 Rd. 21, MA,
350-5284, 376-8232
Creative Dance & Fitness
Center, 13B Rd. 254, Digla,
MA, 352-1252
SACHA, 29 Ahmad Hishmat,
7th fl., ZA, 340-6167
Sport Palace, 159 26th July,
ZA, 340-7631

FISHING & HUNTING
Anglers Federation,
17 Mahmud Basyuni, DT,
fax 570-1055
Fawzia Abu Dief & Co., 168
al-Tahrir, DT, 392-2634/
5244

GOLF
British Golf Society, Capt.
Alan Percival 350-5916 or
378-2202, Vice Capt. Alan
Causer 351-2925 or
354-0298

Mena House Ladies, Lalaine
Noordhuis, 269-7650; Lynne
Borghesius, 290-5055

GYMNASTICS
Gezira Club, 340-6000

HORSES & HORSEBACK RIDING
El Boraq Stables and Breeding,
Zawyat Abu Muslim, GZ,
384-8427
El Ferousseya, Gezira Club,
ZA, 340-6000
El Zahraa Stud Farm, HE,
243-1733
Equicare Co., 2 Bahgat 'Ali,
ZA, 340-6939
Stables in/near Nazlat
al-Simman on Gamal 'Abd
al-Nasir at Giza Pyramids:
AA Stables, 385-0351; owner
'Abdul Aziz
FB Stables, 385-0406; owner
Farouk Breesh
Euro Stables, 385-5849
MG Stables, 385-3823; owner
Muhammad Ghoneim
SA Stables, 385-0629; owner
Salama Abou Aziza

MARTIAL ARTS
Number One Health & Beauty,
Ghadat al-Maadi Towers,
MA, 378-6256/7
Sports Mall, 80 Shehab, MO,
303-0246/7 or 302-6432/3

ROWING
El Nil Sporting Club, near
Kubri 'Abbas, Corniche
al-Nil, GZ, 393-4350

RUGBY
Cairo Rugby Club, Rds. 104
and 161 (behind Maadi
Military College), MA,
clubhouse 375-0840,
chairman Joel Leibner
351-4840, Derek Johnson,
375-9175

RUNNING

Cairo Hash House Harriers,
Matthew 353-0574, Scott
517-3197, Malcolm
347-6663

SNORKELING AND SCUBA

See Diving, Desert & Diving
Safaris

SOFTBALL

Cairo Softball League, men's
commissioner Tom Heck,
376-8333, 357-3856,
women's commissioner
Rhonda Wood, 353-5251

TENNIS

Maadi Ladies Tennis, Karen
Jones, 351-9744

SPORTS EQUIPMENT

A Sports, 14 Gumhuriya, DT,
near Midan Ubira, 390-9775,
Amr Khairy
Alpha Market (above
supermarket), Riyadh
Tower, al-Nil, GZ, 572-6203
Sports Mall, 80 Shihab, MO,
302-6432
Scuba Plus, 1st fl., WTC,
574-7988
World Sport, 17 al-Mathaf
al-Zira'i, DK, 335-2778;
302-5954
Weider, 2A Bahgat 'Ali, ZA;
14 al-Mahrusa (off Ahmad
'Urabi near Midan Sphinx),
MO, 302-7993;
34A al-Higaz, al-Tugariyin
Tower, Mahkama, HE,
242-2227; Maadi Grand
Mall, MA, 518-1848

SPORTS FEDERATIONS

Angling, 17 Mahmud Basyuni,
DT, fax 570-1055

Athletics, Bahari Stadium, NC,
260-7788
Basketball, Bahari Stadium,
NC
Billiards, 83 Ramsis, DT,
574-4934
Body Building, Higher Council
of Youth and Sports, Mit
'Uqba, MO
Boxing, 5 Tal'at Harb, DT,
392-2732
Chess, Arab Contractors Club,
283-2391
Croquet, Gezira Sporting Club,
354-4743
Cycling, Bahari Stadium, NC,
402-6724
Diving, 14 Otostrad al-Bahari,
Rab' al-'Adawiya, NC,
260-5381
Fencing, Fencing Club,
al-Azbekiya Gardens (near
Midan Opera), 392-6120
Field Hockey, Bahari Stadium,
NC, 262-5052
Golf, Gezira Sporting Club,
ZAM, 340-6000/6
Gymnastics, 32 Sabri Abu
'Alam, DT, 392-3526
Handball, Bahari Stadium, NC,
261-0416/7
Horse Racing, 3 'Abd
al-Hamid Badawi (next to El
Salam Hotel), HE, 245-4090
Horseback Riding, 261-6575
Judo, Bahari Stadium, NC,
263-4367/8555
Karate, al-'Ubur Towers, Salah
Salem, NC, 269-1430
Kung Fu, 3 al-Qaddarawi,
Bulaq al-Dakrur, 574-2195
Long-Distance Swimming,
Corniche al-Nil, GC,
354-7158
Olympic Committee, 261-1400,
263-2500; fax 260-5974;
e-mail: eo@idsc.gov-eg
Pole Vaulting, 16 al-Nuzha,
HE, 418-1839

Polo, 13 Qasr al-Nil, DT
(contact Olympic
Committee, above)
Power Lifting, 5 Musaddaq,
DK, 383-3799
Raquetball, 5 Montassir Bldg.,
Faysal, PY, 858-406,
852-098
Rowing, el-Nil Sporting Club,
Corniche al-Nil, GZ,
393-4350
Shooting, Bahari Stadium, NC
Soccer, 5 Gabalaya, ZA,
340-3268/5560, 341-3730
Speedball, Higher Council of
Youth and Sports, Mit
'Uqba, MO, 346-0073
Squash, Cairo Stadium, NC,
262-4273, 401-0237
Swimming, 260-7375
Tae Kwon Do, 64 Ramsis, Apt.
2, HE, 263-1737, 261-7576
Table Tennis, 2 Abu Hif, Bab
el-Luq, DT, 392-5986
Tennis, 13 Qasr al-Nil, DT
Volleyball, Bahari Stadium,
NC, 262-1696
Weightlifting, Bahari Stadium,
NC, 260-9256/63
Wrestling, Bahari Stadium,
NC, 261-0608
Yachting, 82 'Abd al-'Aziz
al-Sa'ud, MN, 364-6763, fax
983-679

STATIONERY

All along 'Abd al-Khaliq
Sarwat, DT
El Fagre, Abu Bakr al-Siddiq
(down from Kanzy Hotel),
DK, 361-0131 (good office
stationery)
Khodeir, 15 Nadi al-Seid, DK,
360-1842; 10 'Ilwi and
3 Huda Sha'rawi (off Qasr
al-Nil), DT; 20 Mansur
Muhammad, ZA

STOPPEURS (RE-WEAVERS)

El Zayat, 4 Brazil, ZA,
340-1064

SUPERMARKETS

Abu Zakry, Muhi al-Din Abu
al-'Izz (at al-Tahrir), DK
Alpha Market, Riyadh Tower,
al-Nil, GZ, 572-6203
Alpha Market, Corniche al-Nil,
MA
Fairway, al-Asari Ibn Nafi',
HE, 258-8551, 259-6570
Sunny, 11 al-'Aziz 'Usman,
ZA, 341-2032, 342-1121
Sunny, 1 Midan Fu'ad al-Din
(on Gam'at al-Duwal
al-'Arabiya), MO, 346-8480,
303-1731

TAXI & LIMOUSINE SERVICES

Maadi Taxi, Rd. 9 and
al-Nahda, MA, 350-1118
Muhammad Naguib, MA,
350-9123
Muhammad Selmi, MA,
352-8706
Mustafa Muhammad, Rd. 10,
MA, 375-1961

TAXI DRIVERS

(English-speaking)
Alexander, 573-8068 (after
7pm)
Diaa, 330-7997 (English &
Italian, 12–6pm)
Reda, 314-9924
Shouki, 318-3344 after 9pm

TELEPHONES

See Appliances

TELEVISION: CABLE & SATELLITE

Cable Network Egypt (CNE)
and Multi-Choice, 3 Rd.
262, Midan Gaza'ir, New
Maadi, 517-0122/1122/1222

TELEVISIONS

See Appliances

TENNIS

See Sports

TENTMAKERS

All along Khayyamiya in Darb
al-Ahmar near KK
Magdy & Salah Farghaly, 2
Khayyamiya, 517-3429

THEATERS

(for movie theaters see
Cinemas)
Al-Salam, Qasr al-'Aini, GC,
355-2484
Ramses Hilton Theater, Annex,
DT, 574-7435
Al-Haram, al-Haram, GZ,
386-3952
Al-Fann, Ramsis, DT,
578-2444
Al-Zamalek, 13 Shagarat
al-Durr, ZA, 341-0660
Qasr al-Nil, Qasr al-Nil, DT,
575-0761
Farid, Farid and 'Imad al-Din,
DT
Balloon, al-Nil, AG, 347-1718,
347-7457
Salah 'Abdel Sabour Hall,
Midan al-'Ataba, 937-948
National Theater, Midan Ataba,
591-7783

Nasr City Theater, Yusuf
'Abbas, NC, 402-0804
Al-Hanager Theater, Opera
Complex, Gezira, 340-6861
Al-Gezira Theater, 'Abd
al-'Aziz al-Sa'ud, MN,
364-4160

TILE

Ceramica Cleopatra,
38 al-Batal Ahmad 'Abd
al-'Aziz, MO, 360-0581,
361-2442
Sharia Salah al-Din, al-Qal'a
(numerous dealers)
Sharia al-Faggala, Ramsis
(numerous dealers)

TOOLS

See Hardware

TOUR GUIDES

See Travel Agents and Desert
& Diving Safaris

TOYS

Top Toys, 40 Musaddaq, DK,
337-0441
Toys & Joy, 3 Musaddaq, DK

TRANSLATORS

See Business Services Centers

TRAVEL & TOURISM AGENTS

Akhnaton Travel,
70 al-Husayn, MO,
360-5683, 348-6719, fax
360-0934

Basata, Sherif al-Ghamrawy,
350-1829 or, in Basata, at
062-500-481
Elegantes Voyages, 23 Yahya
Ibrahim, ZA, 341-2145
See Egypt–See the World,
26 Rd. 87, MA, 350-9146
(same fax), 378-0972
Ted Cookson (Egypt Panorama
Tours), 4 Rd. 79, MA,
350-5880, 351-0200, fax
351-1199

THOMAS COOK

DT: 17 Mahmud Basyuni,
574-3955, 762-750, 767-920
GC: 12 Midan al-Shaykh
Yusuf, 356-4650/4651/
4934-5-6, fax 356-4654
GZ: Forte Grand Pyramids
Hotel, 383-1441, 383-0383
ext 4090, fax 383-1730
HE: 7 Baghdad, 417-3511-2,
290-7310, fax 291-6215
MA: 88 Rd. 9, Midan
al-Mahatta, 351-1419/1438,
351-0232, fax 350-2651
MO: 10 26th July, 344-0008,
346-2429/7187, fax
303-4530
Semiramis Hotel, 355-8162/
8544, fax 355-7061
WTC: 578-0808-9, same fax

TRIMMINGS

See Sewing Supplies

TUTORS

Check with Schools and in
Middle East Times classified
ads
Diane Stainton, BA, MA,
385-4432 (ESL, Eng, Soc)
Helen Deakin, 347-4703
(TEFL, Eng, Math)

UNIFORMS

See Sports Equipment

UNIVERSITIES

See Schools, University-level

VCR & TELEVISION RENTAL

Telehire, 3 Hasan 'Asim 1st fl.,
ZA, 341-0183, 263-8131

VETERINARIANS

Brooke Hospital for Animals,
2 Bayram al-Tunsi, Sayyida
Zaynab, DT, 364-9312
People's Dispensary for Sick
Animals (PDSA),
60 al-Sikka al-Bayda,
'Abbasiya, DT; clinic,
772-227; hospital, 482-2294,
Dr. Farouk, Dr. Osama
Safar, Dr. Ahmed Obeida
Dr. Osama Safar, PDSA Clinic,
772-227, hospital 482-2294,
home 284-3123
New Maadi Veterinary Clinic,
5 Rd. 278, New MA,
352-6693, 352-8882, Drs.
Magdi & Magda Boutros

VOLUNTEERING

Al Nour Wal Amal (Light and
Hope Assoc. for Blind
Girls), 16 Abu Bakr
al-Siddiq, HE, Amal
Hashem, 340-4991, or
Malek El-Sherbini,
244-1929.
Al Nour Institute for Girls,
22 al-Kawsar, MO; director
Muhammad El-Zeidi,
348-0465 (blind children)

Awladi Orphanage, 29 Rd. 206,
Digla, MA, 351-0128
Befrienders Cairo, 209 26th
July, Midan Sphinx, MO,
344-8200; 303-6025/35
Center for Children with
Disabilities, 42 'Abdallah
Diraz, HE, 417-2084/5/6/7
Egyptian Red Crescent Society,
29 al-Galaa, DT, 575-0558
Egyptian Museum Library,
Midan al-Tahrir, DT,
772-352 (direct), 574-4267
Friends of Children with
Cancer, Marguerite Kelly,
353-1390, Elizabeth Naylor,
340-8619; mailings:
Shalakany Law Office,
12 Mar'ashli, ZA, 340-3331.
HOPE and IQRA'A (Help
Orphans Pursue Education
and Read), 345-8440 and at
Jameel Center, AUC,
357-5039
Hope Village Society, 14
Ahmad al-Khashab, NC,
272-4563
SOS Children's Village, end of
'Abbas al-'Aqqad (next to
MB Petroleum Co.), NC,
274-3339/2286
UNICEF, 8 & 11 'Adnan
'Umar Sidqi (off Musaddaq
just past Club Med office),
DK, 361-6346

WALKING TOURS

See Organizations

WALL HANGINGS

See Arts & Crafts

WATCH & CLOCK REPAIRS

See Clock and Watch Repairs

WATER FILTERS

Life Trend-Egypt (Instapure),
3 al-Diwan, GC, 356-4461,
fax 355-6344
Laser, Ramses Hilton Annex,
2nd fl., 574-4400, 577-7444

WATER PIPES

See Shisha Supplies

WEIGHT CONTROL

See also Health Clubs
Beauty Essentials, 14 Ahmad
Hishmat, 341-2927

WINDOW SCREENS

Hassan Hilmy, 50 Musaddaq,
DK, 348-1925

WINDSURFING

See Sports

WHIRLING DERVISHES

Al Tannoura Dancers, Wikalat
al-Ghuri Cultural Palace,
al-Azhar, Wed & Sat around
9pm

WIRE SERVICES

See News Agencies

WOMEN'S GROUPS

See Organizations

WOOD

See Lumber

WROUGHT IRON (FER FORGÉ)

See also Furniture
Shops along al-Sabtiya and
Ramsis

X-RAYS

See Laboratories

YACHTING

See Boating

YOGA

Indian Cultural Center,
23 Tal'at Harb, 393-3396
Leslie at CSA, 350-5284,
376-8232
Leslie Garcia, 353-2467
Linda Allam, 418-6226
Marie Louise Ibrahim,
337-1655
The Swiss Club, al-Salam,
Imbaba, 314-2811; or
contact Tessie al-Gabi,
349-1116

ZIPPERS

See Sewing Supplies

ZOO

See Children's Entertainment

INDEX